RED SONJA®

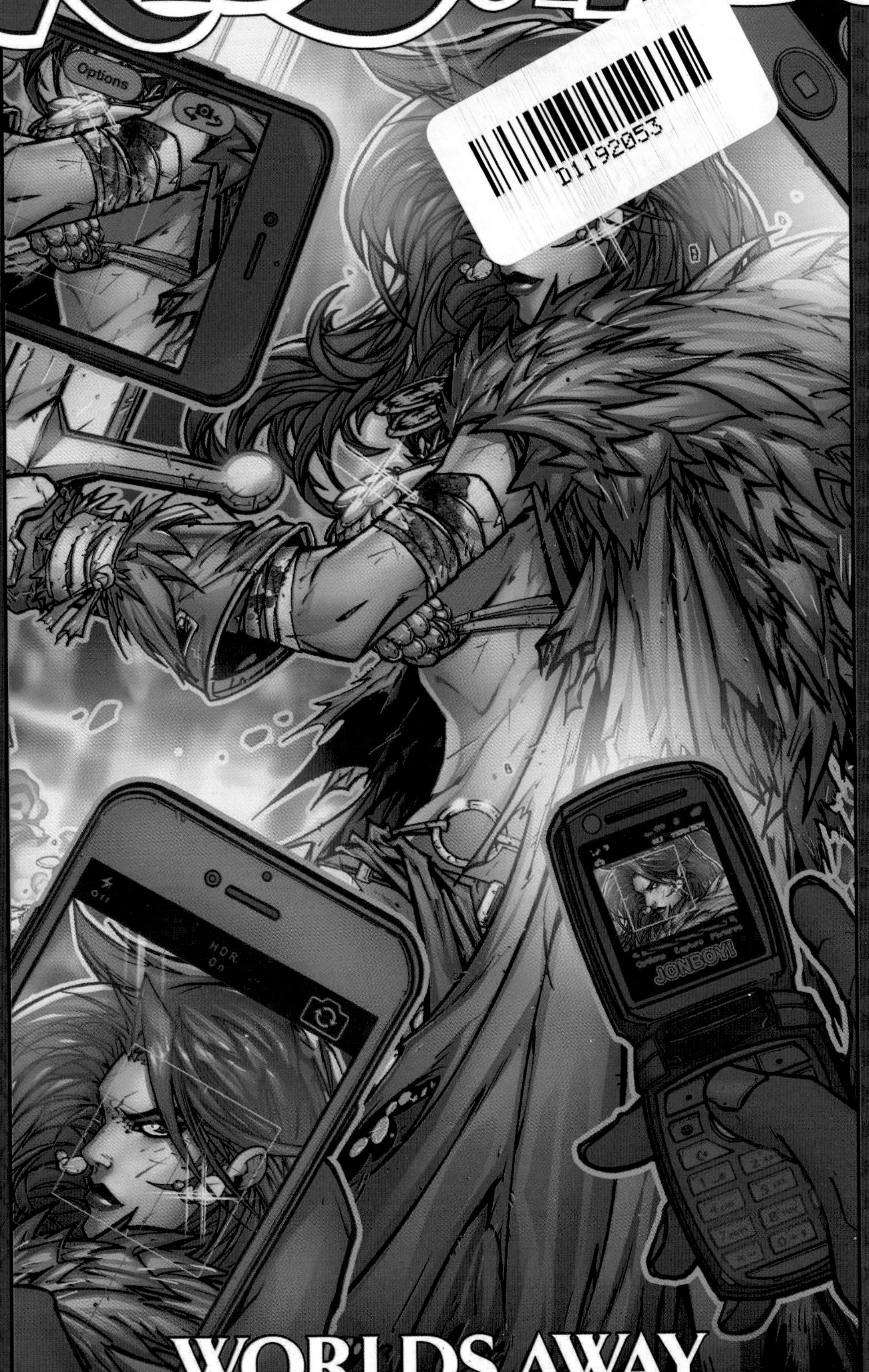
Options
Off
HDR On
JONBOY!

WORLDS AWAY
VOLUME 2

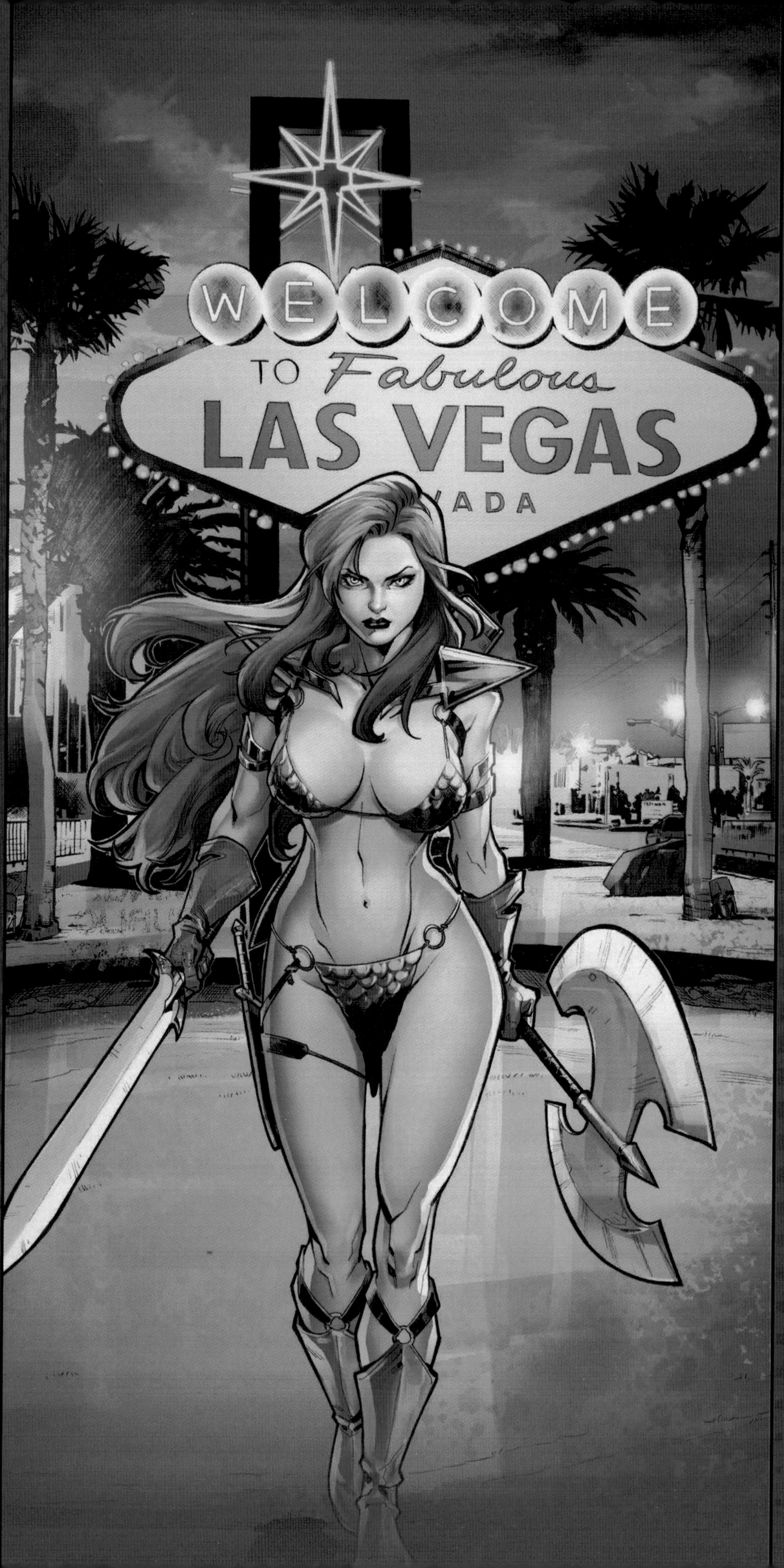
WELCOME
TO Fabulous
LAS VEGAS

RED SONJA® WORLDS AWAY, VOLUME 2: BACK ROADS

written by
AMY CHU

illustrated by
CARLOS GOMEZ

colored by
MOHAN

issues 7, 8, 10, 11 lettered by
SIMON BOWLAND

issue 9 lettered by
TOM NAPOLITANO

collection cover art by
MIKE McKONE

RED SONJA: LONG WALK TO OBLIVION

written by
ERIK BURNHAM

illustrated by
TOM MANDRAKE

colored by
MOHAN

lettered by
TOM NAPOLITANO

co-executive editors JOSEPH RYBANDT & LUKE LIEBERMAN
associate editor ANTHONY MARQUES
book design by CATHLEEN HEARD

based on the heroine created by
ROBERT E. HOWARD

in memory of
ARTHUR LIEBERMAN

special thanks to
SHANNON KINGSTON

DYNAMITE®

Online at www.DYNAMITE.com
On Facebook /Dynamitecomics
On Instagram /Dynamitecomics
On Tumblr dynamitecomics.tumblr.com
On Twitter @dynamitecomics
On YouTube /Dynamitecomics

Nick Barrucci, CEO / Publisher
Juan Collado, President / COO

Joe Rybandt, Executive Editor
Matt Idelson, Senior Editor
Anthony Marques, Associate Editor
Kevin Ketner, Assistant Editor

Jason Ullmeyer, Art Director
Geoff Harkins, Senior Graphic Designer
Cathleen Heard, Graphic Designer
Alexis Persson, Graphic Designer

Chris Caniano, Digital Associate
Rachel Kilbury, Digital Multimedia Associate

Brandon Dante Primavera, V.P. of IT and Operations
Rich Young, Director of Business Development

Alan Payne, V.P. of Sales and Marketing
Janie Mackenzie, Marketing Coordinator
Pat O'Connell, Sales Manager

For media rights, foreign rights, promotions, licensing, and advertising:
marketing@dynamite.com.

ISBN13: 978-1-5241-0582-2
First Printing   10 9 8 7 6 5 4 3 2 1

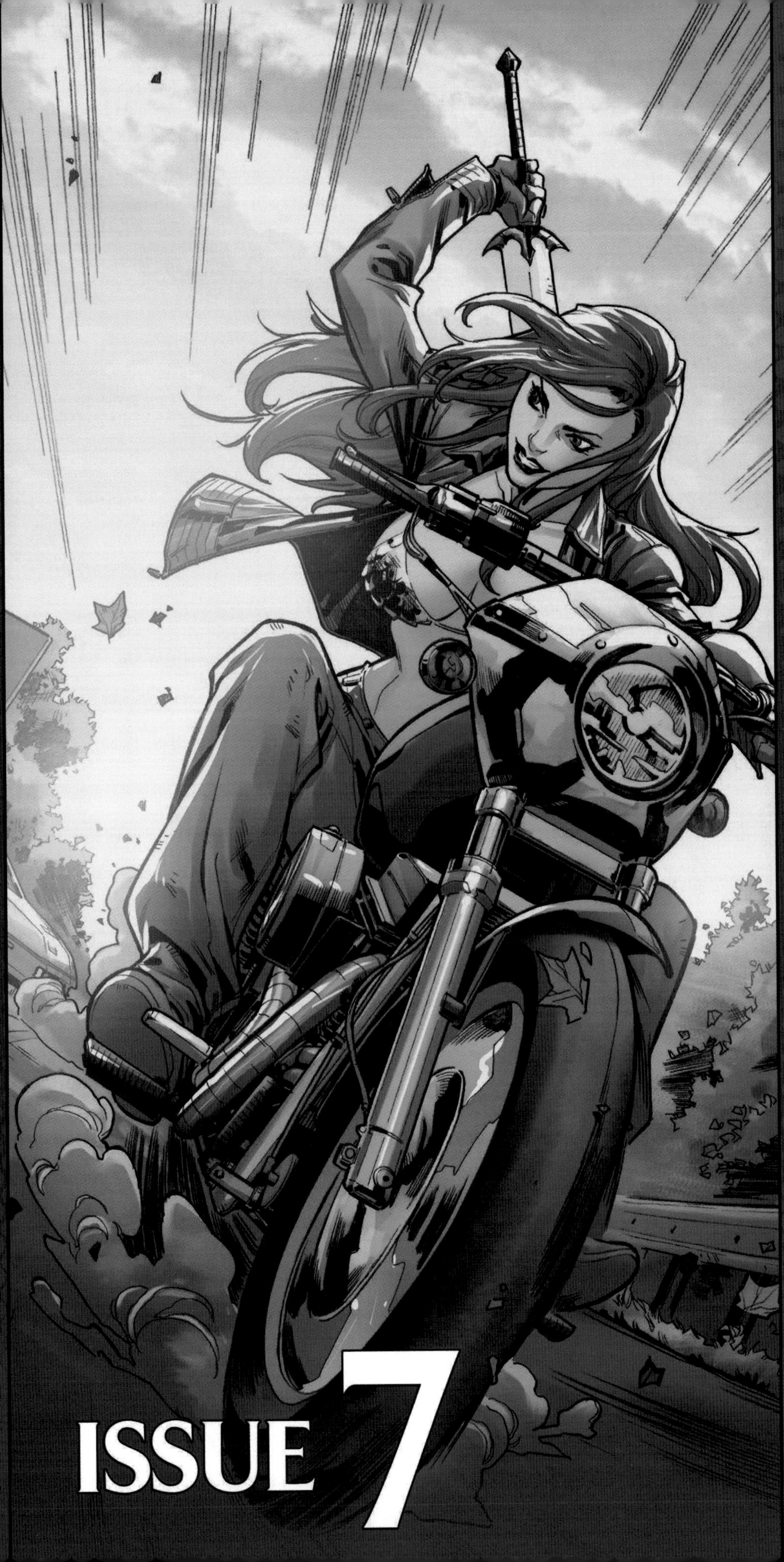
ISSUE 7

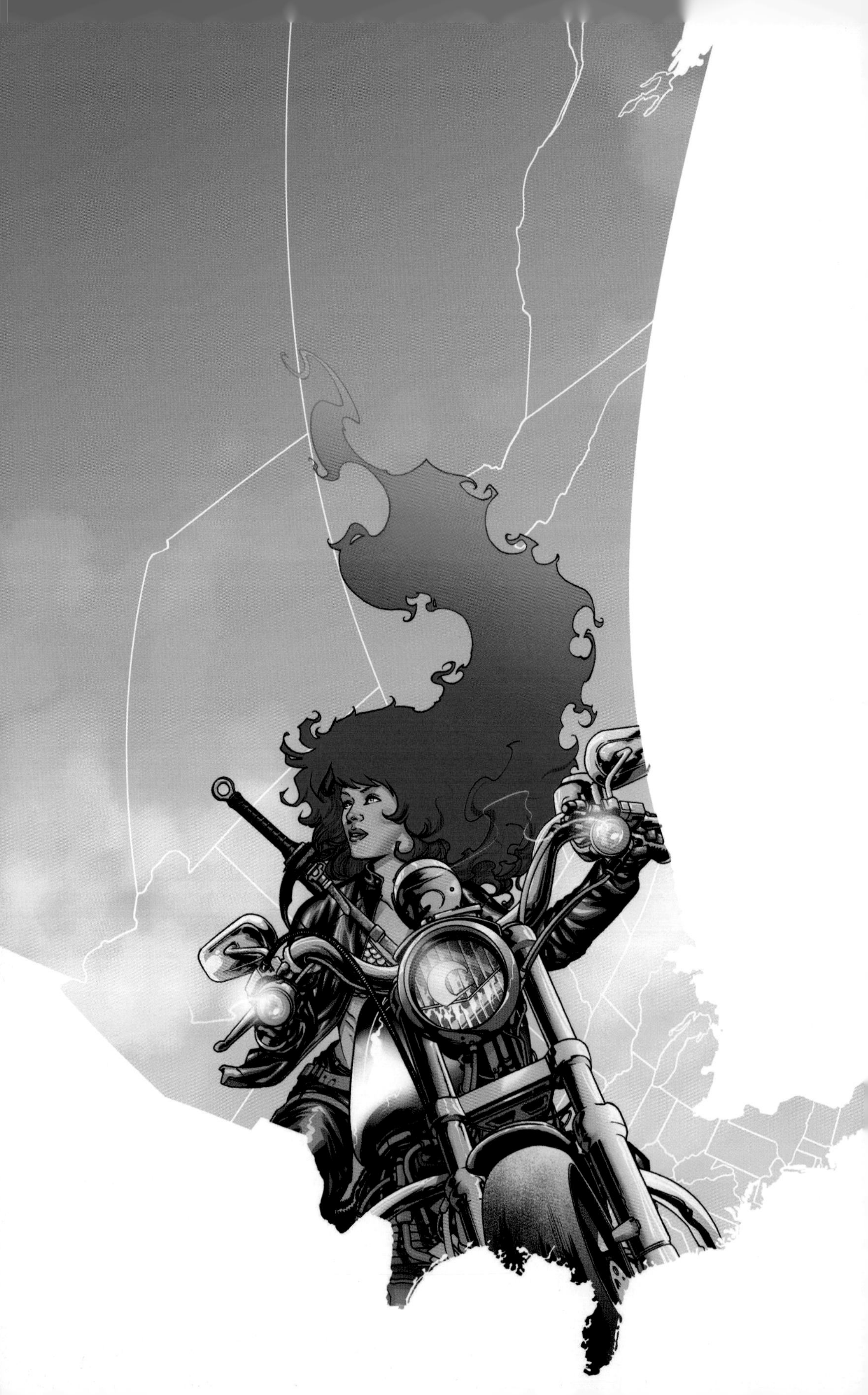

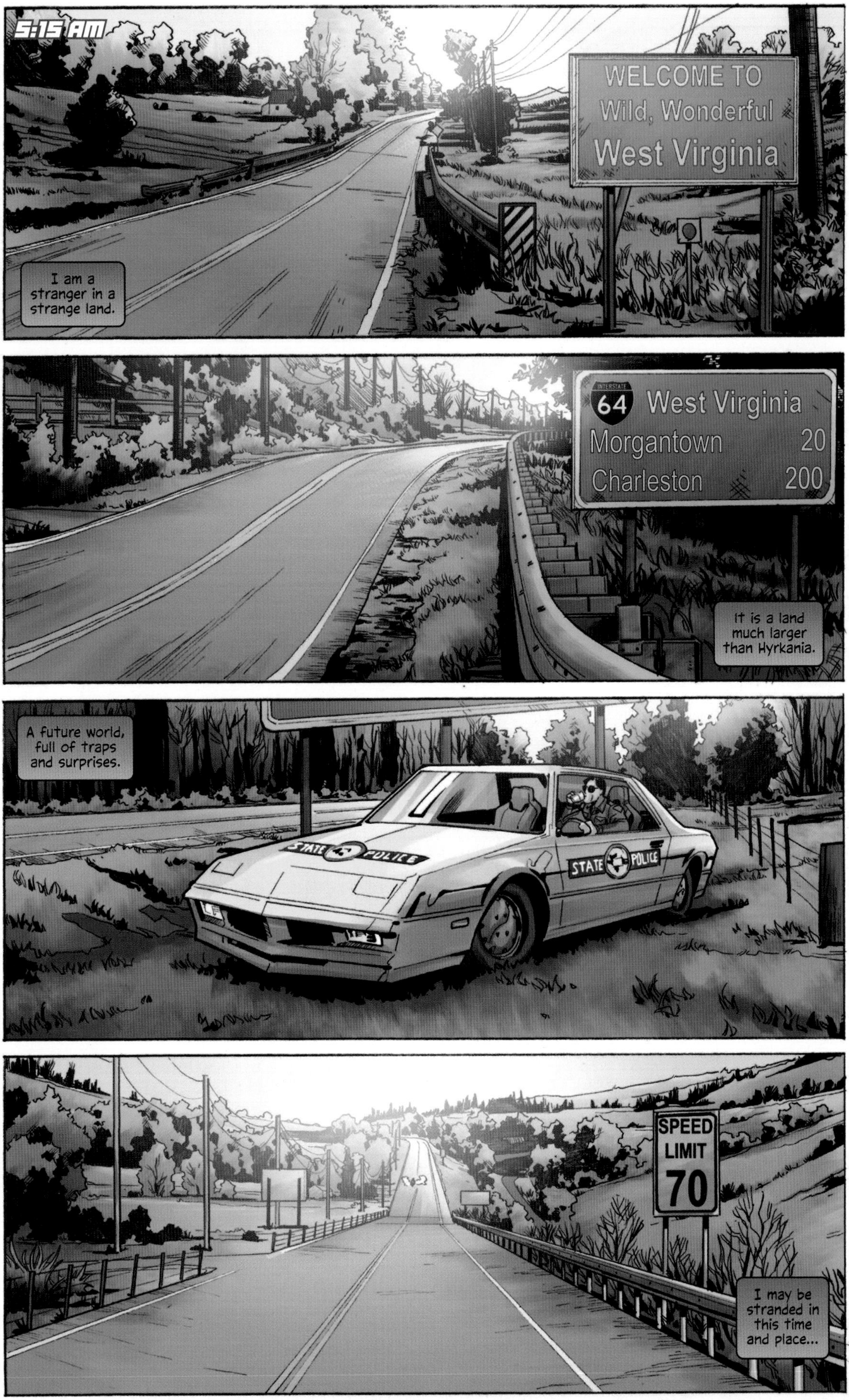

5:15 AM
WELCOME TO
Wild, Wonderful
West Virginia
I am a stranger in a strange land.
INTERSTATE
64
West Virginia
Morgantown 20
Charleston 200
It is a land much larger than Hyrkania.
A future world, full of traps and surprises.
STATE POLICE
STATE POLICE
SPEED
LIMIT
70
I may be stranded in this time and place...

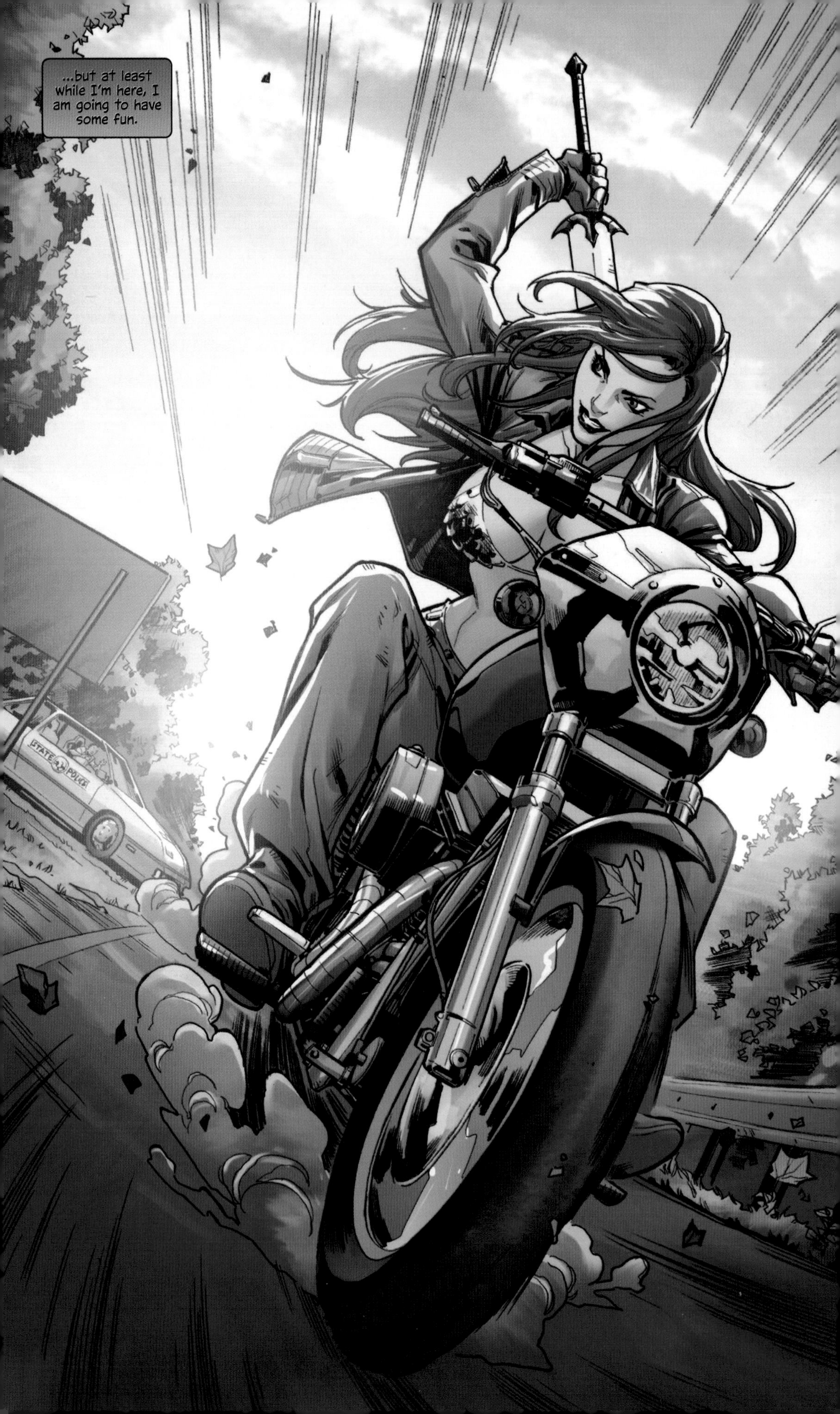
...but at least while I'm here, I am going to have some fun.
STATE POLICE

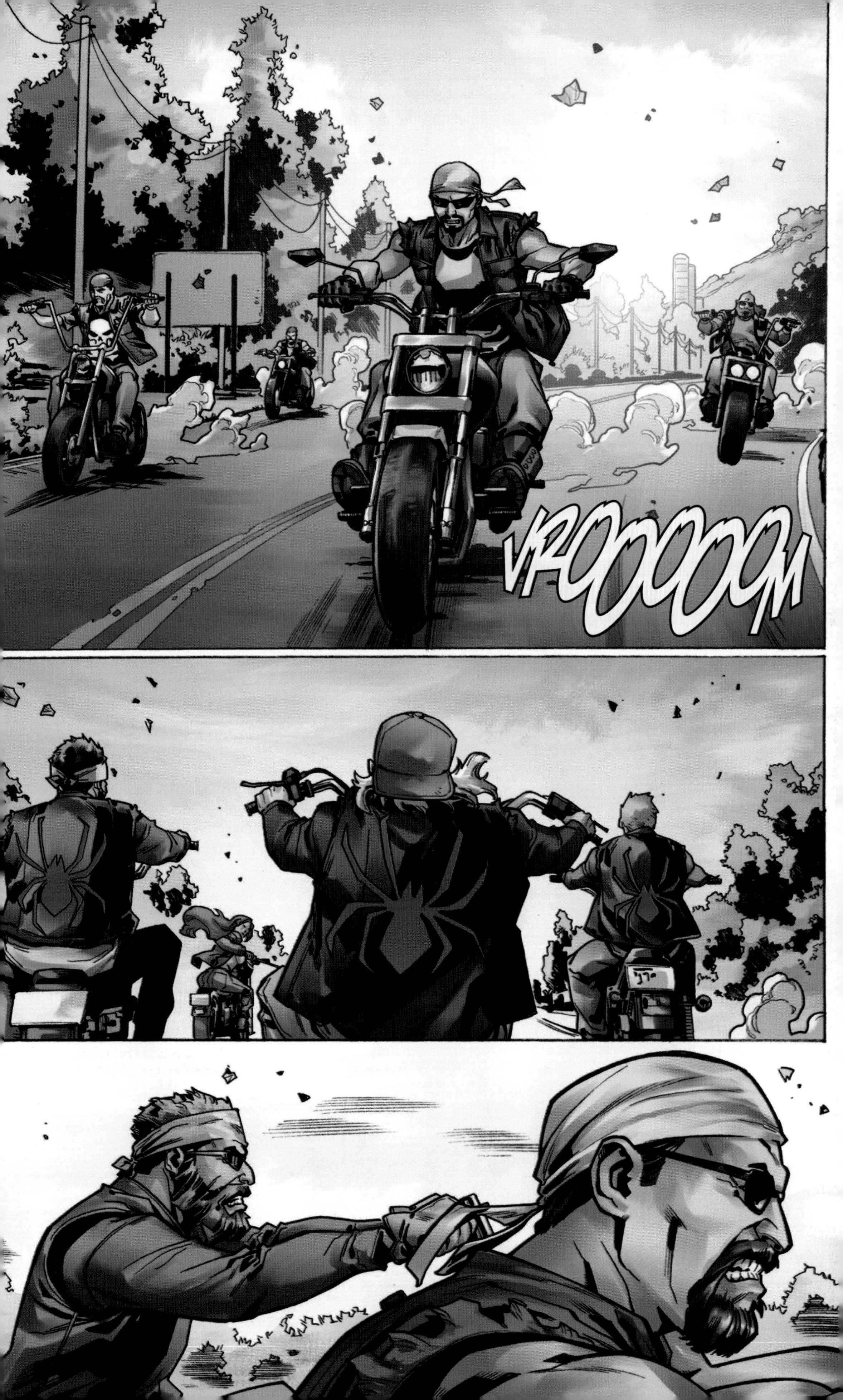
VROOOOOM

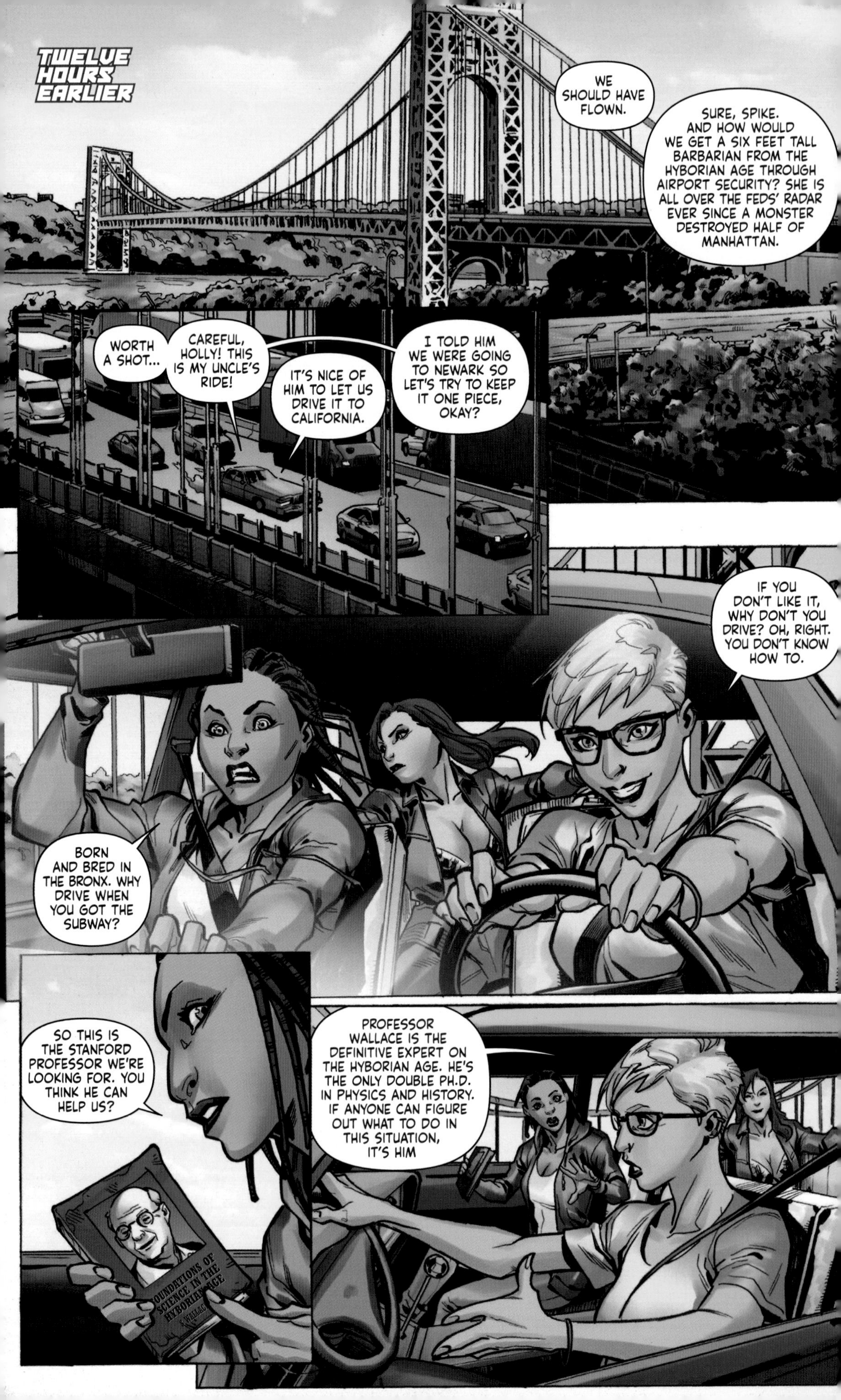
TWELVE HOURS EARLIER
WE SHOULD HAVE FLOWN.
SURE, SPIKE. AND HOW WOULD WE GET A SIX FEET TALL BARBARIAN FROM THE HYBORIAN AGE THROUGH AIRPORT SECURITY? SHE IS ALL OVER THE FEDS' RADAR EVER SINCE A MONSTER DESTROYED HALF OF MANHATTAN.
WORTH A SHOT...
CAREFUL, HOLLY! THIS IS MY UNCLE'S RIDE!
IT'S NICE OF HIM TO LET US DRIVE IT TO CALIFORNIA.
I TOLD HIM WE WERE GOING TO NEWARK SO LET'S TRY TO KEEP IT ONE PIECE, OKAY?
IF YOU DON'T LIKE IT, WHY DON'T YOU DRIVE? OH, RIGHT. YOU DON'T KNOW HOW TO.
BORN AND BRED IN THE BRONX. WHY DRIVE WHEN YOU GOT THE SUBWAY?
SO THIS IS THE STANFORD PROFESSOR WE'RE LOOKING FOR. YOU THINK HE CAN HELP US?
PROFESSOR WALLACE IS THE DEFINITIVE EXPERT ON THE HYBORIAN AGE. HE'S THE ONLY DOUBLE PH.D. IN PHYSICS AND HISTORY. IF ANYONE CAN FIGURE OUT WHAT TO DO IN THIS SITUATION, IT'S HIM
FOUNDATIONS OF SCIENCE IN THE HYBORIAN AGE

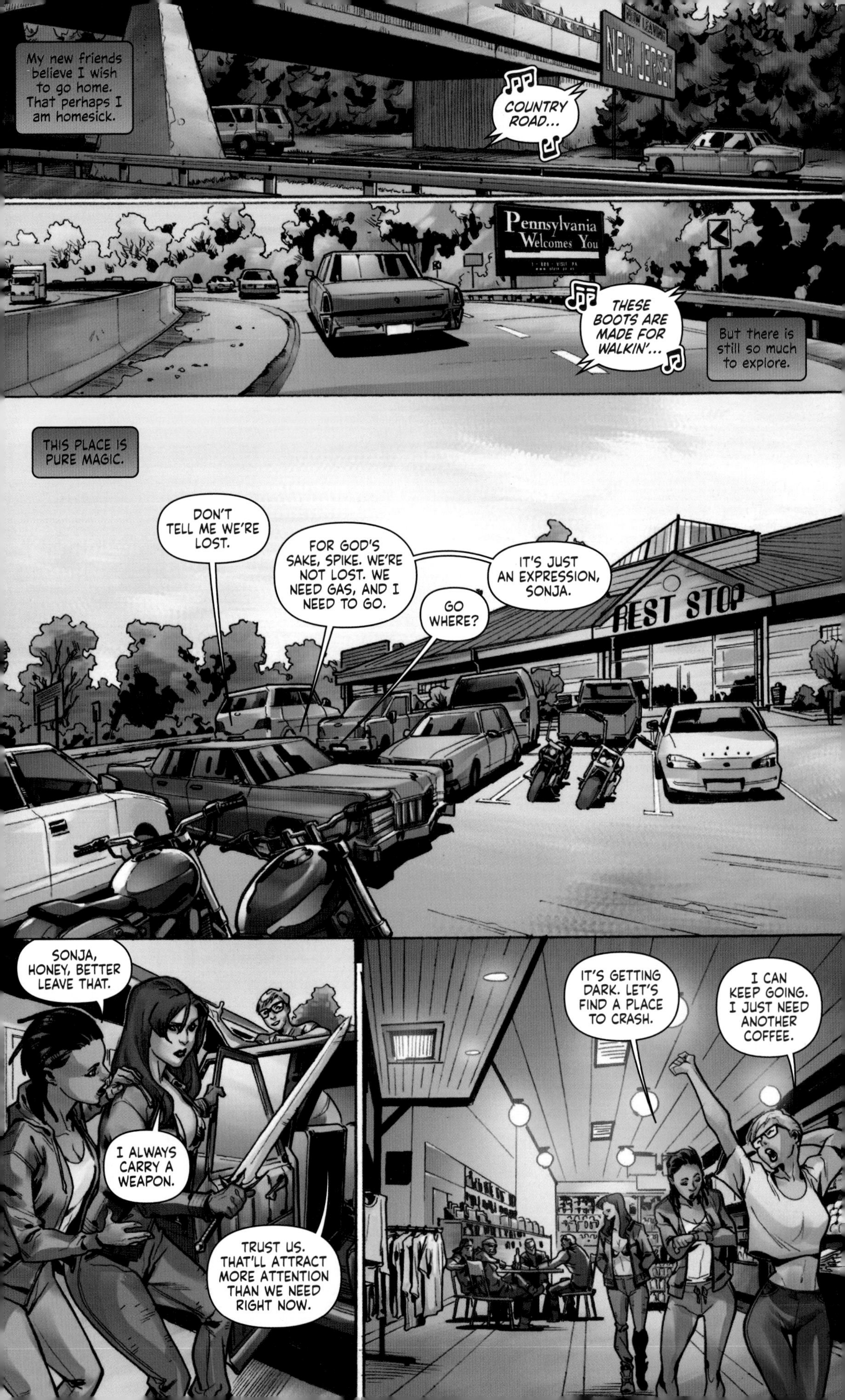
My new friends believe I wish to go home. That perhaps I am homesick.
NEW JERSEY
COUNTRY ROAD...
Pennsylvania Welcomes You
THESE BOOTS ARE MADE FOR WALKIN'...
But there is still so much to explore.
THIS PLACE IS PURE MAGIC.
DON'T TELL ME WE'RE LOST.
FOR GOD'S SAKE, SPIKE. WE'RE NOT LOST. WE NEED GAS, AND I NEED TO GO.
GO WHERE?
IT'S JUST AN EXPRESSION, SONJA.
REST STOP
SONJA, HONEY, BETTER LEAVE THAT.
I ALWAYS CARRY A WEAPON.
TRUST US. THAT'LL ATTRACT MORE ATTENTION THAN WE NEED RIGHT NOW.
IT'S GETTING DARK. LET'S FIND A PLACE TO CRASH.
I CAN KEEP GOING. I JUST NEED ANOTHER COFFEE.

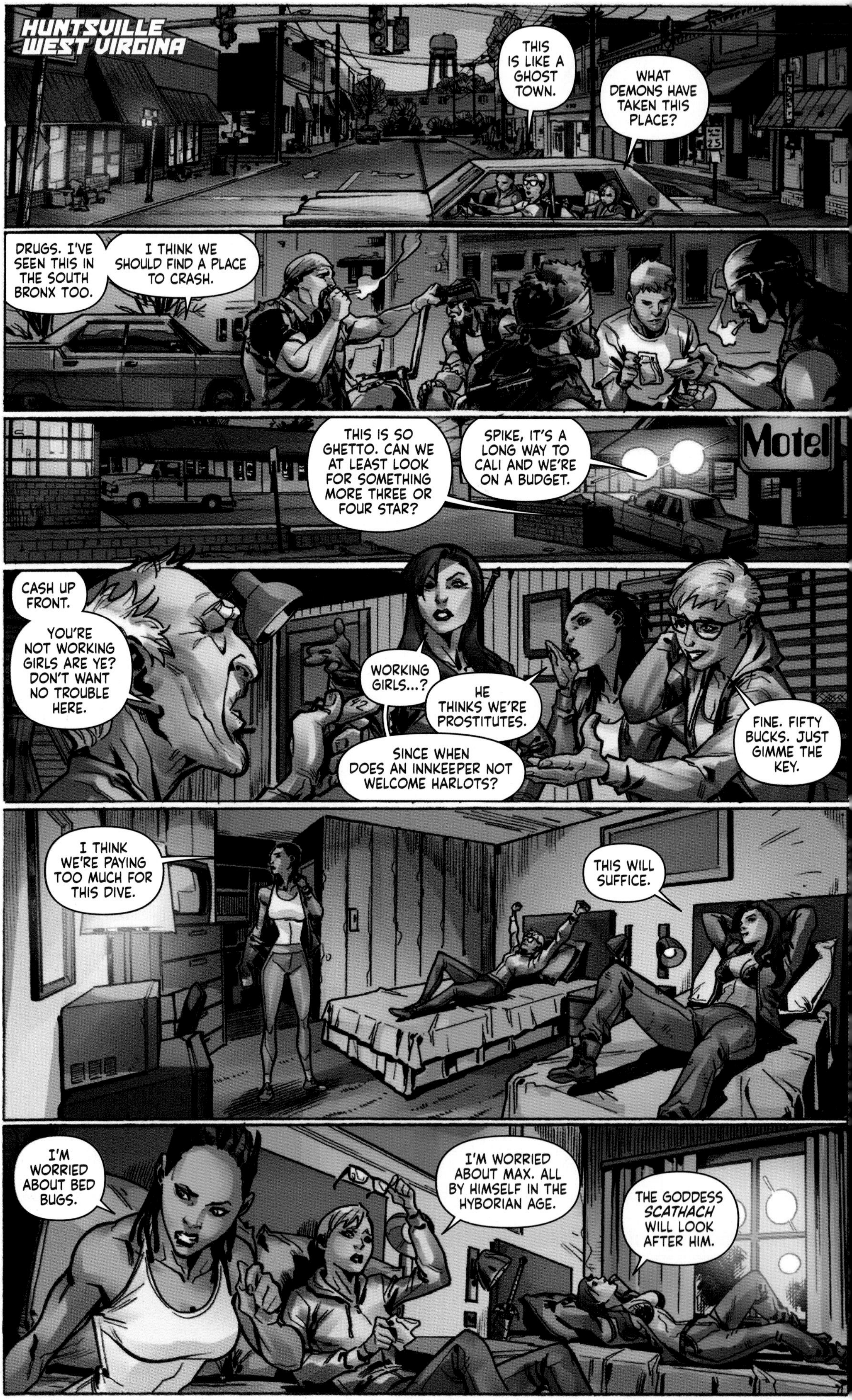
HUNTSVILLE WEST VIRGINA
THIS IS LIKE A GHOST TOWN.
WHAT DEMONS HAVE TAKEN THIS PLACE?
25
DRUGS. I'VE SEEN THIS IN THE SOUTH BRONX TOO.
I THINK WE SHOULD FIND A PLACE TO CRASH.
Motel
THIS IS SO GHETTO. CAN WE AT LEAST LOOK FOR SOMETHING MORE THREE OR FOUR STAR?
SPIKE, IT'S A LONG WAY TO CALI AND WE'RE ON A BUDGET.
CASH UP FRONT.
YOU'RE NOT WORKING GIRLS ARE YE? DON'T WANT NO TROUBLE HERE.
WORKING GIRLS...?
HE THINKS WE'RE PROSTITUTES.
SINCE WHEN DOES AN INNKEEPER NOT WELCOME HARLOTS?
FINE. FIFTY BUCKS. JUST GIMME THE KEY.
I THINK WE'RE PAYING TOO MUCH FOR THIS DIVE.
THIS WILL SUFFICE.
I'M WORRIED ABOUT BED BUGS.
I'M WORRIED ABOUT MAX. ALL BY HIMSELF IN THE HYBORIAN AGE.
THE GODDESS *SCATHACH* WILL LOOK AFTER HIM.

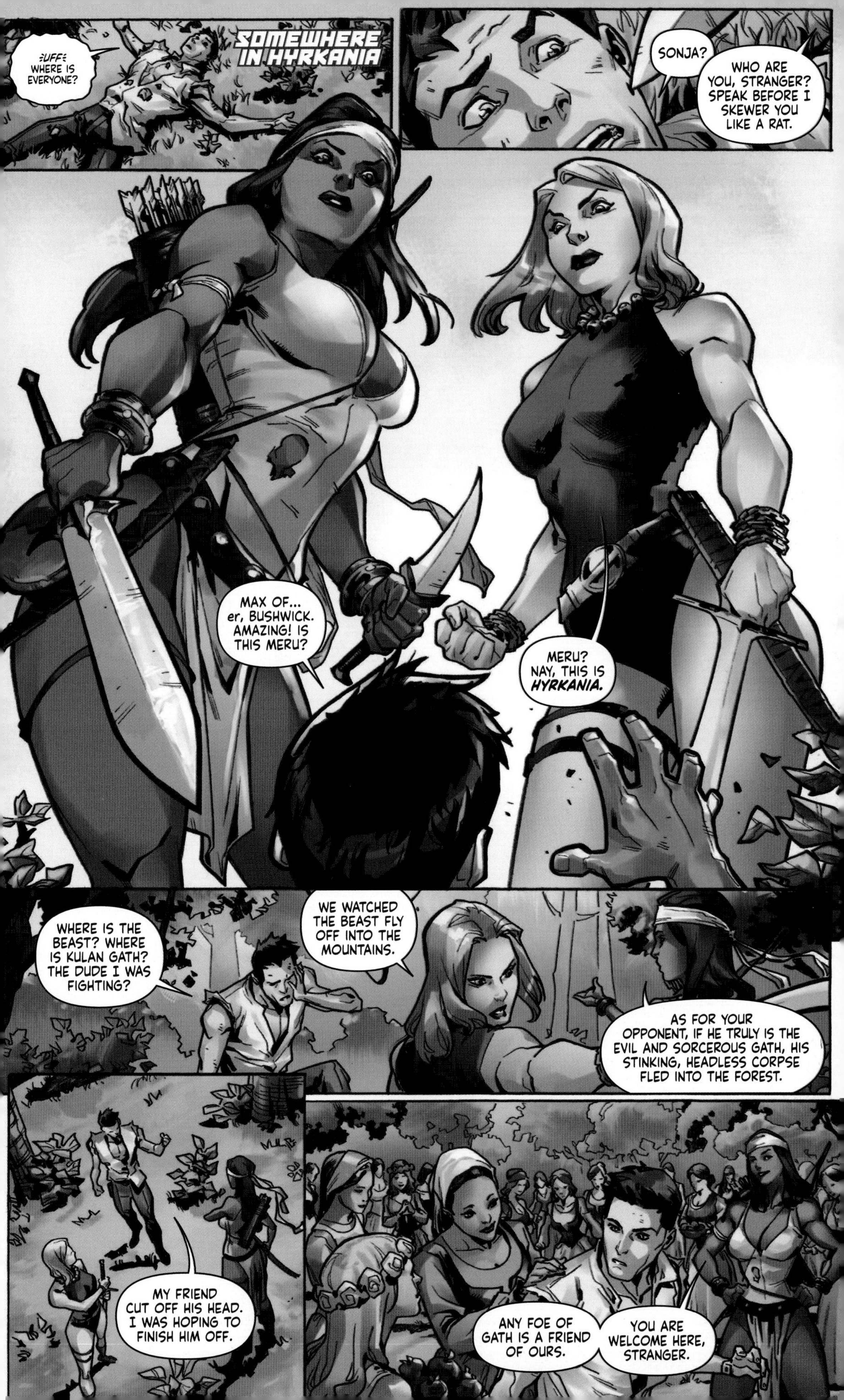
SOMEWHERE IN HYRKANIA
=UFF= WHERE IS EVERYONE?
SONJA?
WHO ARE YOU, STRANGER? SPEAK BEFORE I SKEWER YOU LIKE A RAT.
MAX OF... er, BUSHWICK. AMAZING! IS THIS MERU?
MERU? NAY, THIS IS HYRKANIA.
WHERE IS THE BEAST? WHERE IS KULAN GATH? THE DUDE I WAS FIGHTING?
WE WATCHED THE BEAST FLY OFF INTO THE MOUNTAINS.
AS FOR YOUR OPPONENT, IF HE TRULY IS THE EVIL AND SORCEROUS GATH, HIS STINKING, HEADLESS CORPSE FLED INTO THE FOREST.
MY FRIEND CUT OFF HIS HEAD. I WAS HOPING TO FINISH HIM OFF.
ANY FOE OF GATH IS A FRIEND OF OURS.
YOU ARE WELCOME HERE, STRANGER.

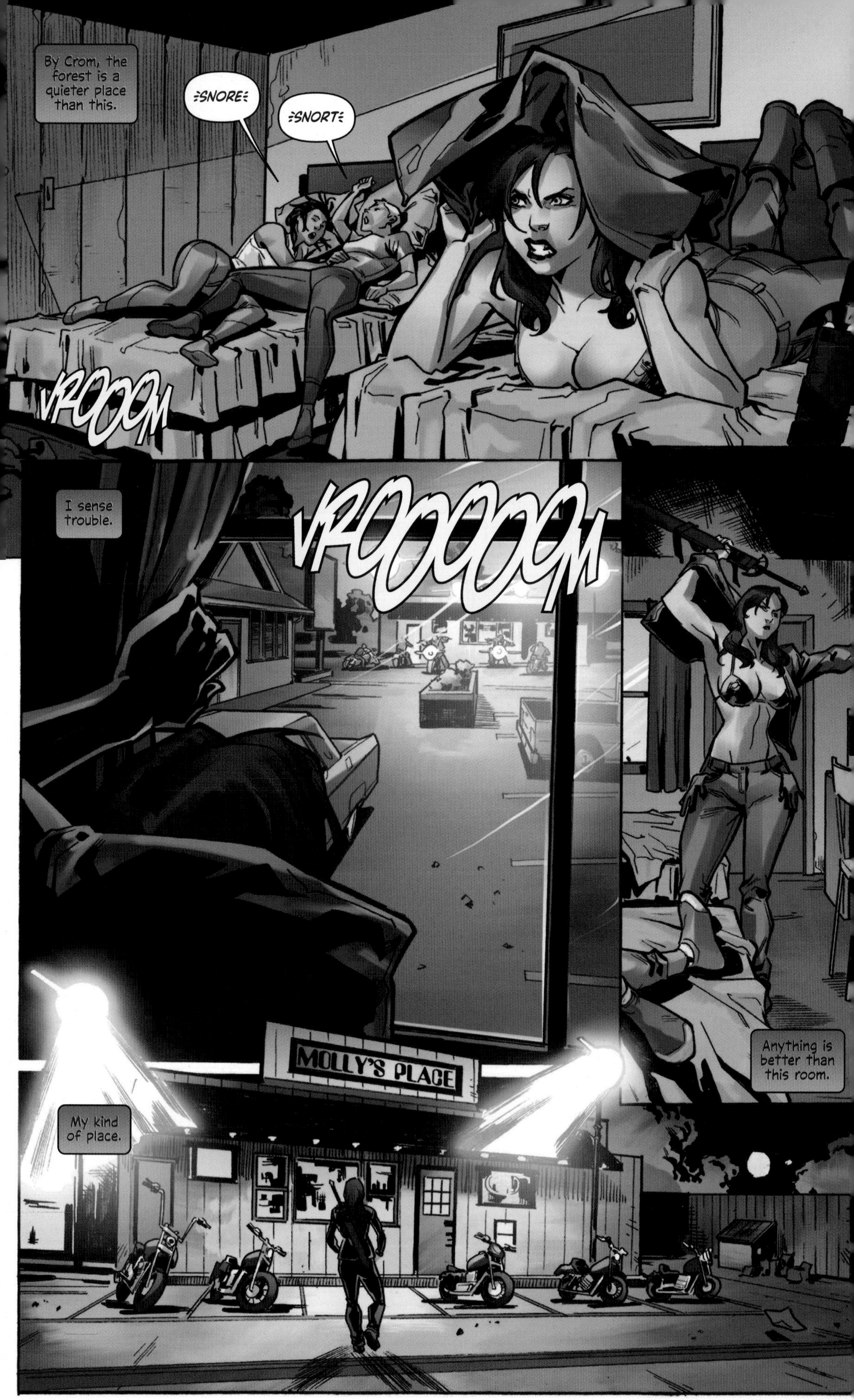
By Crom, the forest is a quieter place than this.
SNORE
SNORT
VROOOM
I sense trouble.
VROOOOOM
Anything is better than this room.
MOLLY'S PLACE
My kind of place.

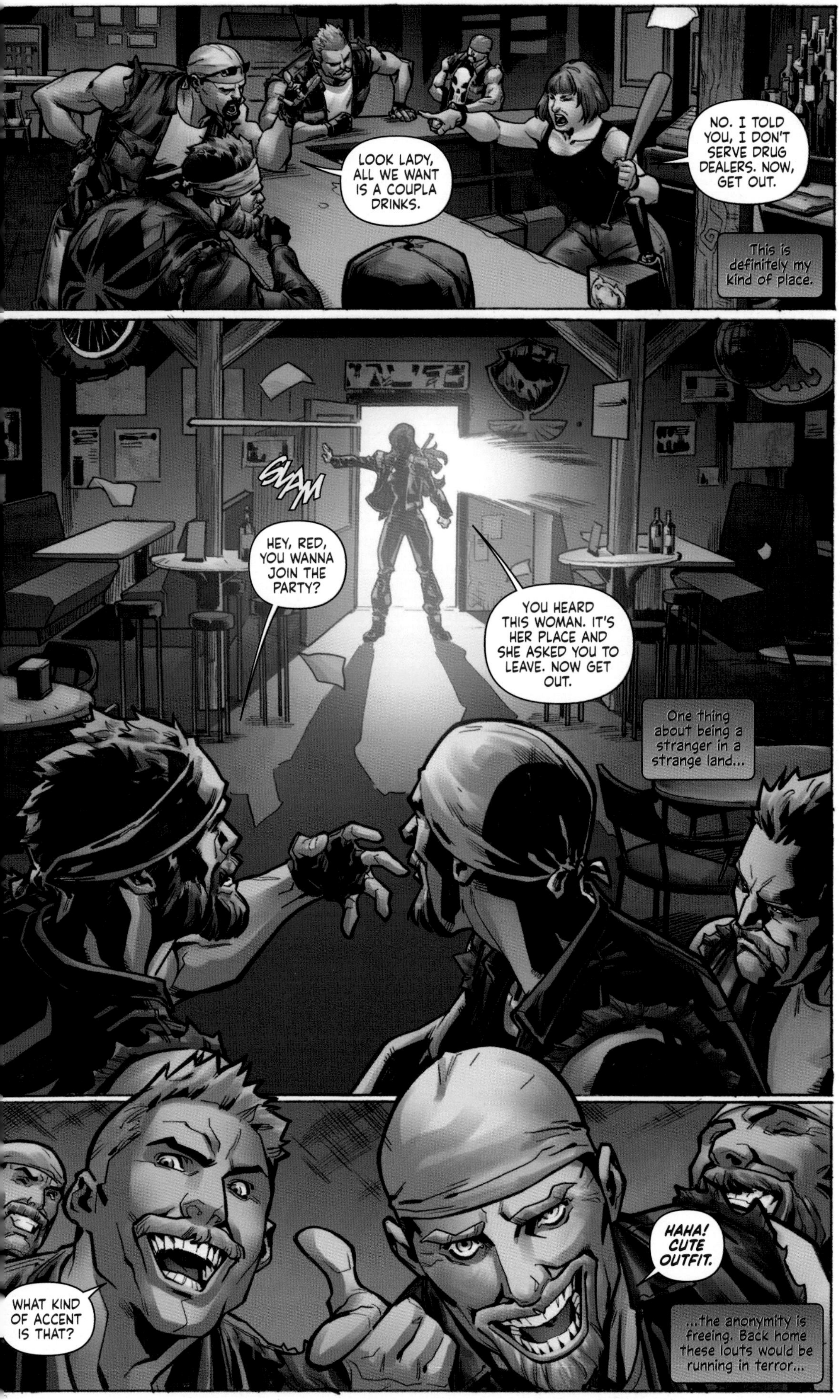
LOOK LADY, ALL WE WANT IS A COUPLA DRINKS.
NO. I TOLD YOU, I DON'T SERVE DRUG DEALERS. NOW, GET OUT.
This is definitely my kind of place.
SLAM
HEY, RED, YOU WANNA JOIN THE PARTY?
YOU HEARD THIS WOMAN. IT'S HER PLACE AND SHE ASKED YOU TO LEAVE. NOW GET OUT.
One thing about being a stranger in a strange land...
WHAT KIND OF ACCENT IS THAT?
HAHA! CUTE OUTFIT.
...the anonymity is freeing. Back home these louts would be running in terror...

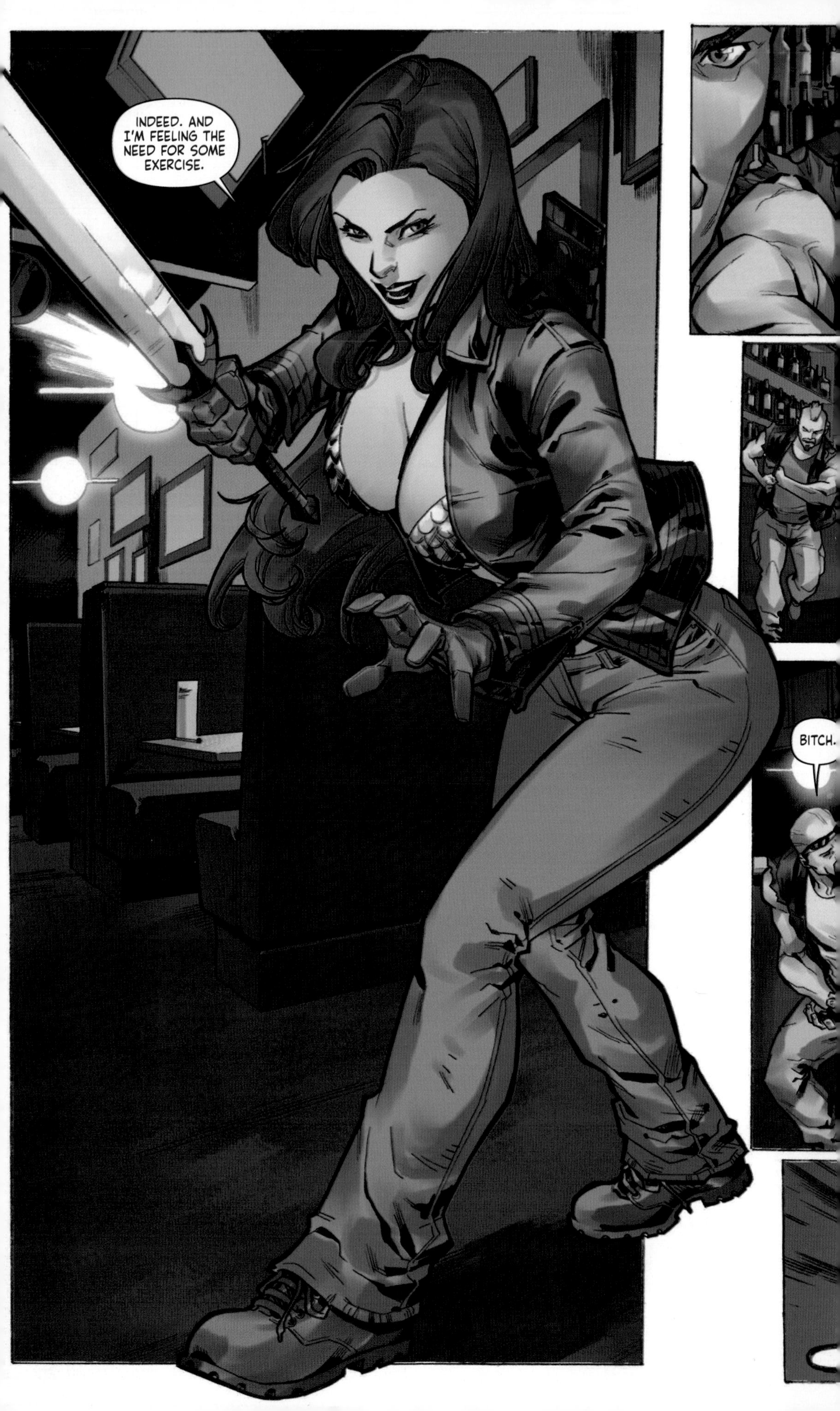
INDEED. AND I'M FEELING THE NEED FOR SOME EXERCISE.
BITCH.

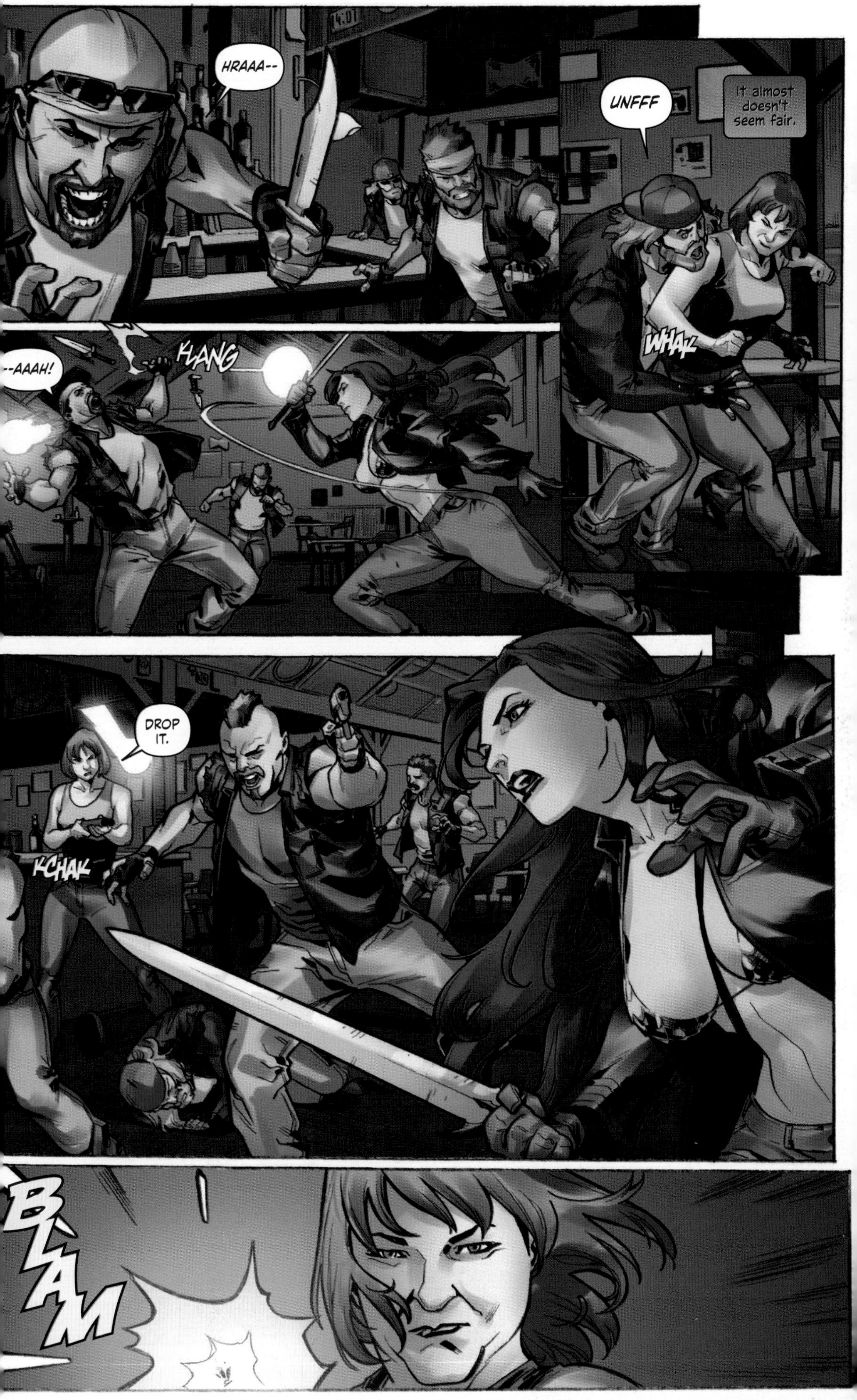
HRAAA--
UNFFF
It almost doesn't seem fair.
WHAK
--AAAH!
KLANG
DROP IT.
KCHAK
BLAM

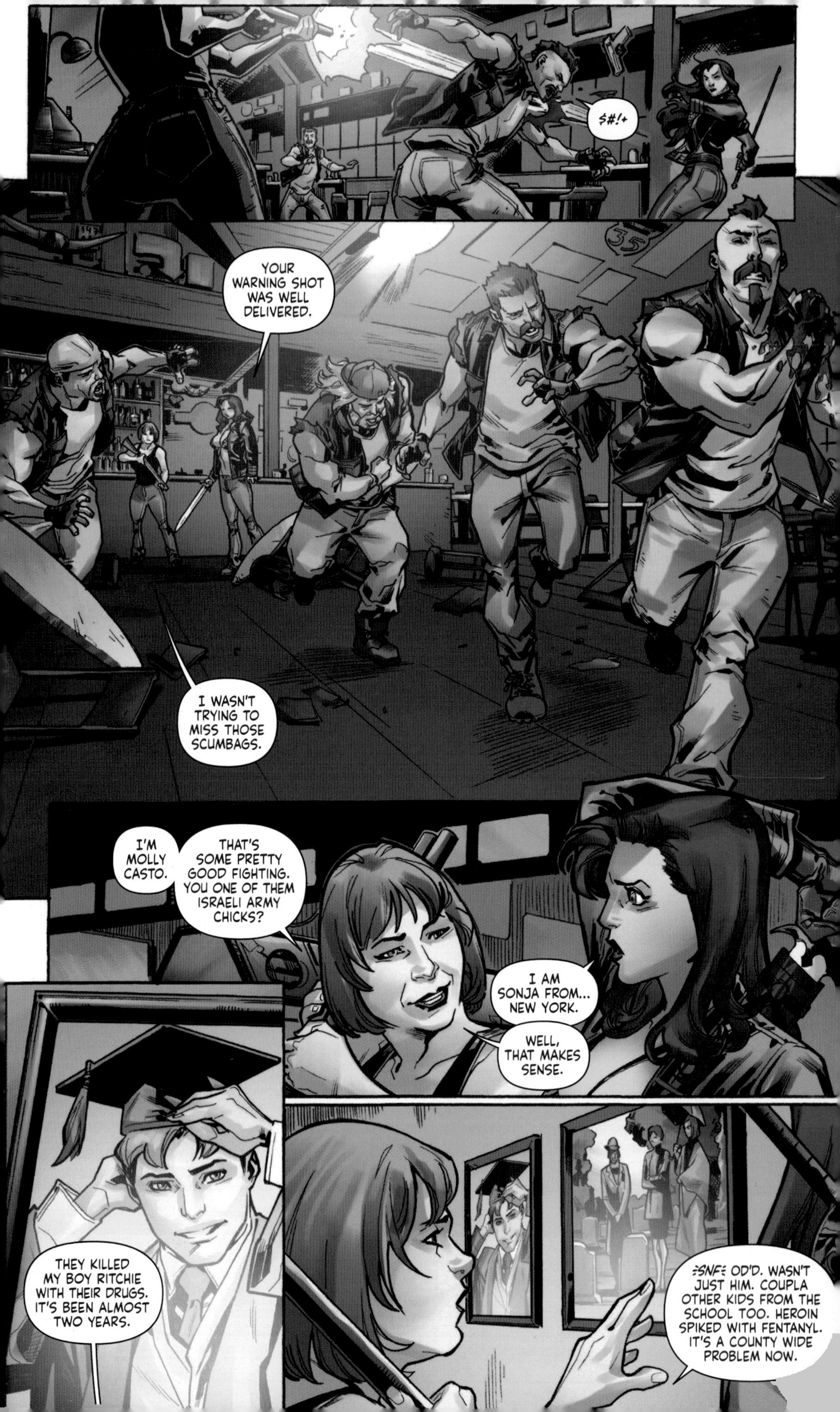
$#!+
YOUR WARNING SHOT WAS WELL DELIVERED.
I WASN'T TRYING TO MISS THOSE SCUMBAGS.
I'M MOLLY CASTO.
THAT'S SOME PRETTY GOOD FIGHTING. YOU ONE OF THEM ISRAELI ARMY CHICKS?
I AM SONJA FROM... NEW YORK.
WELL, THAT MAKES SENSE.
THEY KILLED MY BOY RITCHIE WITH THEIR DRUGS. IT'S BEEN ALMOST TWO YEARS.
SNF OD'D. WASN'T JUST HIM. COUPLA OTHER KIDS FROM THE SCHOOL TOO. HEROIN SPIKED WITH FENTANYL. IT'S A COUNTY WIDE PROBLEM NOW.

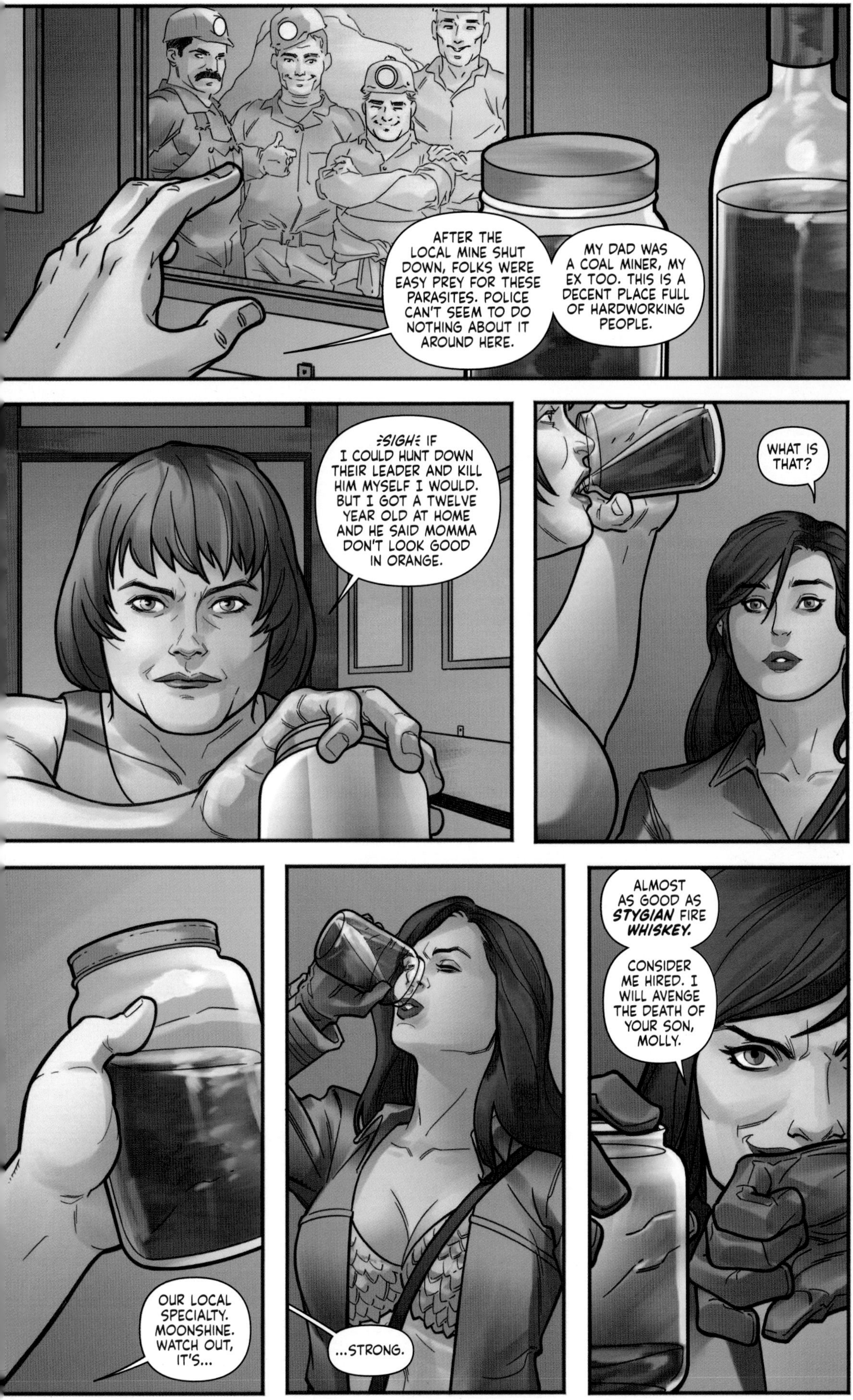

AFTER THE LOCAL MINE SHUT DOWN, FOLKS WERE EASY PREY FOR THESE PARASITES. POLICE CAN'T SEEM TO DO NOTHING ABOUT IT AROUND HERE.
MY DAD WAS A COAL MINER, MY EX TOO. THIS IS A DECENT PLACE FULL OF HARDWORKING PEOPLE.
SIGH IF I COULD HUNT DOWN THEIR LEADER AND KILL HIM MYSELF I WOULD. BUT I GOT A TWELVE YEAR OLD AT HOME AND HE SAID MOMMA DON'T LOOK GOOD IN ORANGE.
WHAT IS THAT?
OUR LOCAL SPECIALTY. MOONSHINE. WATCH OUT, IT'S...
...STRONG.
ALMOST AS GOOD AS STYGIAN FIRE WHISKEY.
CONSIDER ME HIRED. I WILL AVENGE THE DEATH OF YOUR SON, MOLLY.

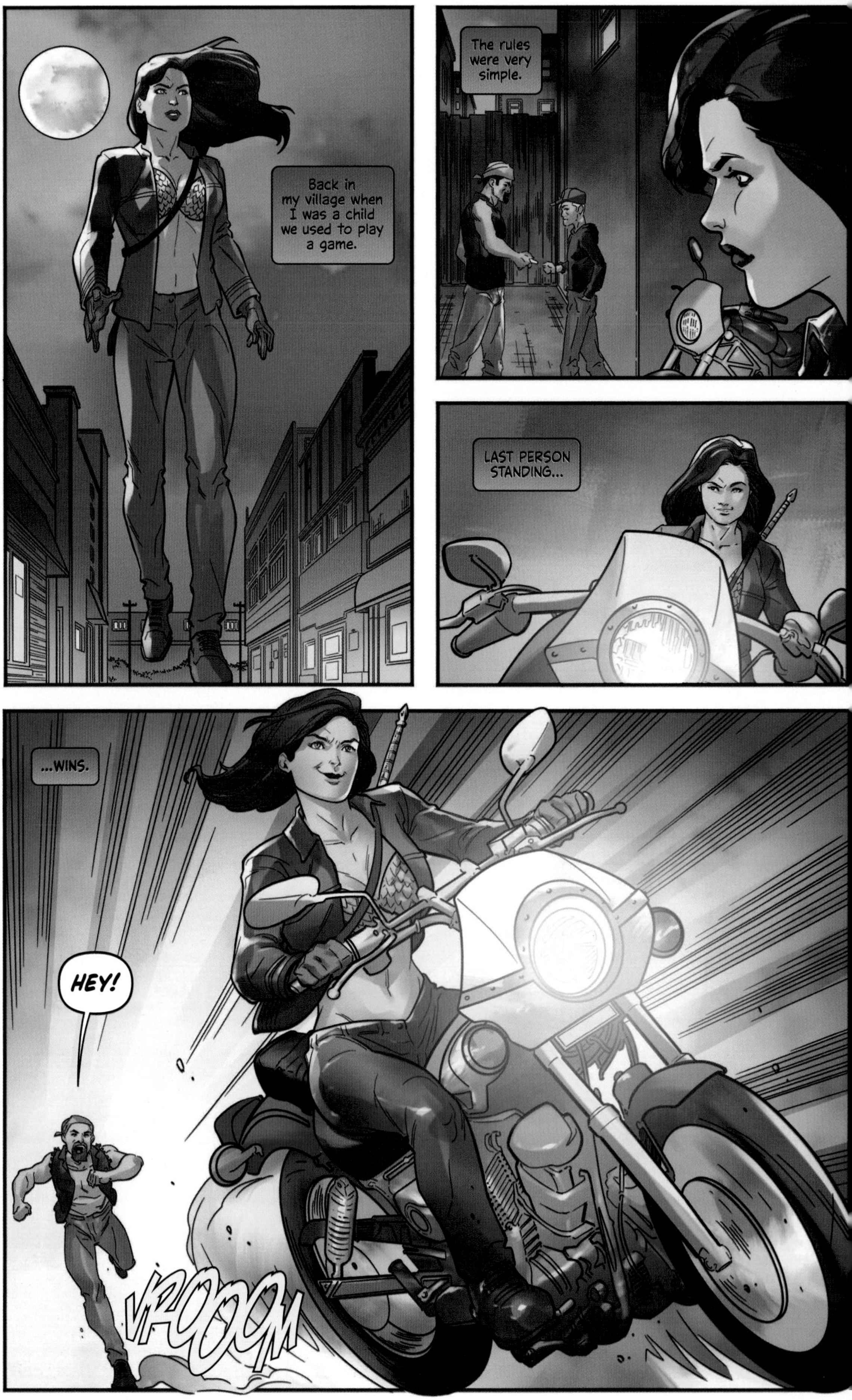
Back in my village when I was a child we used to play a game.
The rules were very simple.
LAST PERSON STANDING...
...WINS.
HEY!
VROOOM

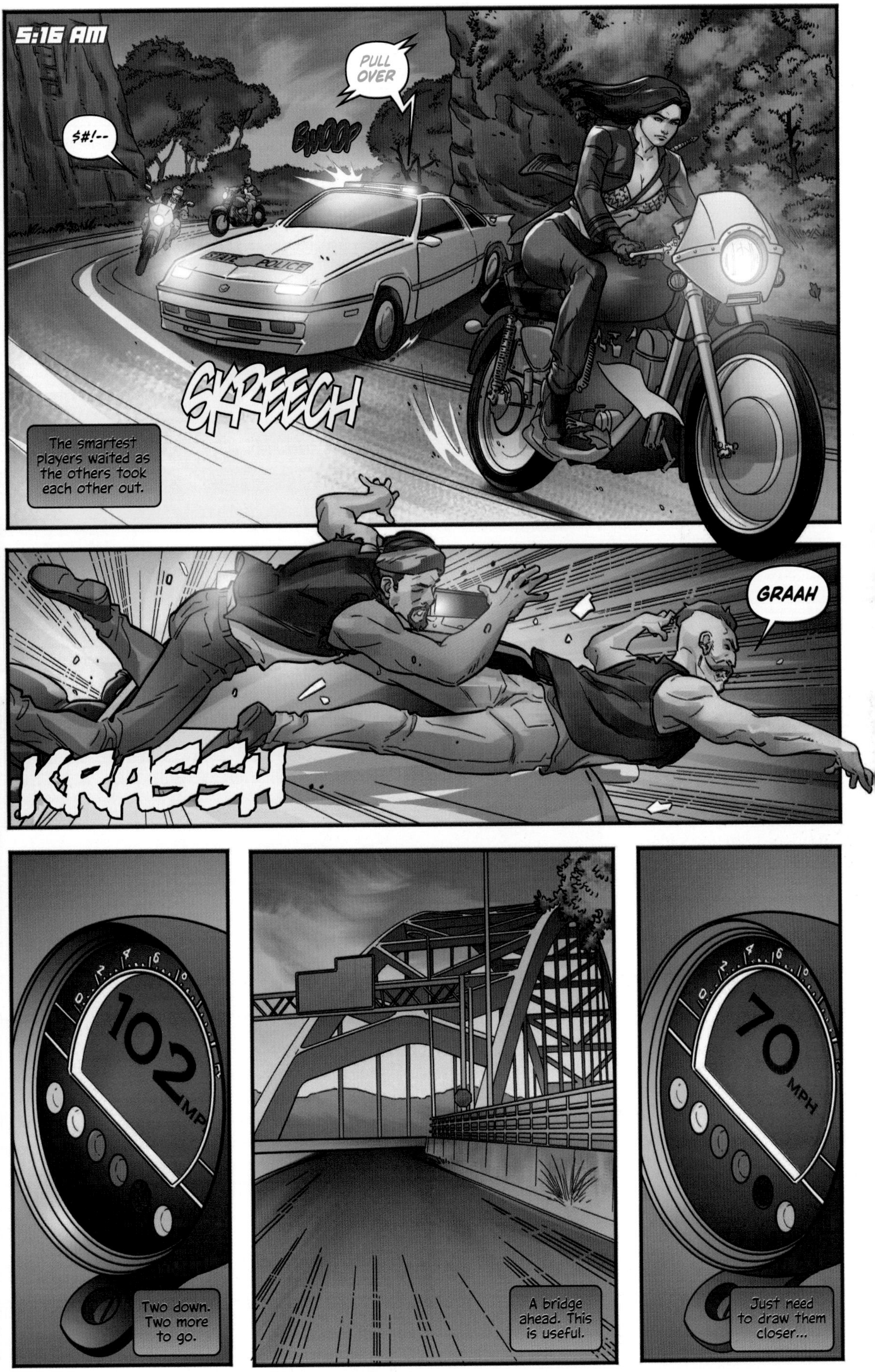
5:16 AM
$#!--
PULL OVER
BWOOP
STATE POLICE
SKREECH
The smartest players waited as the others took each other out.
GRAAH
KRASSH
102 MP
Two down. Two more to go.
A bridge ahead. This is useful.
70 MPH
Just need to draw them closer...

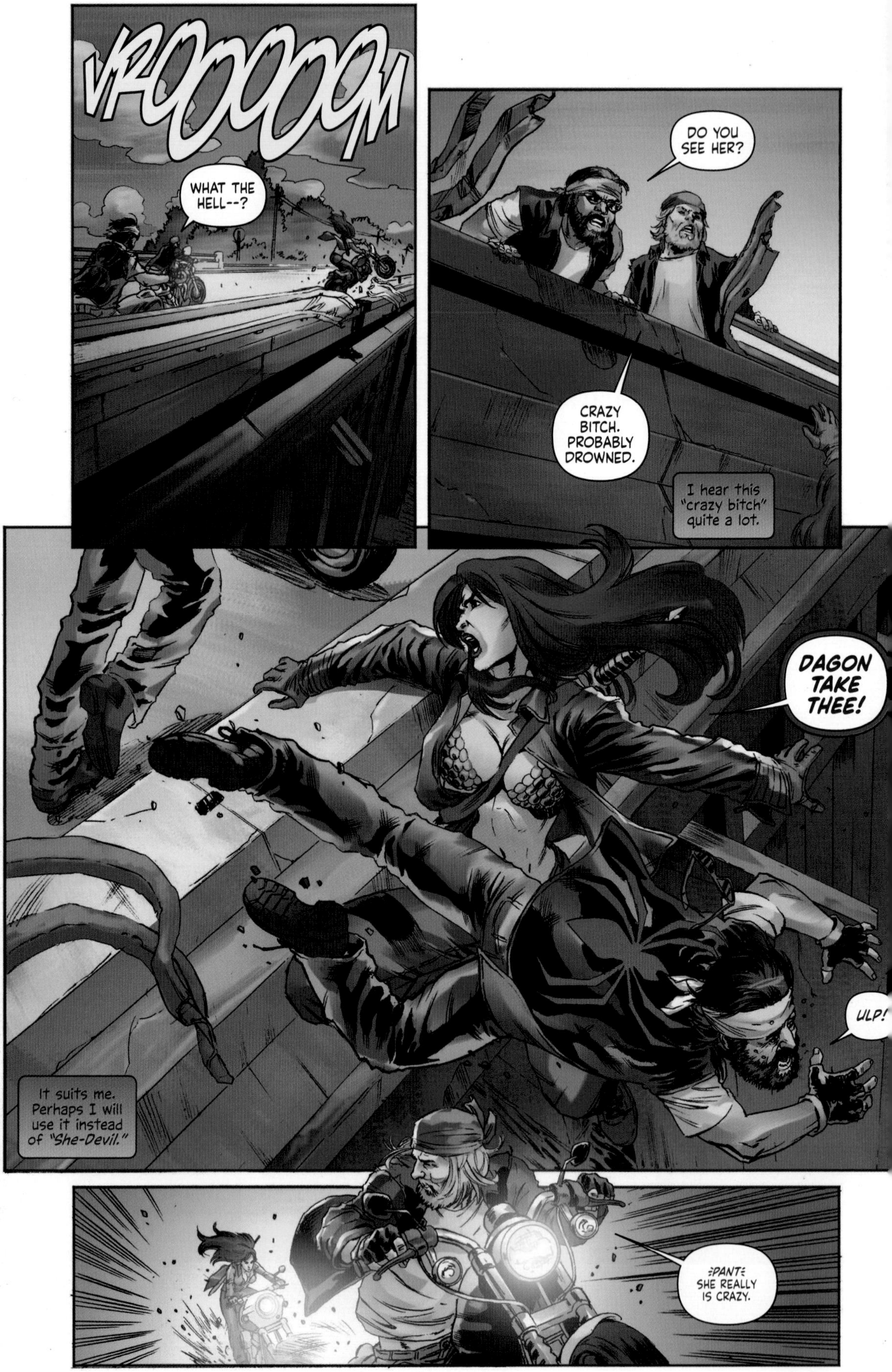
VROOOOOM
WHAT THE HELL--?
DO YOU SEE HER?
CRAZY BITCH. PROBABLY DROWNED.
I hear this "crazy bitch" quite a lot.
DAGON TAKE THEE!
ULP!
It suits me. Perhaps I will use it instead of "She-Devil."
PANT
SHE REALLY IS CRAZY.

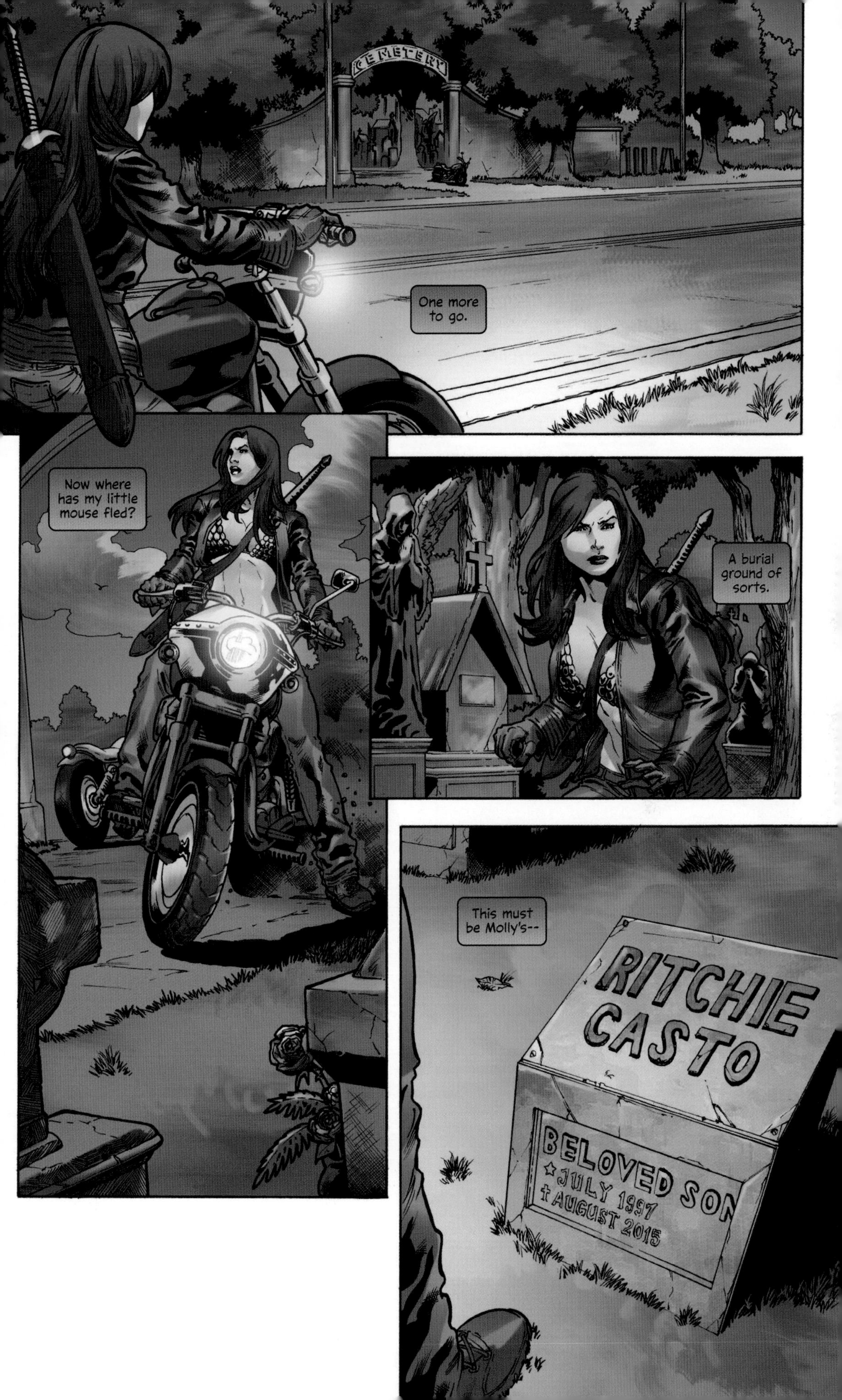
CEMETERY
One more to go.
Now where has my little mouse fled?
A burial ground of sorts.
This must be Molly's--
RITCHIE CASTO
BELOVED SON
JULY 1997
AUGUST 2015

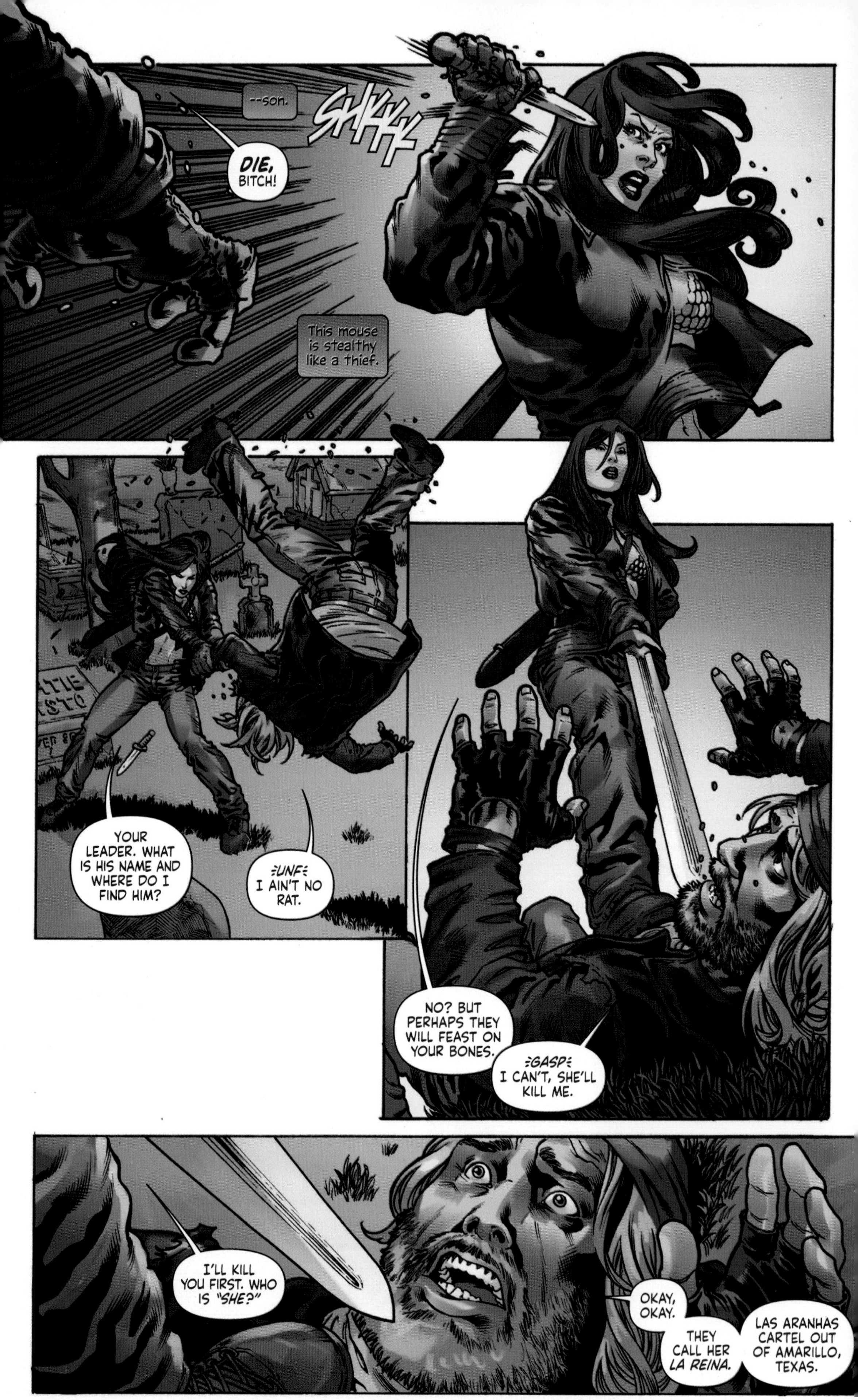
--son.
DIE, BITCH!
SHKKK
This mouse is stealthy like a thief.
YOUR LEADER. WHAT IS HIS NAME AND WHERE DO I FIND HIM?
UNF I AIN'T NO RAT.
NO? BUT PERHAPS THEY WILL FEAST ON YOUR BONES.
GASP I CAN'T, SHE'LL KILL ME.
I'LL KILL YOU FIRST. WHO IS "SHE?"
OKAY, OKAY.
THEY CALL HER LA REINA.
LAS ARANHAS CARTEL OUT OF AMARILLO, TEXAS.

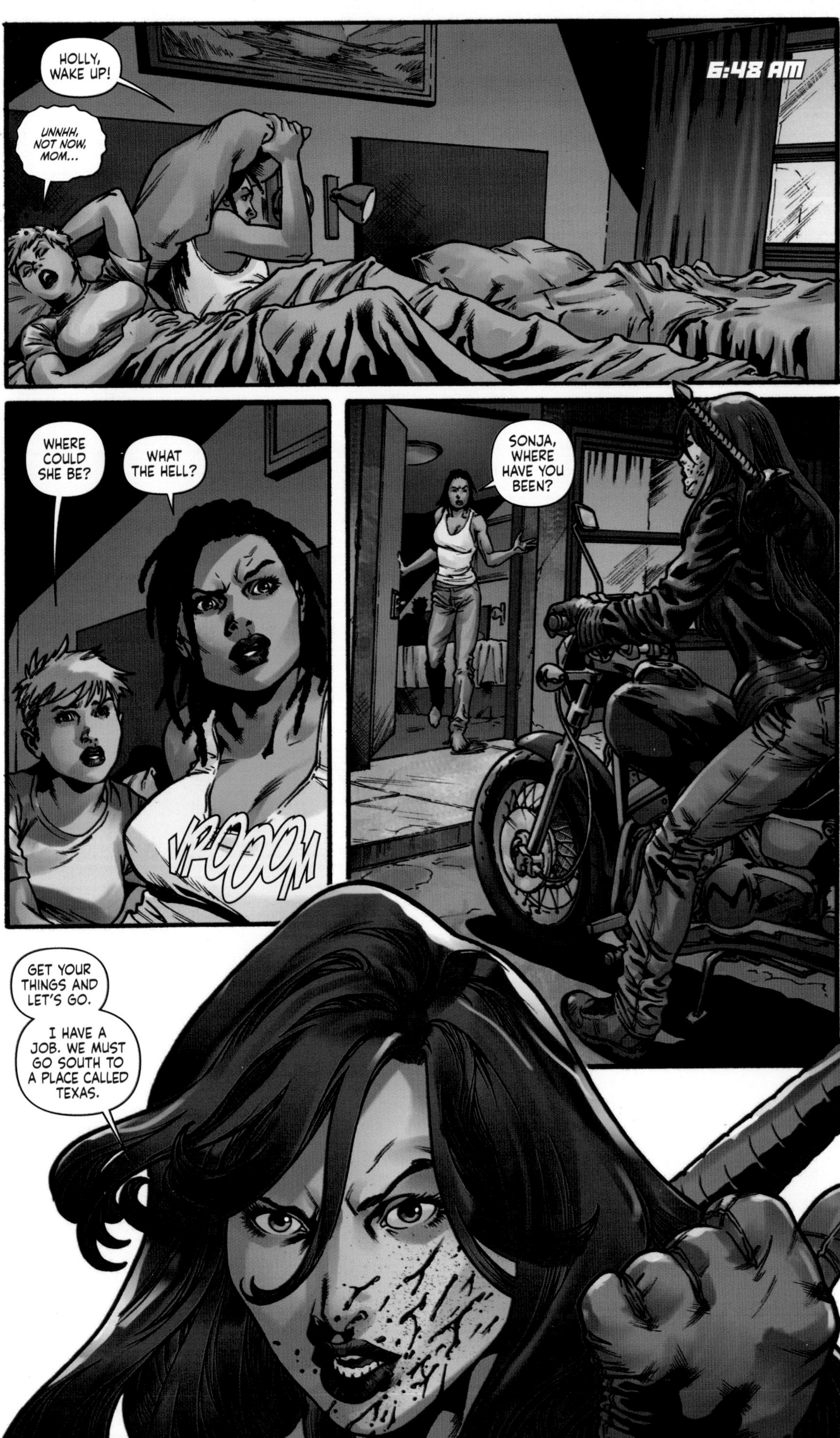
6:48 AM
HOLLY, WAKE UP!
UNNHH, NOT NOW, MOM...
WHERE COULD SHE BE?
WHAT THE HELL?
VROOOM
SONJA, WHERE HAVE YOU BEEN?
GET YOUR THINGS AND LET'S GO.
I HAVE A JOB. WE MUST GO SOUTH TO A PLACE CALLED TEXAS.

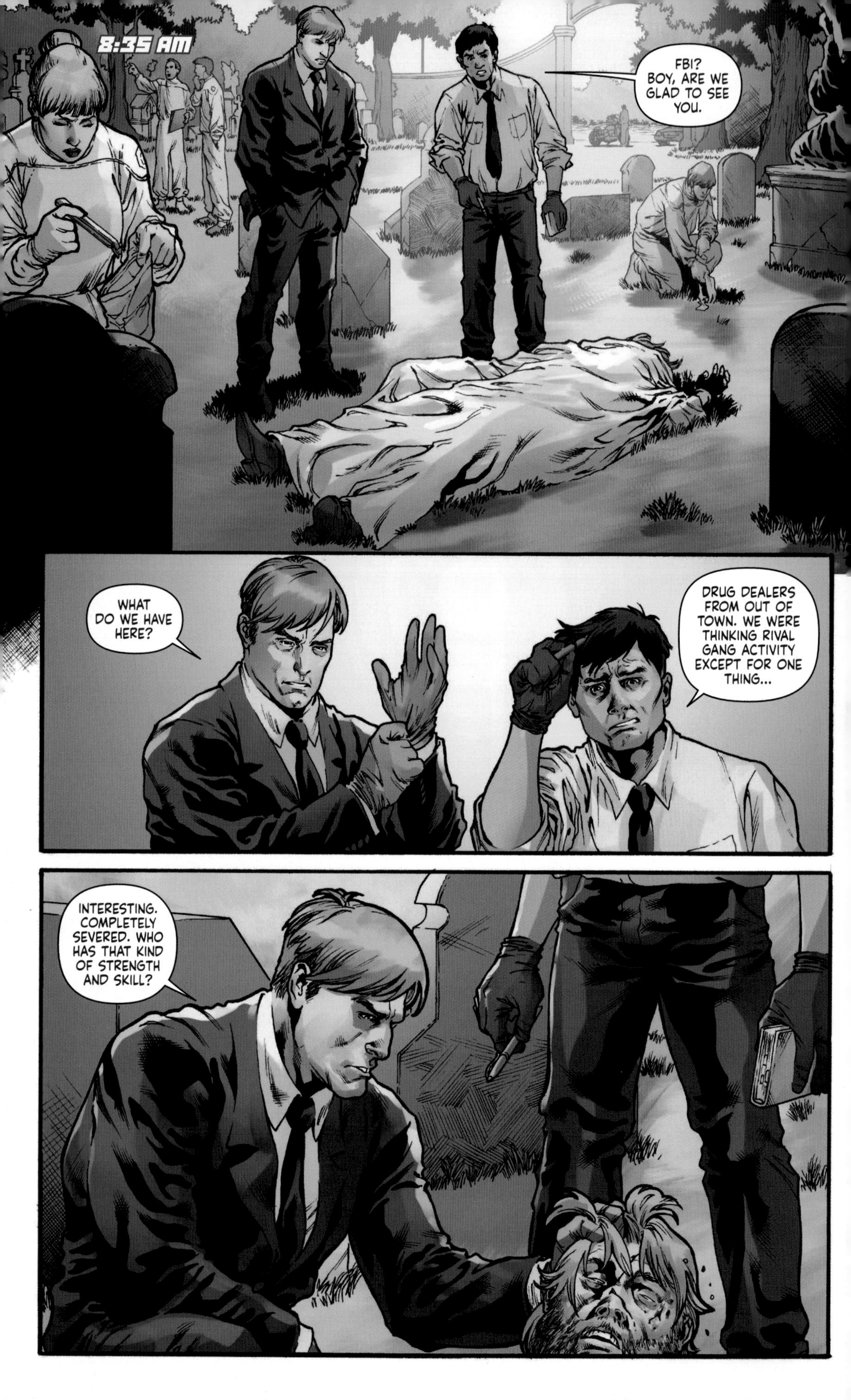
8:35 AM
FBI? BOY, ARE WE GLAD TO SEE YOU.
WHAT DO WE HAVE HERE?
DRUG DEALERS FROM OUT OF TOWN. WE WERE THINKING RIVAL GANG ACTIVITY EXCEPT FOR ONE THING...
INTERESTING. COMPLETELY SEVERED. WHO HAS THAT KIND OF STRENGTH AND SKILL?

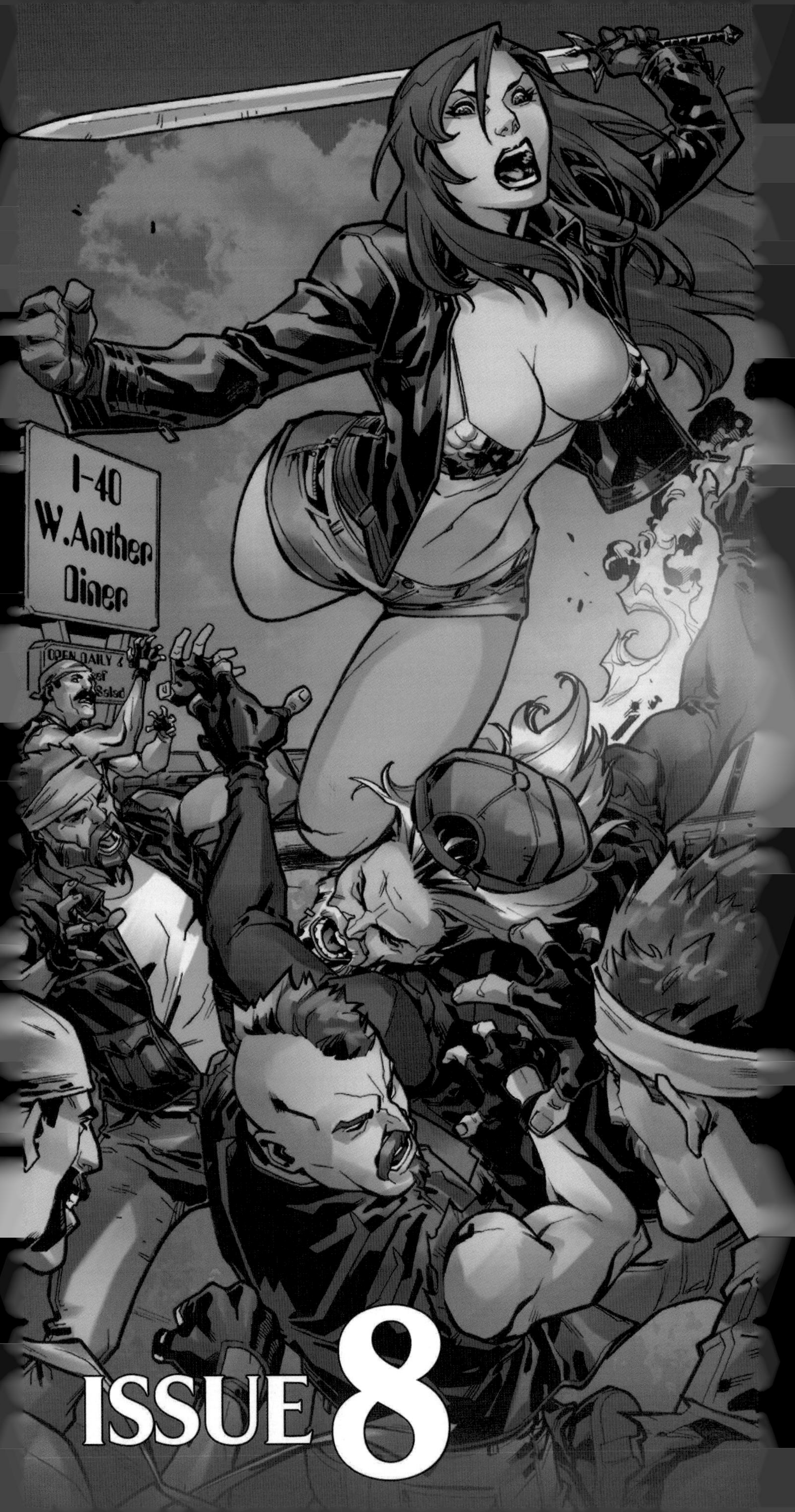
I-40
W.Anther
Diner

ISSUE 8

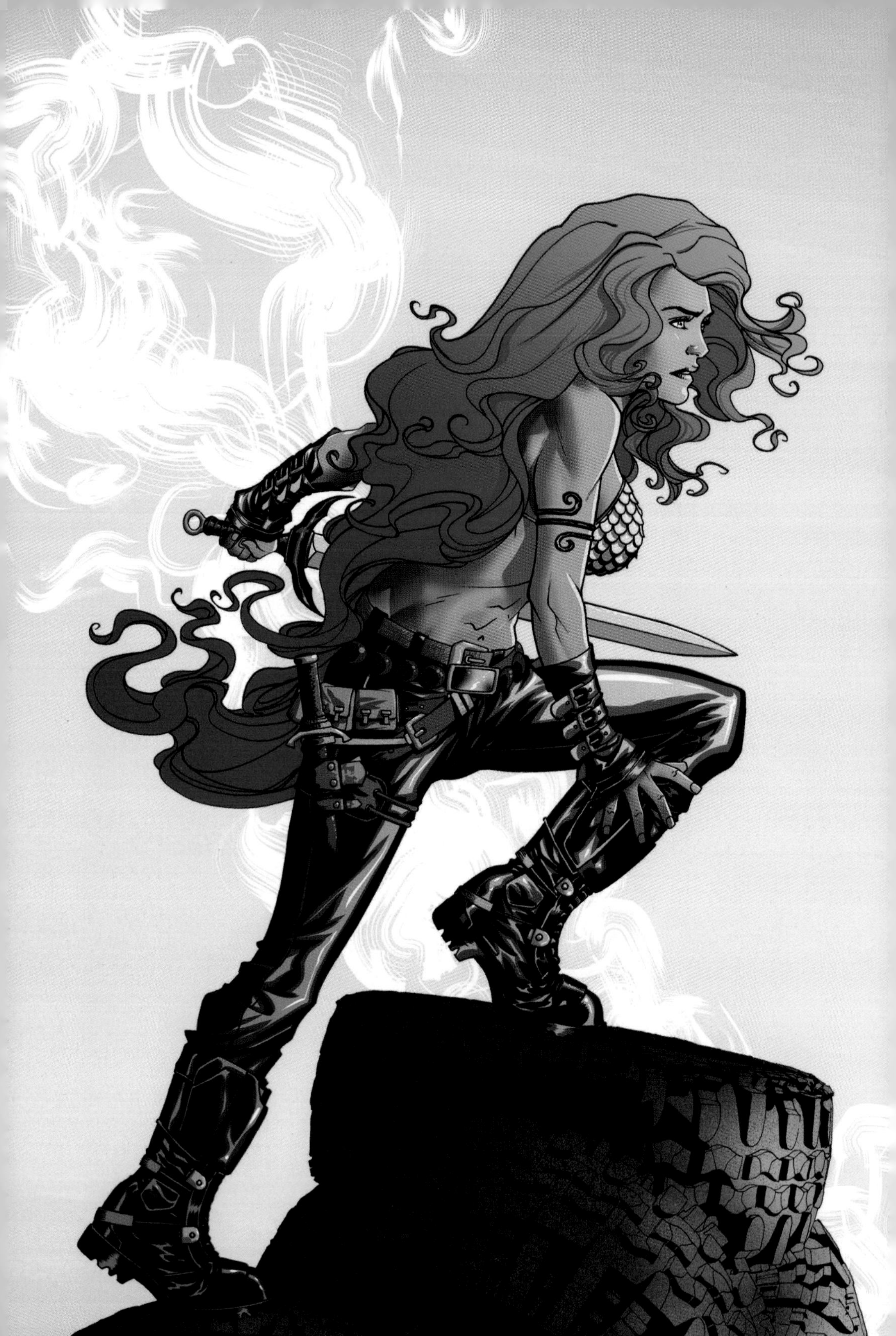

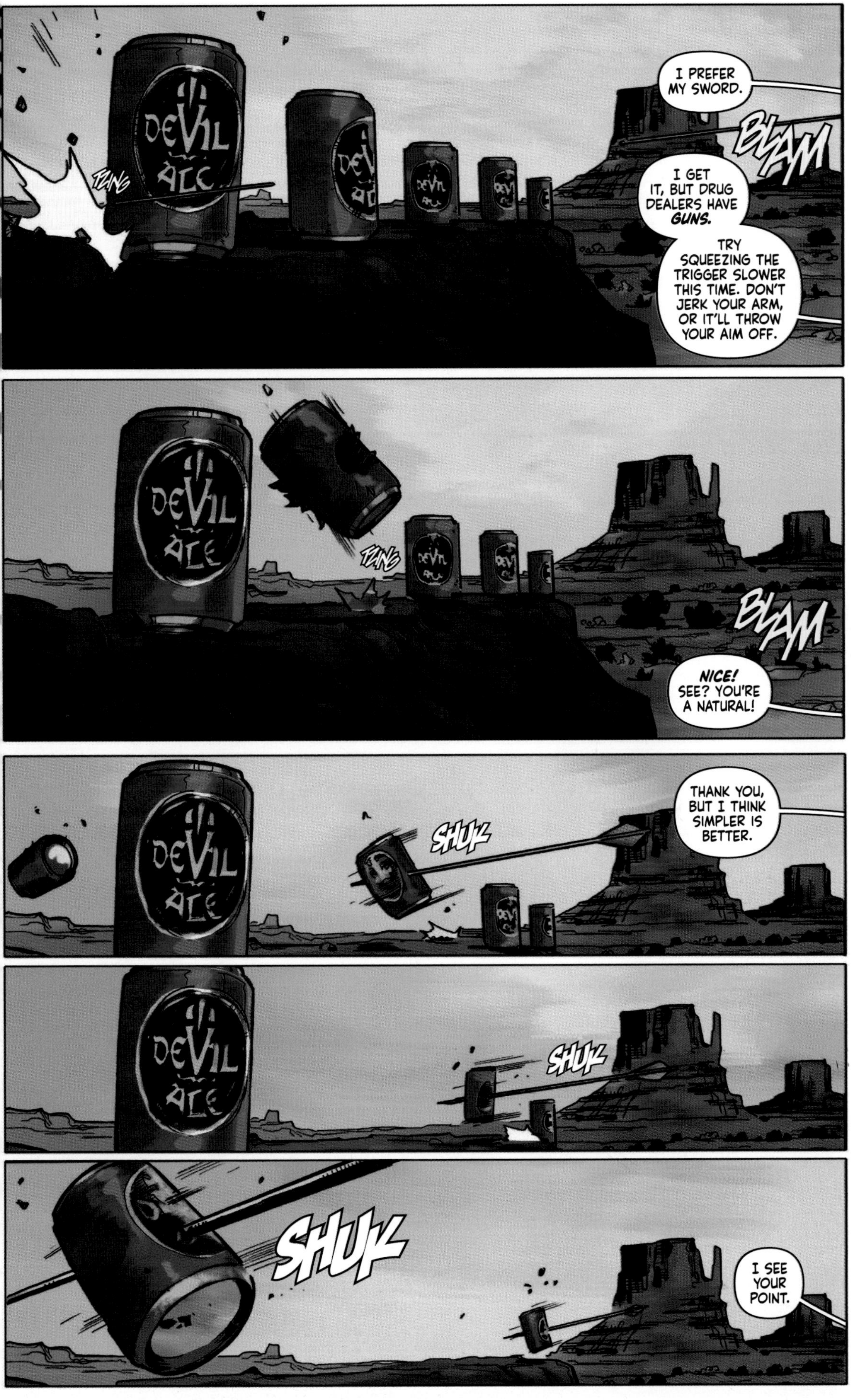
I PREFER MY SWORD.
BLAM
PTANG
I GET IT, BUT DRUG DEALERS HAVE GUNS.
TRY SQUEEZING THE TRIGGER SLOWER THIS TIME. DON'T JERK YOUR ARM, OR IT'LL THROW YOUR AIM OFF.
PTANG
BLAM
NICE! SEE? YOU'RE A NATURAL!
SHUK
THANK YOU, BUT I THINK SIMPLER IS BETTER.
SHUK
SHUK
I SEE YOUR POINT.

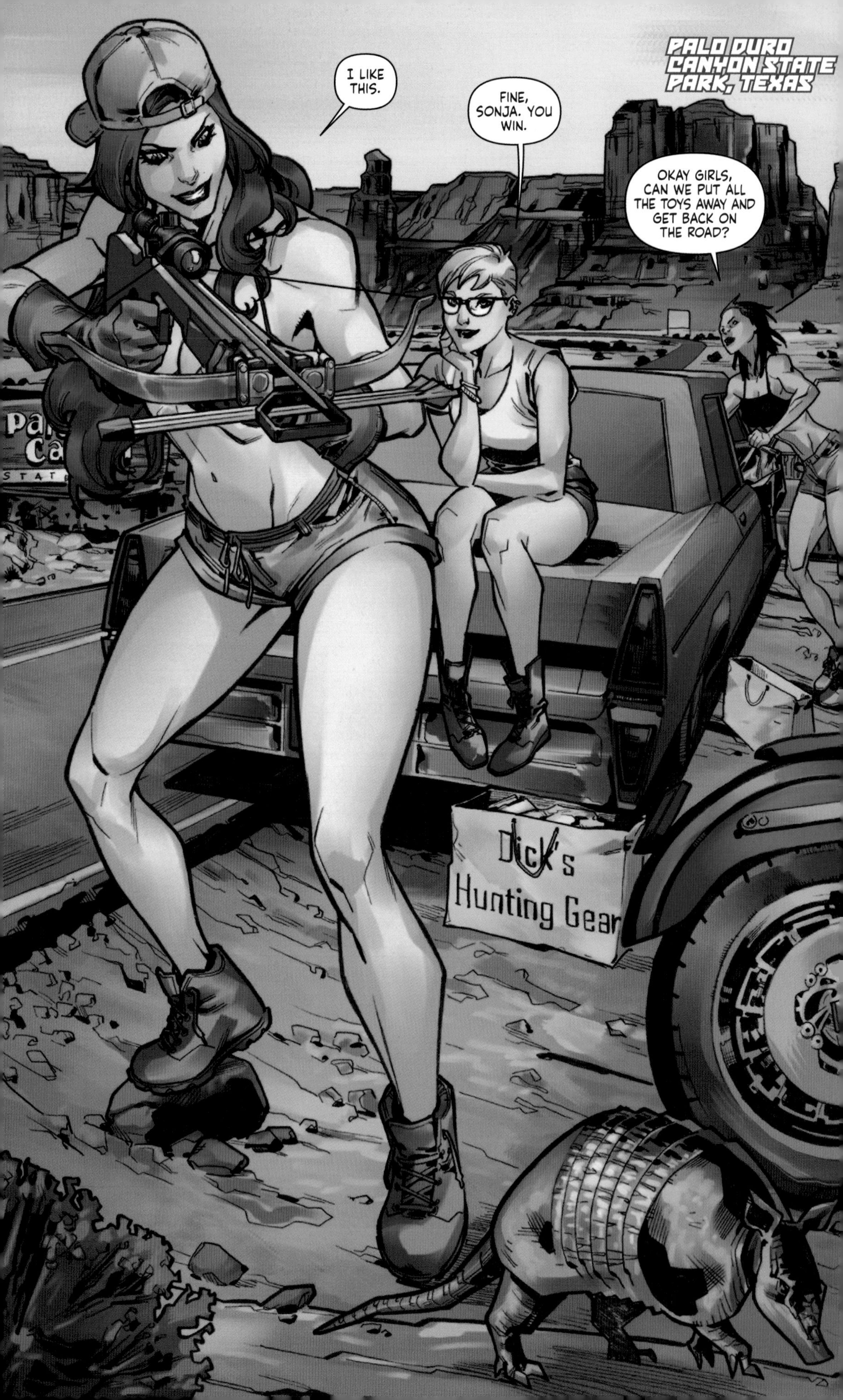
PALO DURO CANYON STATE PARK, TEXAS
I LIKE THIS.
FINE, SONJA. YOU WIN.
OKAY GIRLS, CAN WE PUT ALL THE TOYS AWAY AND GET BACK ON THE ROAD?
Dick's Hunting Gear

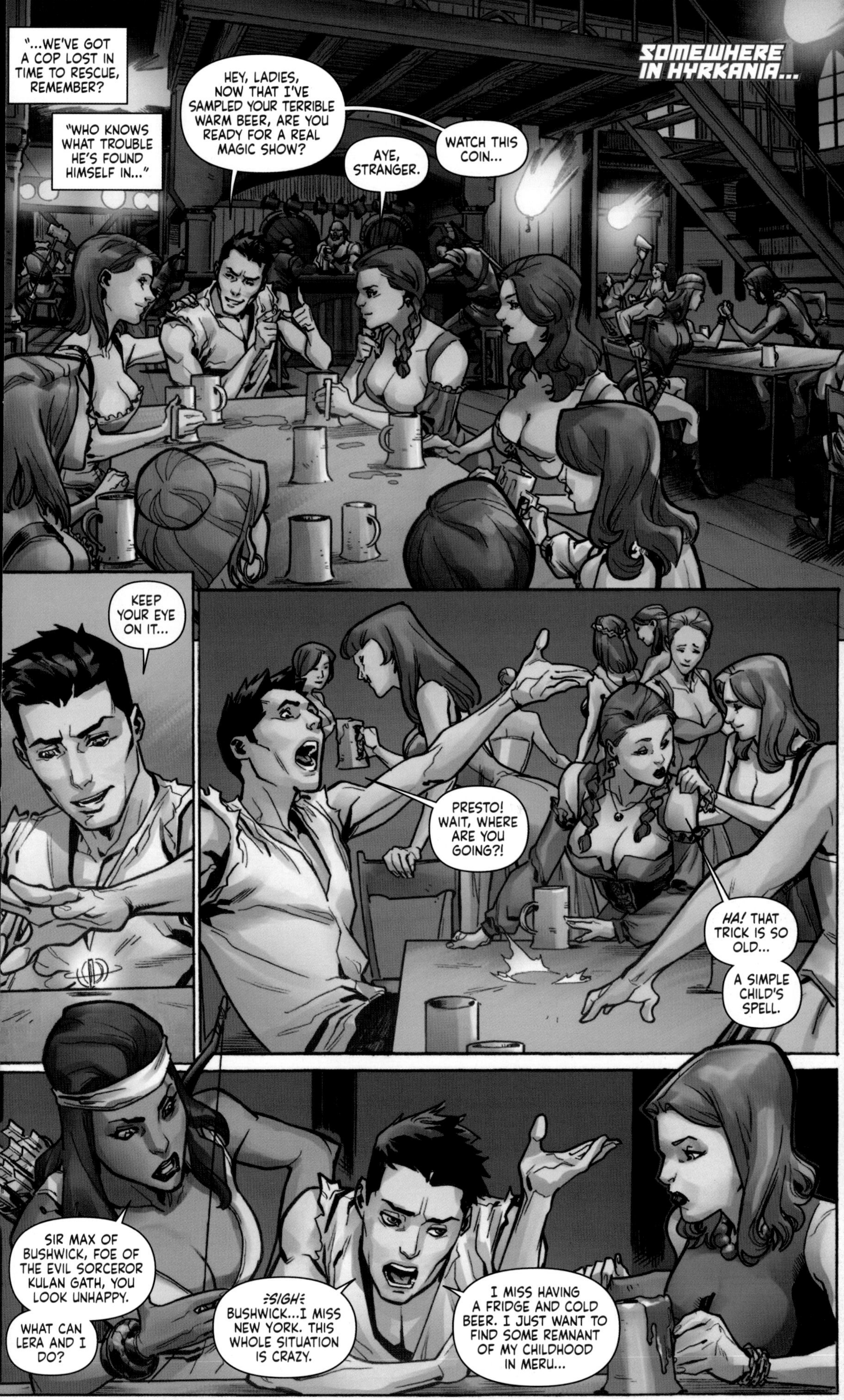

"...WE'VE GOT A COP LOST IN TIME TO RESCUE, REMEMBER?
"WHO KNOWS WHAT TROUBLE HE'S FOUND HIMSELF IN..."
SOMEWHERE IN HYRKANIA...
HEY, LADIES, NOW THAT I'VE SAMPLED YOUR TERRIBLE WARM BEER, ARE YOU READY FOR A REAL MAGIC SHOW?
AYE, STRANGER.
WATCH THIS COIN...
KEEP YOUR EYE ON IT...
PRESTO! WAIT, WHERE ARE YOU GOING?!
HA! THAT TRICK IS SO OLD...
A SIMPLE CHILD'S SPELL.
SIR MAX OF BUSHWICK, FOE OF THE EVIL SORCEROR KULAN GATH, YOU LOOK UNHAPPY.
WHAT CAN LERA AND I DO?
SIGH
BUSHWICK...I MISS NEW YORK. THIS WHOLE SITUATION IS CRAZY.
I MISS HAVING A FRIDGE AND COLD BEER. I JUST WANT TO FIND SOME REMNANT OF MY CHILDHOOD IN MERU...

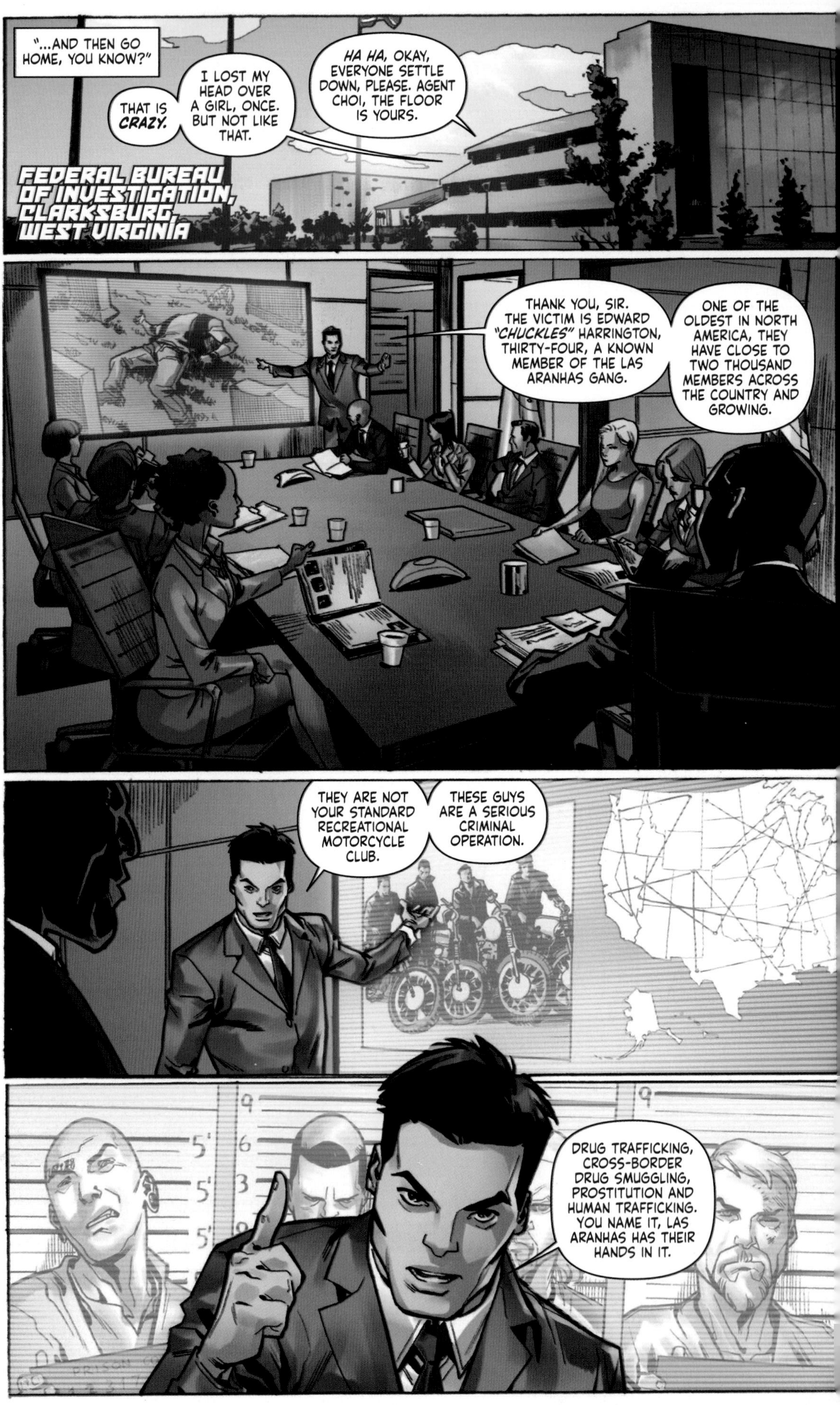
"...AND THEN GO HOME, YOU KNOW?"
THAT IS *CRAZY.*
I LOST MY HEAD OVER A GIRL, ONCE. BUT NOT LIKE THAT.
HA HA, OKAY, EVERYONE SETTLE DOWN, PLEASE. AGENT CHOI, THE FLOOR IS YOURS.
FEDERAL BUREAU OF INVESTIGATION, CLARKSBURG, WEST VIRGINIA
THANK YOU, SIR. THE VICTIM IS EDWARD *"CHUCKLES"* HARRINGTON, THIRTY-FOUR, A KNOWN MEMBER OF THE LAS ARANHAS GANG.
ONE OF THE OLDEST IN NORTH AMERICA, THEY HAVE CLOSE TO TWO THOUSAND MEMBERS ACROSS THE COUNTRY AND GROWING.
THEY ARE NOT YOUR STANDARD RECREATIONAL MOTORCYCLE CLUB.
THESE GUYS ARE A SERIOUS CRIMINAL OPERATION.
DRUG TRAFFICKING, CROSS-BORDER DRUG SMUGGLING, PROSTITUTION AND HUMAN TRAFFICKING. YOU NAME IT, LAS ARANHAS HAS THEIR HANDS IN IT.

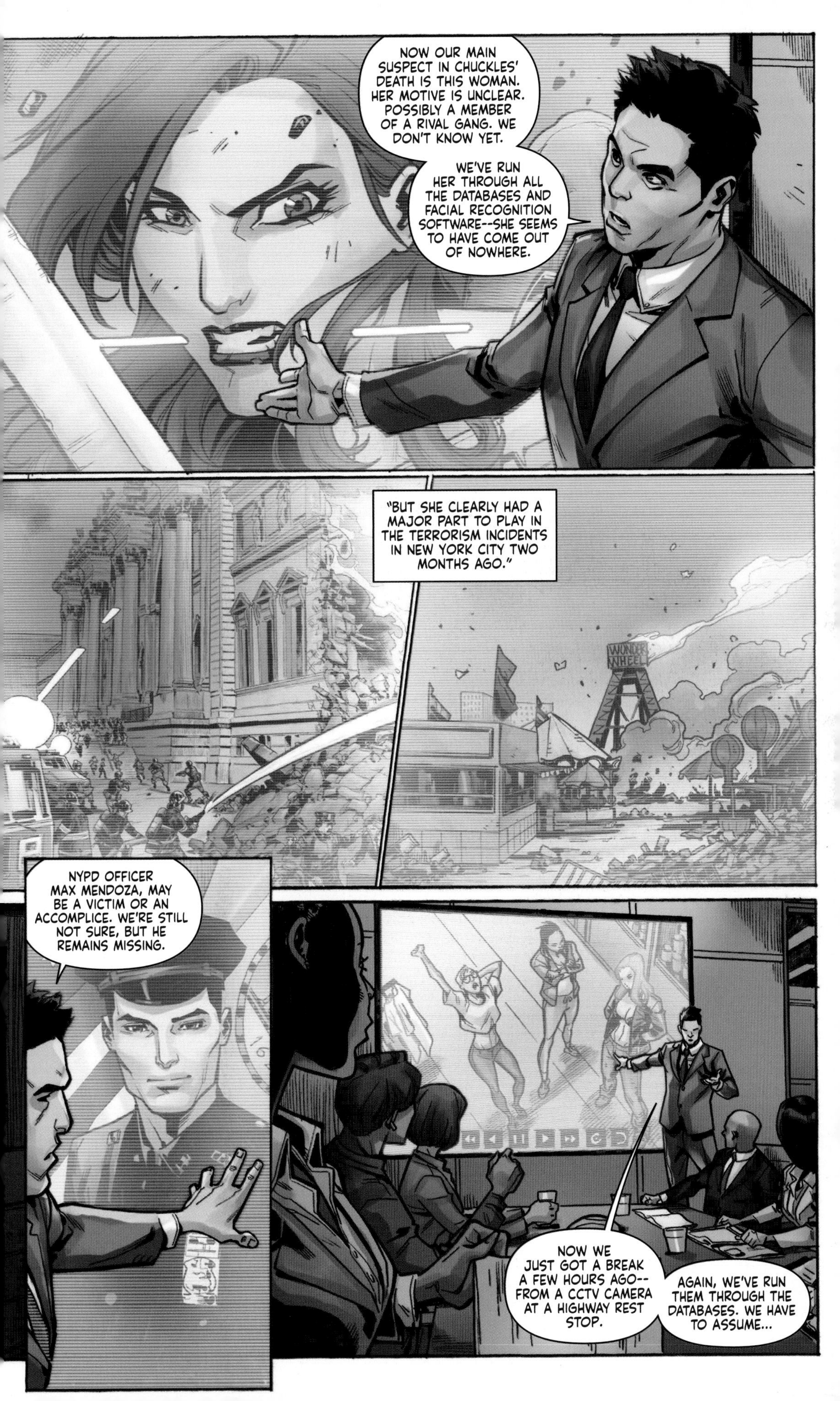
NOW OUR MAIN SUSPECT IN CHUCKLES' DEATH IS THIS WOMAN. HER MOTIVE IS UNCLEAR. POSSIBLY A MEMBER OF A RIVAL GANG. WE DON'T KNOW YET.
WE'VE RUN HER THROUGH ALL THE DATABASES AND FACIAL RECOGNITION SOFTWARE--SHE SEEMS TO HAVE COME OUT OF NOWHERE.
"BUT SHE CLEARLY HAD A MAJOR PART TO PLAY IN THE TERRORISM INCIDENTS IN NEW YORK CITY TWO MONTHS AGO."
WONDER WHEEL
NYPD OFFICER MAX MENDOZA, MAY BE A VICTIM OR AN ACCOMPLICE. WE'RE STILL NOT SURE, BUT HE REMAINS MISSING.
NOW WE JUST GOT A BREAK A FEW HOURS AGO-- FROM A CCTV CAMERA AT A HIGHWAY REST STOP.
AGAIN, WE'VE RUN THEM THROUGH THE DATABASES. WE HAVE TO ASSUME...

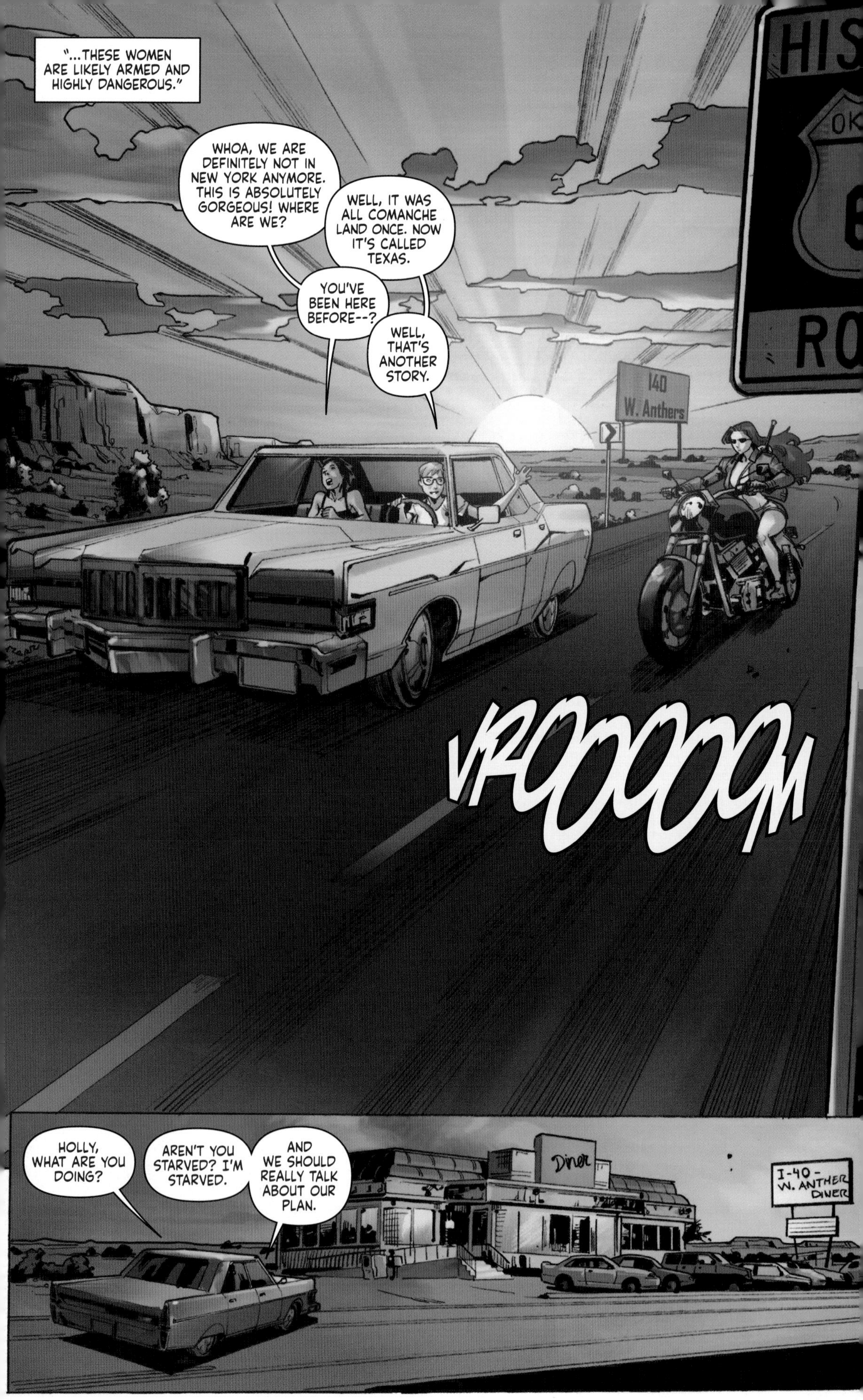
"...THESE WOMEN ARE LIKELY ARMED AND HIGHLY DANGEROUS."
WHOA, WE ARE DEFINITELY NOT IN NEW YORK ANYMORE. THIS IS ABSOLUTELY GORGEOUS! WHERE ARE WE?
WELL, IT WAS ALL COMANCHE LAND ONCE. NOW IT'S CALLED TEXAS.
YOU'VE BEEN HERE BEFORE--?
WELL, THAT'S ANOTHER STORY.
140
W. Anthers
VROOOOM
HOLLY, WHAT ARE YOU DOING?
AREN'T YOU STARVED? I'M STARVED.
AND WE SHOULD REALLY TALK ABOUT OUR PLAN.
Diner
I-40 - W. ANTHER DINER

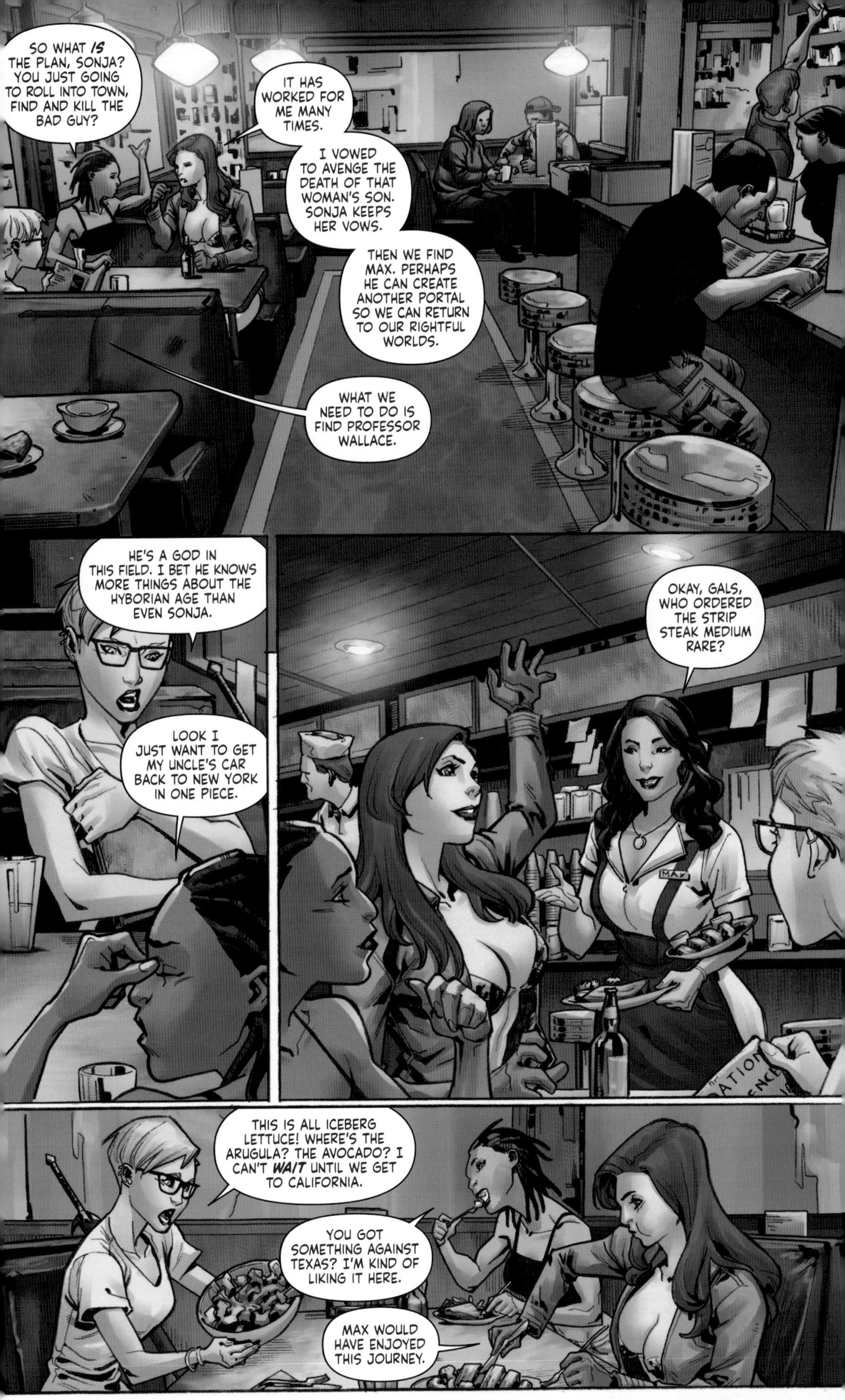
SO WHAT *IS* THE PLAN, SONJA? YOU JUST GOING TO ROLL INTO TOWN, FIND AND KILL THE BAD GUY?
IT HAS WORKED FOR ME MANY TIMES.
I VOWED TO AVENGE THE DEATH OF THAT WOMAN'S SON. SONJA KEEPS HER VOWS.
THEN WE FIND MAX. PERHAPS HE CAN CREATE ANOTHER PORTAL SO WE CAN RETURN TO OUR RIGHTFUL WORLDS.
WHAT WE NEED TO DO IS FIND PROFESSOR WALLACE.
HE'S A GOD IN THIS FIELD. I BET HE KNOWS MORE THINGS ABOUT THE HYBORIAN AGE THAN EVEN SONJA.
LOOK I JUST WANT TO GET MY UNCLE'S CAR BACK TO NEW YORK IN ONE PIECE.
OKAY, GALS, WHO ORDERED THE STRIP STEAK MEDIUM RARE?
MAX
THIS IS ALL ICEBERG LETTUCE! WHERE'S THE ARUGULA? THE AVOCADO? I CAN'T *WAIT* UNTIL WE GET TO CALIFORNIA.
YOU GOT SOMETHING AGAINST TEXAS? I'M KIND OF LIKING IT HERE.
MAX WOULD HAVE ENJOYED THIS JOURNEY.

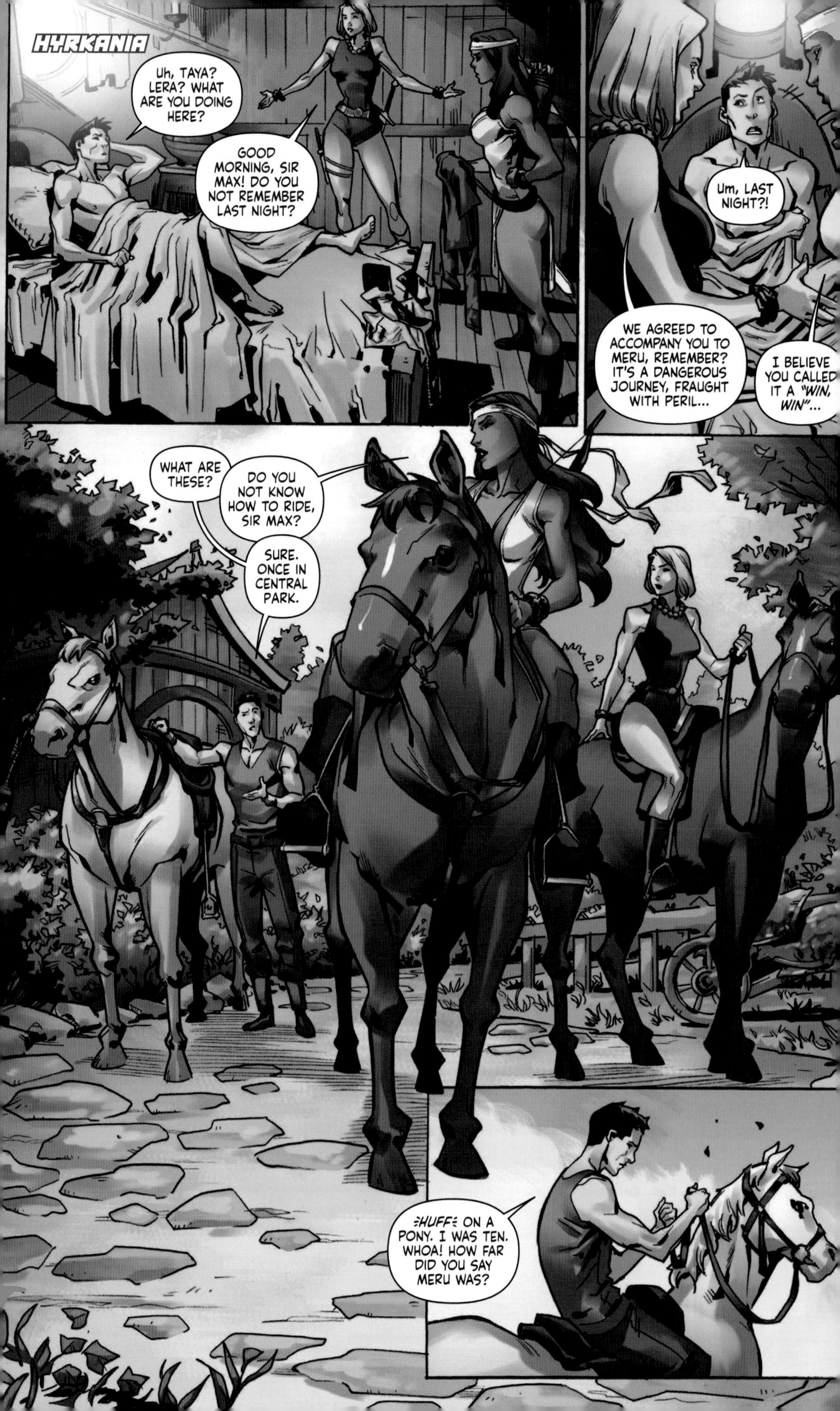
HYRKANIA
Uh, TAYA? LERA? WHAT ARE YOU DOING HERE?
GOOD MORNING, SIR MAX! DO YOU NOT REMEMBER LAST NIGHT?
Um, LAST NIGHT?!
WE AGREED TO ACCOMPANY YOU TO MERU, REMEMBER? IT'S A DANGEROUS JOURNEY, FRAUGHT WITH PERIL...
I BELIEVE YOU CALLED IT A "WIN, WIN"...
WHAT ARE THESE?
DO YOU NOT KNOW HOW TO RIDE, SIR MAX?
SURE. ONCE IN CENTRAL PARK.
HUFF ON A PONY. I WAS TEN. WHOA! HOW FAR DID YOU SAY MERU WAS?

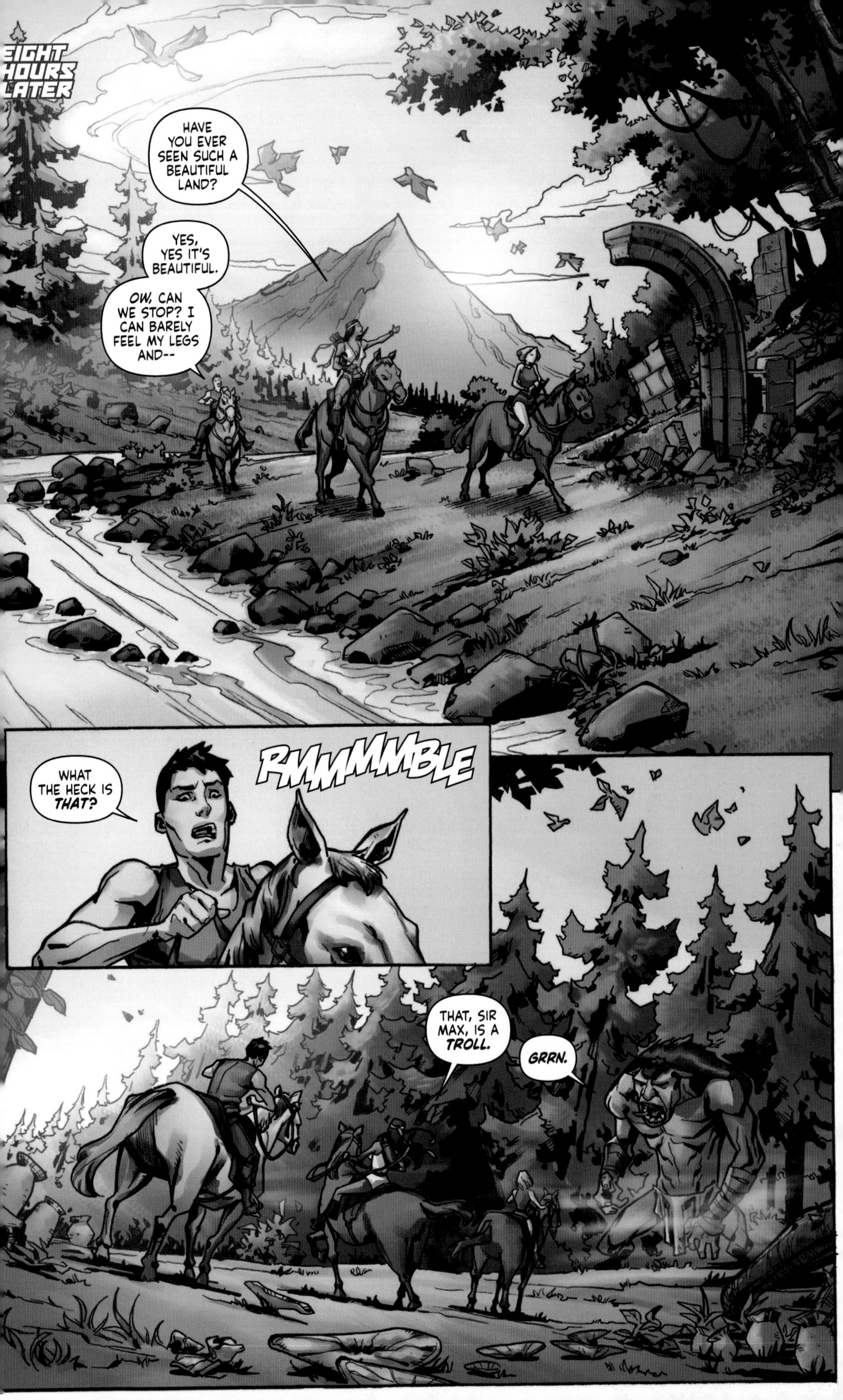
EIGHT HOURS LATER
HAVE YOU EVER SEEN SUCH A BEAUTIFUL LAND?
YES, YES IT'S BEAUTIFUL.
OW, CAN WE STOP? I CAN BARELY FEEL MY LEGS AND--
RMMMMBLE
WHAT THE HECK IS *THAT?*
THAT, SIR MAX, IS A *TROLL.*
GRRN.

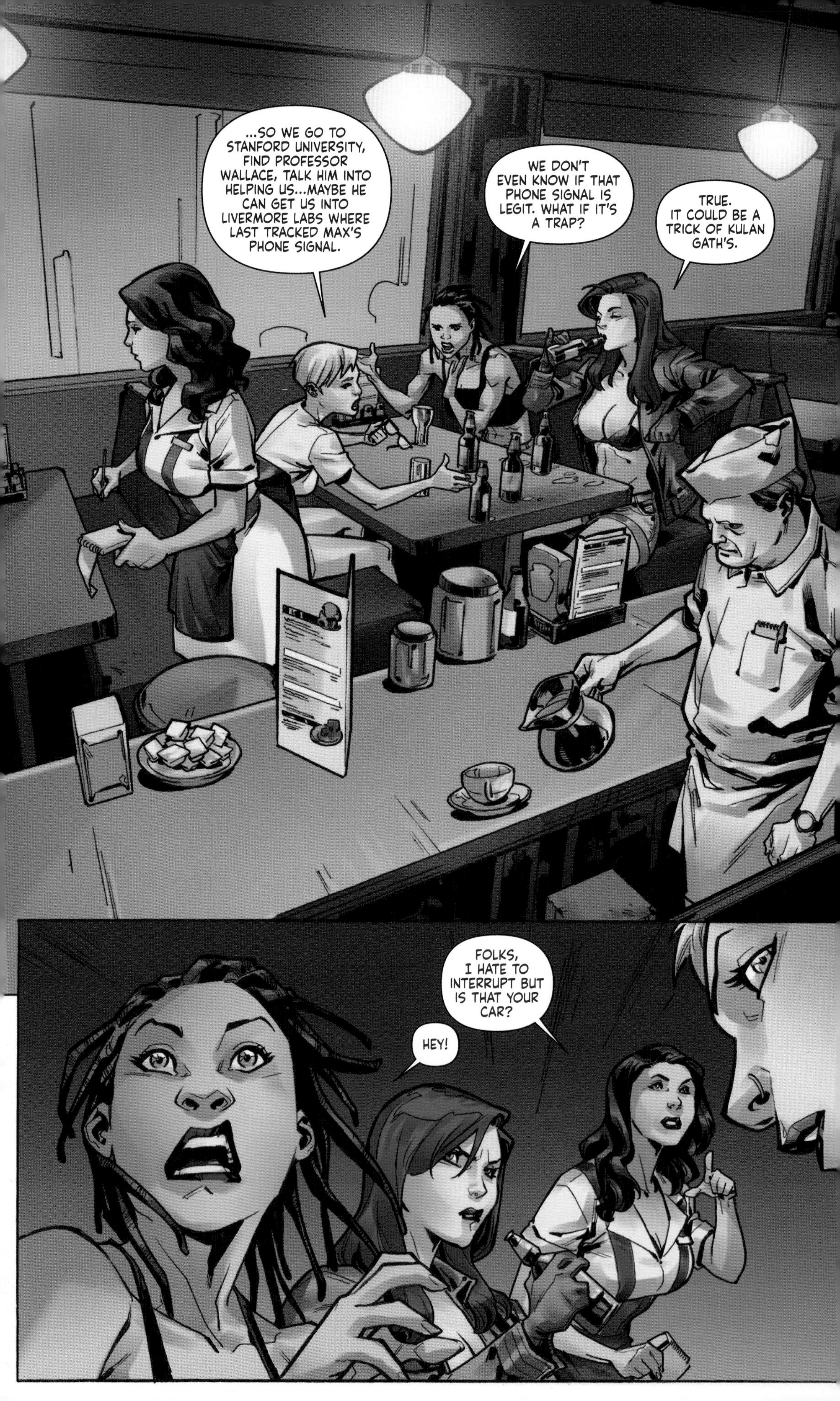
...SO WE GO TO STANFORD UNIVERSITY, FIND PROFESSOR WALLACE, TALK HIM INTO HELPING US...MAYBE HE CAN GET US INTO LIVERMORE LABS WHERE LAST TRACKED MAX'S PHONE SIGNAL.
WE DON'T EVEN KNOW IF THAT PHONE SIGNAL IS LEGIT. WHAT IF IT'S A TRAP?
TRUE. IT COULD BE A TRICK OF KULAN GATH'S.
FOLKS, I HATE TO INTERRUPT BUT IS THAT YOUR CAR?
HEY!

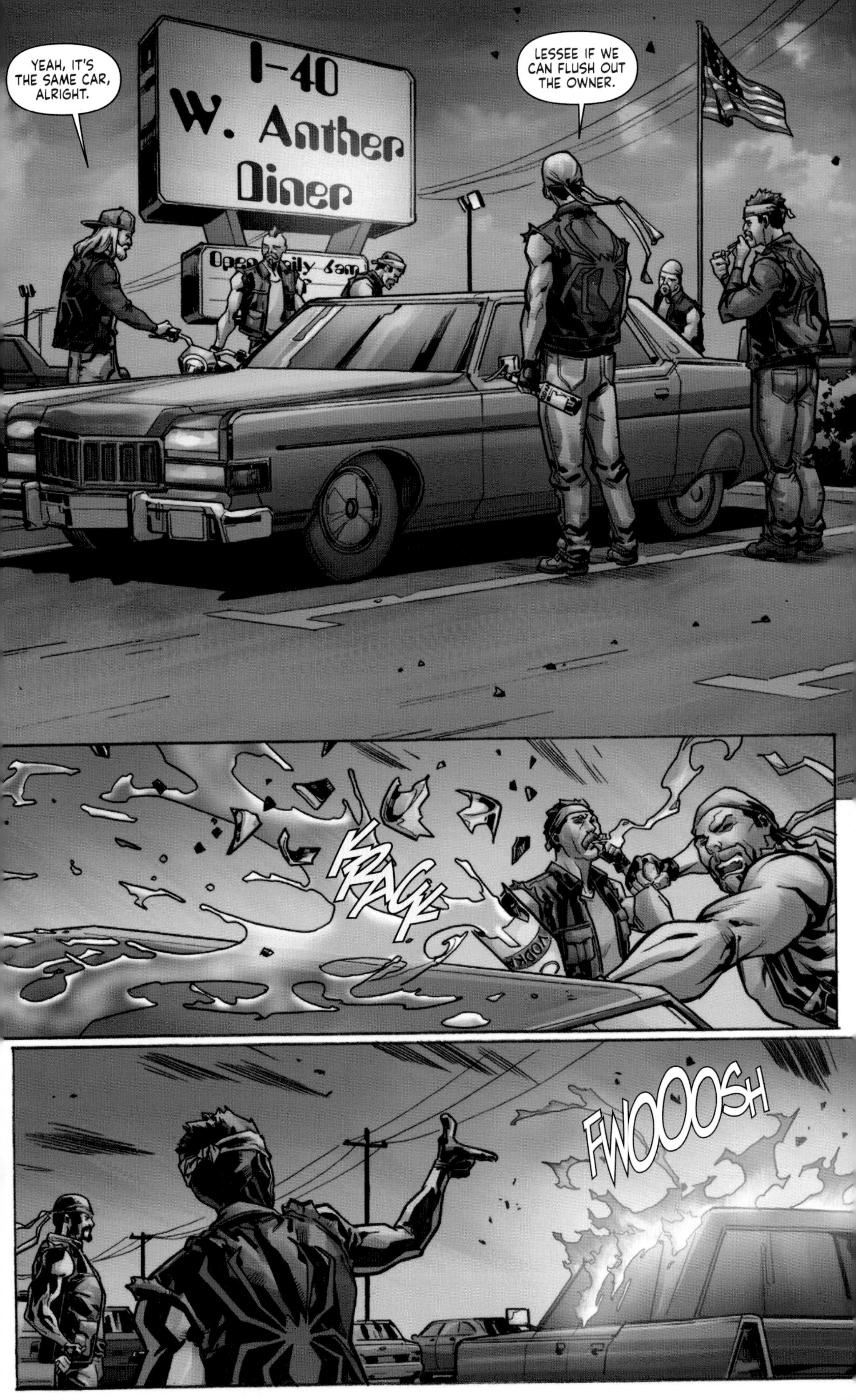
YEAH, IT'S THE SAME CAR, ALRIGHT.
I-40
W. Anther
Diner
LESSEE IF WE CAN FLUSH OUT THE OWNER.
KRACK
VODKA
FWOOOSH

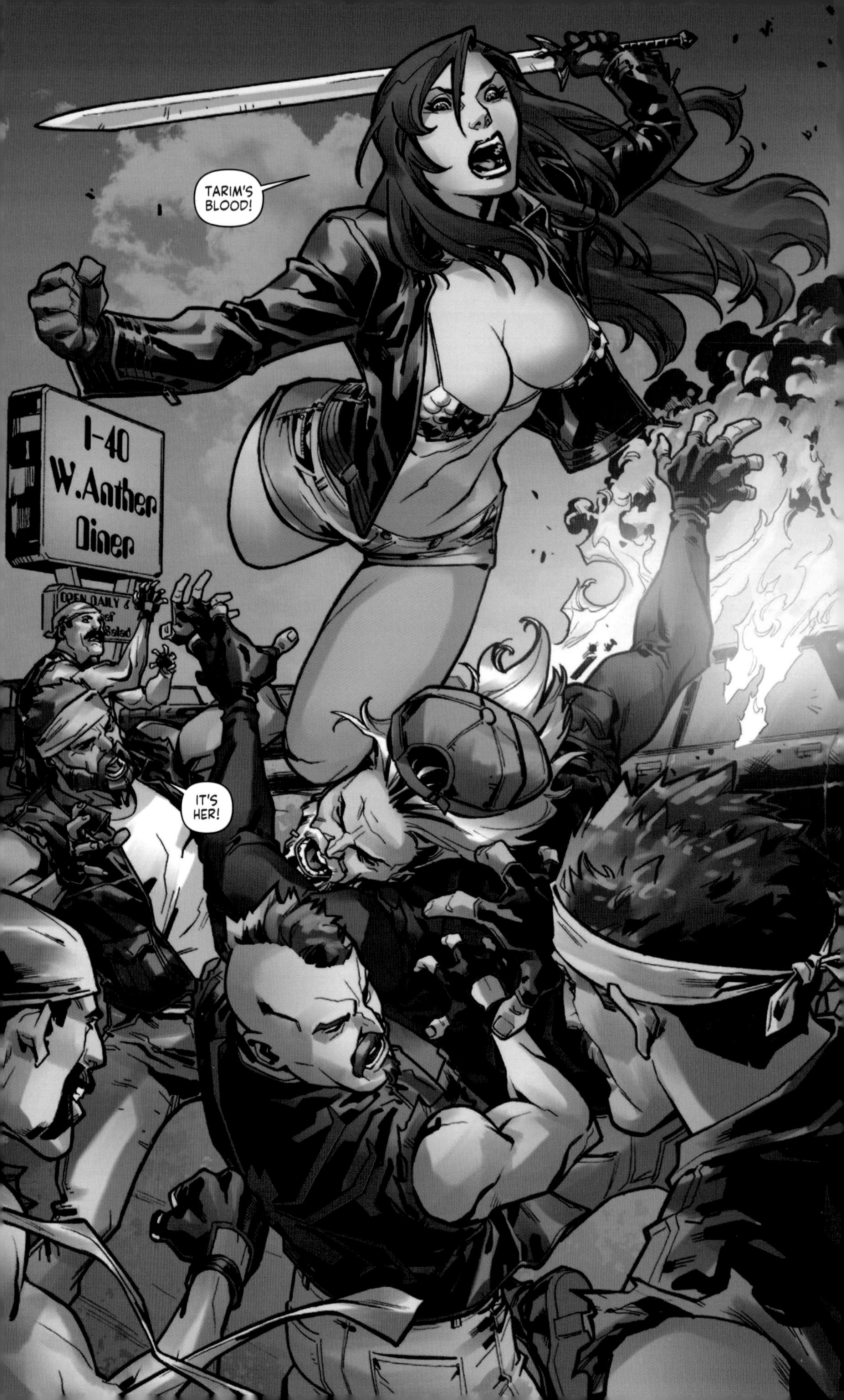
TARIM'S BLOOD!
I-40 W.Anther Diner
IT'S HER!

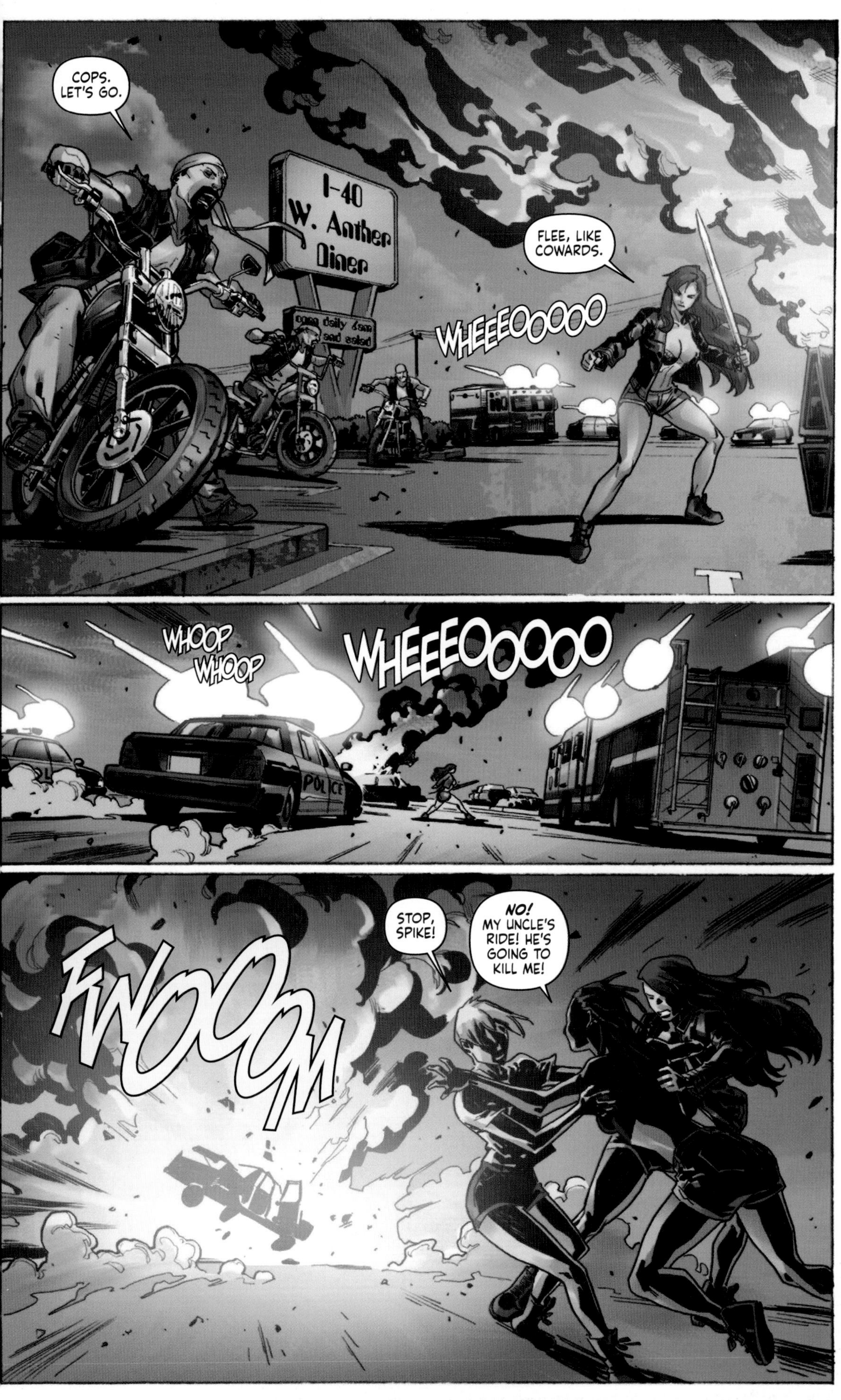

COPS. LET'S GO.
I-40
W. Anther
Diner
FLEE, LIKE COWARDS.
WHEEEOOOOO
WHOOP WHOOP
WHEEEOOOOO
POLICE
FWOOOM
STOP, SPIKE!
NO! MY UNCLE'S RIDE! HE'S GOING TO KILL ME!

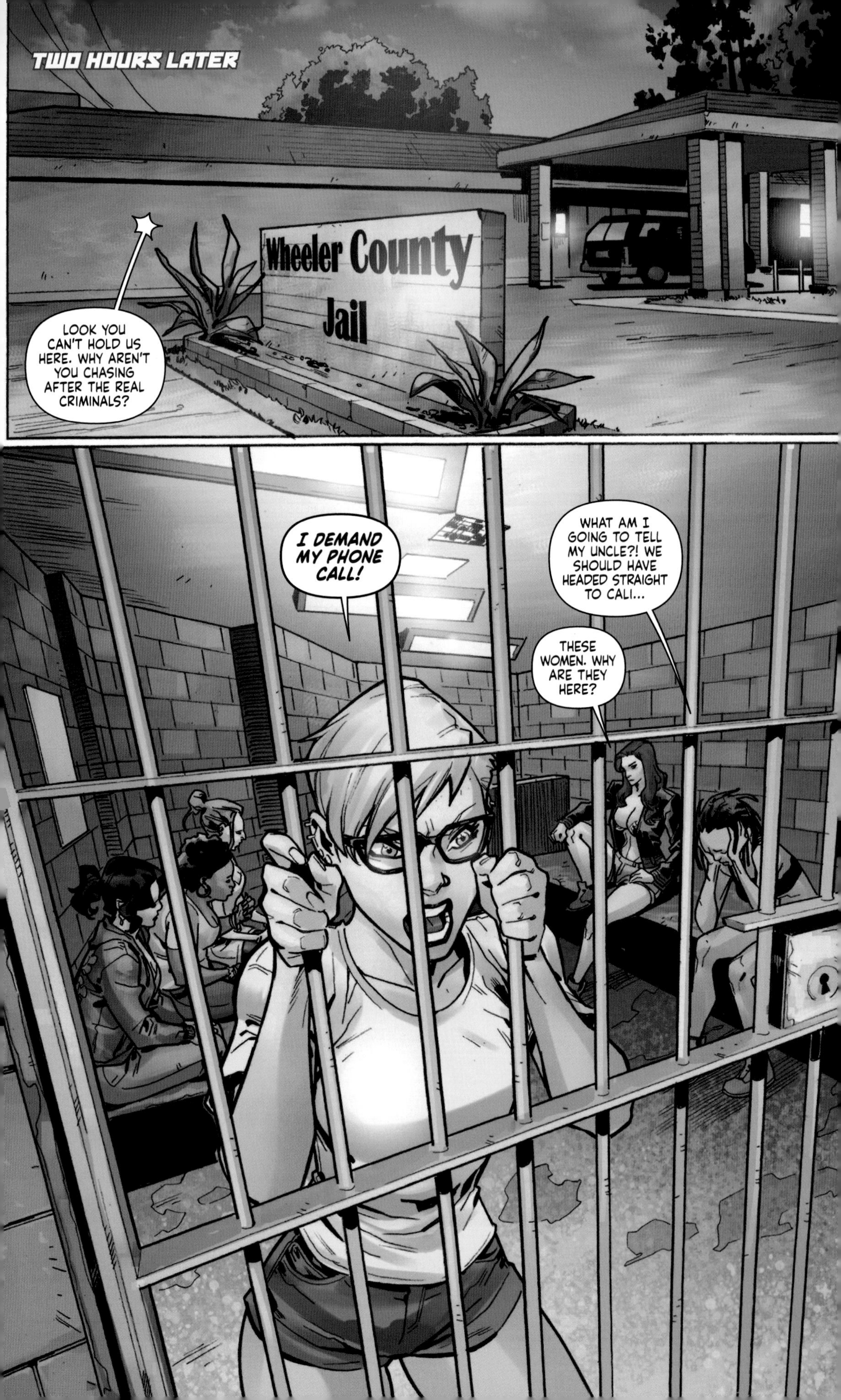
TWO HOURS LATER
Wheeler County Jail
LOOK YOU CAN'T HOLD US HERE. WHY AREN'T YOU CHASING AFTER THE REAL CRIMINALS?
I DEMAND MY PHONE CALL!
WHAT AM I GOING TO TELL MY UNCLE?! WE SHOULD HAVE HEADED STRAIGHT TO CALI...
THESE WOMEN. WHY ARE THEY HERE?

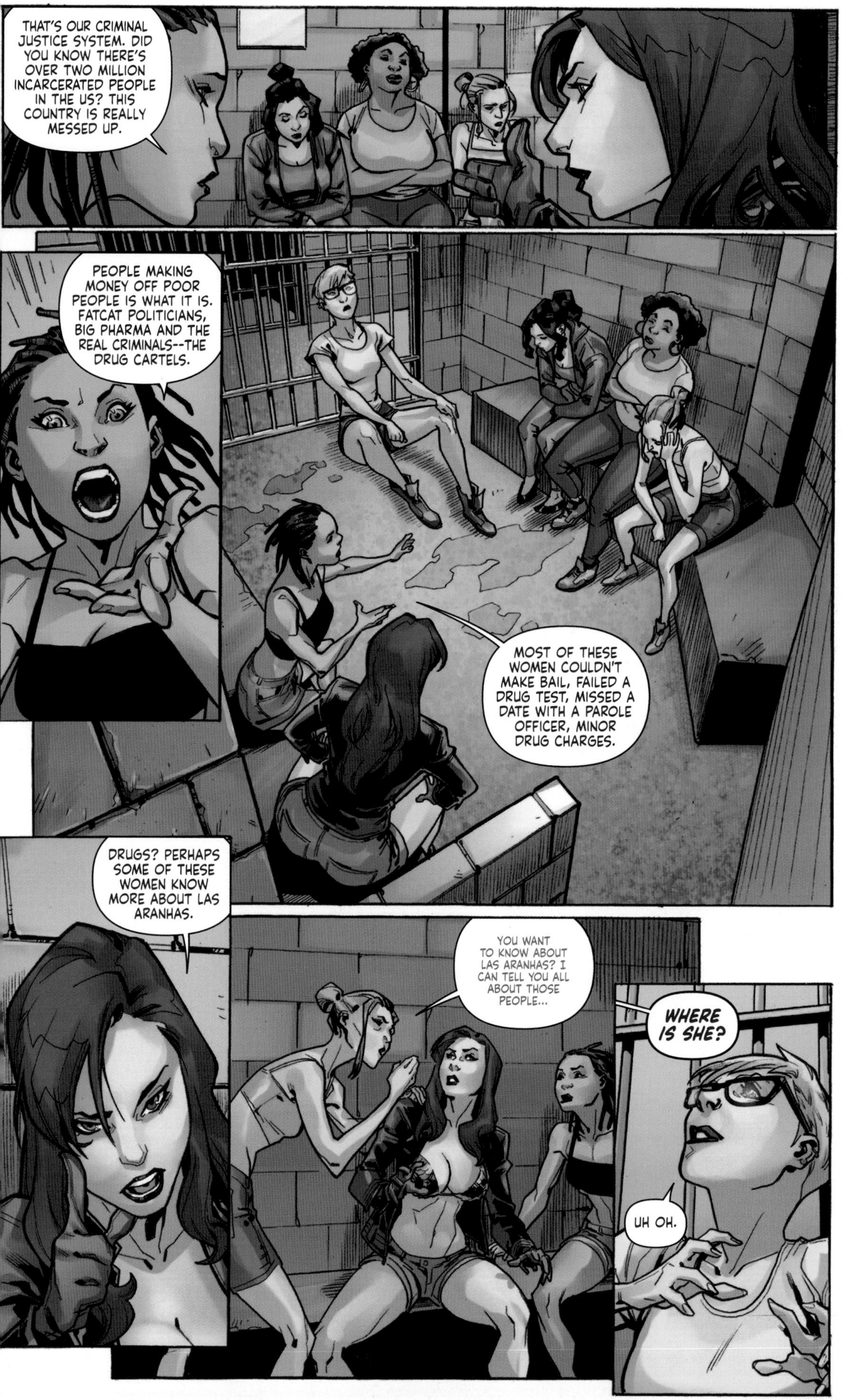

THAT'S OUR CRIMINAL JUSTICE SYSTEM. DID YOU KNOW THERE'S OVER TWO MILLION INCARCERATED PEOPLE IN THE US? THIS COUNTRY IS REALLY MESSED UP.
PEOPLE MAKING MONEY OFF POOR PEOPLE IS WHAT IT IS. FATCAT POLITICIANS, BIG PHARMA AND THE REAL CRIMINALS--THE DRUG CARTELS.
MOST OF THESE WOMEN COULDN'T MAKE BAIL, FAILED A DRUG TEST, MISSED A DATE WITH A PAROLE OFFICER, MINOR DRUG CHARGES.
DRUGS? PERHAPS SOME OF THESE WOMEN KNOW MORE ABOUT LAS ARANHAS.
YOU WANT TO KNOW ABOUT LAS ARANHAS? I CAN TELL YOU ALL ABOUT THOSE PEOPLE...
WHERE IS SHE?
UH OH.

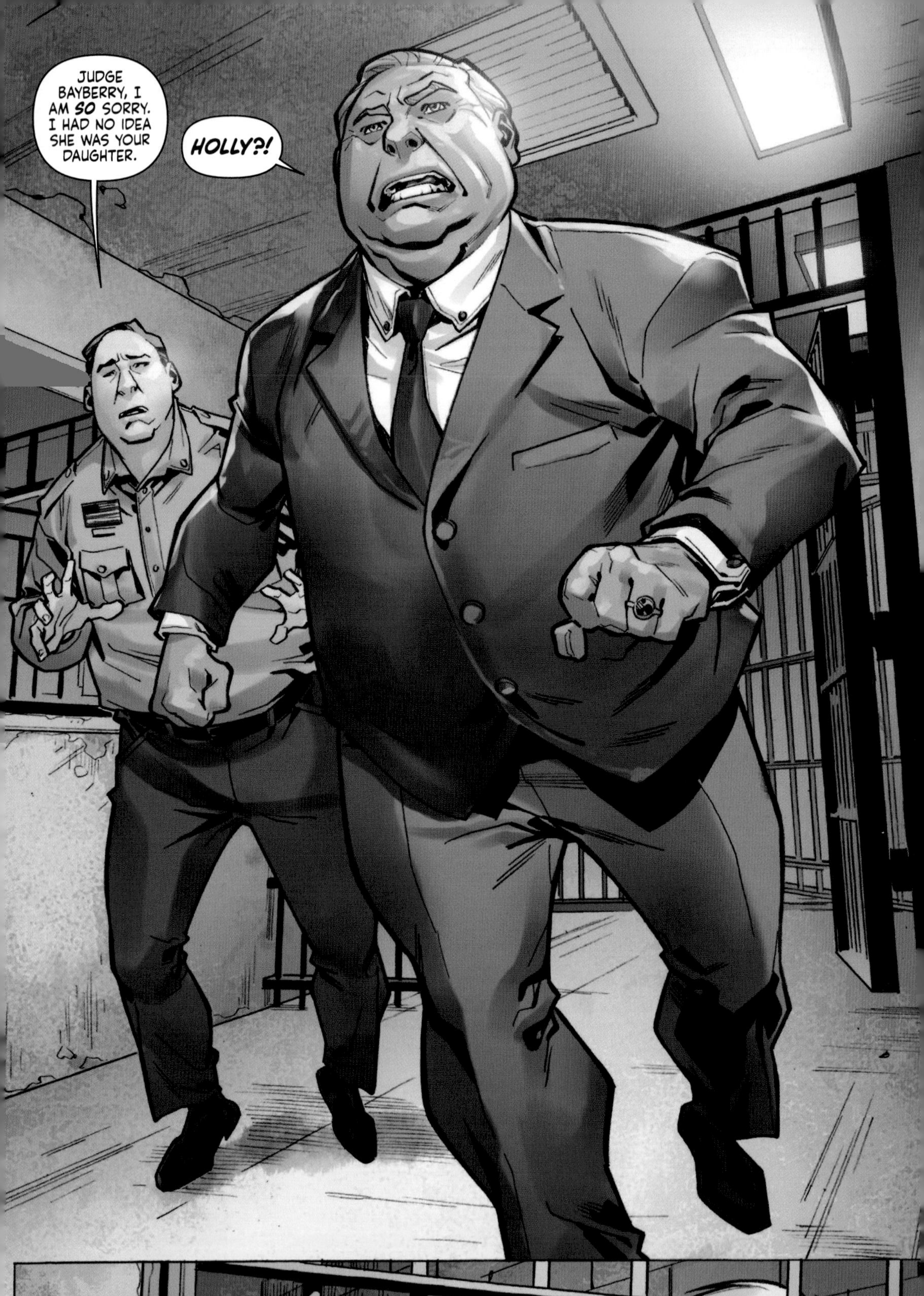
JUDGE BAYBERRY, I AM SO SORRY. I HAD NO IDEA SHE WAS YOUR DAUGHTER.
HOLLY?!

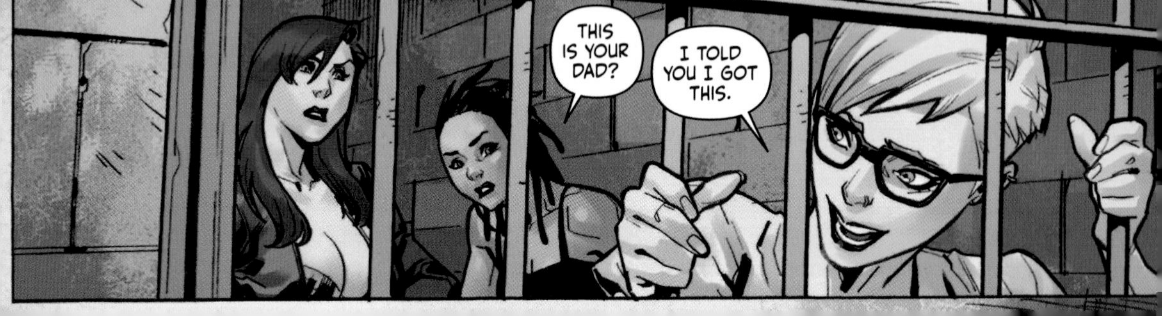
THIS IS YOUR DAD?
I TOLD YOU I GOT THIS.

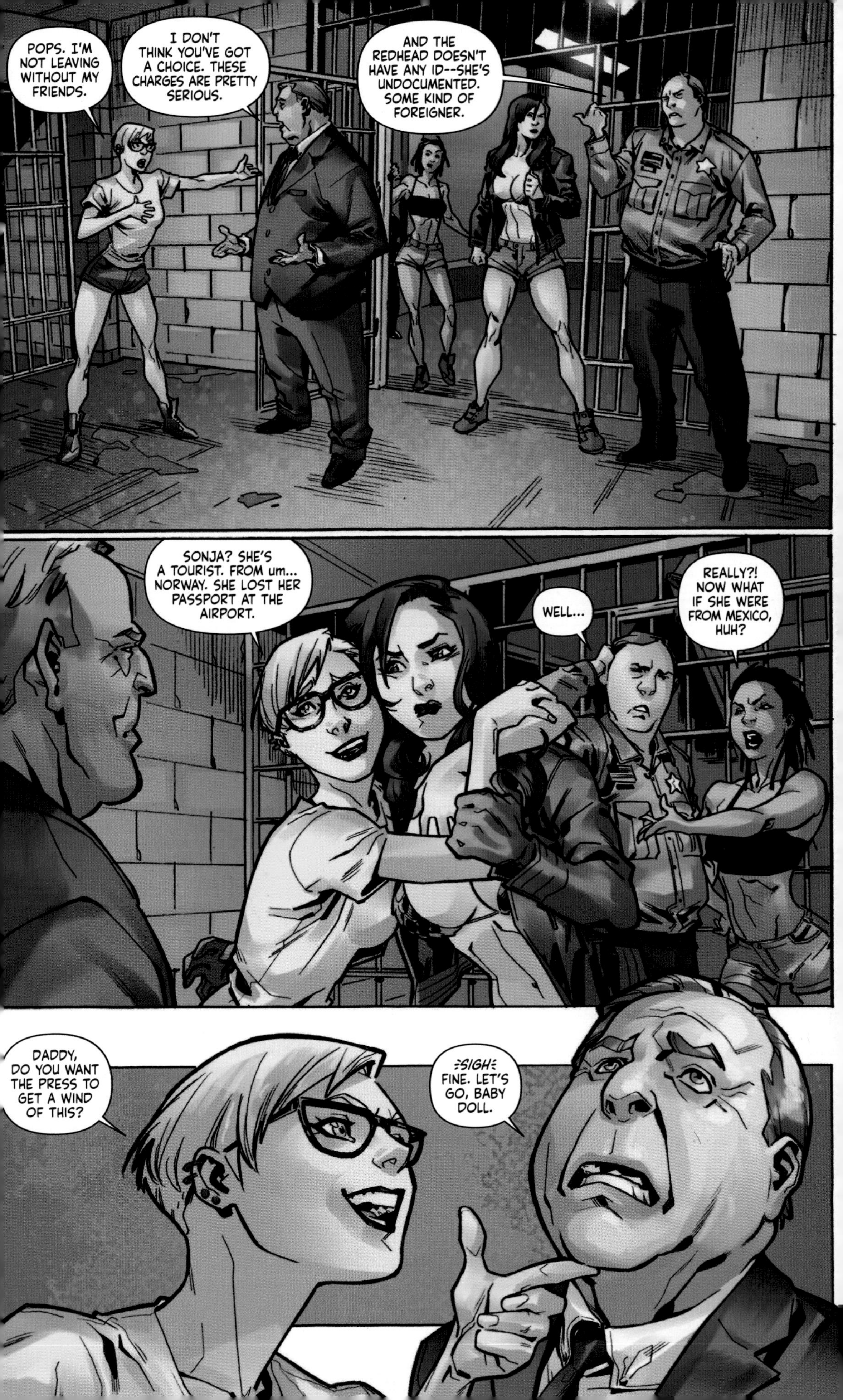
POPS. I'M NOT LEAVING WITHOUT MY FRIENDS.
I DON'T THINK YOU'VE GOT A CHOICE. THESE CHARGES ARE PRETTY SERIOUS.
AND THE REDHEAD DOESN'T HAVE ANY ID--SHE'S UNDOCUMENTED. SOME KIND OF FOREIGNER.
SONJA? SHE'S A TOURIST. FROM um... NORWAY. SHE LOST HER PASSPORT AT THE AIRPORT.
WELL...
REALLY?! NOW WHAT IF SHE WERE FROM MEXICO, HUH?
DADDY, DO YOU WANT THE PRESS TO GET A WIND OF THIS?
SIGH
FINE. LET'S GO, BABY DOLL.

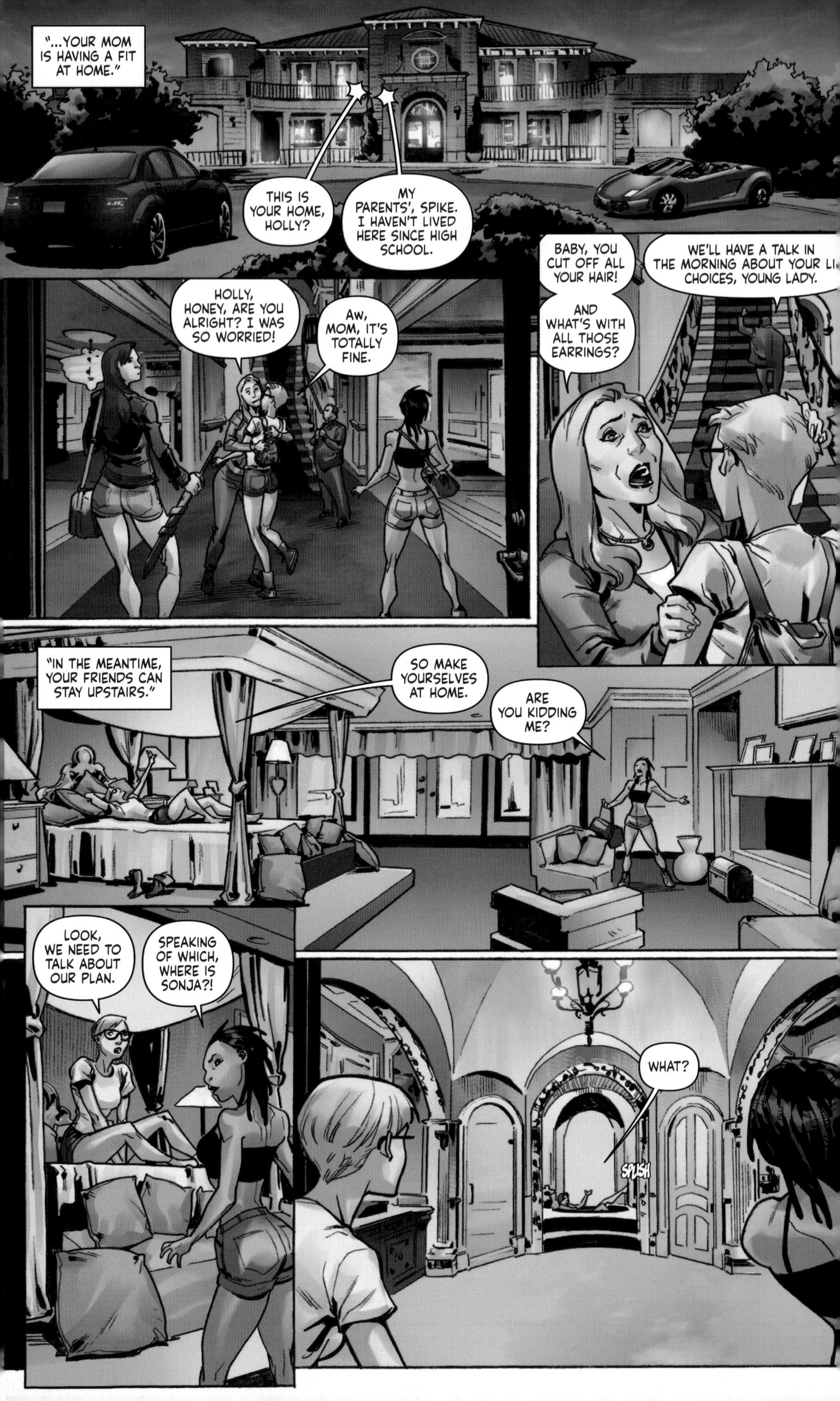
"...YOUR MOM IS HAVING A FIT AT HOME."
THIS IS YOUR HOME, HOLLY?
MY PARENTS', SPIKE. I HAVEN'T LIVED HERE SINCE HIGH SCHOOL.
HOLLY, HONEY, ARE YOU ALRIGHT? I WAS SO WORRIED!
AW, MOM, IT'S TOTALLY FINE.
BABY, YOU CUT OFF ALL YOUR HAIR!
AND WHAT'S WITH ALL THOSE EARRINGS?
WE'LL HAVE A TALK IN THE MORNING ABOUT YOUR LI CHOICES, YOUNG LADY.
"IN THE MEANTIME, YOUR FRIENDS CAN STAY UPSTAIRS."
SO MAKE YOURSELVES AT HOME.
ARE YOU KIDDING ME?
LOOK, WE NEED TO TALK ABOUT OUR PLAN.
SPEAKING OF WHICH, WHERE IS SONJA?!
WHAT?
SPLSH

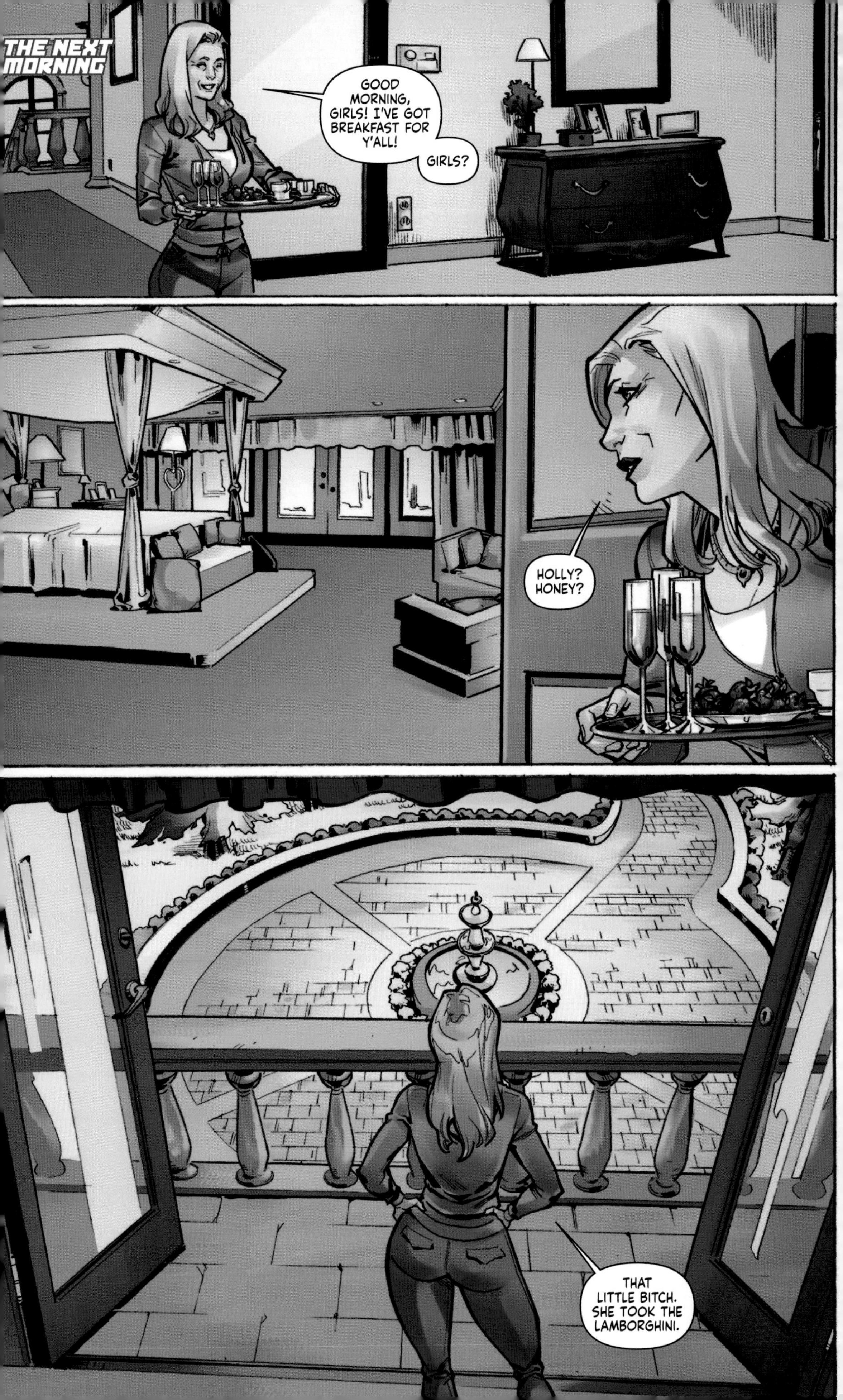
THE NEXT MORNING
GOOD MORNING, GIRLS! I'VE GOT BREAKFAST FOR Y'ALL!
GIRLS?
HOLLY? HONEY?
THAT LITTLE BITCH. SHE TOOK THE LAMBORGHINI.

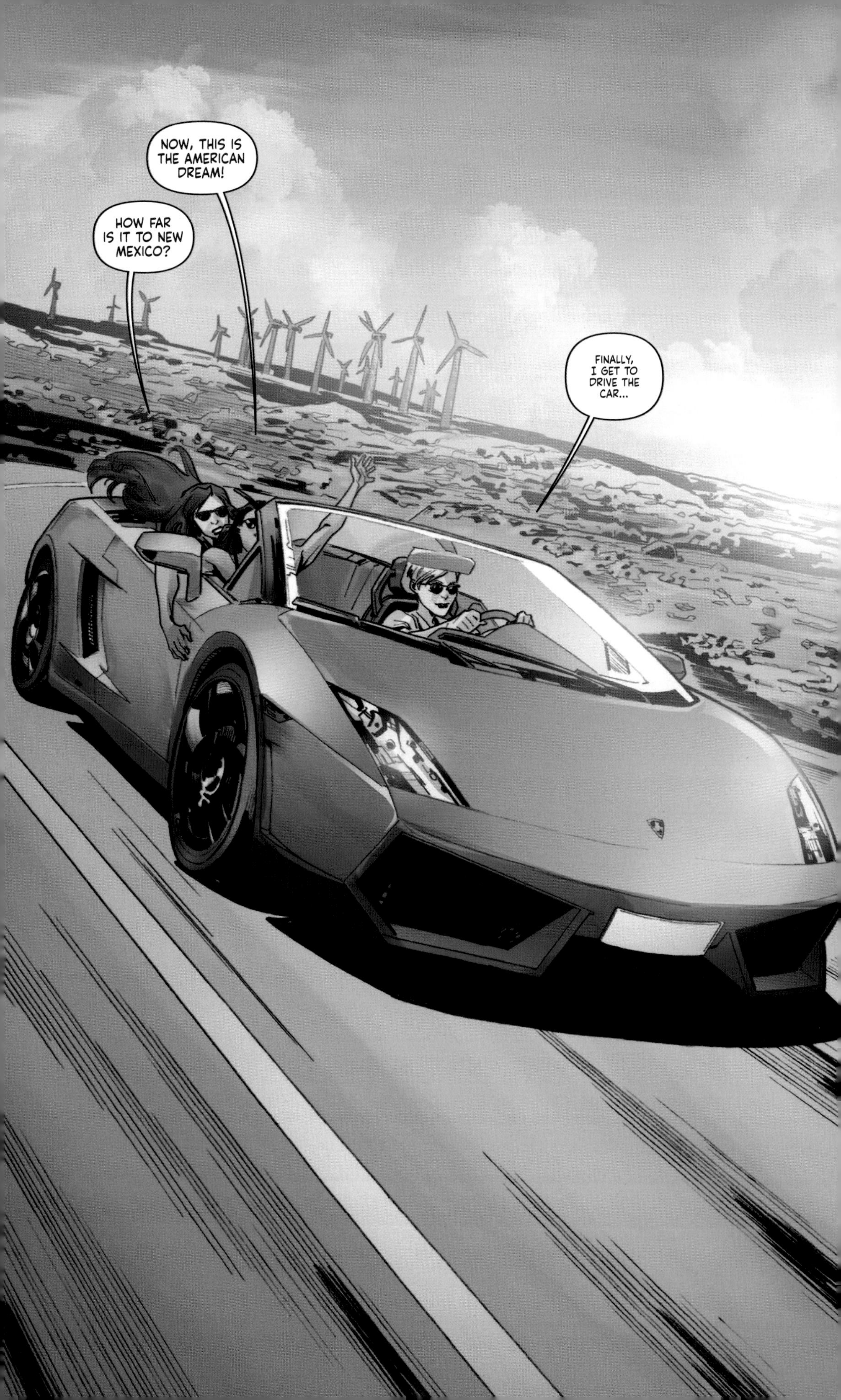
HOW FAR IS IT TO NEW MEXICO?
NOW, THIS IS THE AMERICAN DREAM!
FINALLY, I GET TO DRIVE THE CAR...

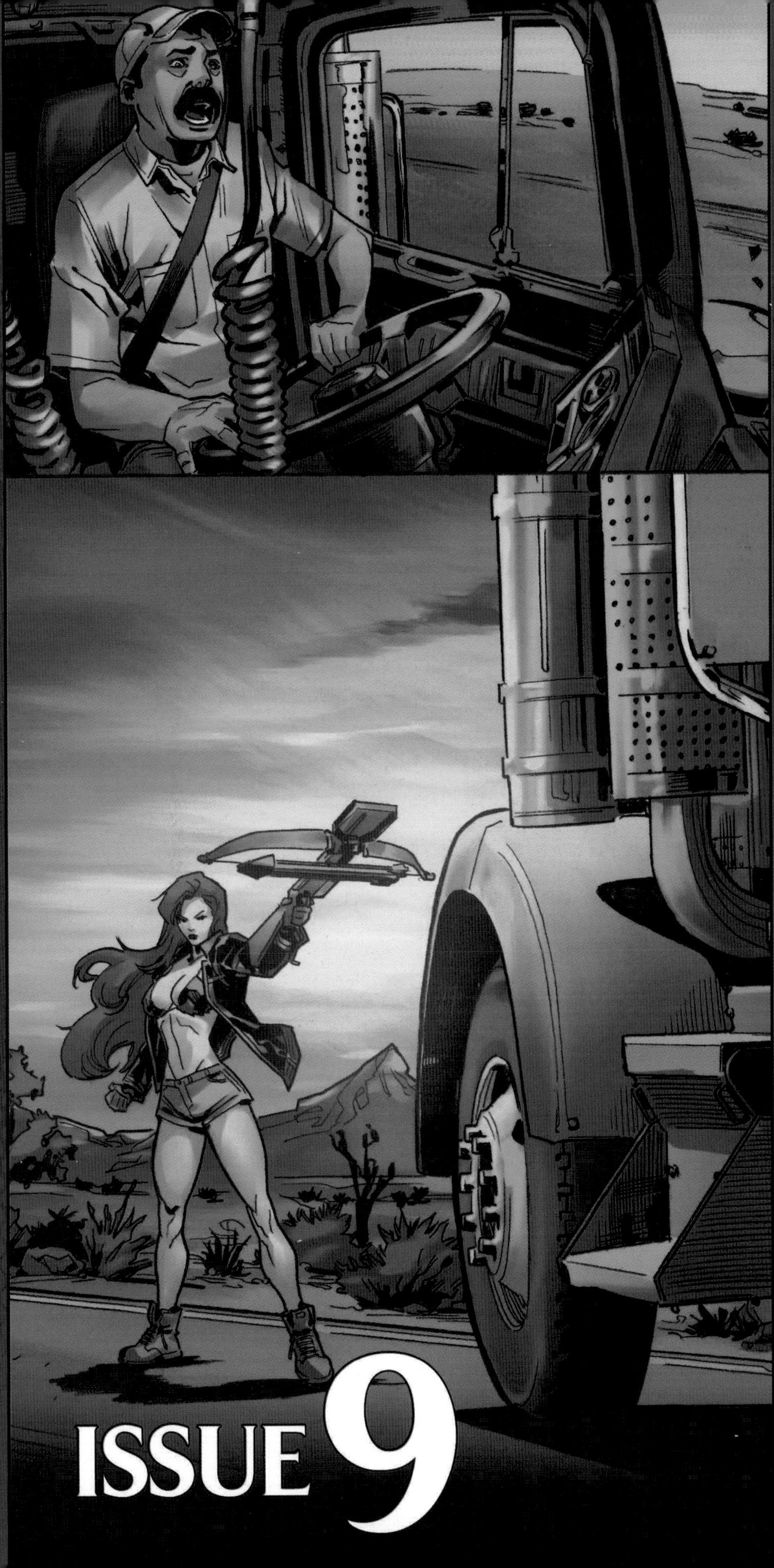
ISSUE 9

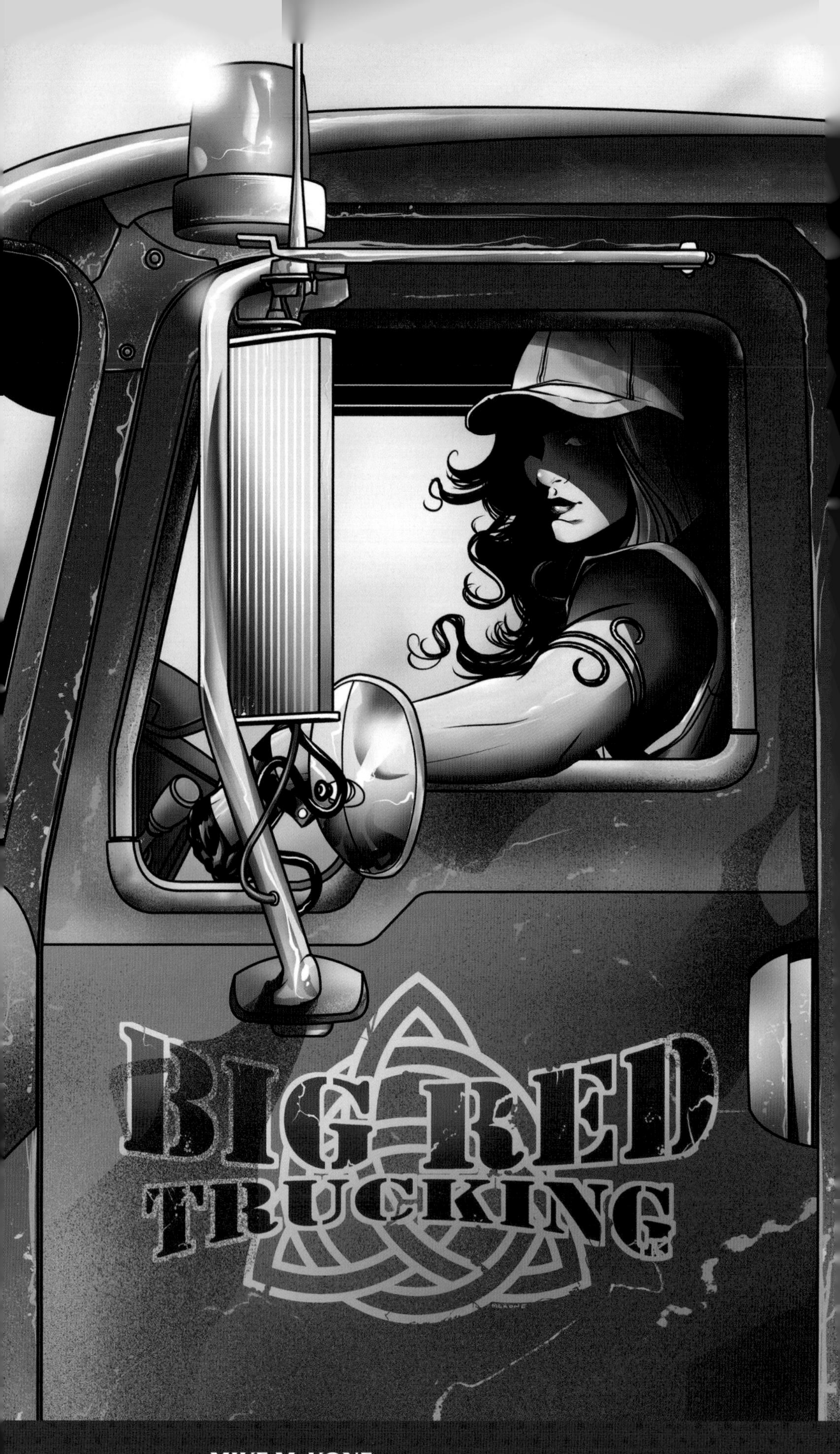
BIG RED
TRUCKING
MCKONE

SSUE #9: COVER ART BY **MIKE McKONE**

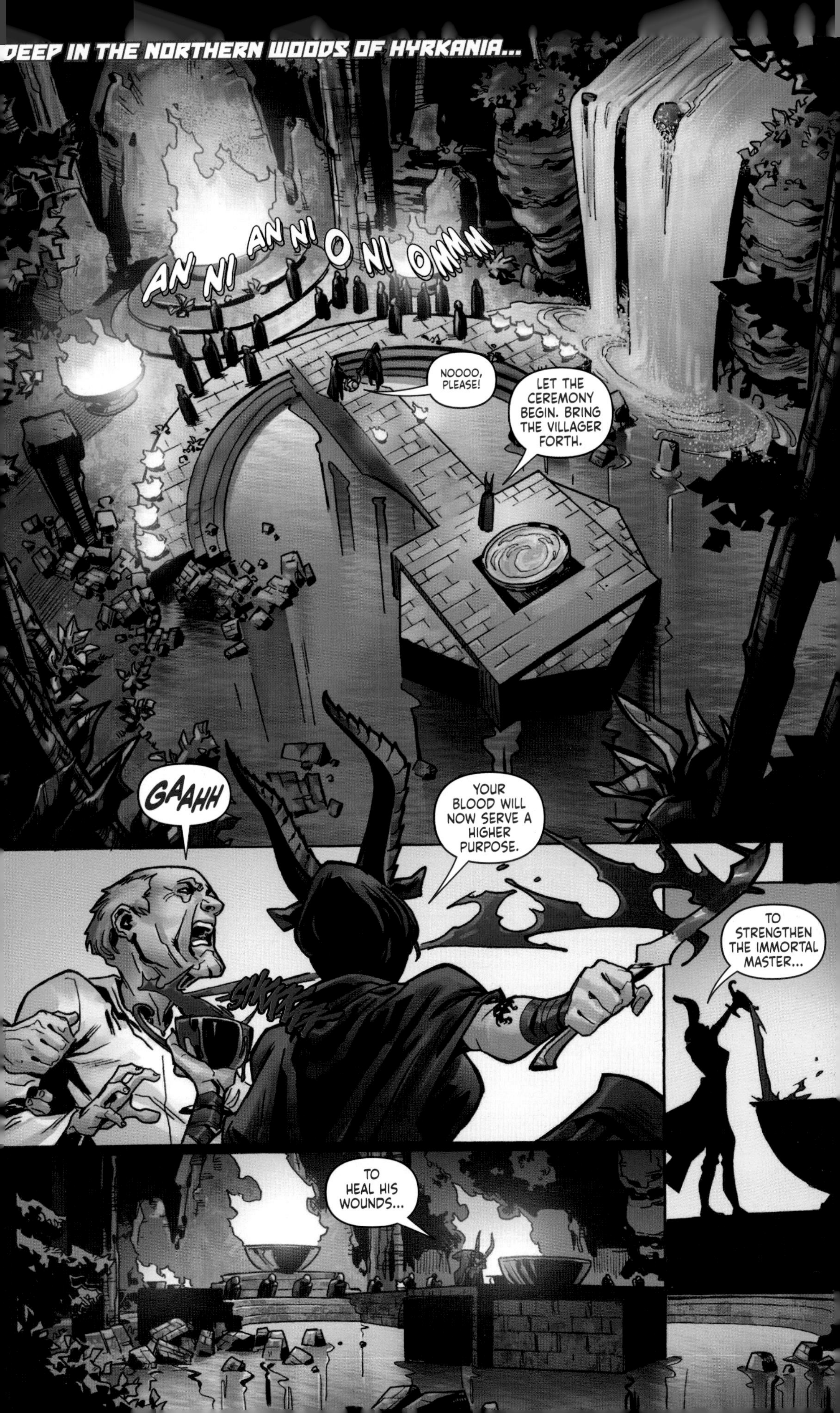
DEEP IN THE NORTHERN WOODS OF HYRKANIA...
AN NI AN NI O NI OMMM
NOOOO, PLEASE!
LET THE CEREMONY BEGIN. BRING THE VILLAGER FORTH.
GAAHH
YOUR BLOOD WILL NOW SERVE A HIGHER PURPOSE.
TO STRENGTHEN THE IMMORTAL MASTER...
TO HEAL HIS WOUNDS...

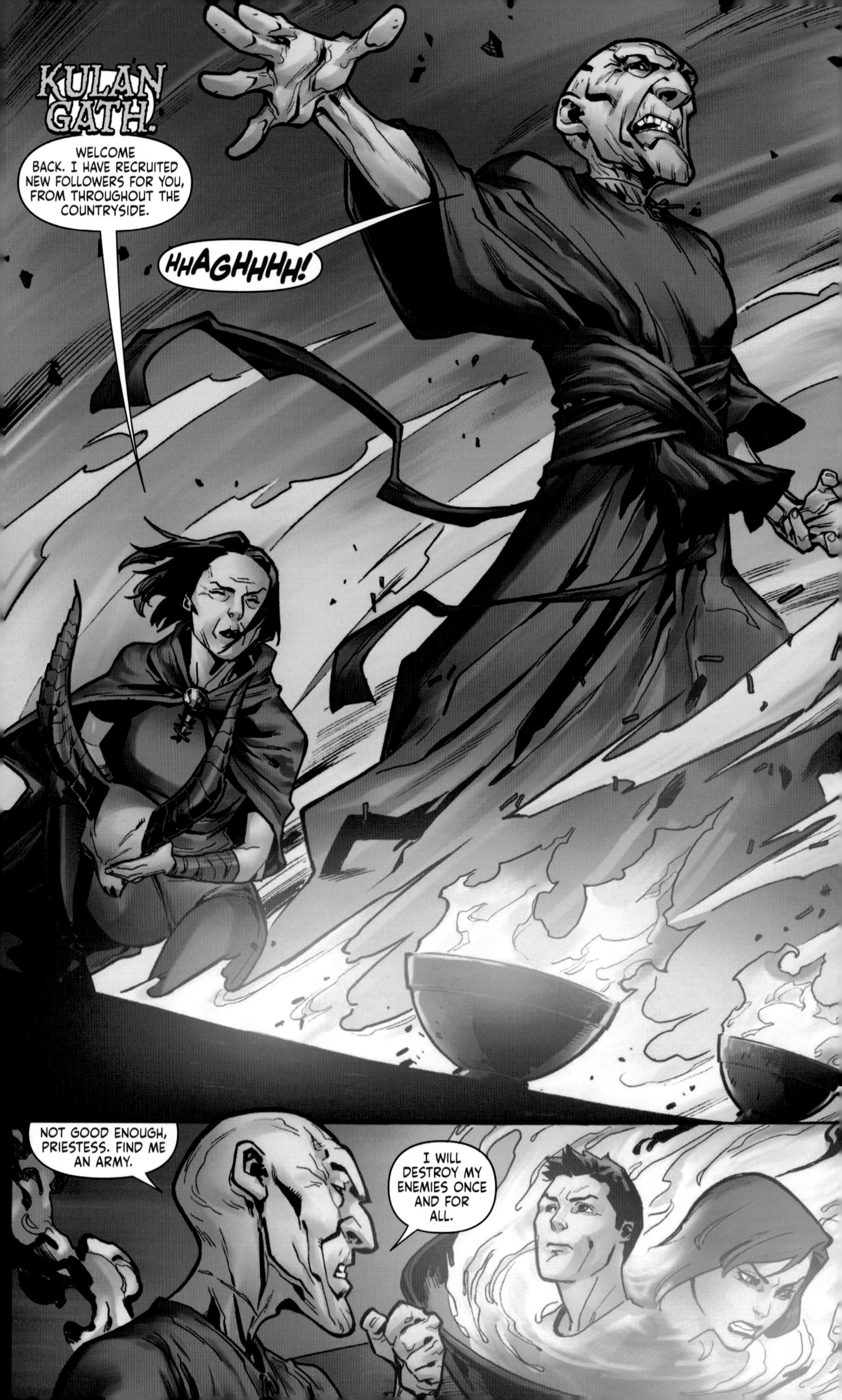
KULAN GATH.
WELCOME BACK. I HAVE RECRUITED NEW FOLLOWERS FOR YOU, FROM THROUGHOUT THE COUNTRYSIDE.
HHAGHHHH!
NOT GOOD ENOUGH, PRIESTESS. FIND ME AN ARMY.
I WILL DESTROY MY ENEMIES ONCE AND FOR ALL.

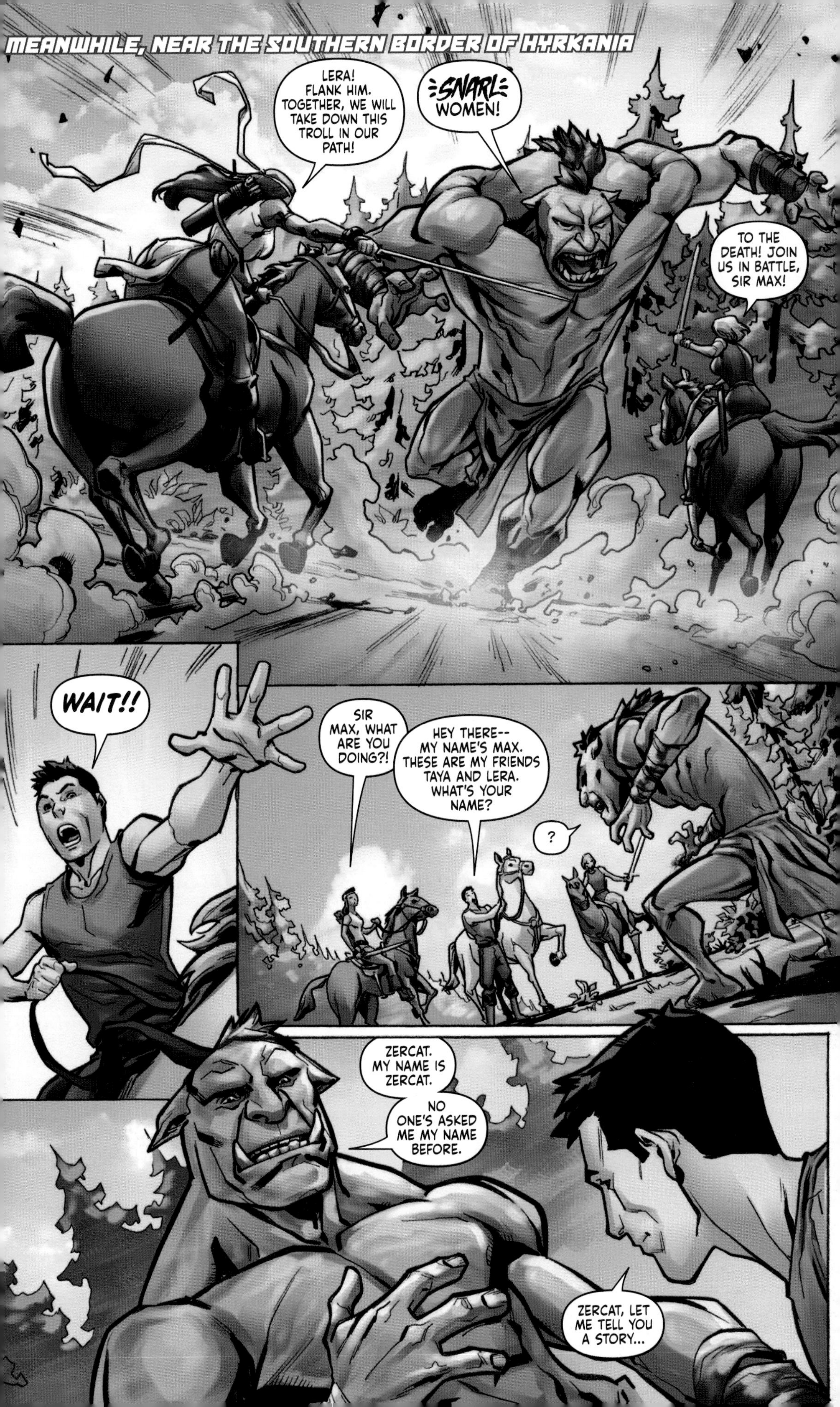
MEANWHILE, NEAR THE SOUTHERN BORDER OF HYRKANIA
LERA! FLANK HIM. TOGETHER, WE WILL TAKE DOWN THIS TROLL IN OUR PATH!
SNARL WOMEN!
TO THE DEATH! JOIN US IN BATTLE, SIR MAX!
WAIT!!
SIR MAX, WHAT ARE YOU DOING?!
HEY THERE-- MY NAME'S MAX. THESE ARE MY FRIENDS TAYA AND LERA. WHAT'S YOUR NAME?
?
ZERCAT. MY NAME IS ZERCAT.
NO ONE'S ASKED ME MY NAME BEFORE.
ZERCAT, LET ME TELL YOU A STORY...

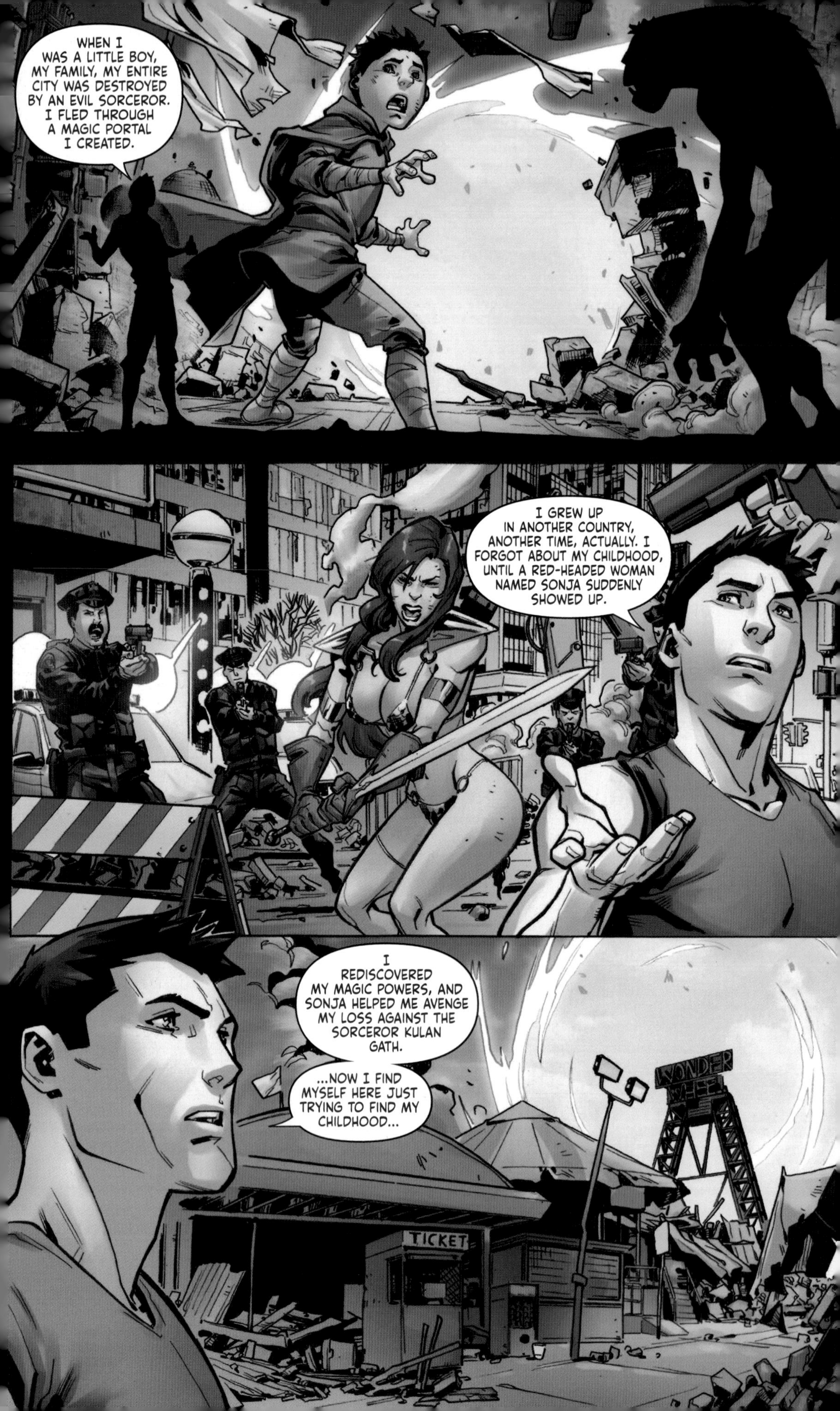

WHEN I WAS A LITTLE BOY, MY FAMILY, MY ENTIRE CITY WAS DESTROYED BY AN EVIL SORCEROR. I FLED THROUGH A MAGIC PORTAL I CREATED.
I GREW UP IN ANOTHER COUNTRY, ANOTHER TIME, ACTUALLY. I FORGOT ABOUT MY CHILDHOOD, UNTIL A RED-HEADED WOMAN NAMED SONJA SUDDENLY SHOWED UP.
I REDISCOVERED MY MAGIC POWERS, AND SONJA HELPED ME AVENGE MY LOSS AGAINST THE SORCEROR KULAN GATH.
...NOW I FIND MYSELF HERE JUST TRYING TO FIND MY CHILDHOOD...
WONDER
TICKET

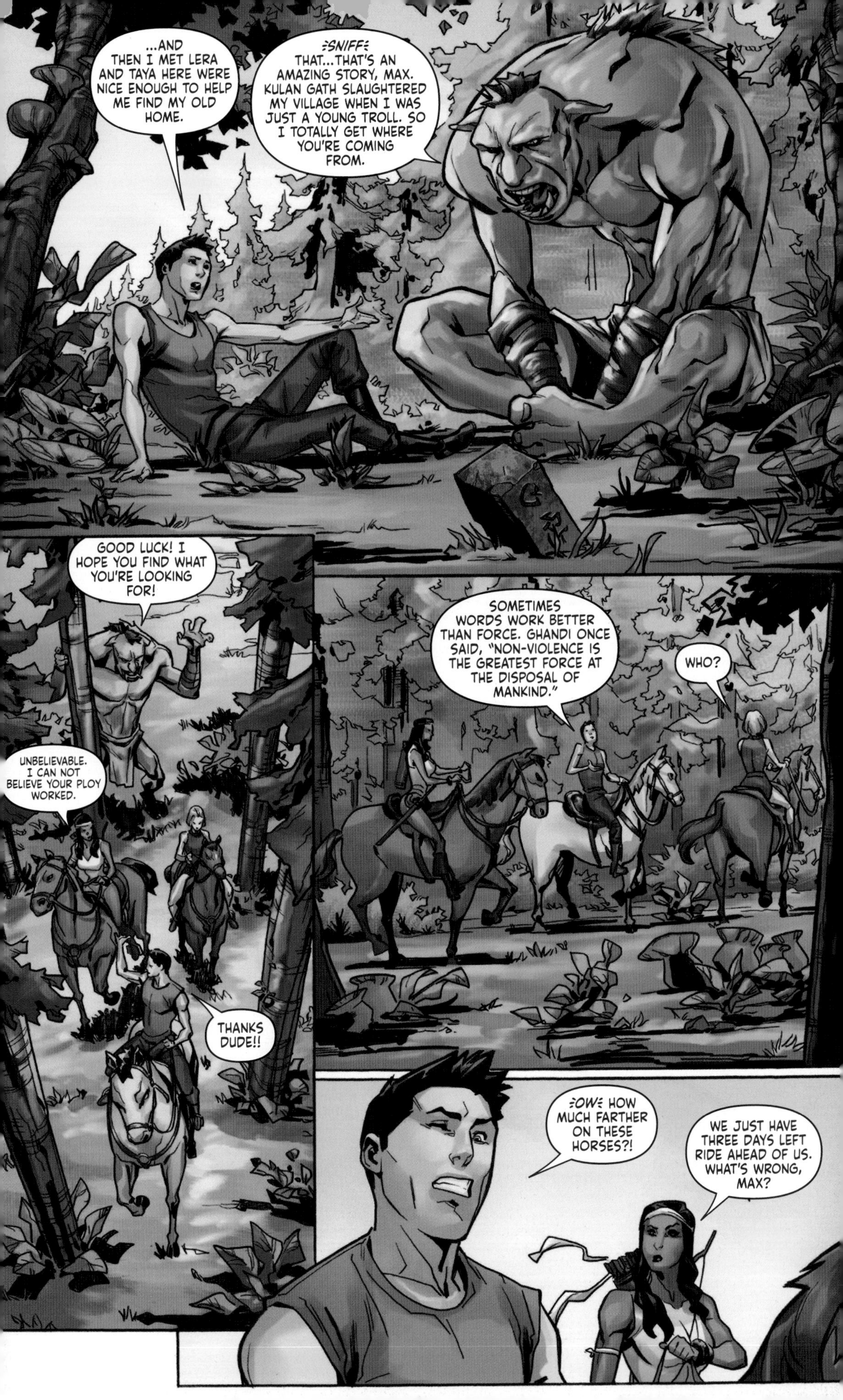
...AND THEN I MET LERA AND TAYA HERE WERE NICE ENOUGH TO HELP ME FIND MY OLD HOME.
SNIFF
THAT...THAT'S AN AMAZING STORY, MAX. KULAN GATH SLAUGHTERED MY VILLAGE WHEN I WAS JUST A YOUNG TROLL. SO I TOTALLY GET WHERE YOU'RE COMING FROM.
GOOD LUCK! I HOPE YOU FIND WHAT YOU'RE LOOKING FOR!
UNBELIEVABLE. I CAN NOT BELIEVE YOUR PLOY WORKED.
THANKS DUDE!!
SOMETIMES WORDS WORK BETTER THAN FORCE. GHANDI ONCE SAID, "NON-VIOLENCE IS THE GREATEST FORCE AT THE DISPOSAL OF MANKIND."
WHO?
OW HOW MUCH FARTHER ON THESE HORSES?!
WE JUST HAVE THREE DAYS LEFT RIDE AHEAD OF US. WHAT'S WRONG, MAX?

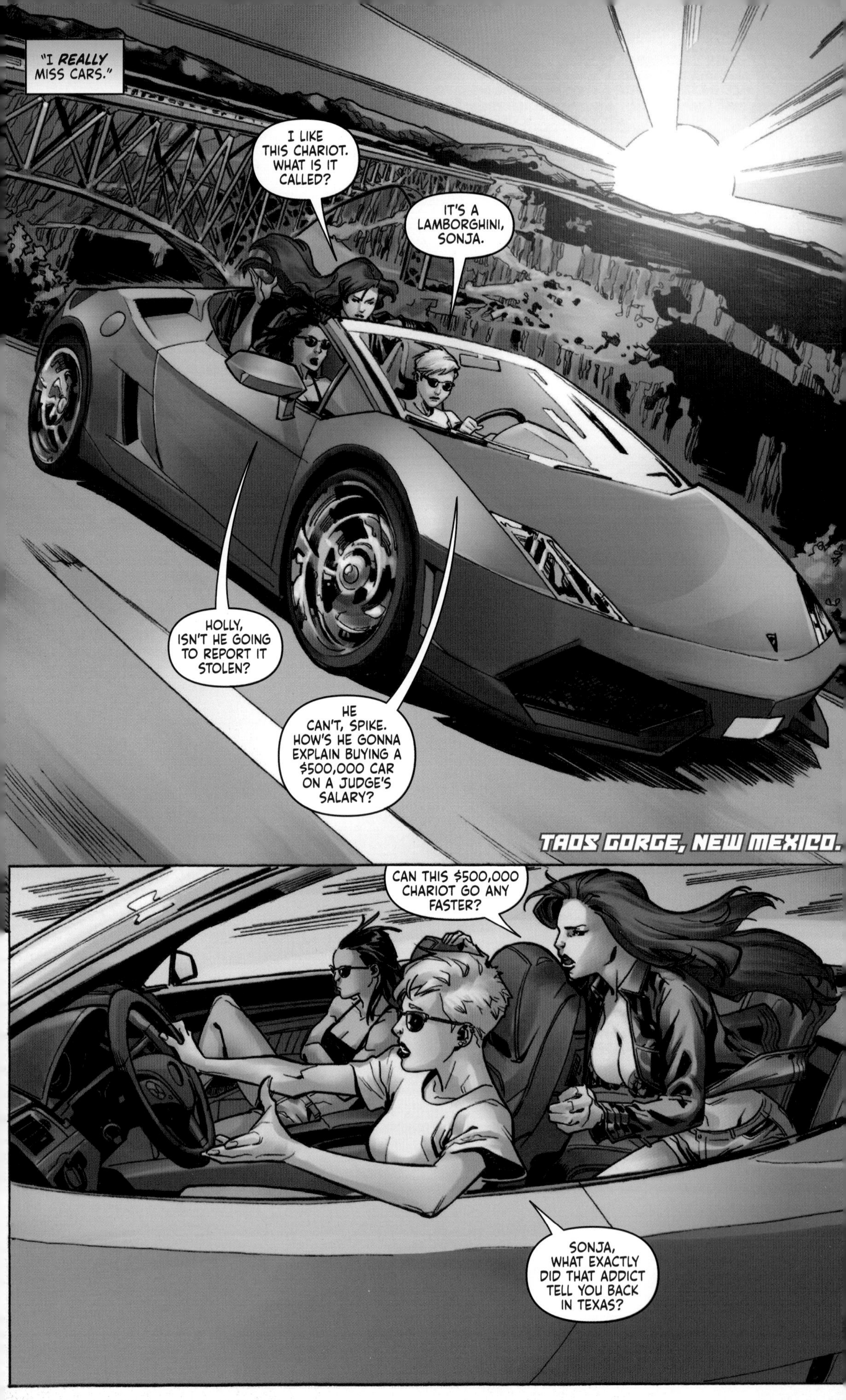
"I REALLY MISS CARS."
I LIKE THIS CHARIOT. WHAT IS IT CALLED?
IT'S A LAMBORGHINI, SONJA.
HOLLY, ISN'T HE GOING TO REPORT IT STOLEN?
HE CAN'T, SPIKE. HOW'S HE GONNA EXPLAIN BUYING A $500,000 CAR ON A JUDGE'S SALARY?
TAOS GORGE, NEW MEXICO.
CAN THIS $500,000 CHARIOT GO ANY FASTER?
SONJA, WHAT EXACTLY DID THAT ADDICT TELL YOU BACK IN TEXAS?

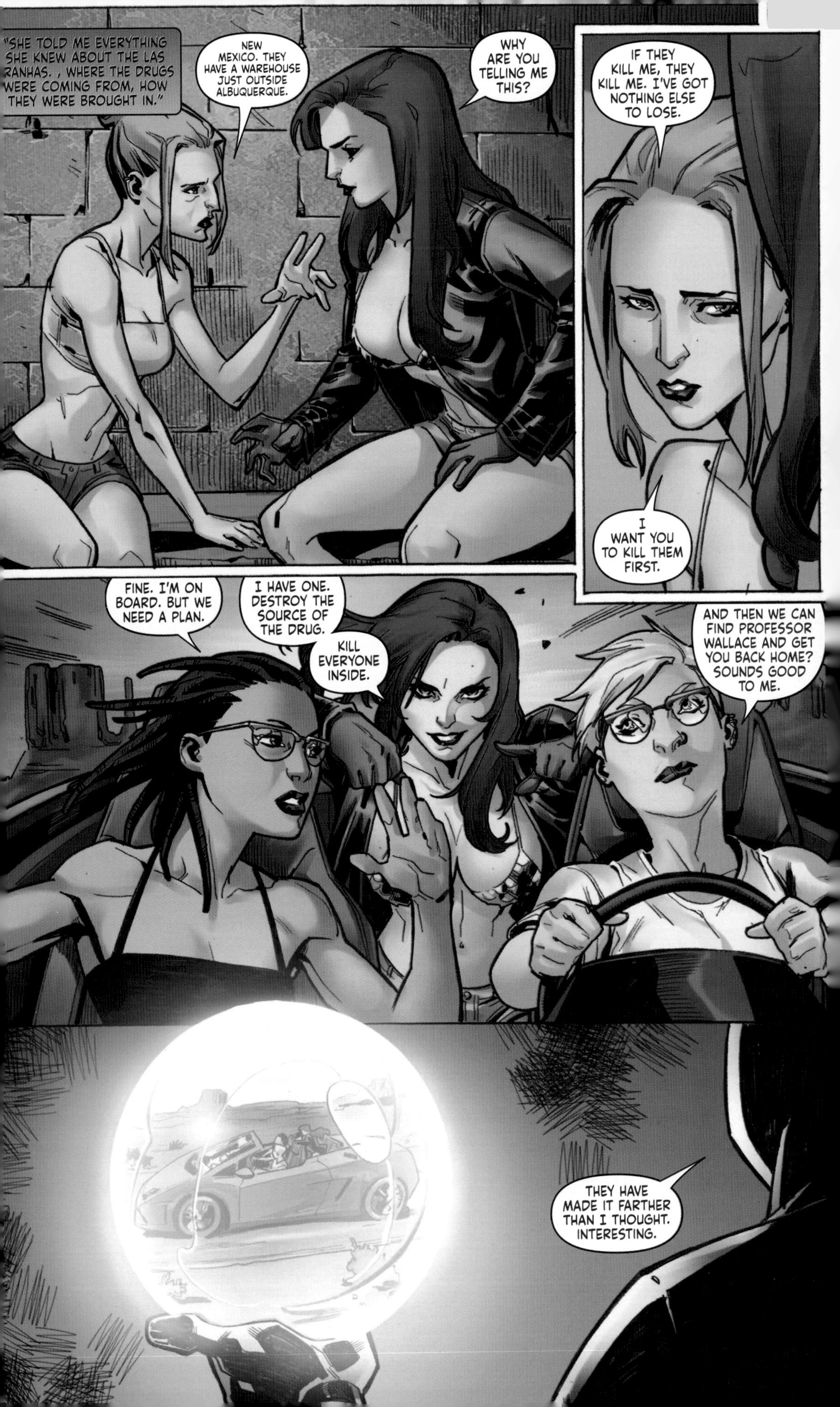
"SHE TOLD ME EVERYTHING SHE KNEW ABOUT THE LAS RANHAS. , WHERE THE DRUGS WERE COMING FROM, HOW THEY WERE BROUGHT IN."
NEW MEXICO. THEY HAVE A WAREHOUSE JUST OUTSIDE ALBUQUERQUE.
WHY ARE YOU TELLING ME THIS?
IF THEY KILL ME, THEY KILL ME. I'VE GOT NOTHING ELSE TO LOSE.
I WANT YOU TO KILL THEM FIRST.
FINE. I'M ON BOARD. BUT WE NEED A PLAN.
I HAVE ONE. DESTROY THE SOURCE OF THE DRUG.
KILL EVERYONE INSIDE.
AND THEN WE CAN FIND PROFESSOR WALLACE AND GET YOU BACK HOME? SOUNDS GOOD TO ME.
THEY HAVE MADE IT FARTHER THAN I THOUGHT. INTERESTING.

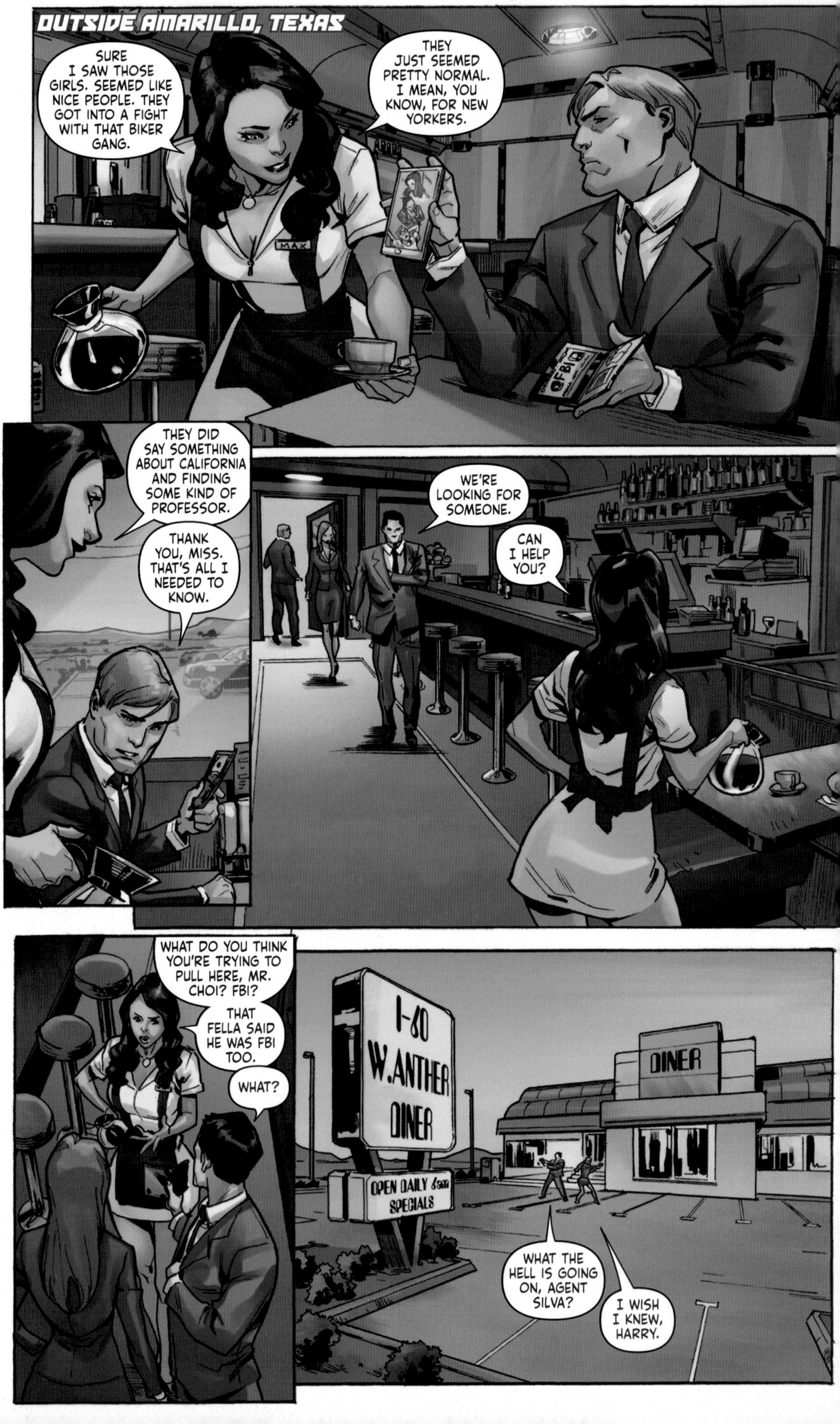
OUTSIDE AMARILLO, TEXAS
SURE I SAW THOSE GIRLS. SEEMED LIKE NICE PEOPLE. THEY GOT INTO A FIGHT WITH THAT BIKER GANG.
THEY JUST SEEMED PRETTY NORMAL. I MEAN, YOU KNOW, FOR NEW YORKERS.
MAX
FBI
THEY DID SAY SOMETHING ABOUT CALIFORNIA AND FINDING SOME KIND OF PROFESSOR.
THANK YOU, MISS. THAT'S ALL I NEEDED TO KNOW.
WE'RE LOOKING FOR SOMEONE.
CAN I HELP YOU?
WHAT DO YOU THINK YOU'RE TRYING TO PULL HERE, MR. CHOI? FBI?
THAT FELLA SAID HE WAS FBI TOO.
WHAT?
I-80
W.ANTHER
DINER
OPEN DAILY 6am
SPECIALS
DINER
WHAT THE HELL IS GOING ON, AGENT SILVA?
I WISH I KNEW, HARRY.

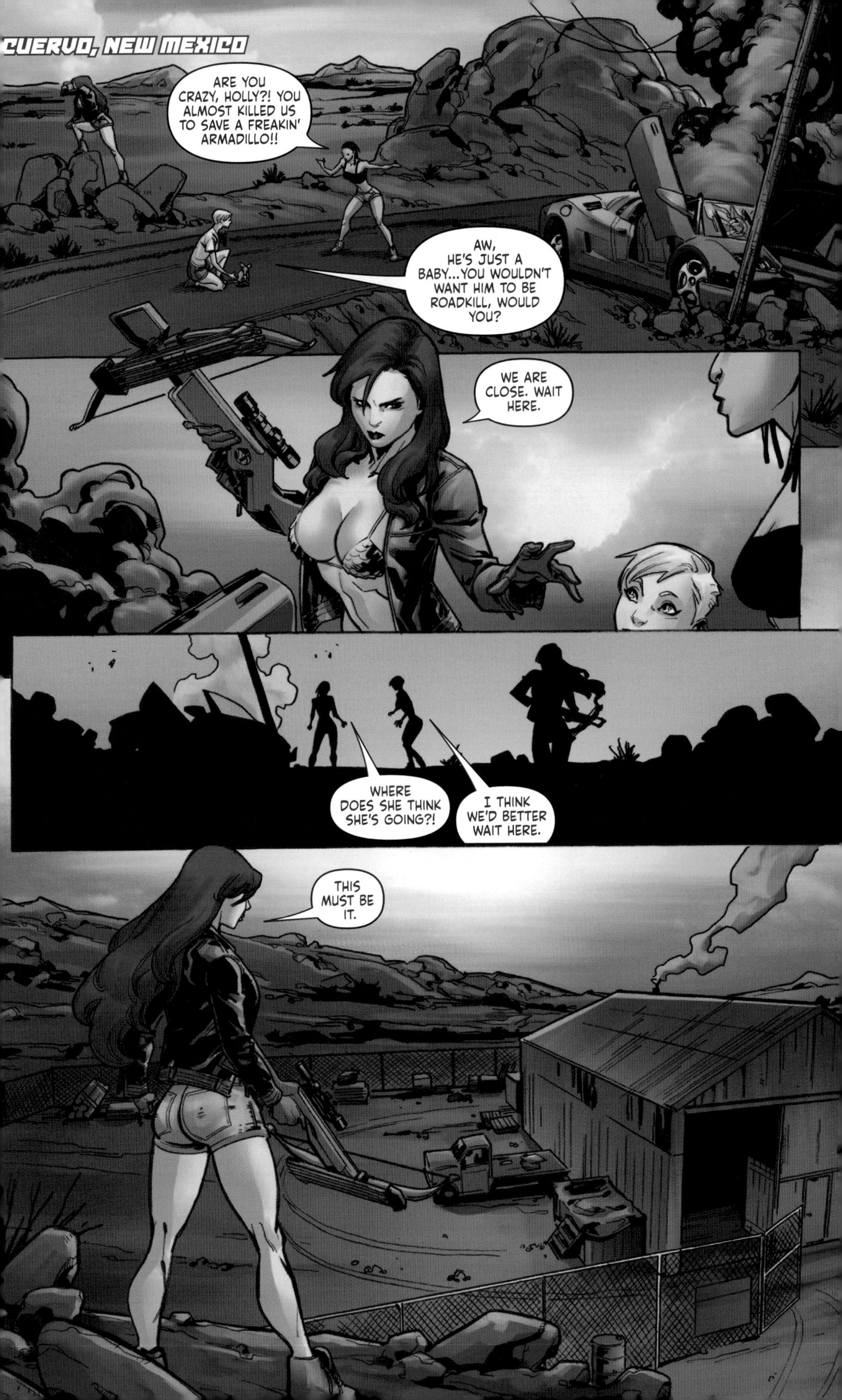
CUERVO, NEW MEXICO
ARE YOU CRAZY, HOLLY?! YOU ALMOST KILLED US TO SAVE A FREAKIN' ARMADILLO!!
AW, HE'S JUST A BABY...YOU WOULDN'T WANT HIM TO BE ROADKILL, WOULD YOU?
WE ARE CLOSE. WAIT HERE.
WHERE DOES SHE THINK SHE'S GOING?!
I THINK WE'D BETTER WAIT HERE.
THIS MUST BE IT.

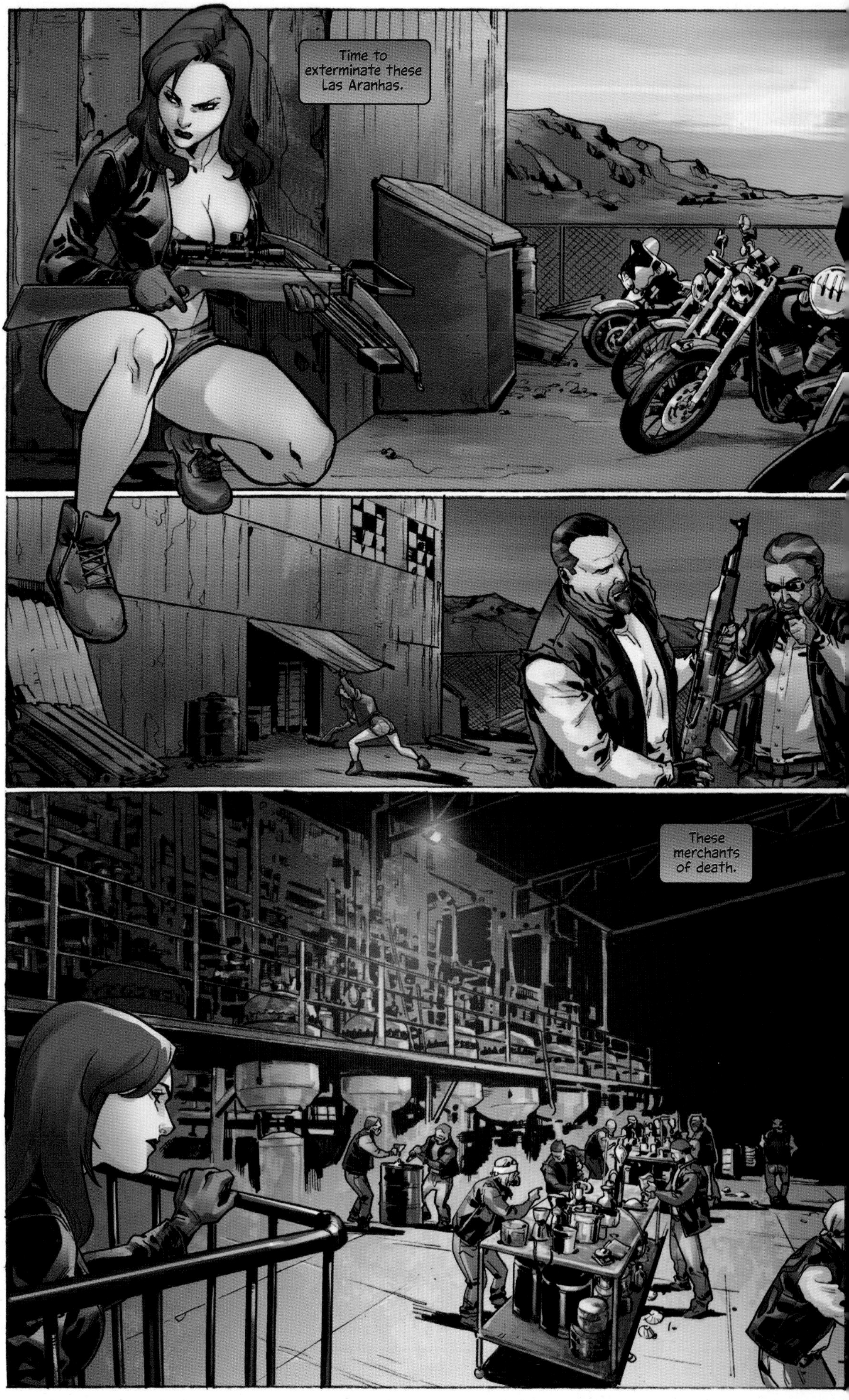

Time to exterminate these Las Aranhas.
These merchants of death.

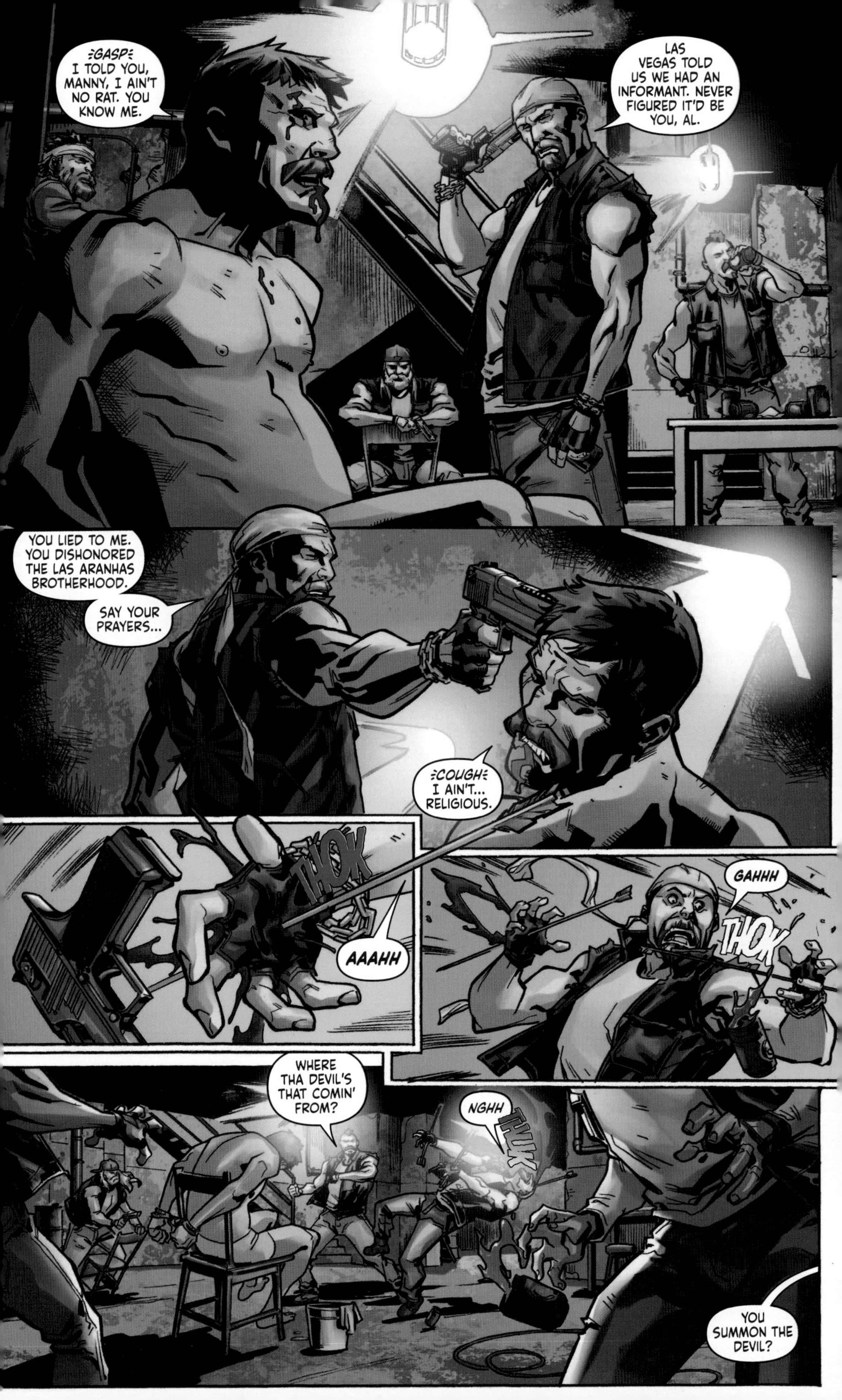

GASP
I TOLD YOU, MANNY, I AIN'T NO RAT. YOU KNOW ME.
LAS VEGAS TOLD US WE HAD AN INFORMANT. NEVER FIGURED IT'D BE YOU, AL.
YOU LIED TO ME. YOU DISHONORED THE LAS ARANHAS BROTHERHOOD.
SAY YOUR PRAYERS...
COUGH
I AIN'T... RELIGIOUS.
THOK
AAAHH
GAHHH
THOK
WHERE THA DEVIL'S THAT COMIN' FROM?
NGHH
THUK
YOU SUMMON THE DEVIL?

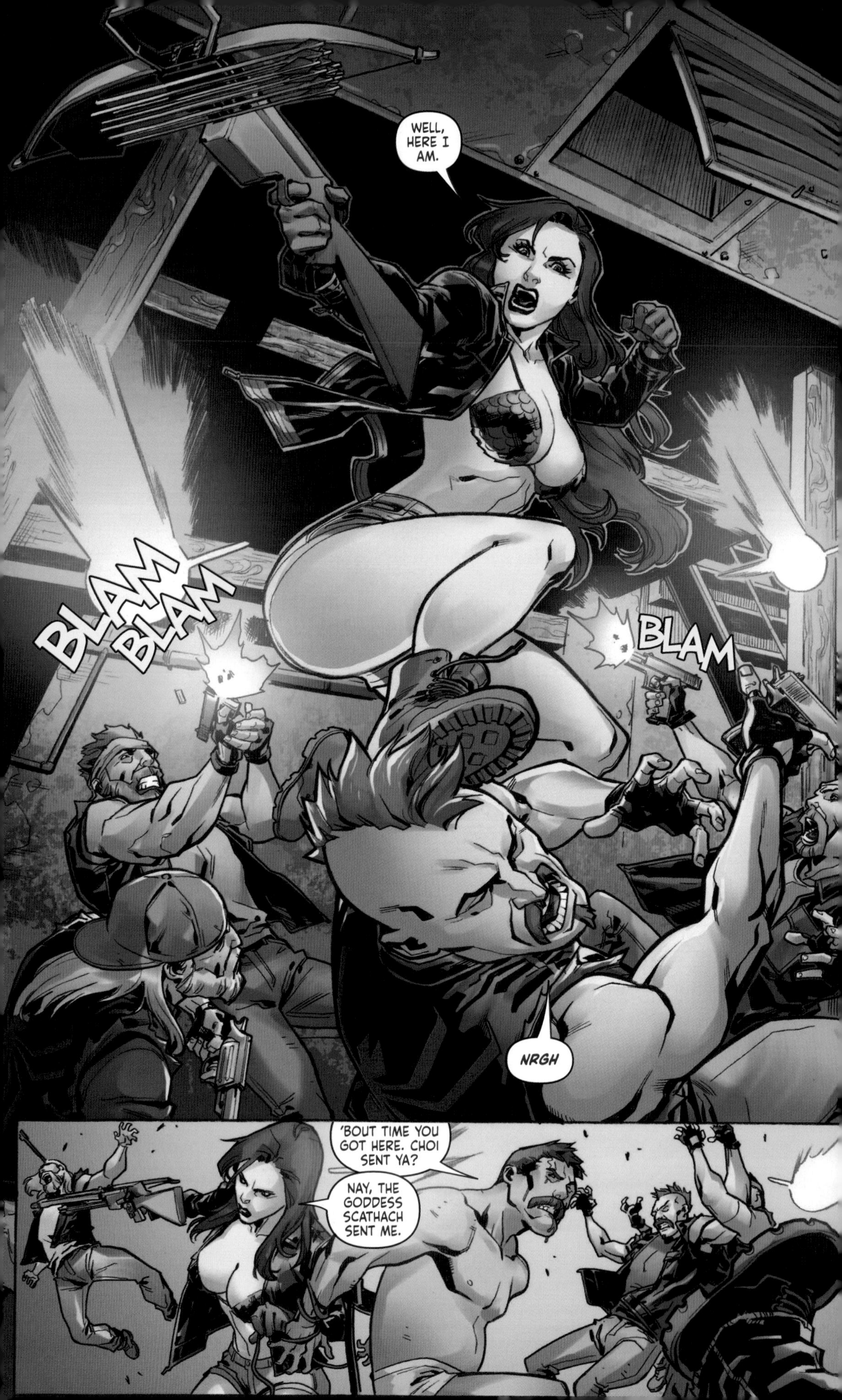

WELL, HERE I AM.
BLAM BLAM
BLAM
NRGH
'BOUT TIME YOU GOT HERE. CHOI SENT YA?
NAY, THE GODDESS SCATHACH SENT ME.

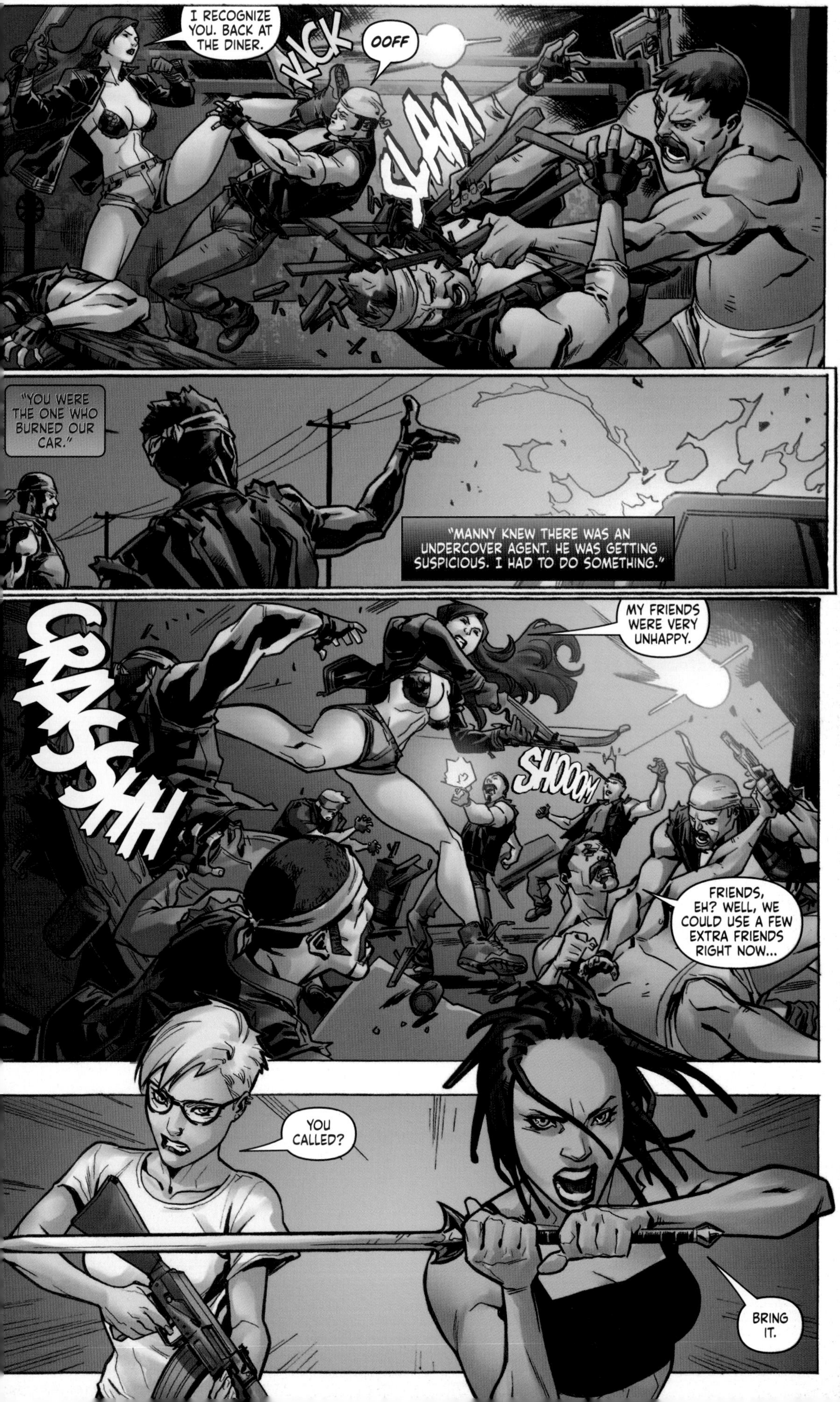
I RECOGNIZE YOU. BACK AT THE DINER.
KICK
OOFF
SLAM
"YOU WERE THE ONE WHO BURNED OUR CAR."
"MANNY KNEW THERE WAS AN UNDERCOVER AGENT. HE WAS GETTING SUSPICIOUS. I HAD TO DO SOMETHING."
CRASSHH
MY FRIENDS WERE VERY UNHAPPY.
SHOOOM
FRIENDS, EH? WELL, WE COULD USE A FEW EXTRA FRIENDS RIGHT NOW...
YOU CALLED?
BRING IT.

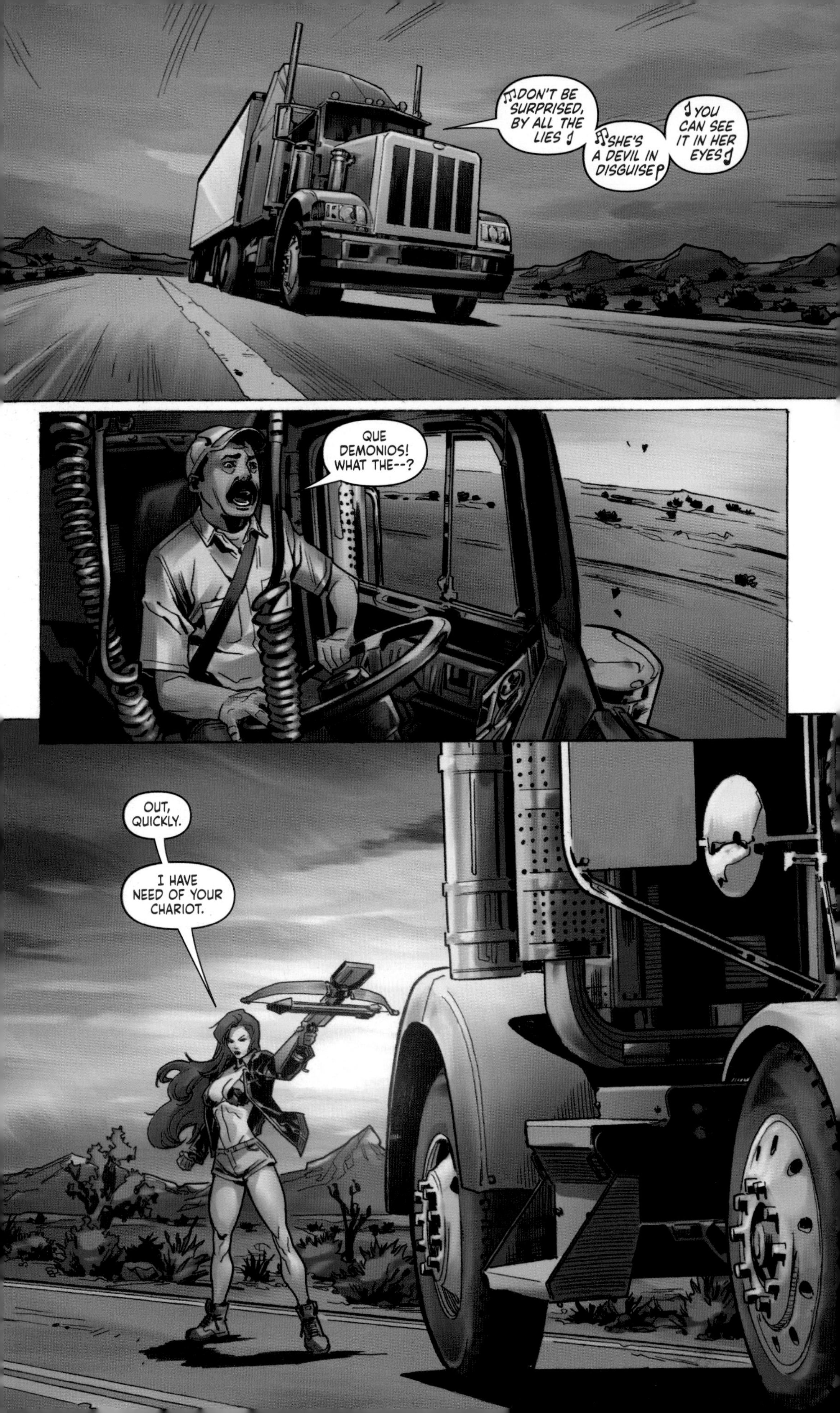
♫DON'T BE SURPRISED, BY ALL THE LIES♩
♫SHE'S A DEVIL IN DISGUISE♪
♩YOU CAN SEE IT IN HER EYES♩
QUE DEMONIOS! WHAT THE--?
OUT, QUICKLY.
I HAVE NEED OF YOUR CHARIOT.

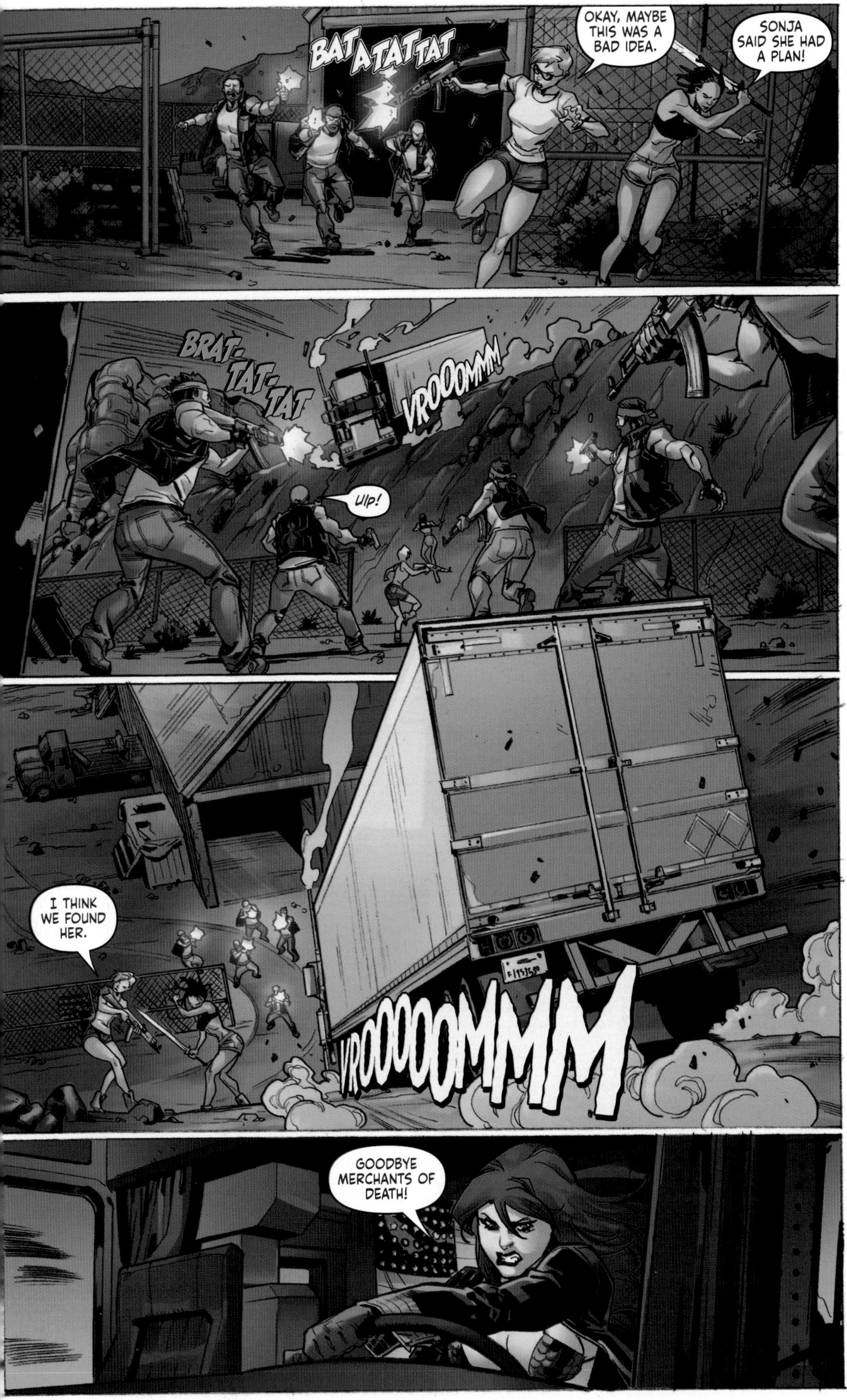
BAT A TAT TAT
OKAY, MAYBE THIS WAS A BAD IDEA.
SONJA SAID SHE HAD A PLAN!
BRAT-TAT-TAT
VROOOMMM
Ulp!
I THINK WE FOUND HER.
VROOOOOMMMM
GOODBYE MERCHANTS OF DEATH!

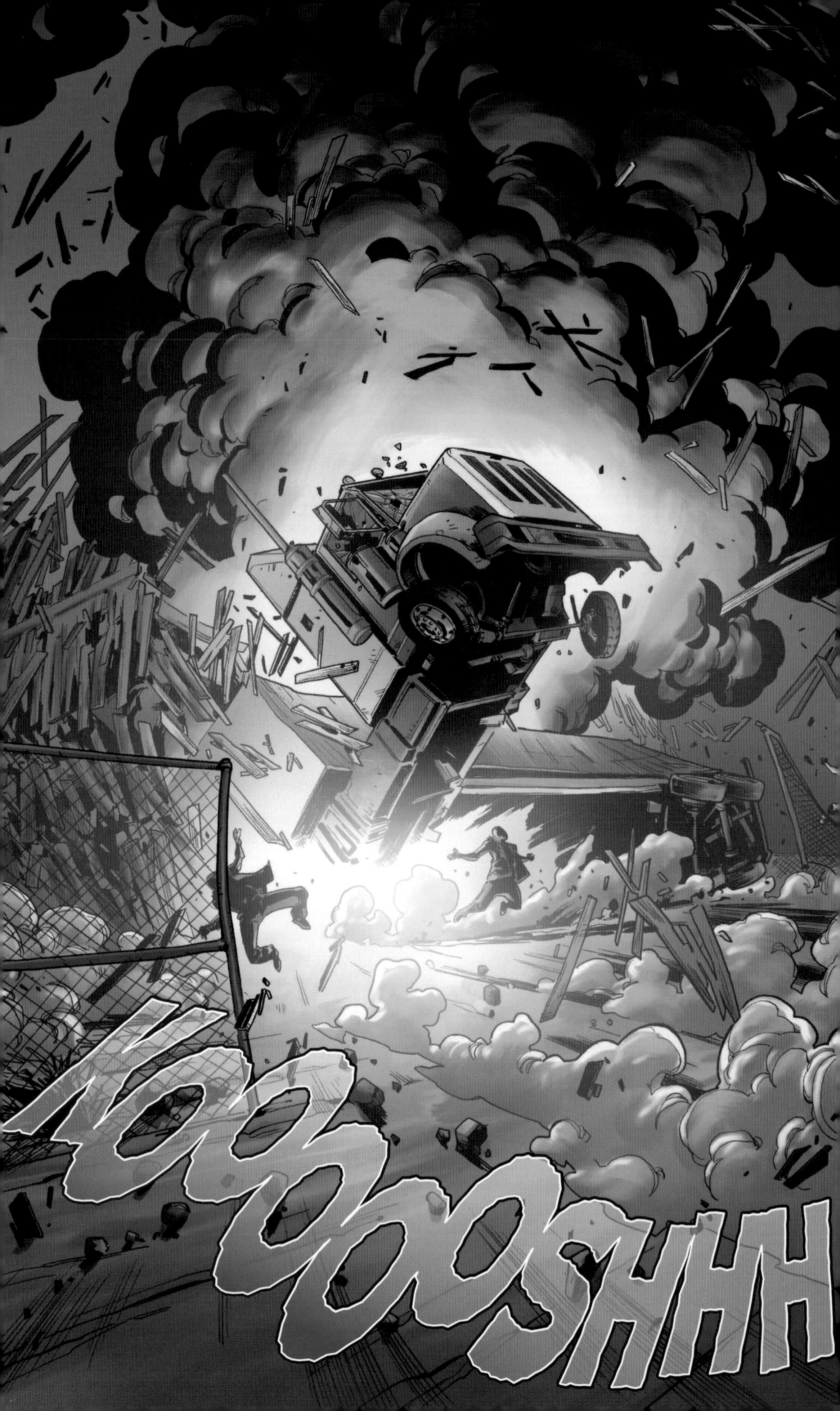
WOOOOOSHHH

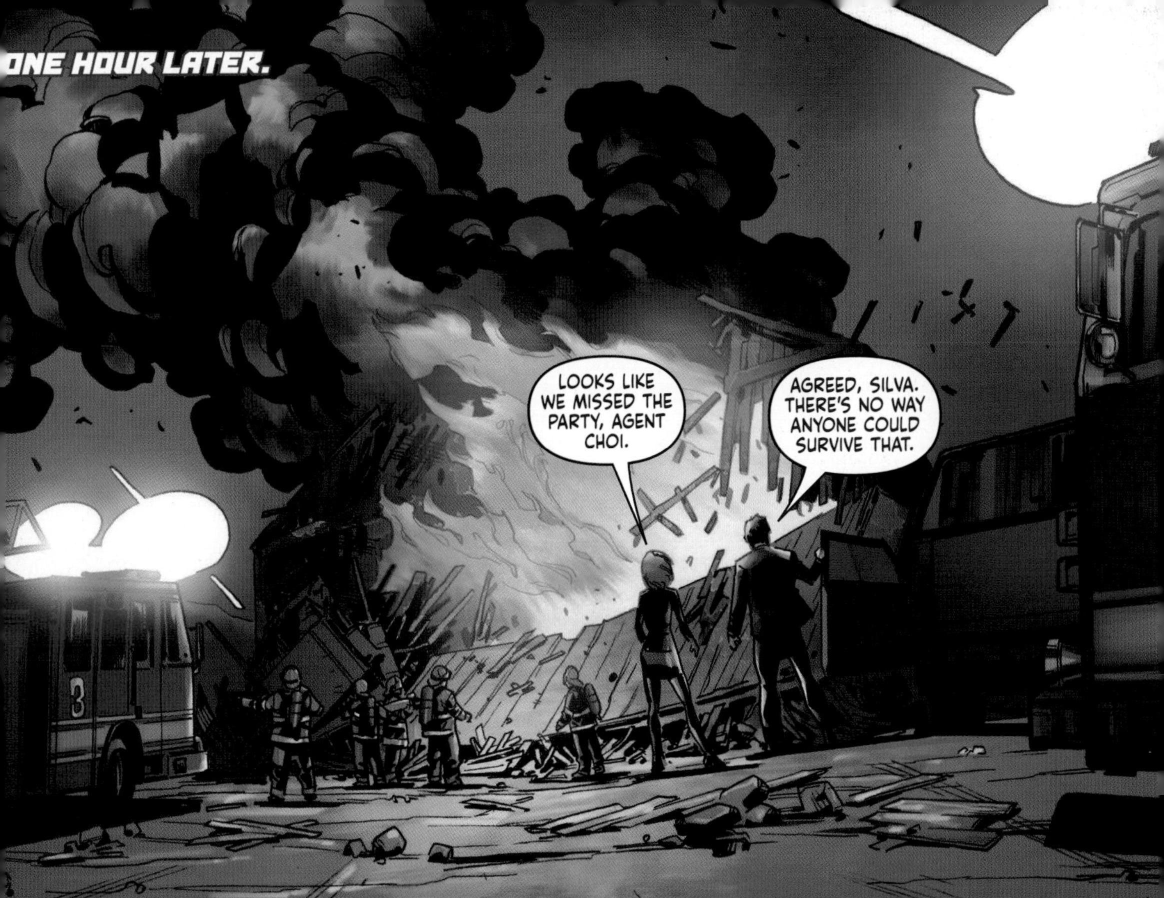
ONE HOUR LATER.
LOOKS LIKE WE MISSED THE PARTY, AGENT CHOI.
AGREED, SILVA. THERE'S NO WAY ANYONE COULD SURVIVE THAT.

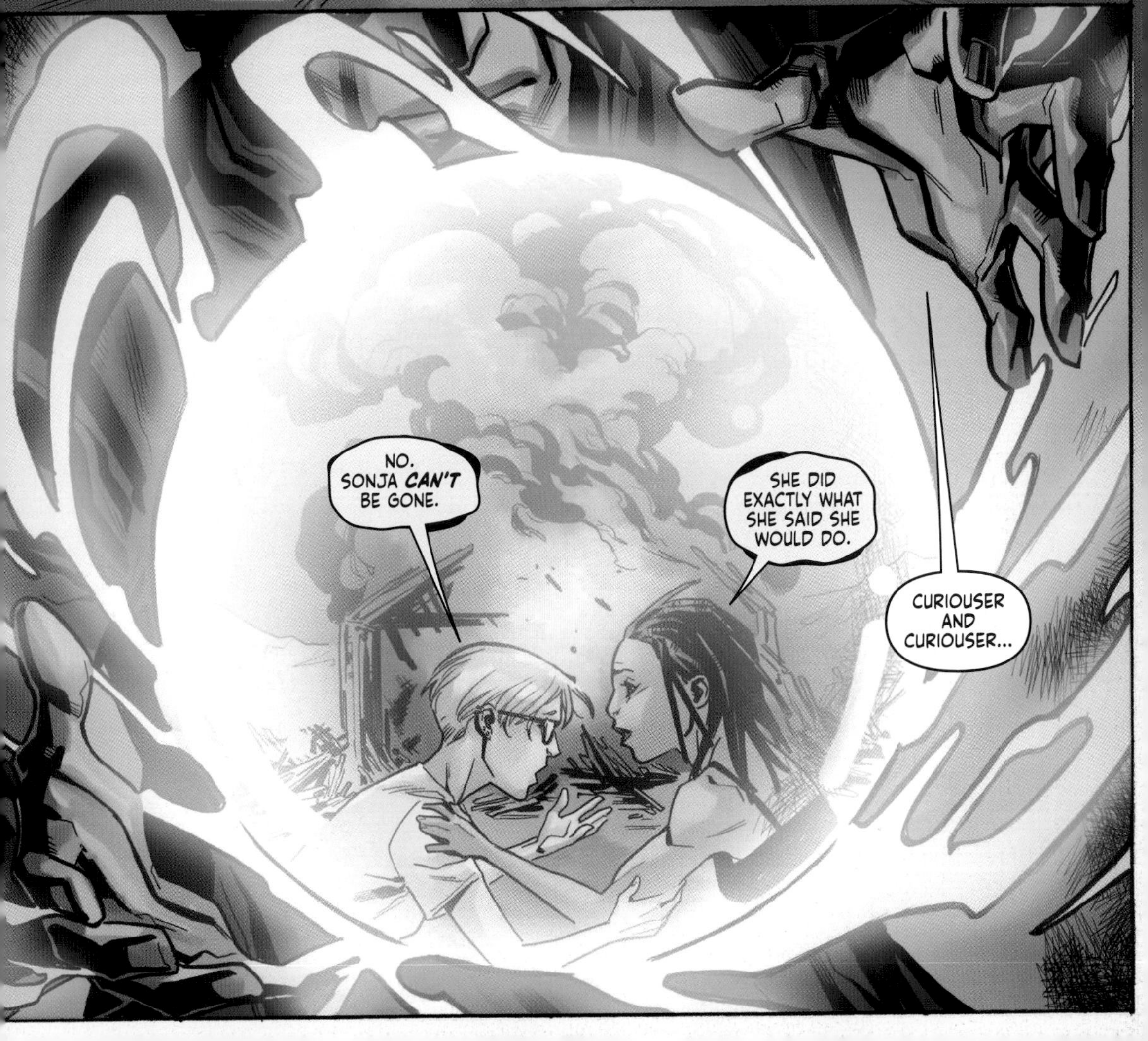
NO. SONJA ***CAN'T*** BE GONE.
SHE DID EXACTLY WHAT SHE SAID SHE WOULD DO.
CURIOUSER AND CURIOUSER...

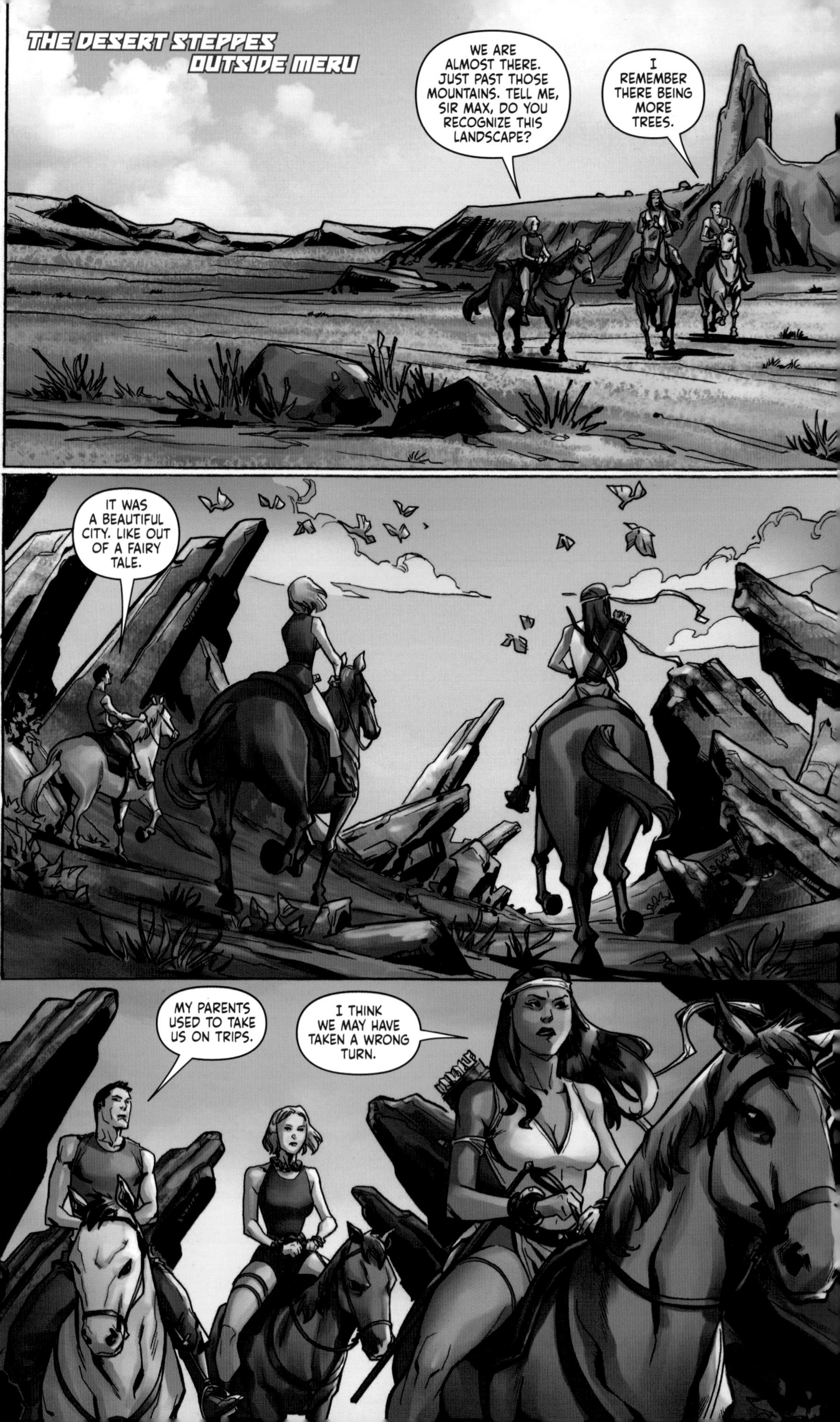
THE DESERT STEPPES OUTSIDE MERU
WE ARE ALMOST THERE. JUST PAST THOSE MOUNTAINS. TELL ME, SIR MAX, DO YOU RECOGNIZE THIS LANDSCAPE?
I REMEMBER THERE BEING MORE TREES.
IT WAS A BEAUTIFUL CITY. LIKE OUT OF A FAIRY TALE.
MY PARENTS USED TO TAKE US ON TRIPS.
I THINK WE MAY HAVE TAKEN A WRONG TURN.

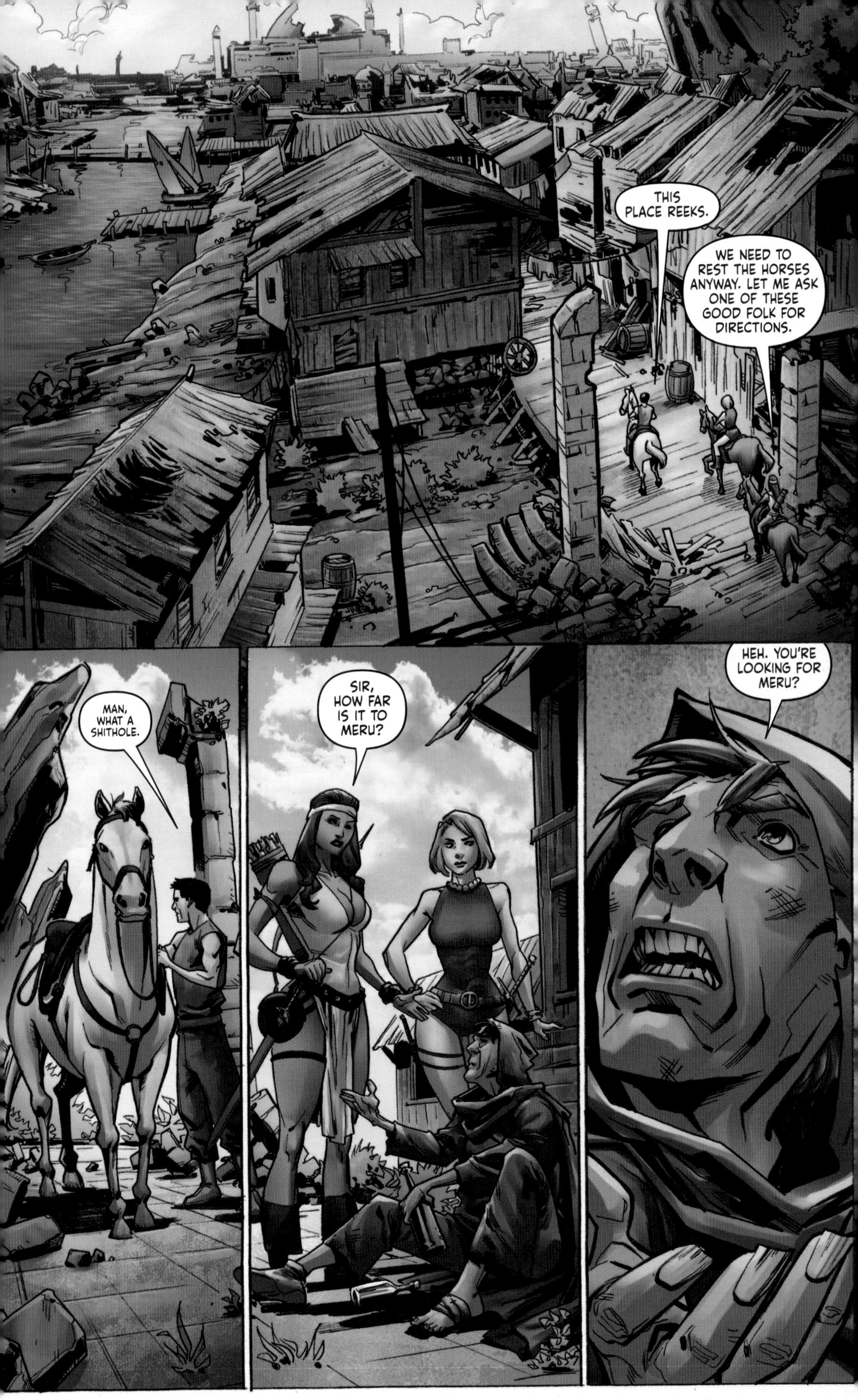
THIS PLACE REEKS.
WE NEED TO REST THE HORSES ANYWAY. LET ME ASK ONE OF THESE GOOD FOLK FOR DIRECTIONS.
MAN, WHAT A SHITHOLE.
SIR, HOW FAR IS IT TO MERU?
HEH. YOU'RE LOOKING FOR MERU?

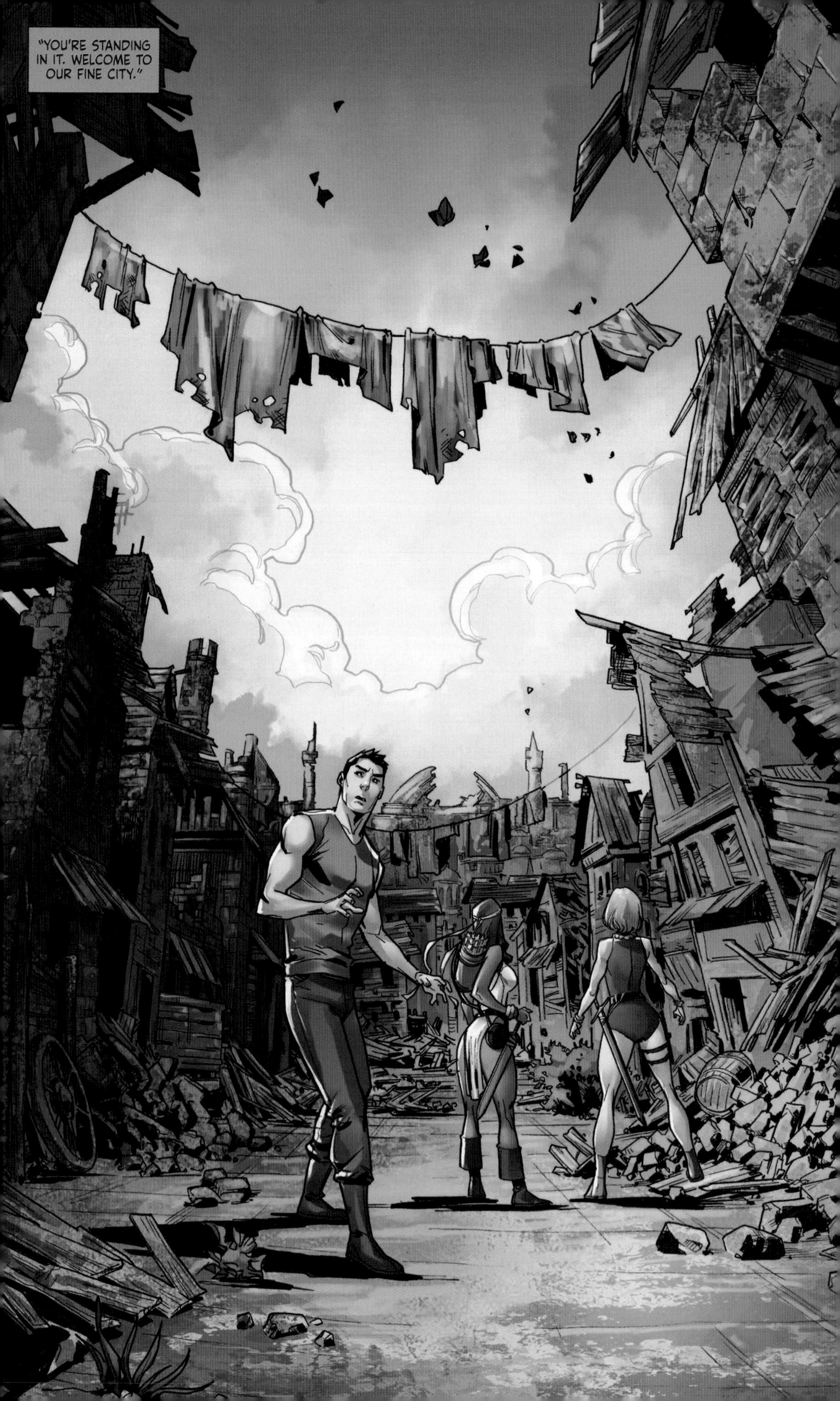
"YOU'RE STANDING IN IT. WELCOME TO OUR FINE CITY."

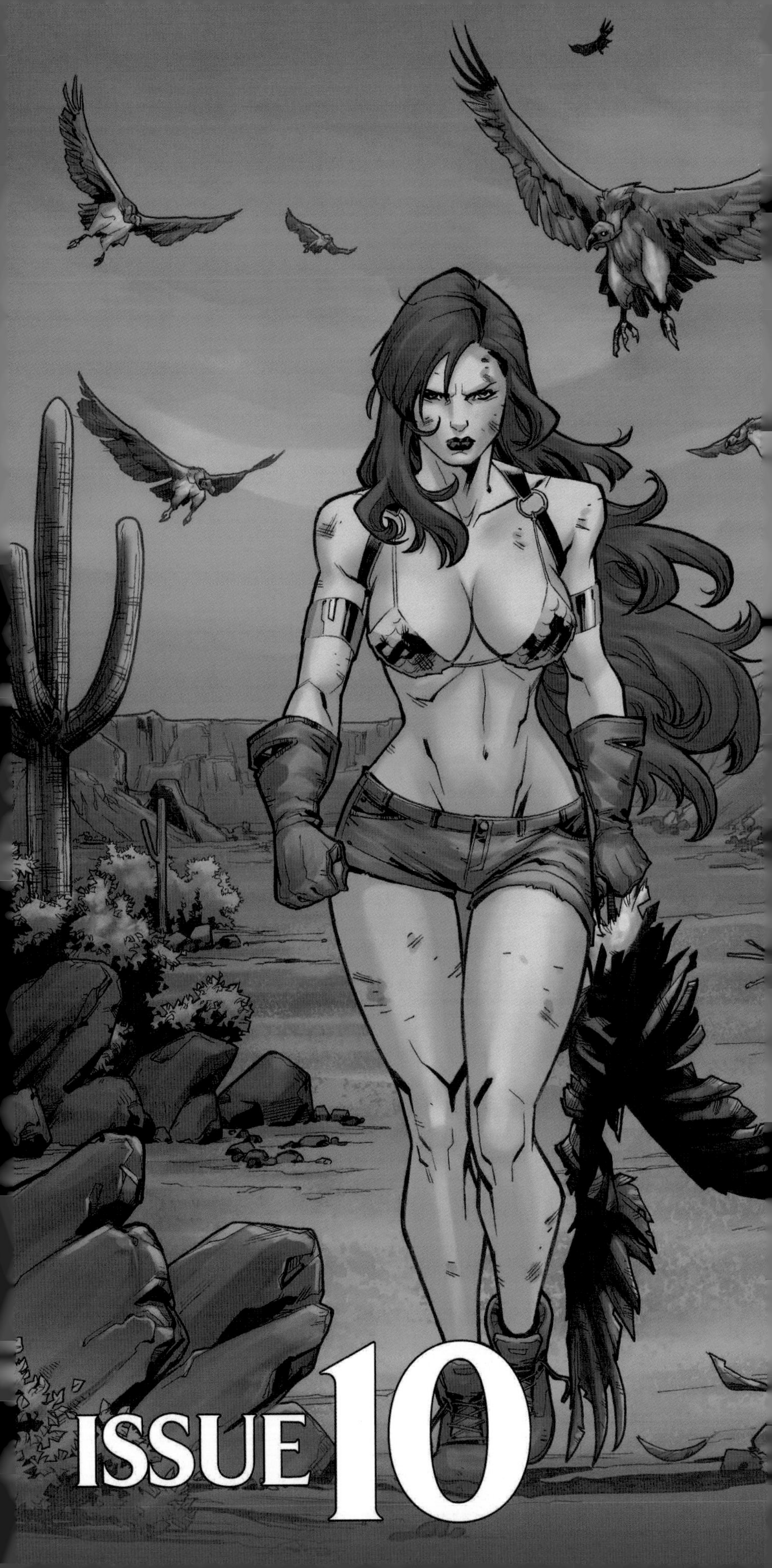
ISSUE 10

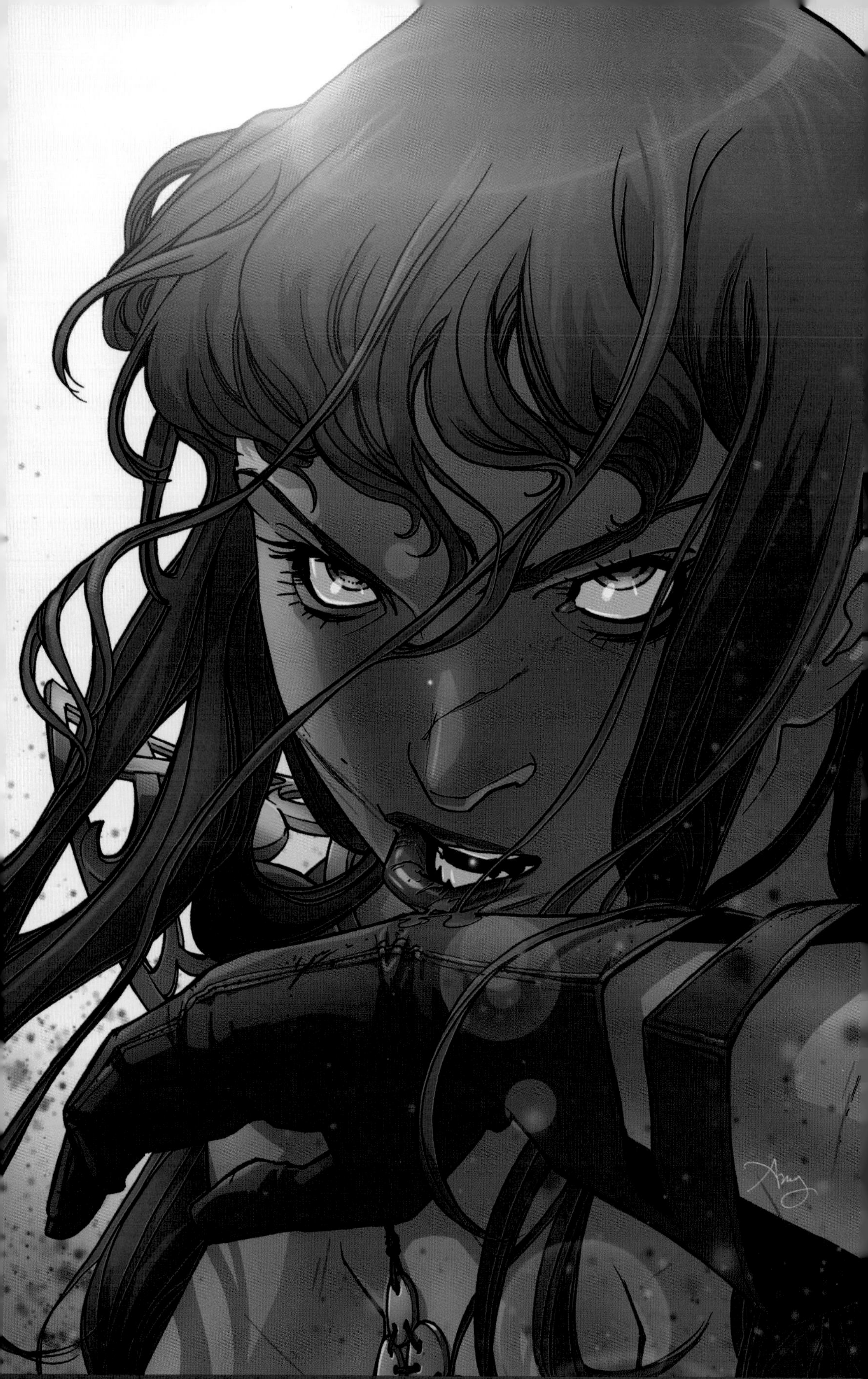

SSUE #10: COVER ART BY **AMY REEDER**

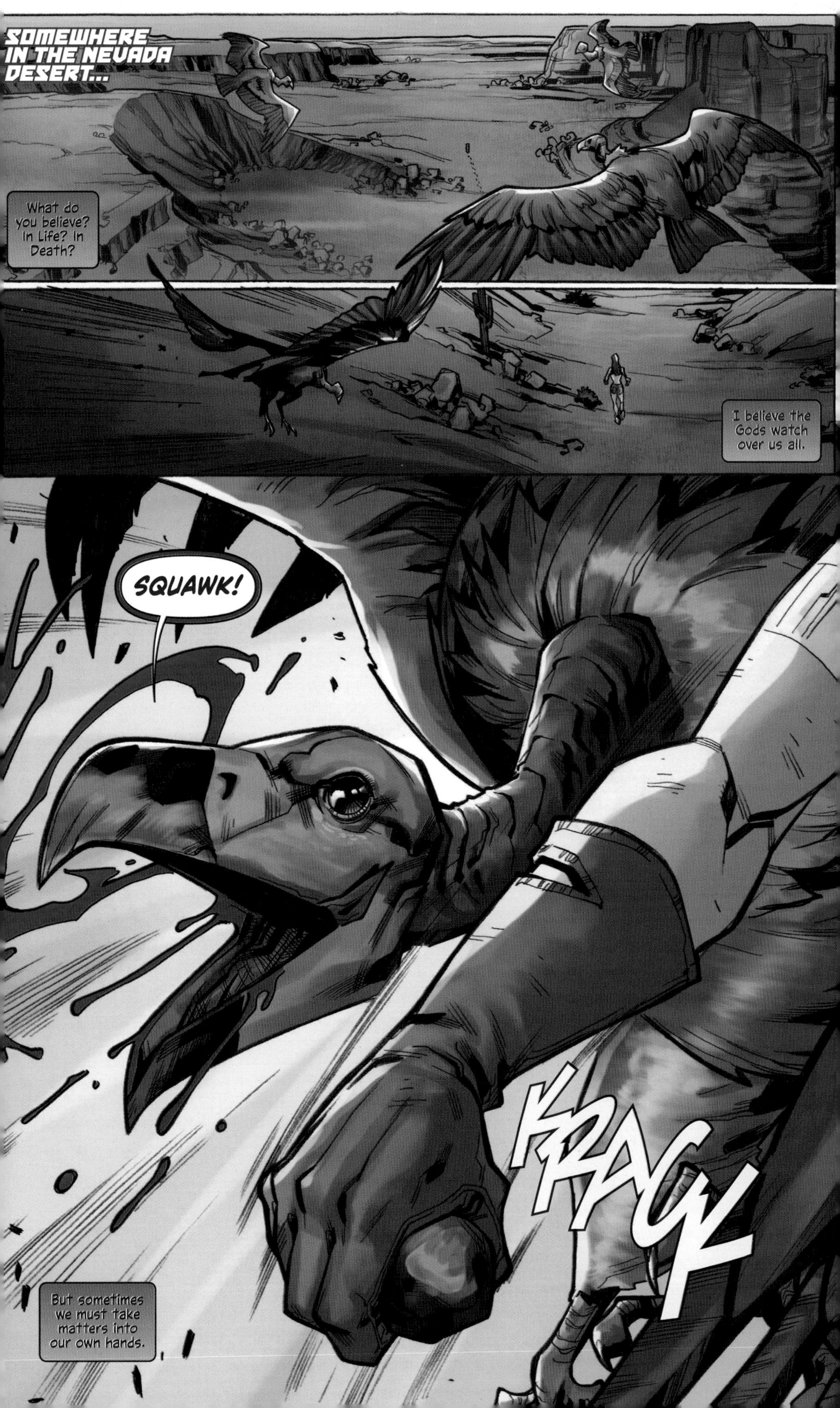

SOMEWHERE IN THE NEVADA DESERT...
What do you believe? In Life? In Death?
I believe the Gods watch over us all.
SQUAWK!
KRACK
But sometimes we must take matters into our own hands.

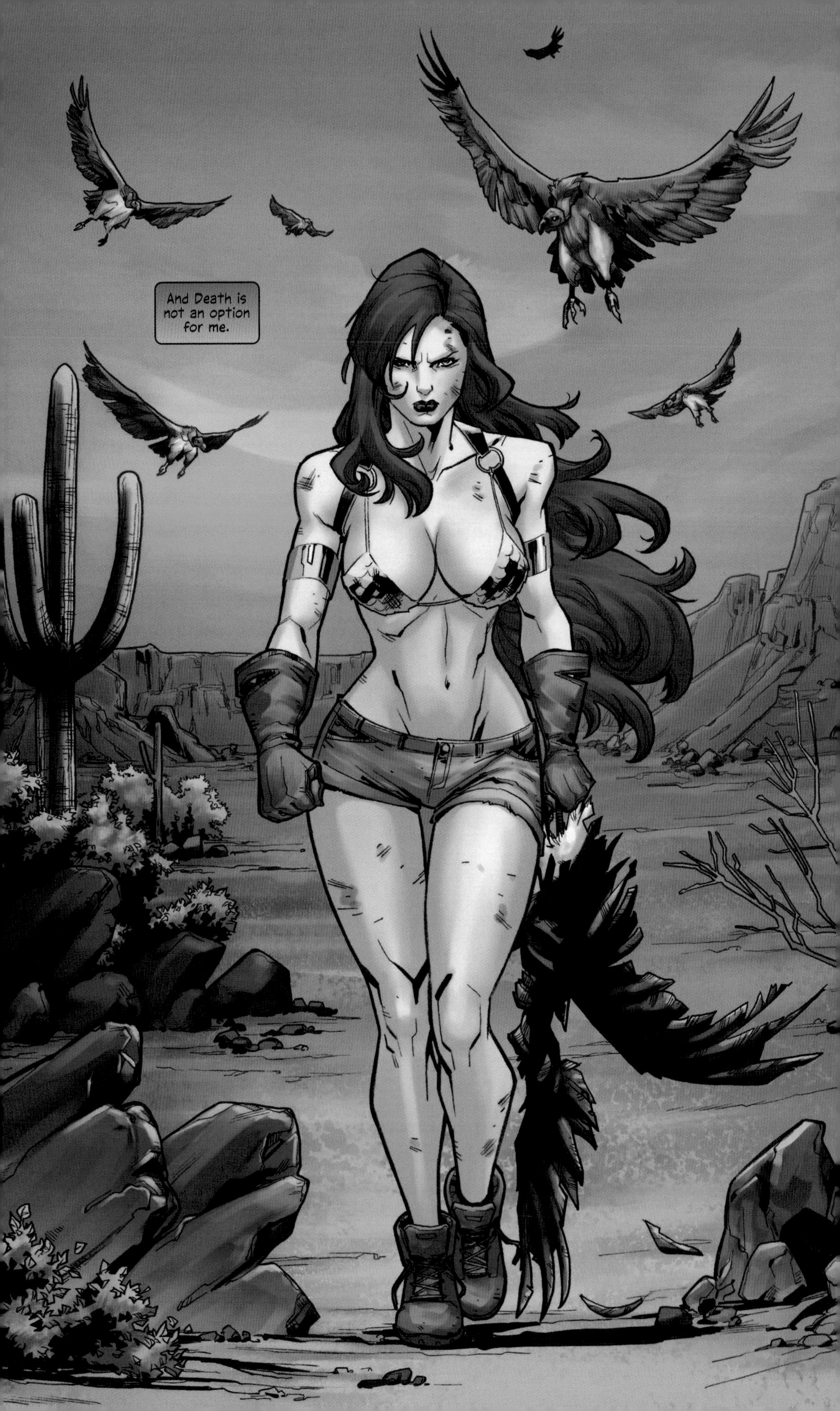
And Death is not an option for me.

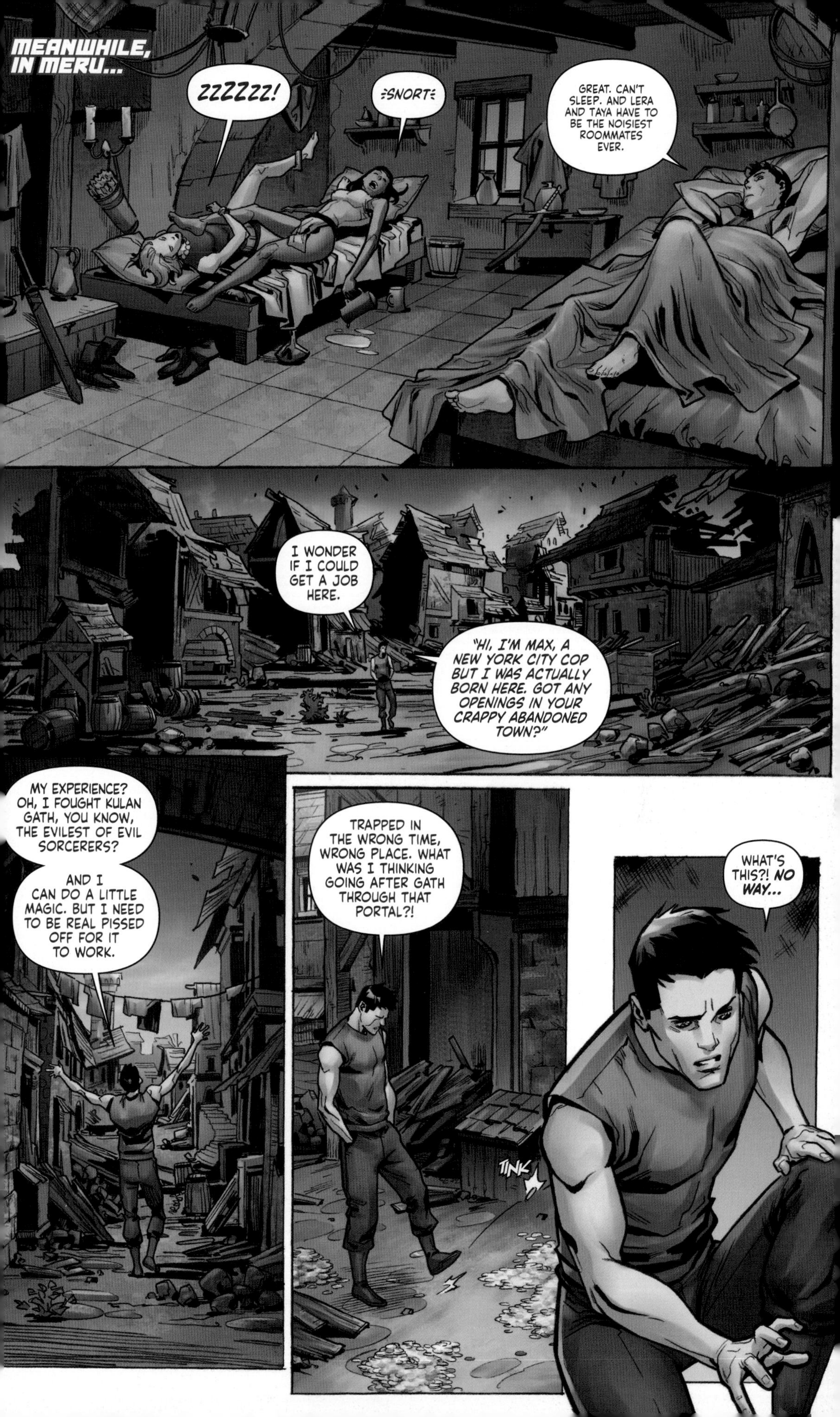
MEANWHILE, IN MERU...
ZZZZZZ!
SNORT
GREAT. CAN'T SLEEP. AND LERA AND TAYA HAVE TO BE THE NOISIEST ROOMMATES EVER.
I WONDER IF I COULD GET A JOB HERE.
"HI, I'M MAX, A NEW YORK CITY COP BUT I WAS ACTUALLY BORN HERE. GOT ANY OPENINGS IN YOUR CRAPPY ABANDONED TOWN?"
MY EXPERIENCE? OH, I FOUGHT KULAN GATH, YOU KNOW, THE EVILEST OF EVIL SORCERERS?
AND I CAN DO A LITTLE MAGIC. BUT I NEED TO BE REAL PISSED OFF FOR IT TO WORK.
TRAPPED IN THE WRONG TIME, WRONG PLACE. WHAT WAS I THINKING GOING AFTER GATH THROUGH THAT PORTAL?!
TINK
WHAT'S THIS?! NO WAY...

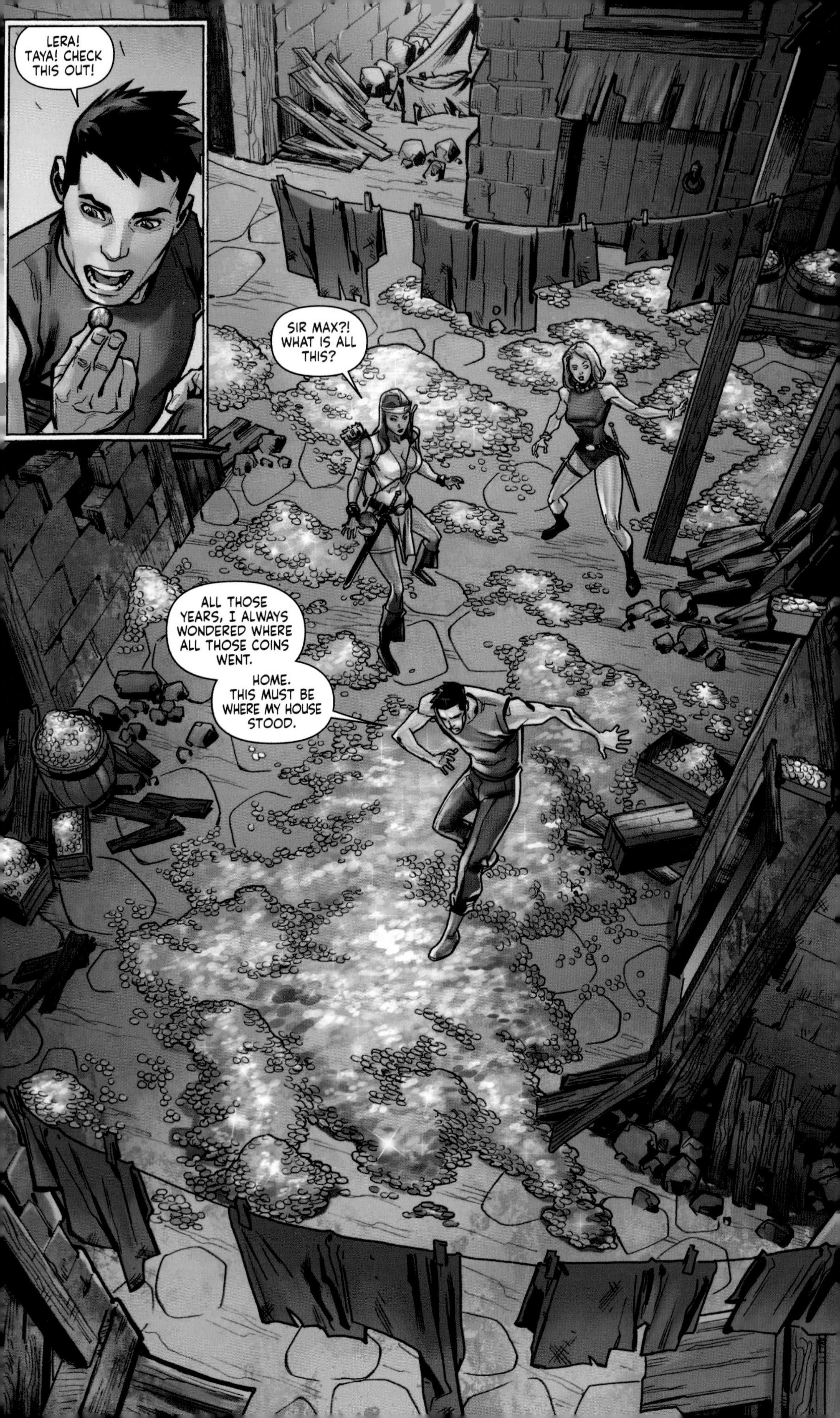
LERA! TAYA! CHECK THIS OUT!
SIR MAX?! WHAT IS ALL THIS?
ALL THOSE YEARS, I ALWAYS WONDERED WHERE ALL THOSE COINS WENT.
HOME. THIS MUST BE WHERE MY HOUSE STOOD.

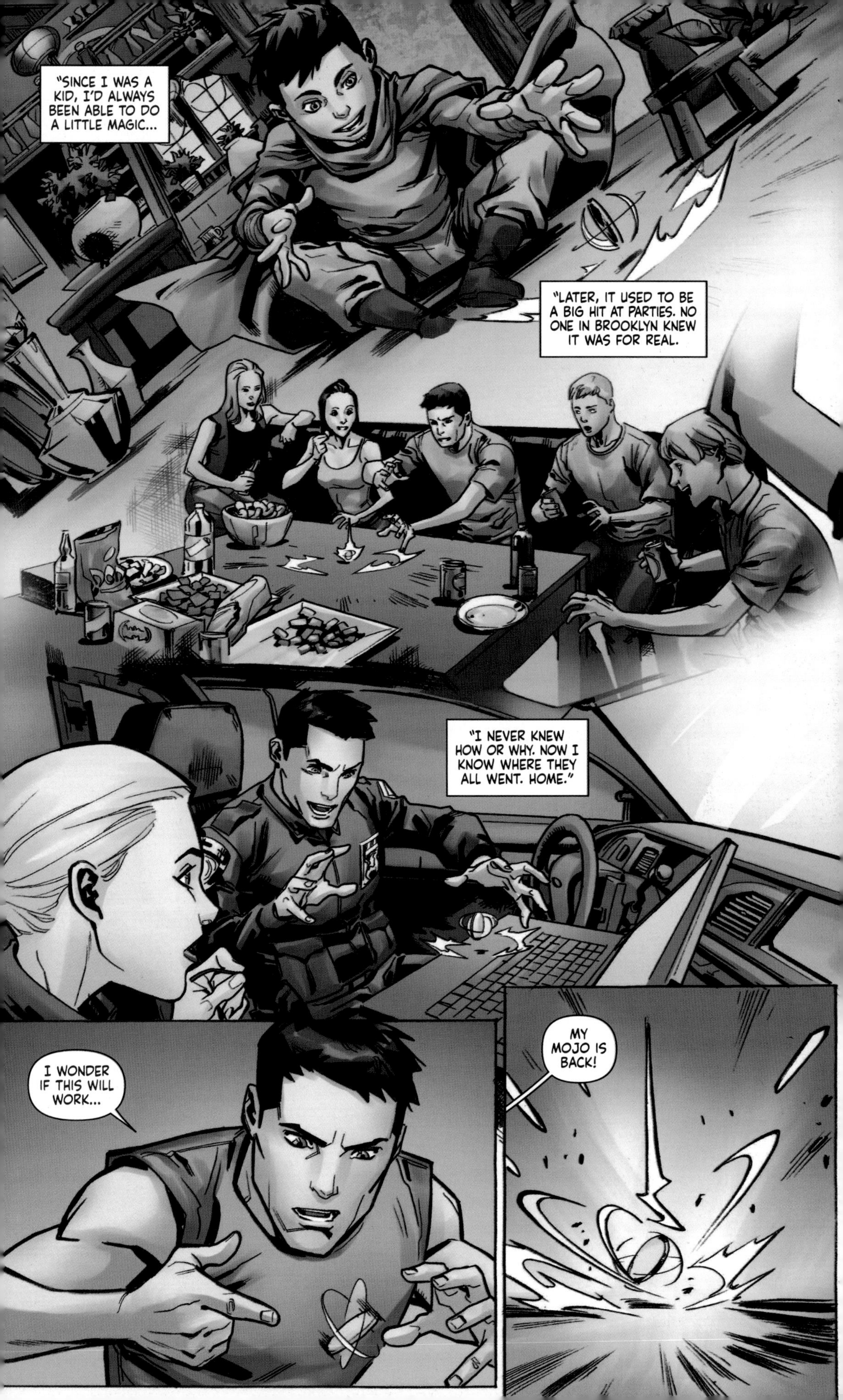
"SINCE I WAS A KID, I'D ALWAYS BEEN ABLE TO DO A LITTLE MAGIC...
"LATER, IT USED TO BE A BIG HIT AT PARTIES. NO ONE IN BROOKLYN KNEW IT WAS FOR REAL.
"I NEVER KNEW HOW OR WHY. NOW I KNOW WHERE THEY ALL WENT. HOME."
I WONDER IF THIS WILL WORK...
MY MOJO IS BACK!

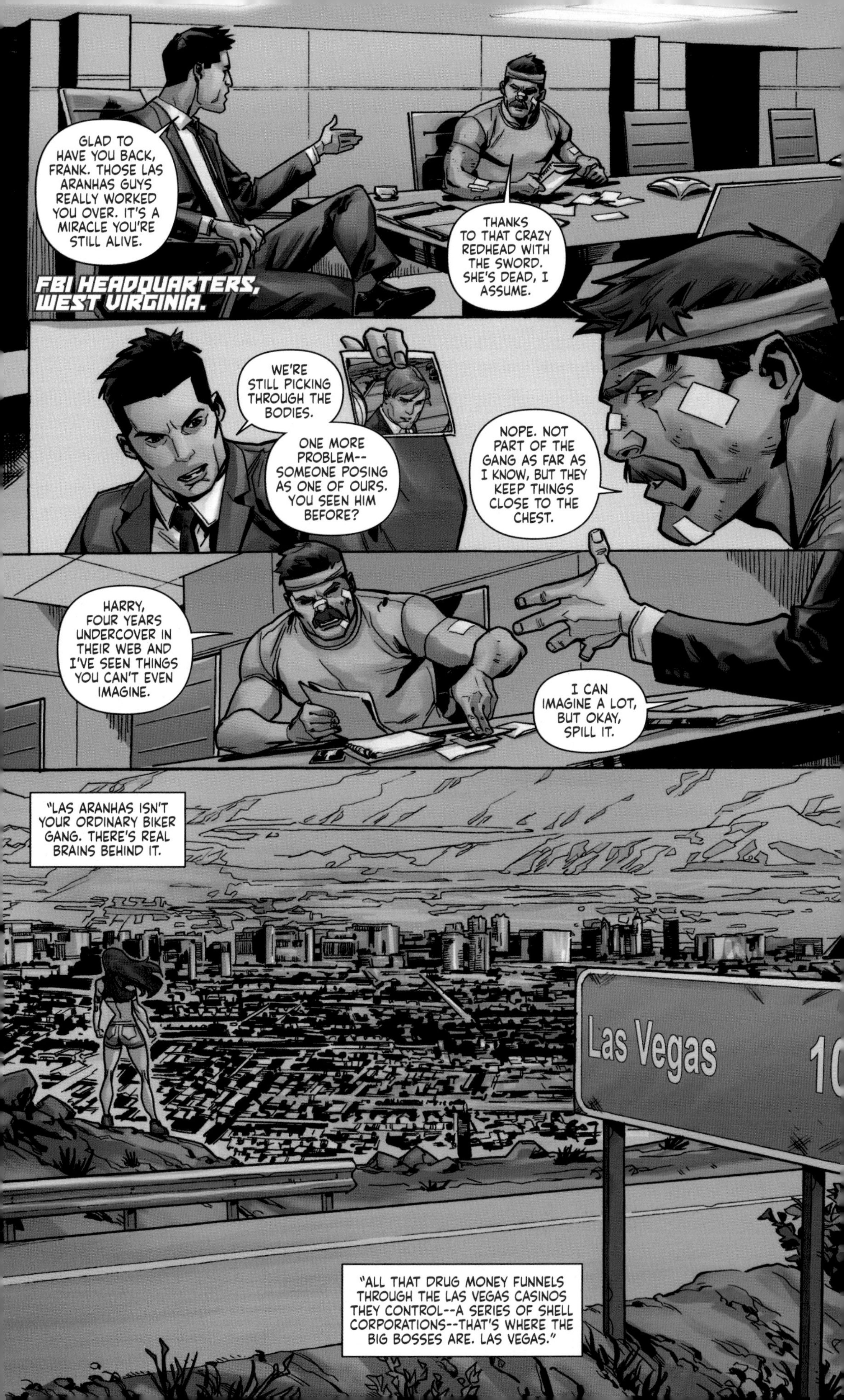
GLAD TO HAVE YOU BACK, FRANK. THOSE LAS ARANHAS GUYS REALLY WORKED YOU OVER. IT'S A MIRACLE YOU'RE STILL ALIVE.
THANKS TO THAT CRAZY REDHEAD WITH THE SWORD. SHE'S DEAD, I ASSUME.
FBI HEADQUARTERS, WEST VIRGINIA.
WE'RE STILL PICKING THROUGH THE BODIES.
ONE MORE PROBLEM-- SOMEONE POSING AS ONE OF OURS. YOU SEEN HIM BEFORE?
NOPE. NOT PART OF THE GANG AS FAR AS I KNOW, BUT THEY KEEP THINGS CLOSE TO THE CHEST.
HARRY, FOUR YEARS UNDERCOVER IN THEIR WEB AND I'VE SEEN THINGS YOU CAN'T EVEN IMAGINE.
I CAN IMAGINE A LOT, BUT OKAY, SPILL IT.
"LAS ARANHAS ISN'T YOUR ORDINARY BIKER GANG. THERE'S REAL BRAINS BEHIND IT.
Las Vegas
"ALL THAT DRUG MONEY FUNNELS THROUGH THE LAS VEGAS CASINOS THEY CONTROL--A SERIES OF SHELL CORPORATIONS--THAT'S WHERE THE BIG BOSSES ARE. LAS VEGAS."

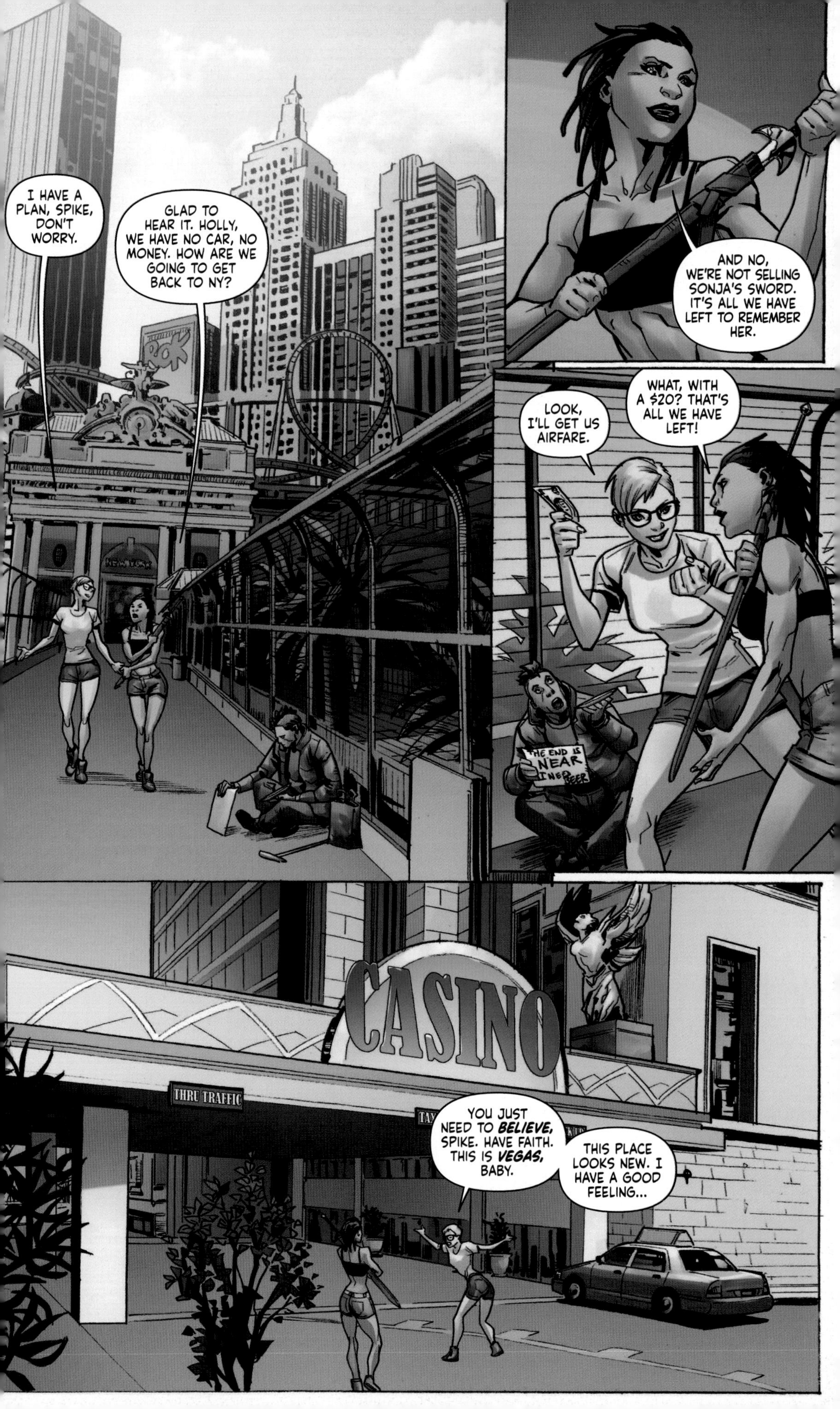
I HAVE A PLAN, SPIKE, DON'T WORRY.
GLAD TO HEAR IT. HOLLY, WE HAVE NO CAR, NO MONEY. HOW ARE WE GOING TO GET BACK TO NY?
AND NO, WE'RE NOT SELLING SONJA'S SWORD. IT'S ALL WE HAVE LEFT TO REMEMBER HER.
LOOK, I'LL GET US AIRFARE.
WHAT, WITH A $20? THAT'S ALL WE HAVE LEFT!
THE END IS NEAR I NEED BEER
CASINO
THRU TRAFFIC
YOU JUST NEED TO ***BELIEVE,*** SPIKE. HAVE FAITH. THIS IS ***VEGAS,*** BABY.
THIS PLACE LOOKS NEW. I HAVE A GOOD FEELING...

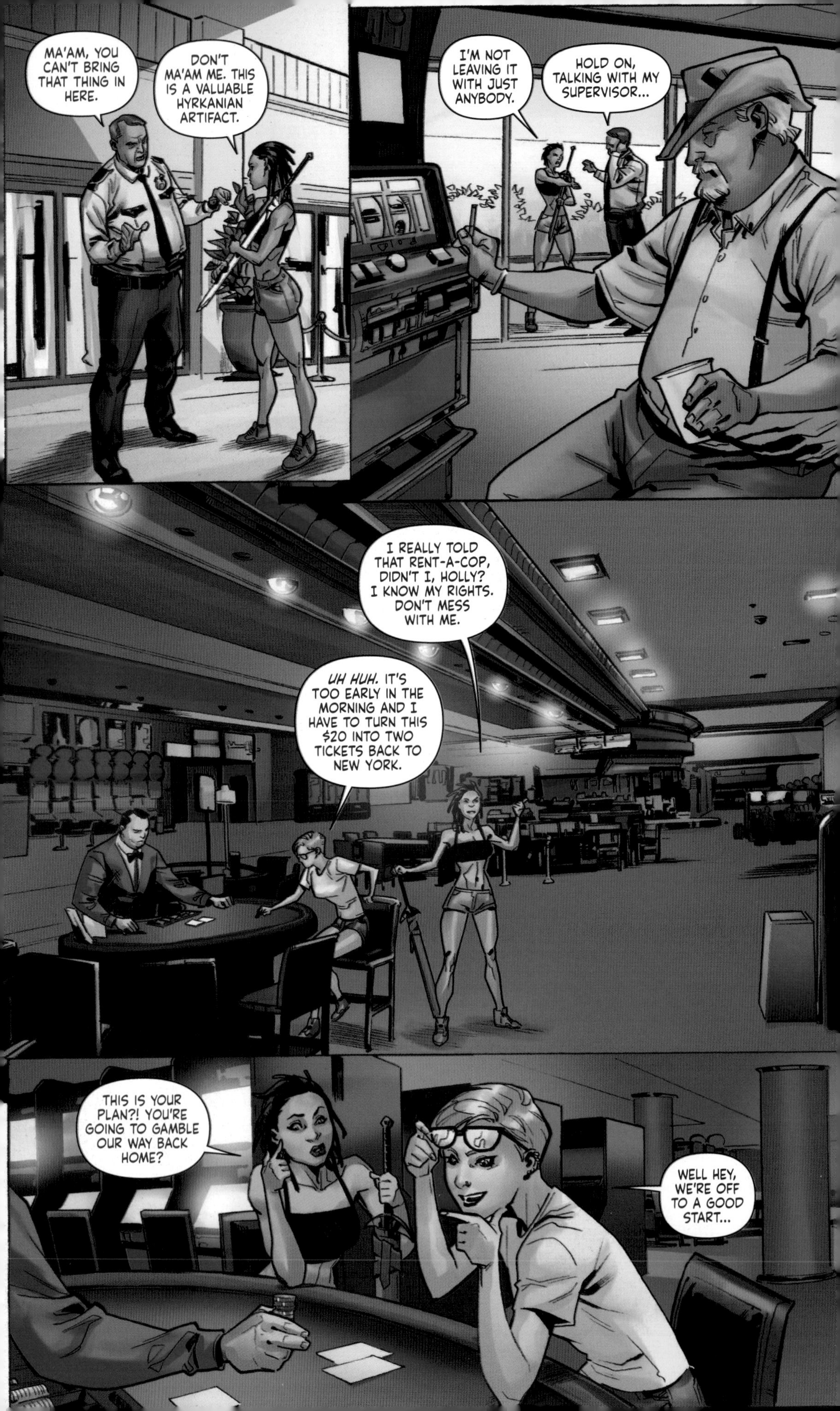
MA'AM, YOU CAN'T BRING THAT THING IN HERE.
DON'T MA'AM ME. THIS IS A VALUABLE HYRKANIAN ARTIFACT.
I'M NOT LEAVING IT WITH JUST ANYBODY.
HOLD ON, TALKING WITH MY SUPERVISOR...
I REALLY TOLD THAT RENT-A-COP, DIDN'T I, HOLLY? I KNOW MY RIGHTS. DON'T MESS WITH ME.
UH HUH. IT'S TOO EARLY IN THE MORNING AND I HAVE TO TURN THIS $20 INTO TWO TICKETS BACK TO NEW YORK.
THIS IS YOUR PLAN?! YOU'RE GOING TO GAMBLE OUR WAY BACK HOME?
WELL HEY, WE'RE OFF TO A GOOD START...

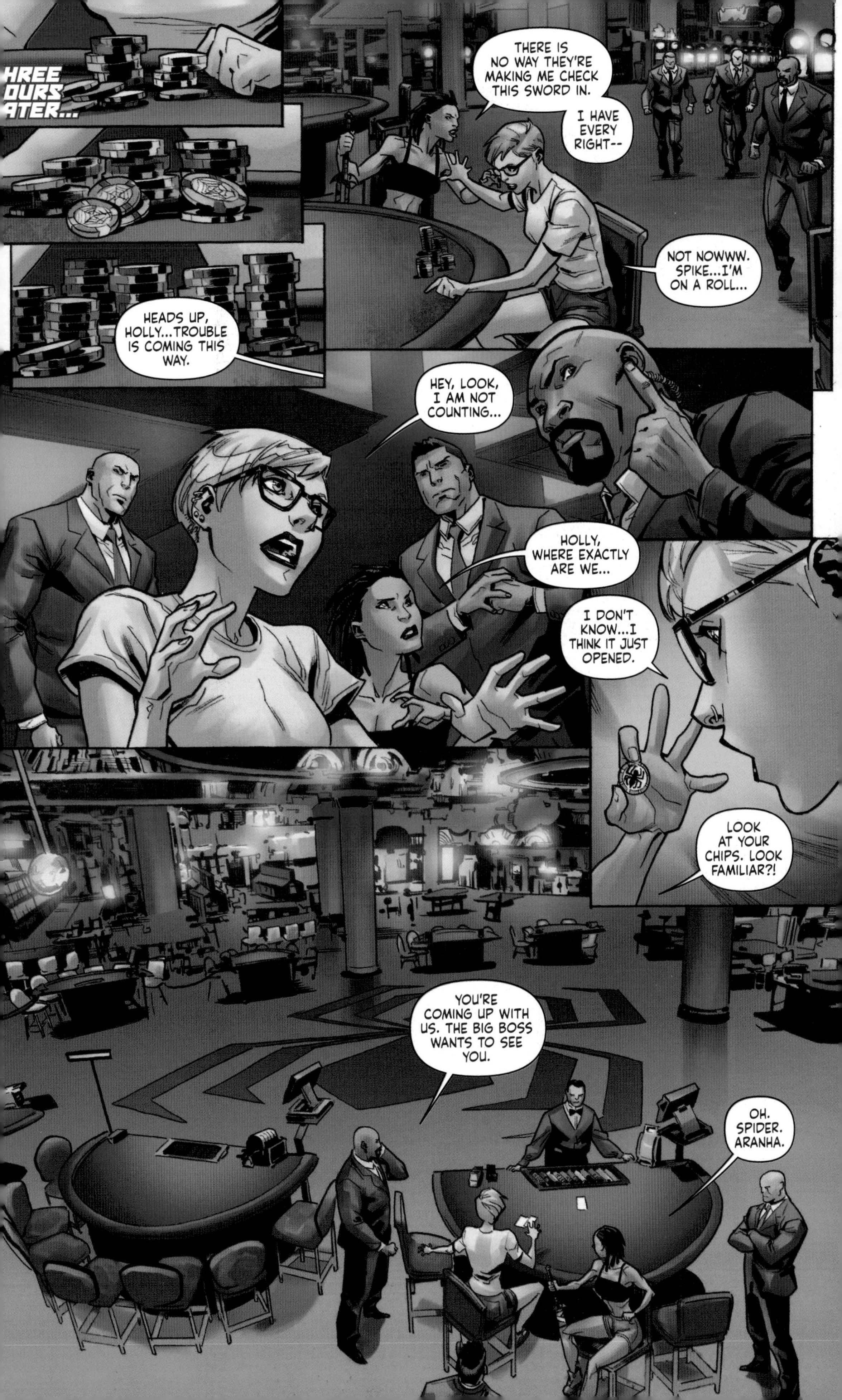

HREE OURS ATER...
HEADS UP, HOLLY...TROUBLE IS COMING THIS WAY.
THERE IS NO WAY THEY'RE MAKING ME CHECK THIS SWORD IN.
I HAVE EVERY RIGHT--
NOT NOWWW. SPIKE...I'M ON A ROLL...
HEY, LOOK, I AM NOT COUNTING...
HOLLY, WHERE EXACTLY ARE WE...
I DON'T KNOW...I THINK IT JUST OPENED.
LOOK AT YOUR CHIPS. LOOK FAMILIAR?!
YOU'RE COMING UP WITH US. THE BIG BOSS WANTS TO SEE YOU.
OH. SPIDER. ARANHA.

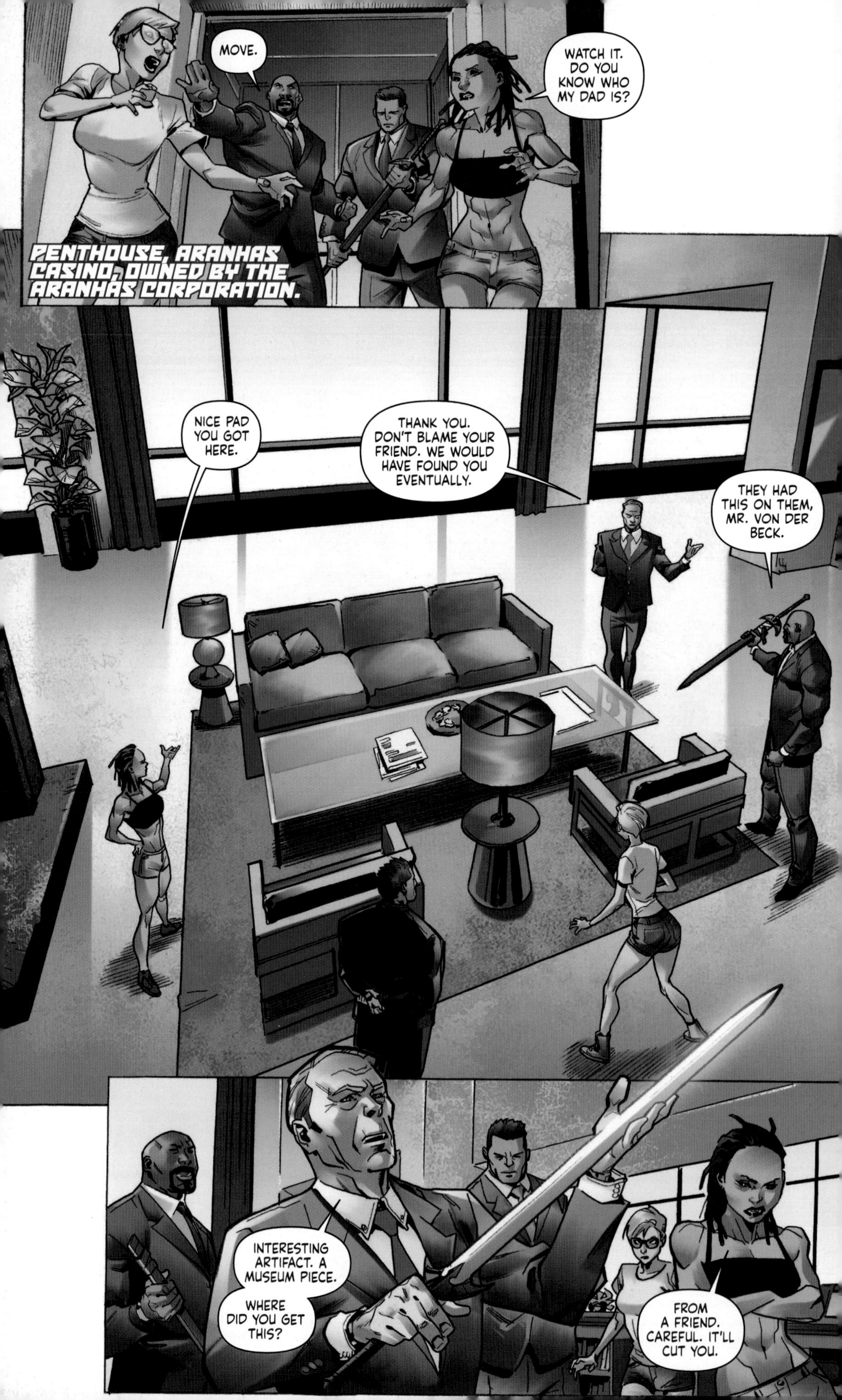
MOVE.
WATCH IT. DO YOU KNOW WHO MY DAD IS?
PENTHOUSE, ARANHAS CASINO, OWNED BY THE ARANHAS CORPORATION.
NICE PAD YOU GOT HERE.
THANK YOU. DON'T BLAME YOUR FRIEND. WE WOULD HAVE FOUND YOU EVENTUALLY.
THEY HAD THIS ON THEM, MR. VON DER BECK.
INTERESTING ARTIFACT. A MUSEUM PIECE.
WHERE DID YOU GET THIS?
FROM A FRIEND. CAREFUL. IT'LL CUT YOU.

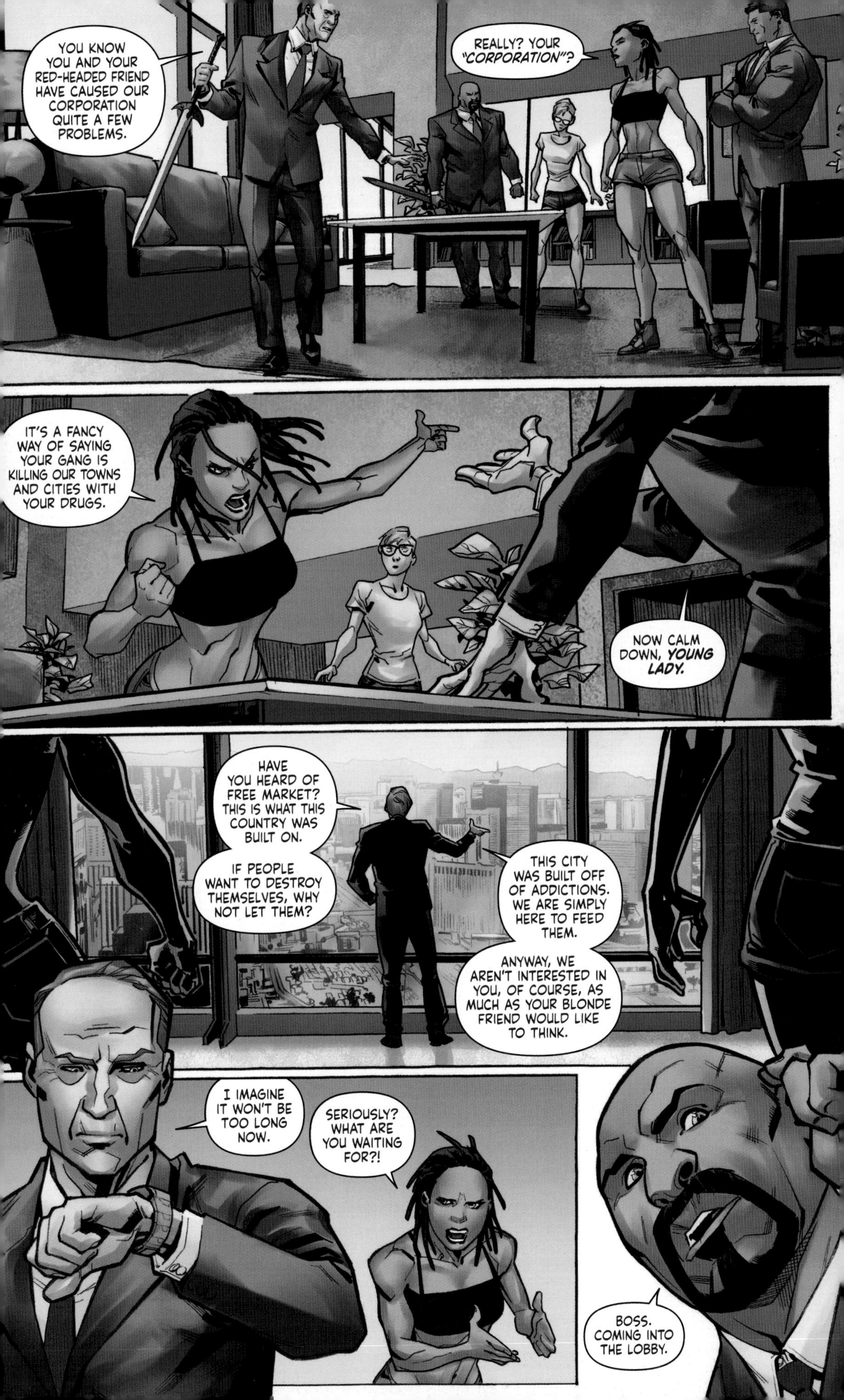
YOU KNOW YOU AND YOUR RED-HEADED FRIEND HAVE CAUSED OUR CORPORATION QUITE A FEW PROBLEMS.
REALLY? YOUR *"CORPORATION"*?
IT'S A FANCY WAY OF SAYING YOUR GANG IS KILLING OUR TOWNS AND CITIES WITH YOUR DRUGS.
NOW CALM DOWN, ***YOUNG LADY.***
HAVE YOU HEARD OF FREE MARKET? THIS IS WHAT THIS COUNTRY WAS BUILT ON.
IF PEOPLE WANT TO DESTROY THEMSELVES, WHY NOT LET THEM?
THIS CITY WAS BUILT OFF OF ADDICTIONS. WE ARE SIMPLY HERE TO FEED THEM.
ANYWAY, WE AREN'T INTERESTED IN YOU, OF COURSE, AS MUCH AS YOUR BLONDE FRIEND WOULD LIKE TO THINK.
I IMAGINE IT WON'T BE TOO LONG NOW.
SERIOUSLY? WHAT ARE YOU WAITING FOR?!
BOSS. COMING INTO THE LOBBY.

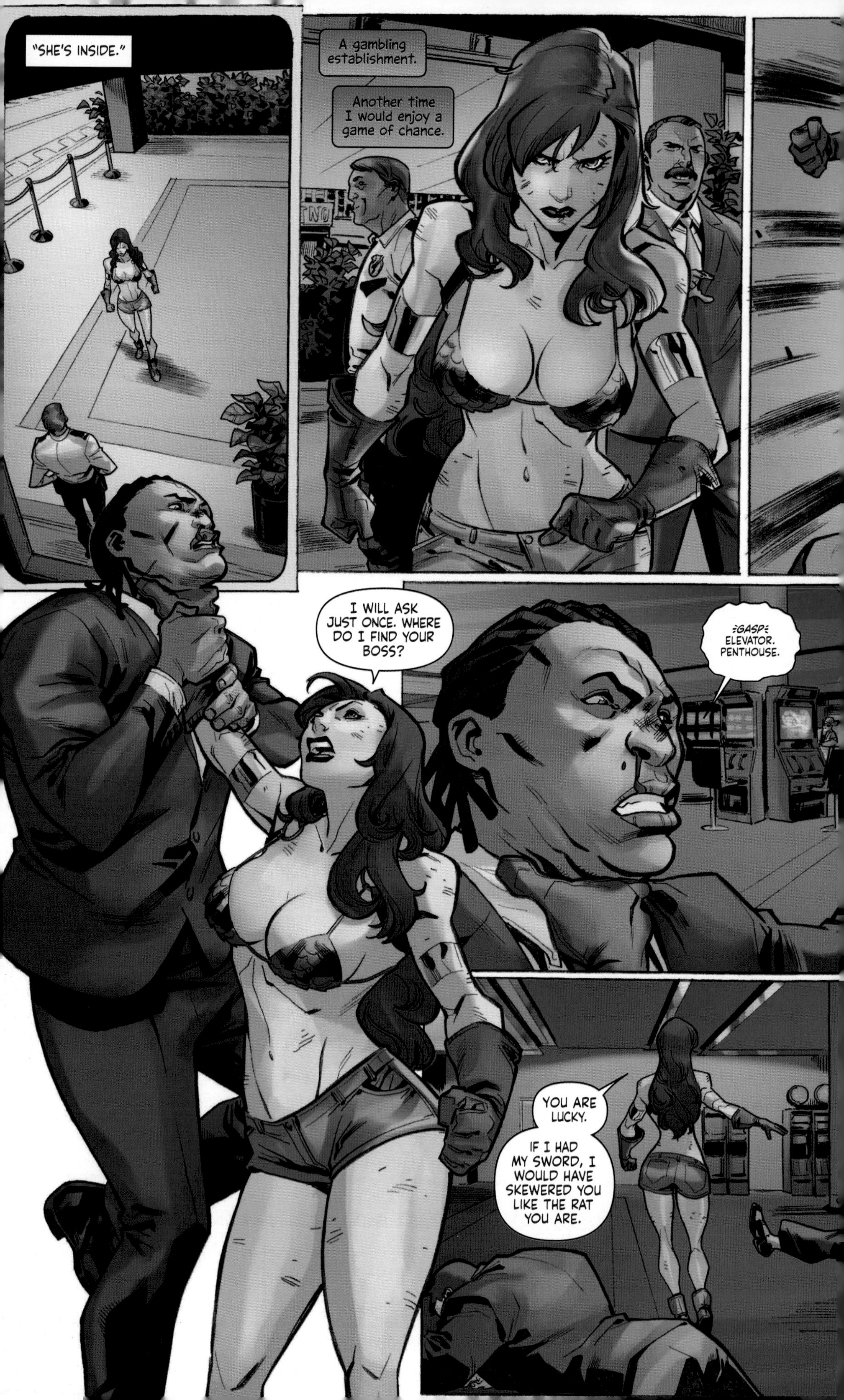
"SHE'S INSIDE."
A gambling establishment.
Another time I would enjoy a game of chance.
I WILL ASK JUST ONCE. WHERE DO I FIND YOUR BOSS?
GASP
ELEVATOR. PENTHOUSE.
YOU ARE LUCKY.
IF I HAD MY SWORD, I WOULD HAVE SKEWERED YOU LIKE THE RAT YOU ARE.

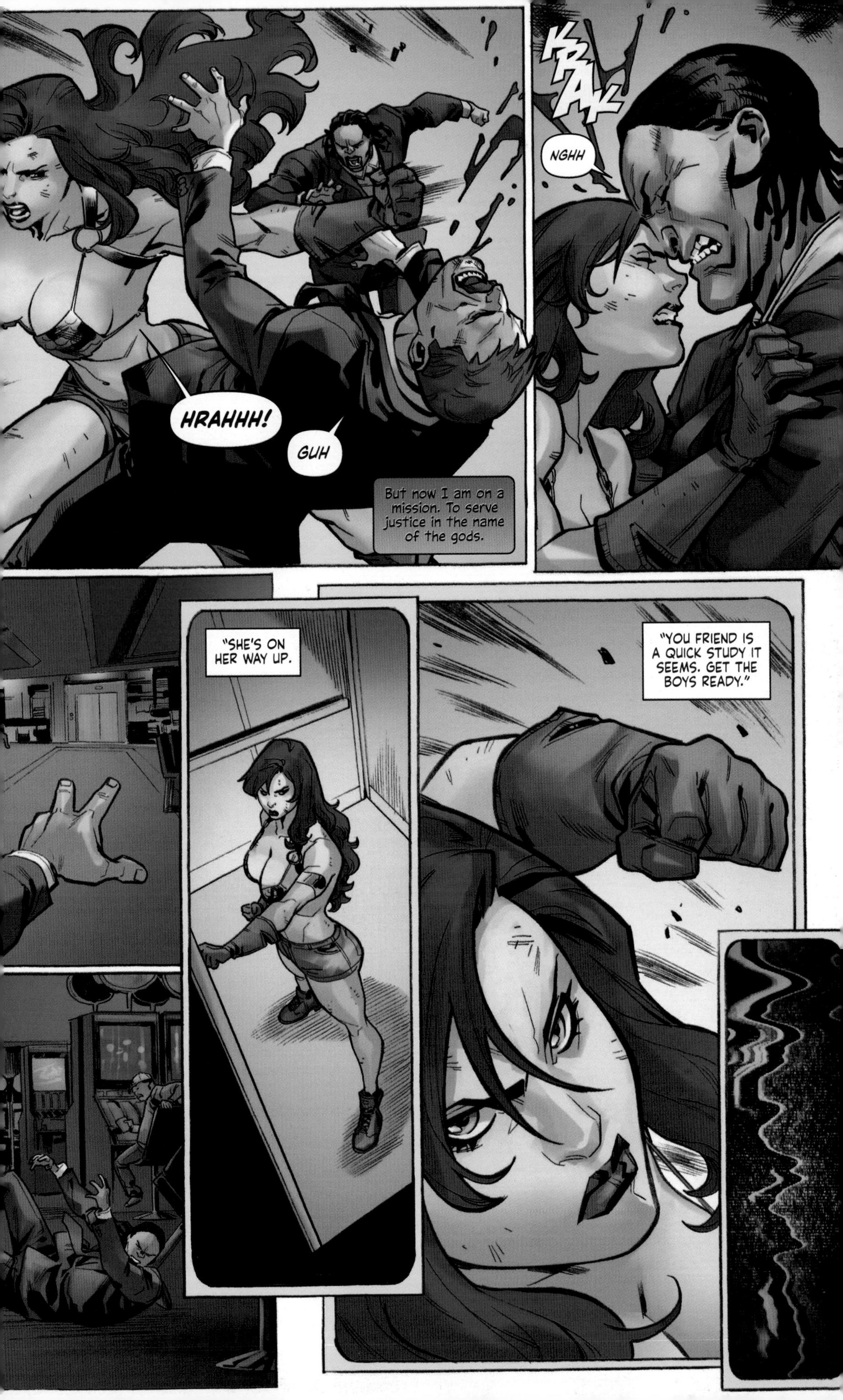
HRAHHH!
GUH
But now I am on a mission. To serve justice in the name of the gods.
KRAK
NGHH
"SHE'S ON HER WAY UP.
"YOU FRIEND IS A QUICK STUDY IT SEEMS. GET THE BOYS READY."

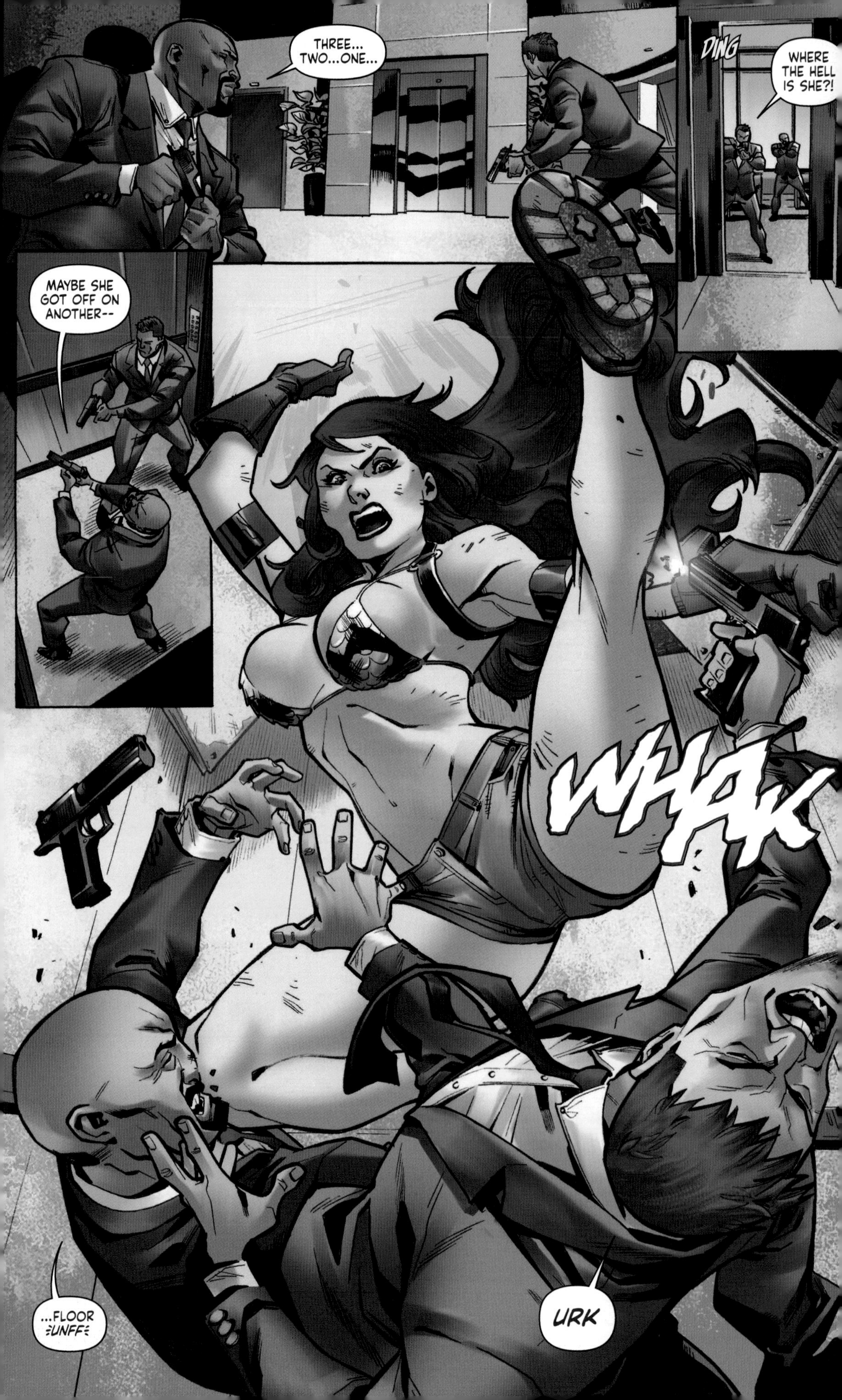
THREE... TWO...ONE...
DING
WHERE THE HELL IS SHE?!
MAYBE SHE GOT OFF ON ANOTHER--
WHAK
...FLOOR UNFF
URK

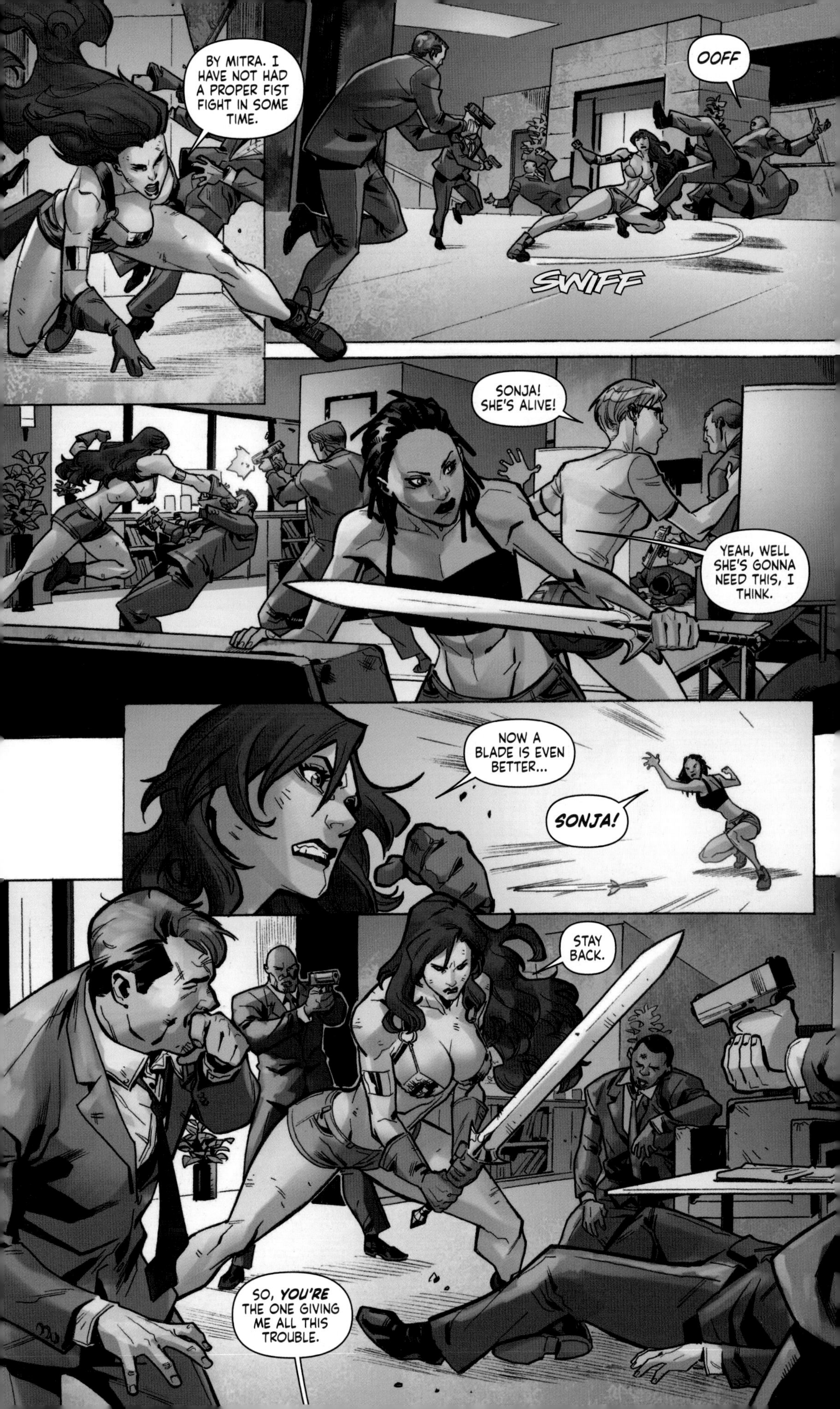
BY MITRA. I HAVE NOT HAD A PROPER FIST FIGHT IN SOME TIME.
OOFF
SWIFF
SONJA! SHE'S ALIVE!
YEAH, WELL SHE'S GONNA NEED THIS, I THINK.
NOW A BLADE IS EVEN BETTER...
SONJA!
STAY BACK.
SO, YOU'RE THE ONE GIVING ME ALL THIS TROUBLE.

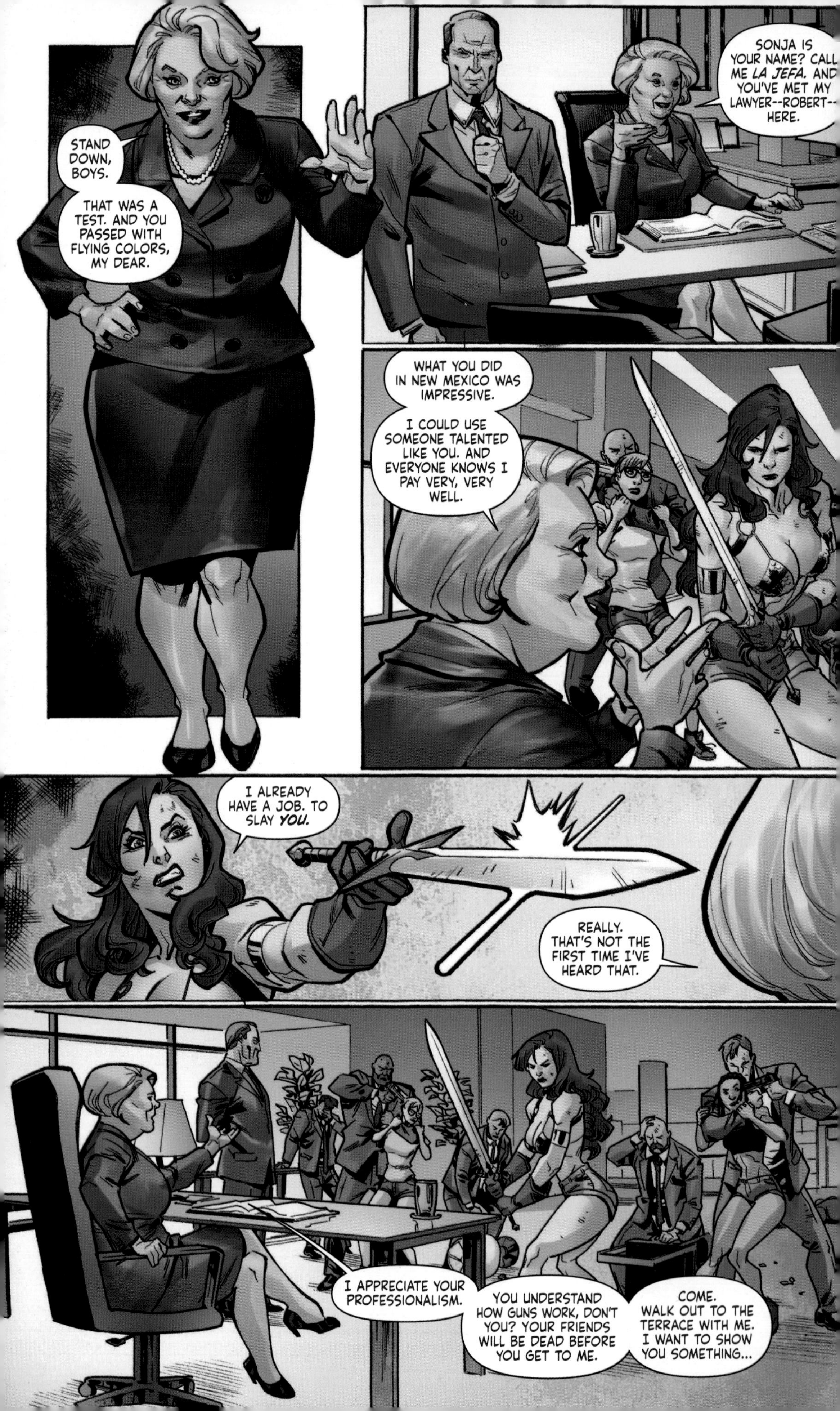

STAND DOWN, BOYS.
THAT WAS A TEST. AND YOU PASSED WITH FLYING COLORS, MY DEAR.
SONJA IS YOUR NAME? CALL ME *LA JEFA.* AND YOU'VE MET MY LAWYER--ROBERT--HERE.
WHAT YOU DID IN NEW MEXICO WAS IMPRESSIVE.
I COULD USE SOMEONE TALENTED LIKE YOU. AND EVERYONE KNOWS I PAY VERY, VERY WELL.
I ALREADY HAVE A JOB. TO SLAY ***YOU.***
REALLY. THAT'S NOT THE FIRST TIME I'VE HEARD THAT.
I APPRECIATE YOUR PROFESSIONALISM.
YOU UNDERSTAND HOW GUNS WORK, DON'T YOU? YOUR FRIENDS WILL BE DEAD BEFORE YOU GET TO ME.
COME. WALK OUT TO THE TERRACE WITH ME. I WANT TO SHOW YOU SOMETHING...

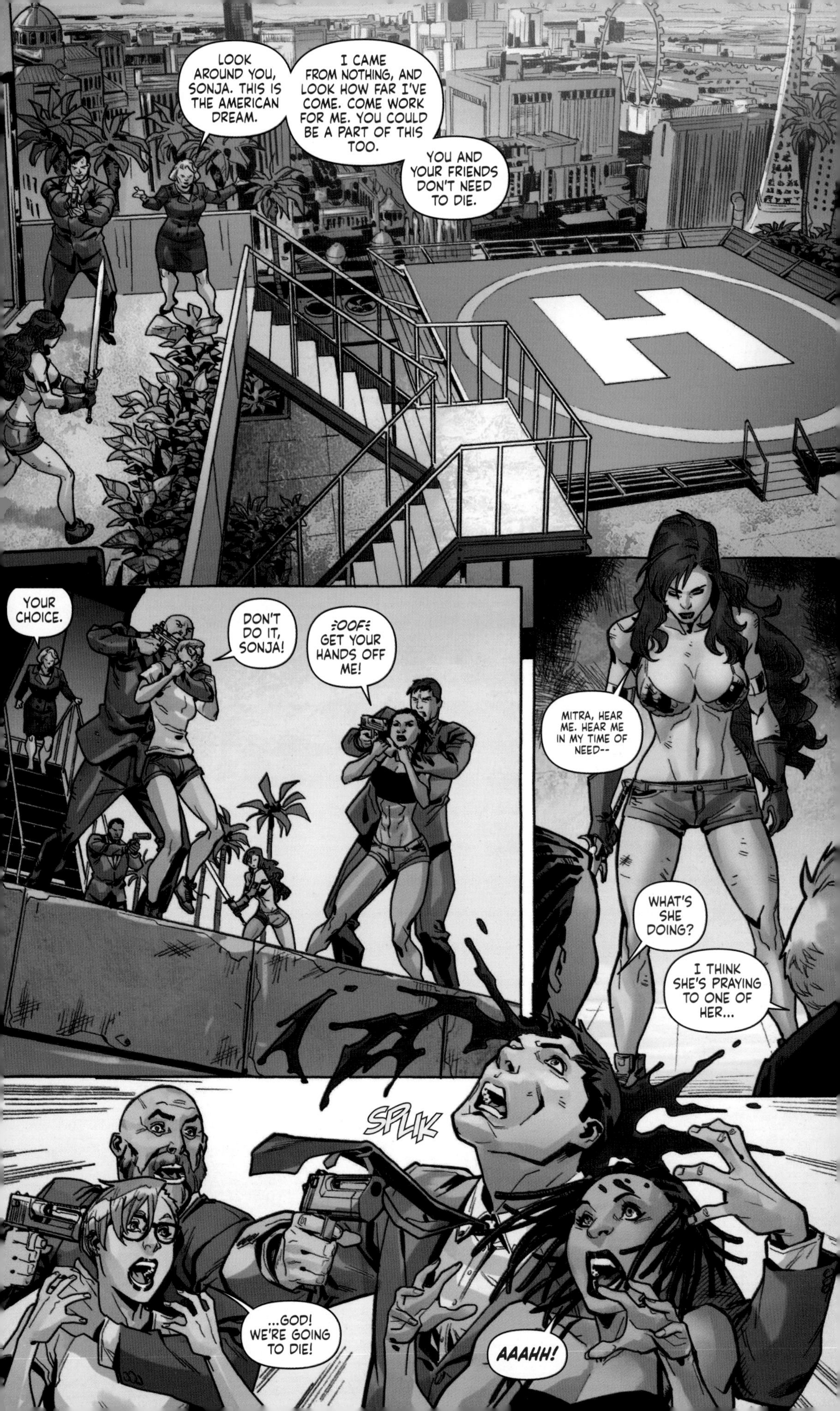
LOOK AROUND YOU, SONJA. THIS IS THE AMERICAN DREAM.
I CAME FROM NOTHING, AND LOOK HOW FAR I'VE COME. COME WORK FOR ME. YOU COULD BE A PART OF THIS TOO.
YOU AND YOUR FRIENDS DON'T NEED TO DIE.
YOUR CHOICE.
DON'T DO IT, SONJA!
OOF GET YOUR HANDS OFF ME!
MITRA, HEAR ME. HEAR ME IN MY TIME OF NEED--
WHAT'S SHE DOING?
I THINK SHE'S PRAYING TO ONE OF HER...
SPLIK
...GOD! WE'RE GOING TO DIE!
AAAHH!

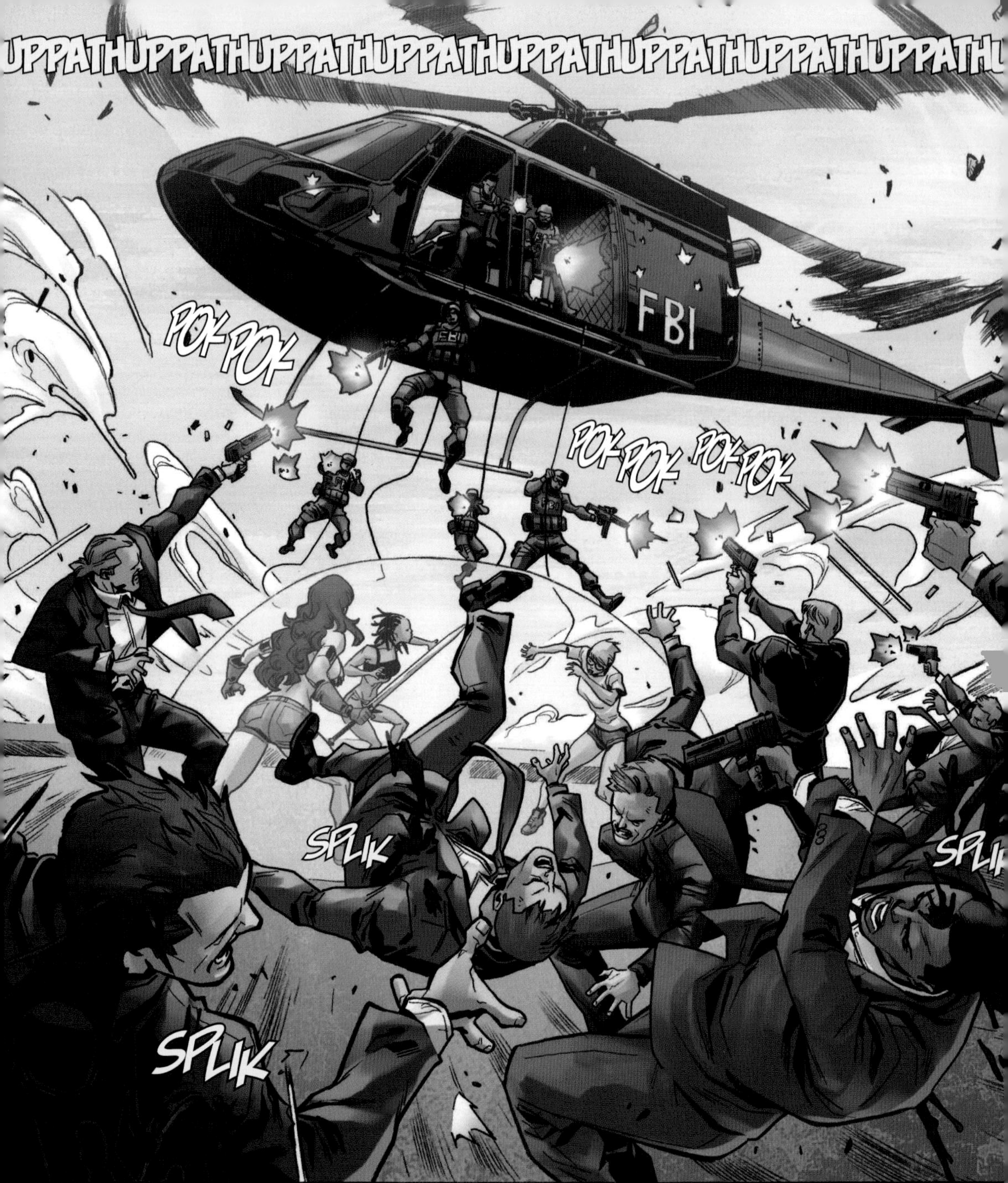
UPPATHUPPATHUPPATHUPPATHUPPATHUPPATHUPPATHU
POK POK
POK POK
POK POK
SPLIK
SPLIK
SPLI

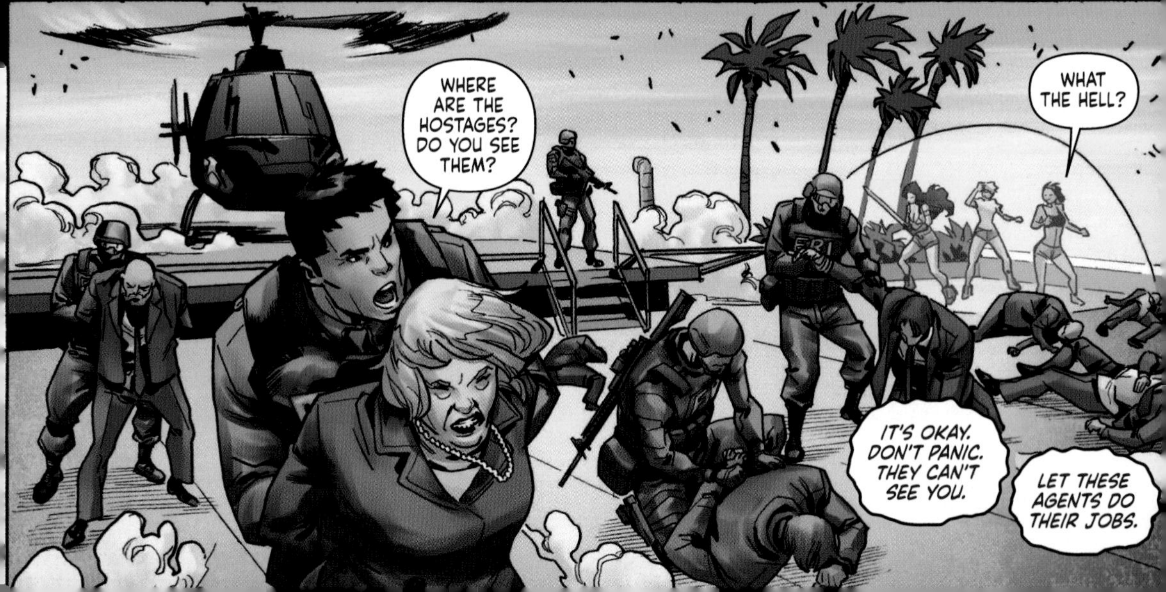
WHERE ARE THE HOSTAGES? DO YOU SEE THEM?
WHAT THE HELL?
IT'S OKAY. DON'T PANIC. THEY CAN'T SEE YOU.
LET THESE AGENTS DO THEIR JOBS.

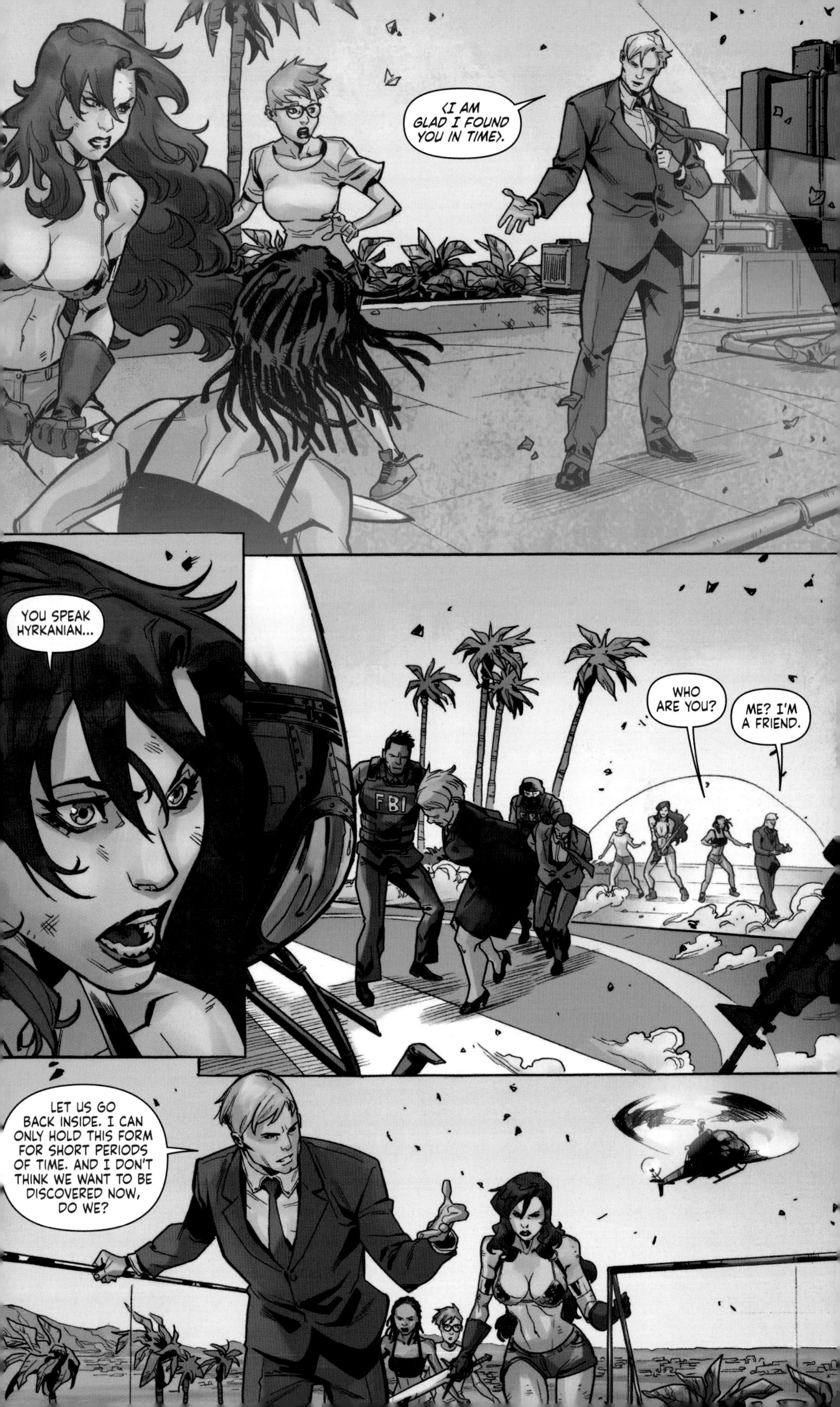

<I AM GLAD I FOUND YOU IN TIME>.
YOU SPEAK HYRKANIAN...
WHO ARE YOU?
ME? I'M A FRIEND.
LET US GO BACK INSIDE. I CAN ONLY HOLD THIS FORM FOR SHORT PERIODS OF TIME. AND I DON'T THINK WE WANT TO BE DISCOVERED NOW, DO WE?
FBI

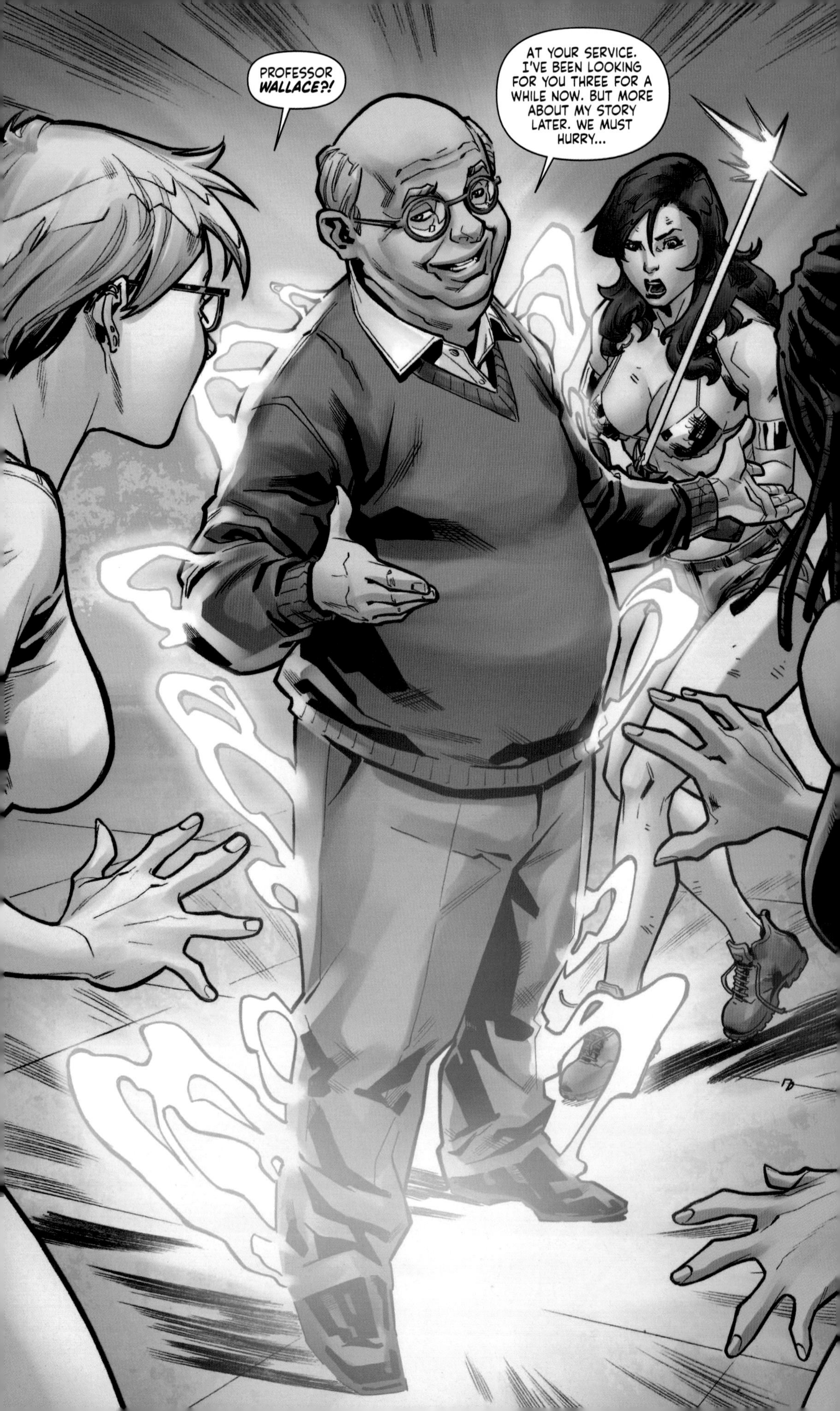
PROFESSOR WALLACE?!
AT YOUR SERVICE. I'VE BEEN LOOKING FOR YOU THREE FOR A WHILE NOW. BUT MORE ABOUT MY STORY LATER. WE MUST HURRY...

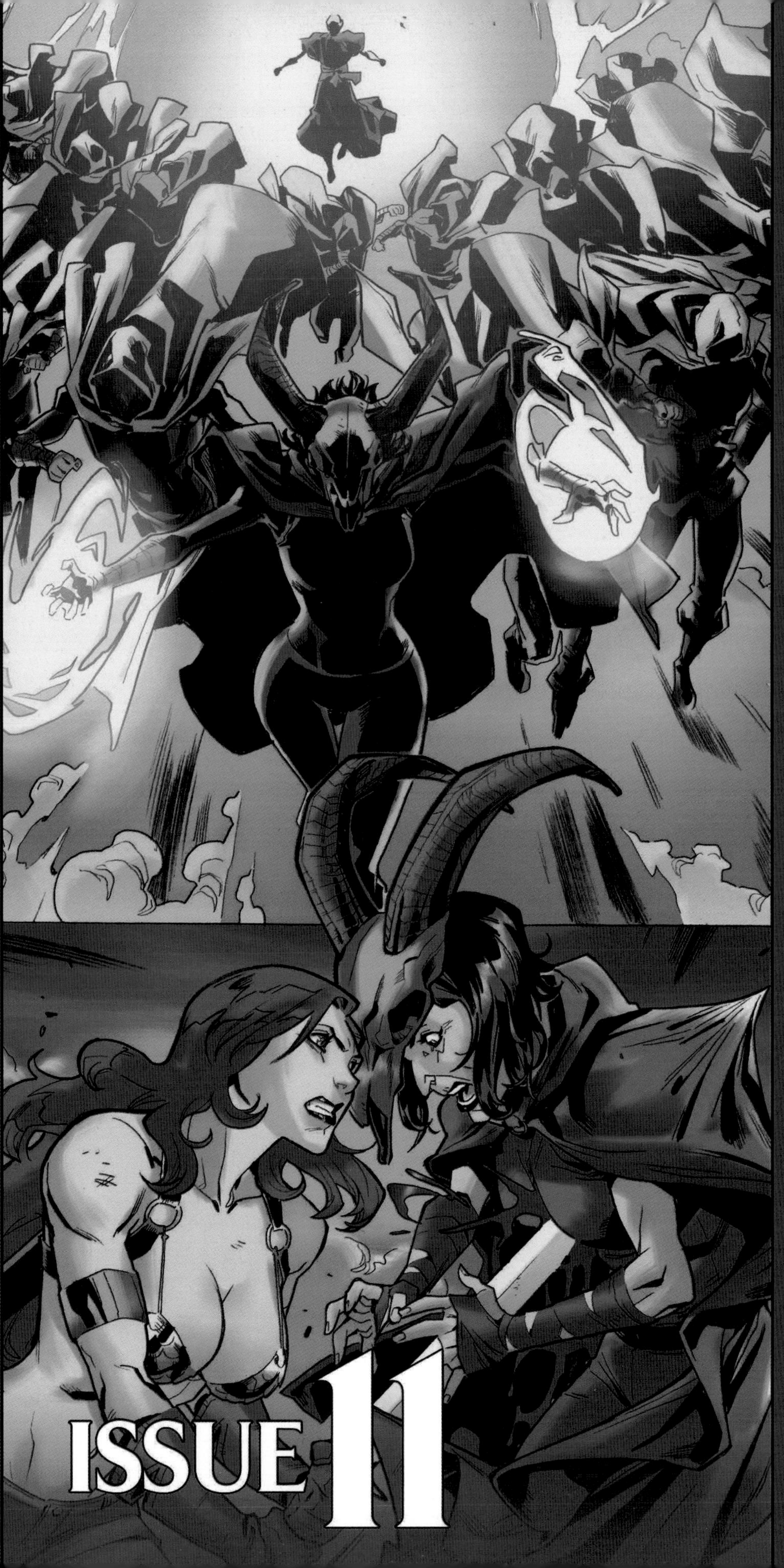
ISSUE 11

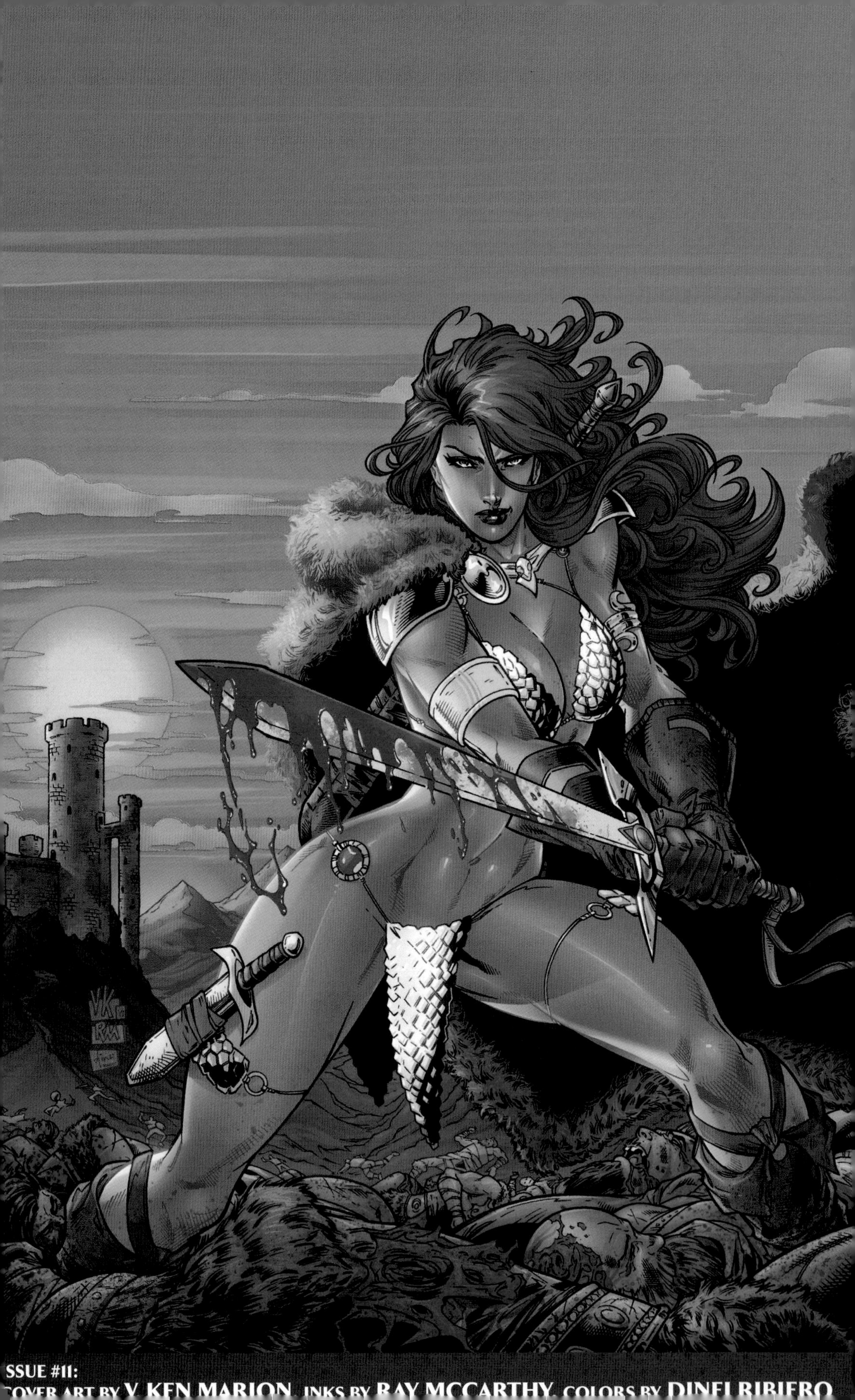

ISSUE #11:
COVER ART BY V. KEN MARION, INKS BY RAY MCCARTHY, COLORS BY DINEI RIBIERO

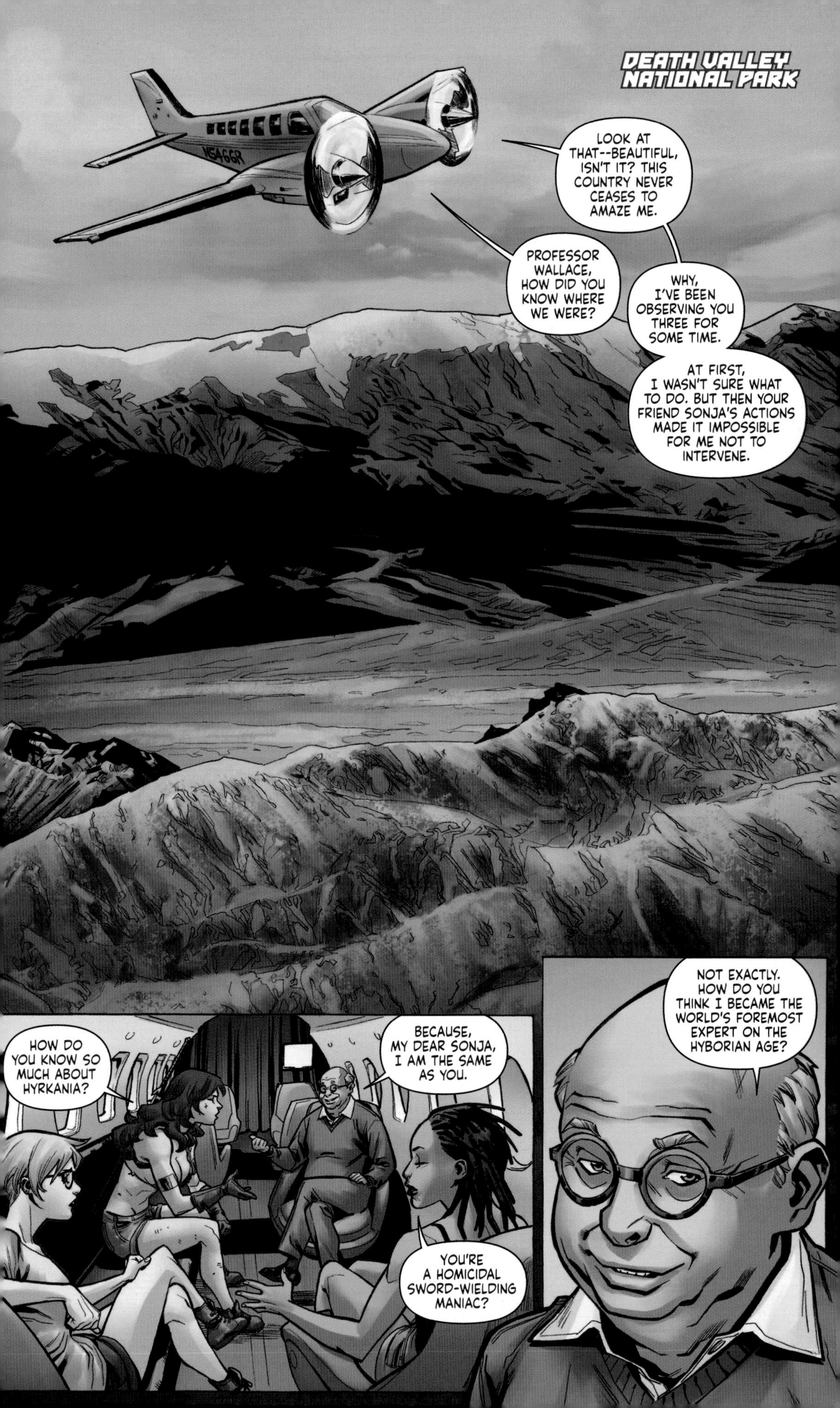
DEATH VALLEY NATIONAL PARK
LOOK AT THAT--BEAUTIFUL, ISN'T IT? THIS COUNTRY NEVER CEASES TO AMAZE ME.
N546GR
PROFESSOR WALLACE, HOW DID YOU KNOW WHERE WE WERE?
WHY, I'VE BEEN OBSERVING YOU THREE FOR SOME TIME.
AT FIRST, I WASN'T SURE WHAT TO DO. BUT THEN YOUR FRIEND SONJA'S ACTIONS MADE IT IMPOSSIBLE FOR ME NOT TO INTERVENE.
HOW DO YOU KNOW SO MUCH ABOUT HYRKANIA?
BECAUSE, MY DEAR SONJA, I AM THE SAME AS YOU.
YOU'RE A HOMICIDAL SWORD-WIELDING MANIAC?
NOT EXACTLY. HOW DO YOU THINK I BECAME THE WORLD'S FOREMOST EXPERT ON THE HYBORIAN AGE?

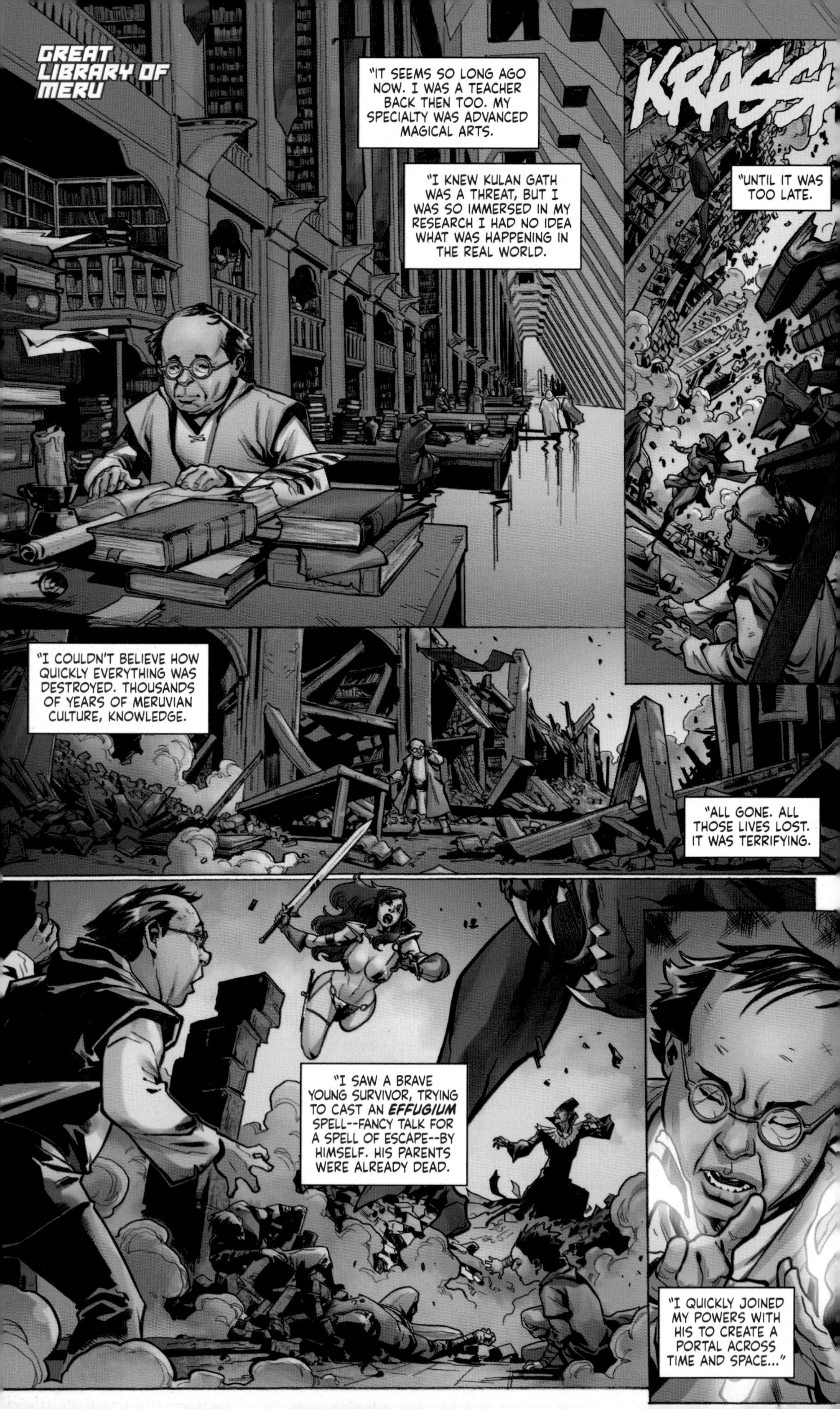
GREAT LIBRARY OF MERU
"IT SEEMS SO LONG AGO NOW. I WAS A TEACHER BACK THEN TOO. MY SPECIALTY WAS ADVANCED MAGICAL ARTS.
"I KNEW KULAN GATH WAS A THREAT, BUT I WAS SO IMMERSED IN MY RESEARCH I HAD NO IDEA WHAT WAS HAPPENING IN THE REAL WORLD.
KRASH
"UNTIL IT WAS TOO LATE.
"I COULDN'T BELIEVE HOW QUICKLY EVERYTHING WAS DESTROYED. THOUSANDS OF YEARS OF MERUVIAN CULTURE, KNOWLEDGE.
"ALL GONE. ALL THOSE LIVES LOST. IT WAS TERRIFYING.
"I SAW A BRAVE YOUNG SURVIVOR, TRYING TO CAST AN *EFFUGIUM* SPELL--FANCY TALK FOR A SPELL OF ESCAPE--BY HIMSELF. HIS PARENTS WERE ALREADY DEAD.
"I QUICKLY JOINED MY POWERS WITH HIS TO CREATE A PORTAL ACROSS TIME AND SPACE..."

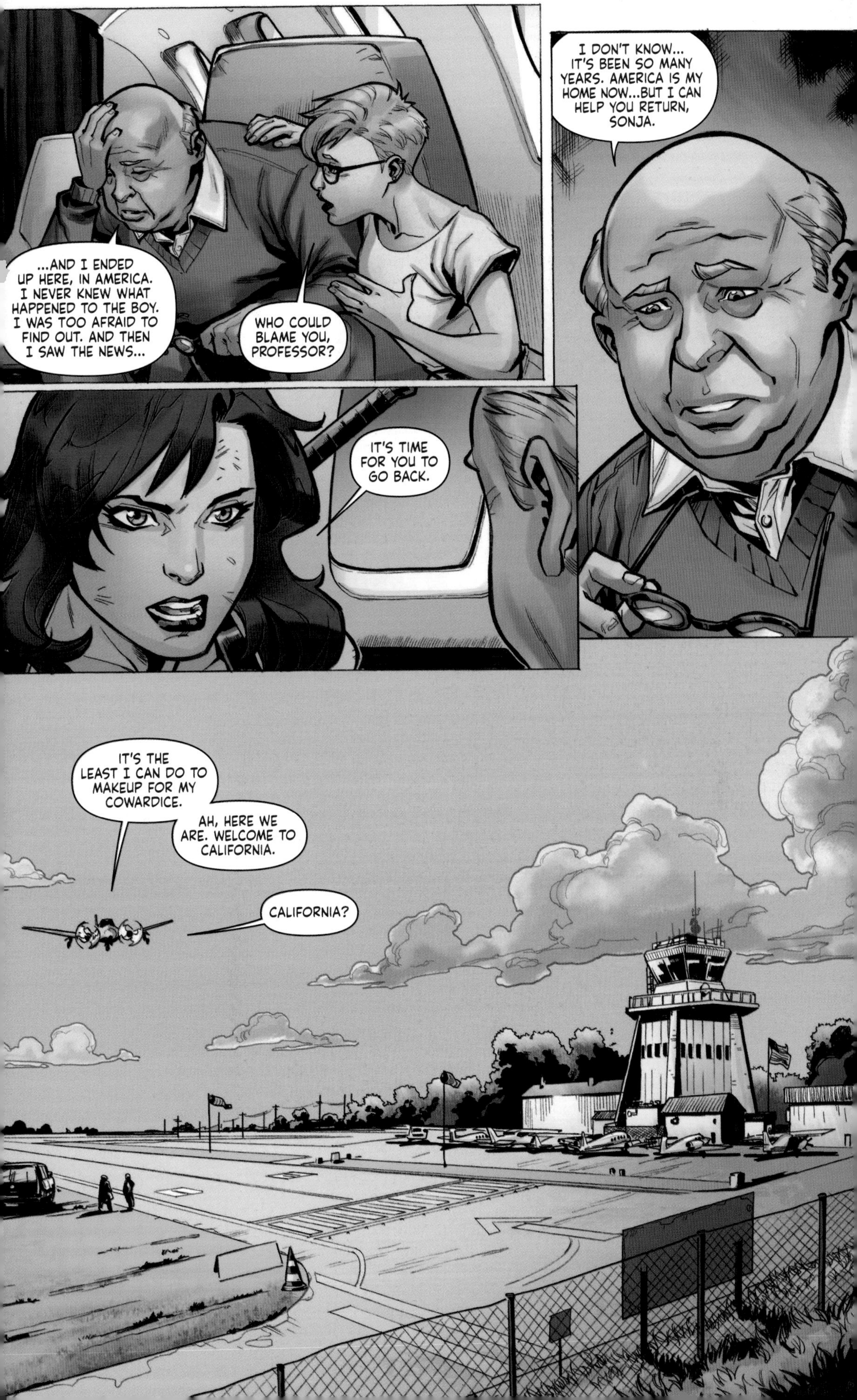
...AND I ENDED UP HERE, IN AMERICA. I NEVER KNEW WHAT HAPPENED TO THE BOY. I WAS TOO AFRAID TO FIND OUT. AND THEN I SAW THE NEWS...
WHO COULD BLAME YOU, PROFESSOR?
I DON'T KNOW... IT'S BEEN SO MANY YEARS. AMERICA IS MY HOME NOW...BUT I CAN HELP YOU RETURN, SONJA.
IT'S TIME FOR YOU TO GO BACK.
IT'S THE LEAST I CAN DO TO MAKEUP FOR MY COWARDICE.
AH, HERE WE ARE. WELCOME TO CALIFORNIA.
CALIFORNIA?

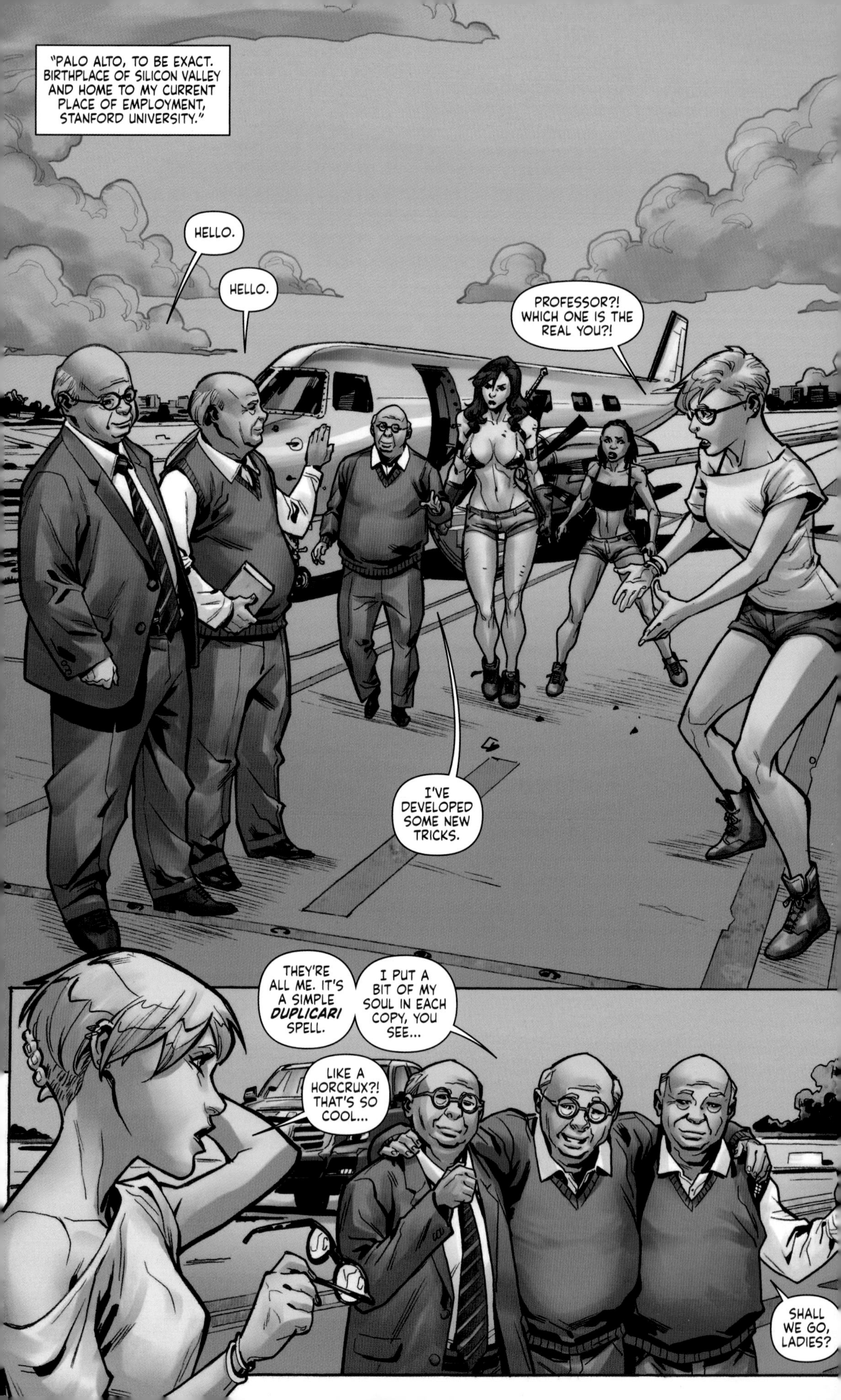
"PALO ALTO, TO BE EXACT. BIRTHPLACE OF SILICON VALLEY AND HOME TO MY CURRENT PLACE OF EMPLOYMENT, STANFORD UNIVERSITY."
HELLO.
HELLO.
PROFESSOR?! WHICH ONE IS THE REAL YOU?!
I'VE DEVELOPED SOME NEW TRICKS.
THEY'RE ALL ME. IT'S A SIMPLE ***DUPLICARI*** SPELL.
I PUT A BIT OF MY SOUL IN EACH COPY, YOU SEE...
LIKE A HORCRUX?! THAT'S SO COOL...
SHALL WE GO, LADIES?

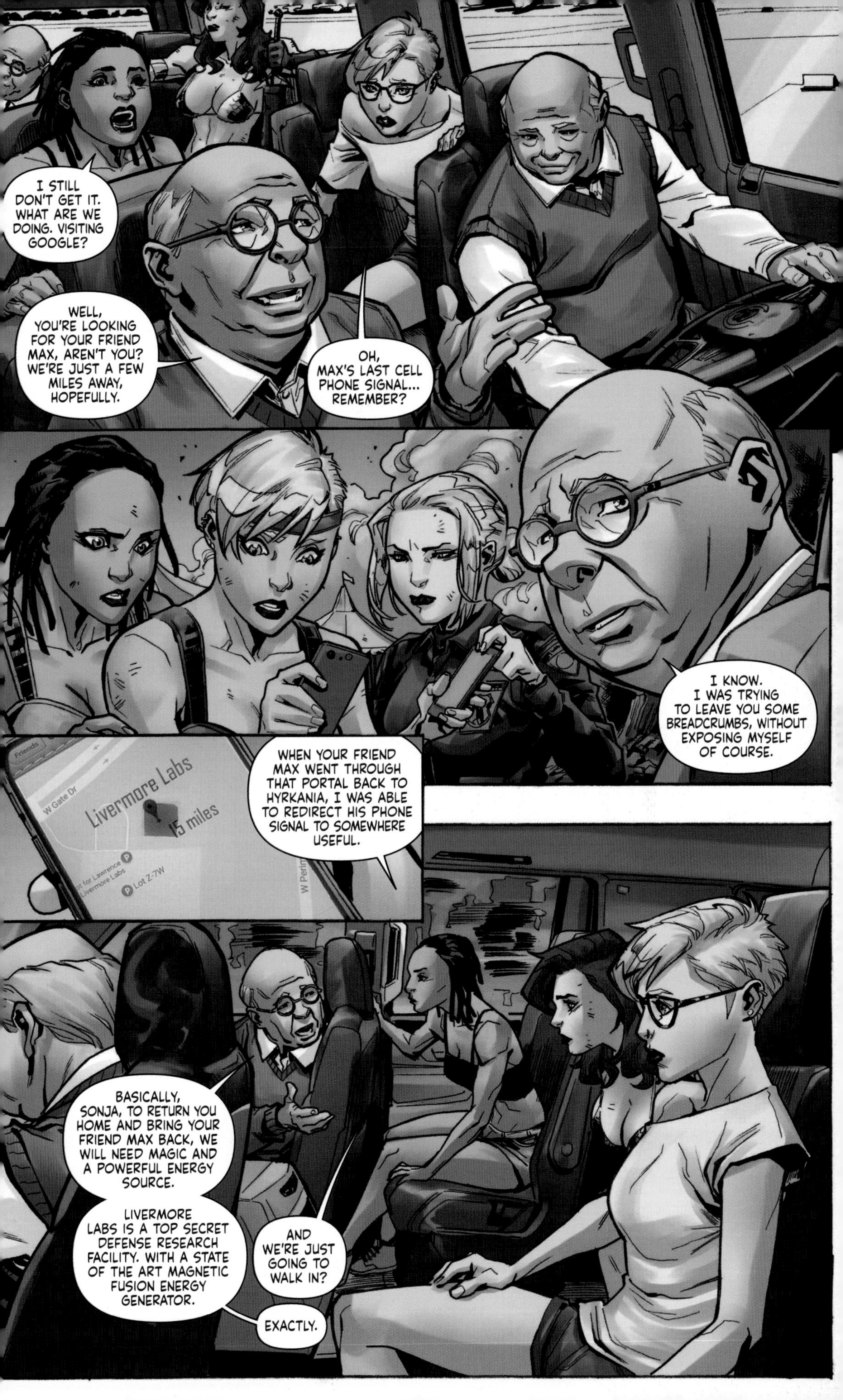

I STILL DON'T GET IT. WHAT ARE WE DOING. VISITING GOOGLE?
WELL, YOU'RE LOOKING FOR YOUR FRIEND MAX, AREN'T YOU? WE'RE JUST A FEW MILES AWAY, HOPEFULLY.
OH, MAX'S LAST CELL PHONE SIGNAL... REMEMBER?
I KNOW. I WAS TRYING TO LEAVE YOU SOME BREADCRUMBS, WITHOUT EXPOSING MYSELF OF COURSE.
Friends
W Gate Dr
Livermore Labs
15 miles
Lot Z-7W
WHEN YOUR FRIEND MAX WENT THROUGH THAT PORTAL BACK TO HYRKANIA, I WAS ABLE TO REDIRECT HIS PHONE SIGNAL TO SOMEWHERE USEFUL.
BASICALLY, SONJA, TO RETURN YOU HOME AND BRING YOUR FRIEND MAX BACK, WE WILL NEED MAGIC AND A POWERFUL ENERGY SOURCE.
LIVERMORE LABS IS A TOP SECRET DEFENSE RESEARCH FACILITY. WITH A STATE OF THE ART MAGNETIC FUSION ENERGY GENERATOR.
AND WE'RE JUST GOING TO WALK IN?
EXACTLY.

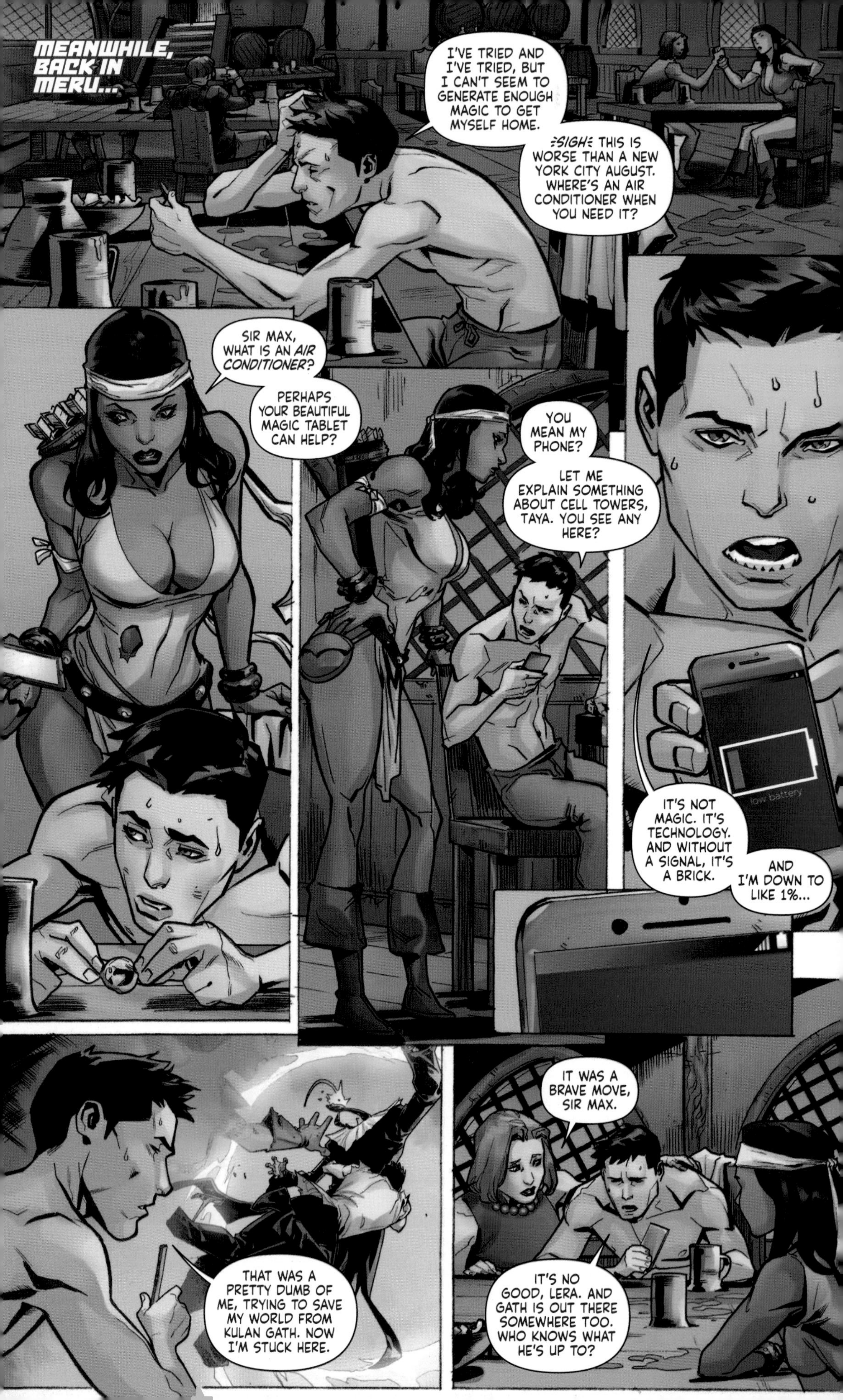
MEANWHILE, BACK IN MERU...
I'VE TRIED AND I'VE TRIED, BUT I CAN'T SEEM TO GENERATE ENOUGH MAGIC TO GET MYSELF HOME.
SIGH THIS IS WORSE THAN A NEW YORK CITY AUGUST. WHERE'S AN AIR CONDITIONER WHEN YOU NEED IT?
SIR MAX, WHAT IS AN AIR CONDITIONER?
PERHAPS YOUR BEAUTIFUL MAGIC TABLET CAN HELP?
YOU MEAN MY PHONE?
LET ME EXPLAIN SOMETHING ABOUT CELL TOWERS, TAYA. YOU SEE ANY HERE?
low battery
IT'S NOT MAGIC. IT'S TECHNOLOGY. AND WITHOUT A SIGNAL, IT'S A BRICK.
AND I'M DOWN TO LIKE 1%...
THAT WAS A PRETTY DUMB OF ME, TRYING TO SAVE MY WORLD FROM KULAN GATH. NOW I'M STUCK HERE.
IT WAS A BRAVE MOVE, SIR MAX.
IT'S NO GOOD, LERA. AND GATH IS OUT THERE SOMEWHERE TOO. WHO KNOWS WHAT HE'S UP TO?

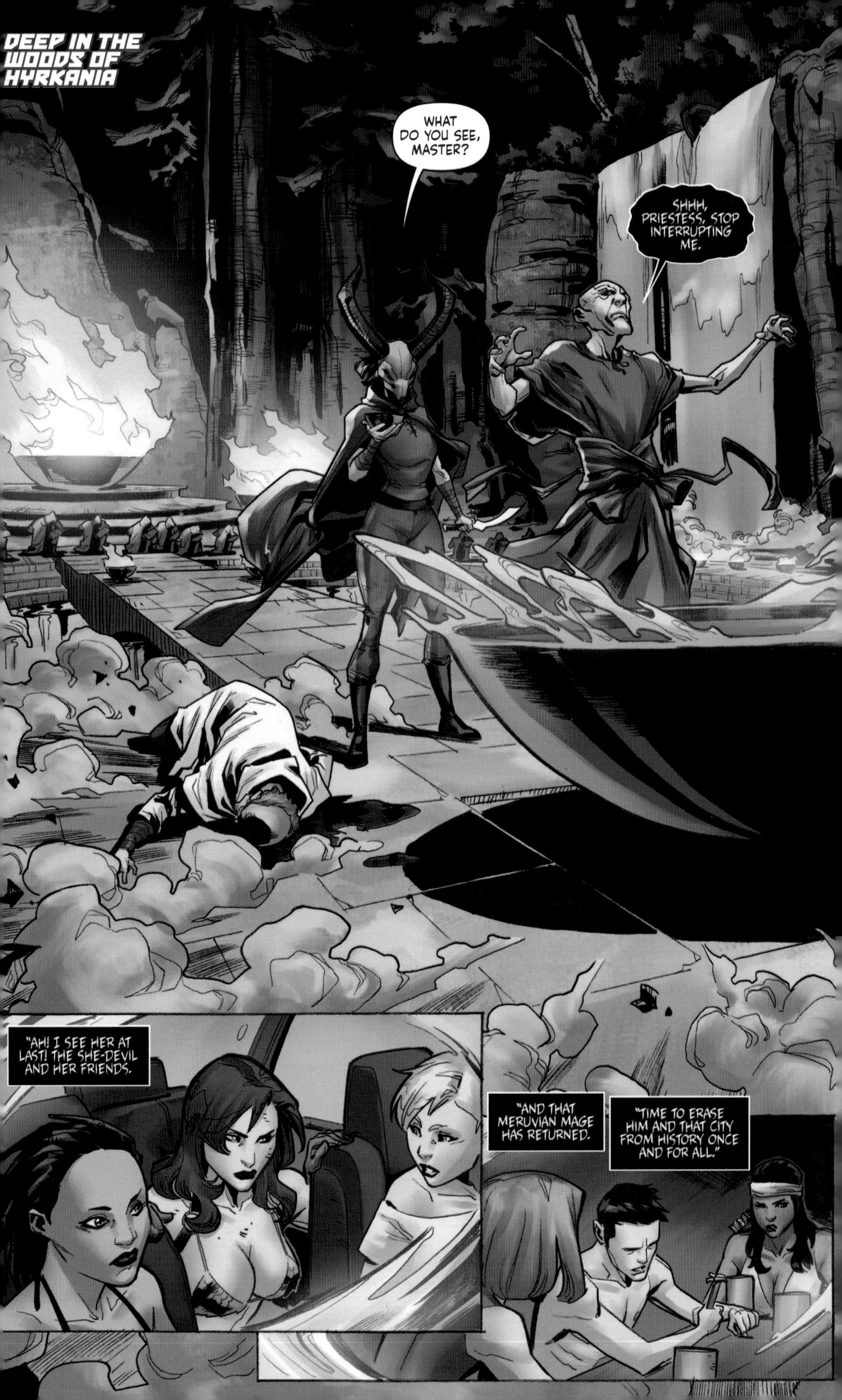

DEEP IN THE WOODS OF HYRKANIA
WHAT DO YOU SEE, MASTER?
SHHH, PRIESTESS, STOP INTERRUPTING ME.
"AH! I SEE HER AT LAST! THE SHE-DEVIL AND HER FRIENDS.
"AND THAT MERUVIAN MAGE HAS RETURNED.
"TIME TO ERASE HIM AND THAT CITY FROM HISTORY ONCE AND FOR ALL."

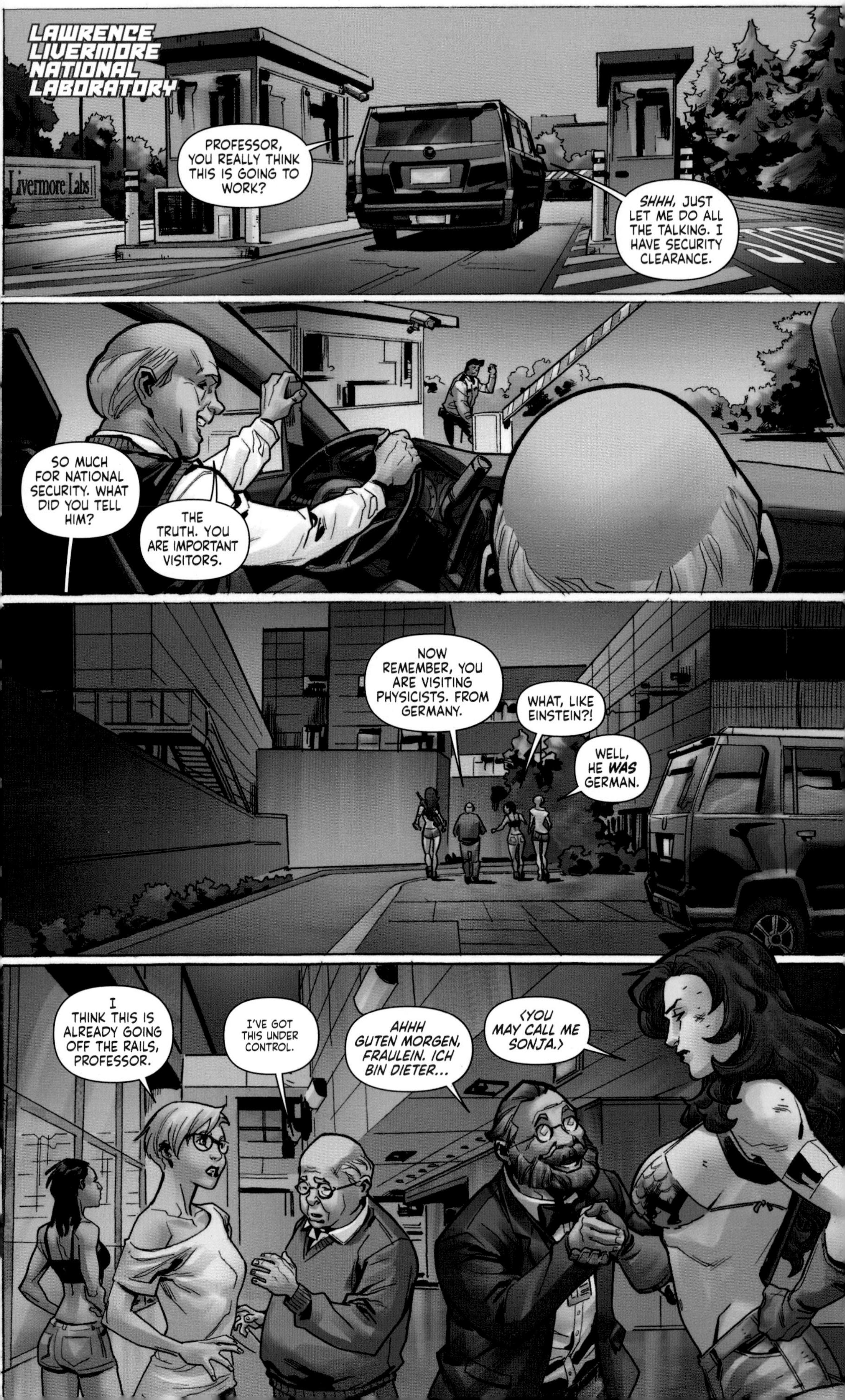
LAWRENCE LIVERMORE NATIONAL LABORATORY
Livermore Labs
PROFESSOR, YOU REALLY THINK THIS IS GOING TO WORK?
SHHH, JUST LET ME DO ALL THE TALKING. I HAVE SECURITY CLEARANCE.
SO MUCH FOR NATIONAL SECURITY. WHAT DID YOU TELL HIM?
THE TRUTH. YOU ARE IMPORTANT VISITORS.
NOW REMEMBER, YOU ARE VISITING PHYSICISTS. FROM GERMANY.
WHAT, LIKE EINSTEIN?!
WELL, HE WAS GERMAN.
I THINK THIS IS ALREADY GOING OFF THE RAILS, PROFESSOR.
I'VE GOT THIS UNDER CONTROL.
AHHH GUTEN MORGEN, FRAULEIN. ICH BIN DIETER...
<YOU MAY CALL ME SONJA.>

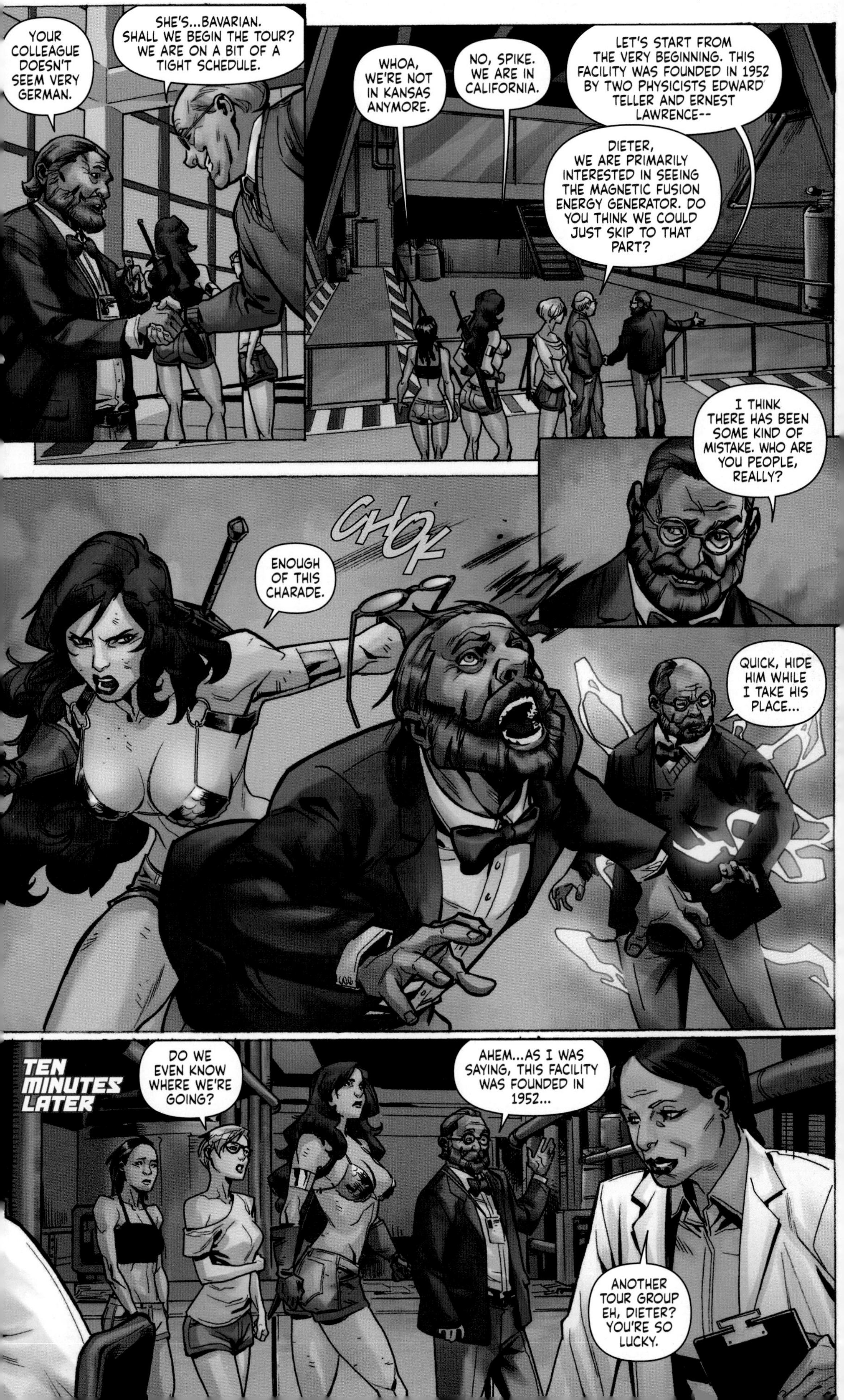
YOUR COLLEAGUE DOESN'T SEEM VERY GERMAN.
SHE'S...BAVARIAN. SHALL WE BEGIN THE TOUR? WE ARE ON A BIT OF A TIGHT SCHEDULE.
WHOA, WE'RE NOT IN KANSAS ANYMORE.
NO, SPIKE. WE ARE IN CALIFORNIA.
LET'S START FROM THE VERY BEGINNING. THIS FACILITY WAS FOUNDED IN 1952 BY TWO PHYSICISTS EDWARD TELLER AND ERNEST LAWRENCE--
DIETER, WE ARE PRIMARILY INTERESTED IN SEEING THE MAGNETIC FUSION ENERGY GENERATOR. DO YOU THINK WE COULD JUST SKIP TO THAT PART?
I THINK THERE HAS BEEN SOME KIND OF MISTAKE. WHO ARE YOU PEOPLE, REALLY?
CHOK
ENOUGH OF THIS CHARADE.
QUICK, HIDE HIM WHILE I TAKE HIS PLACE...
TEN MINUTES LATER
DO WE EVEN KNOW WHERE WE'RE GOING?
AHEM...AS I WAS SAYING, THIS FACILITY WAS FOUNDED IN 1952...
ANOTHER TOUR GROUP EH, DIETER? YOU'RE SO LUCKY.

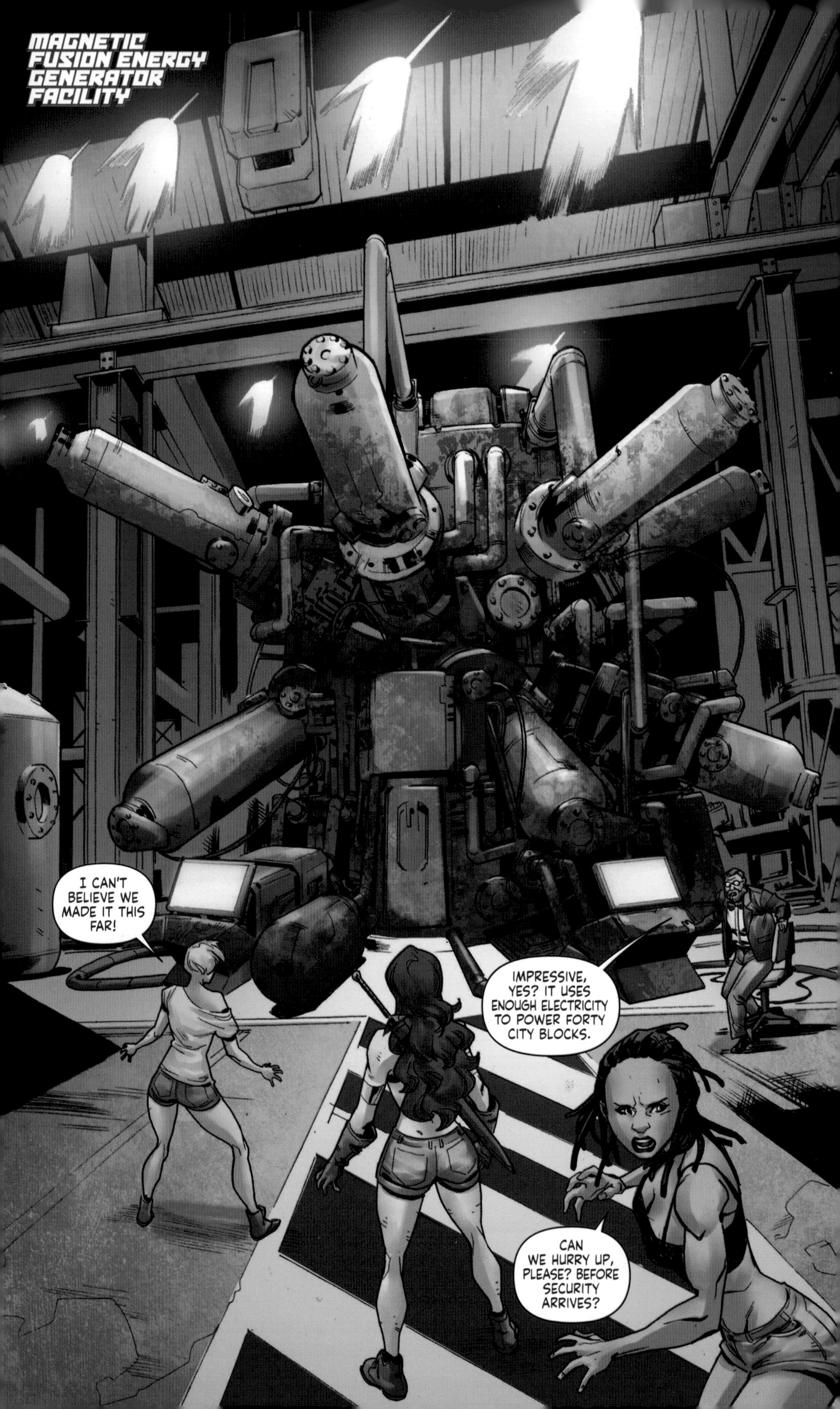
MAGNETIC FUSION ENERGY GENERATOR FACILITY
I CAN'T BELIEVE WE MADE IT THIS FAR!
IMPRESSIVE, YES? IT USES ENOUGH ELECTRICITY TO POWER FORTY CITY BLOCKS.
CAN WE HURRY UP, PLEASE? BEFORE SECURITY ARRIVES?

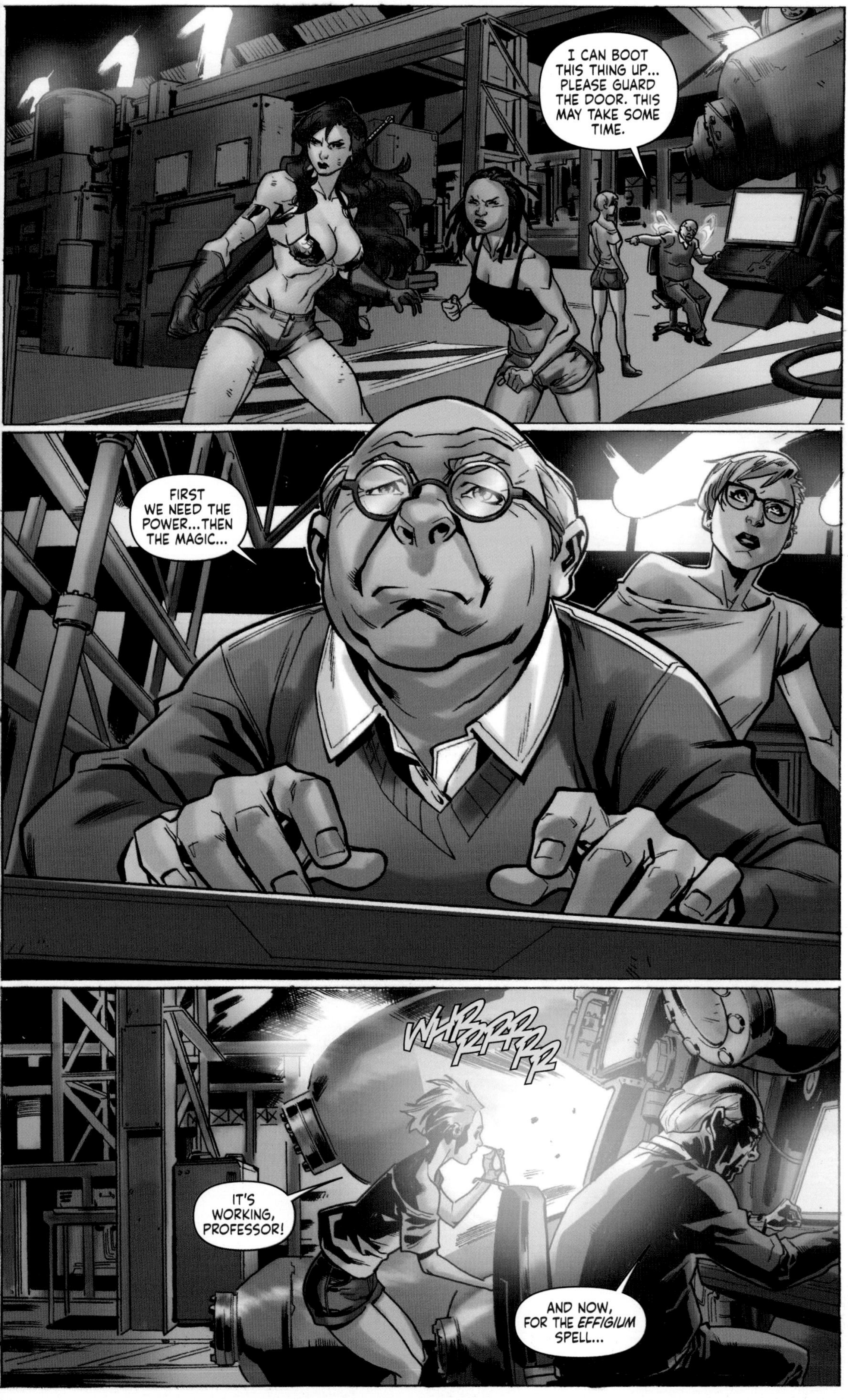
I CAN BOOT THIS THING UP... PLEASE GUARD THE DOOR. THIS MAY TAKE SOME TIME.
FIRST WE NEED THE POWER...THEN THE MAGIC...
WHIRRRRR
IT'S WORKING, PROFESSOR!
AND NOW, FOR THE *EFFIGIUM* SPELL...

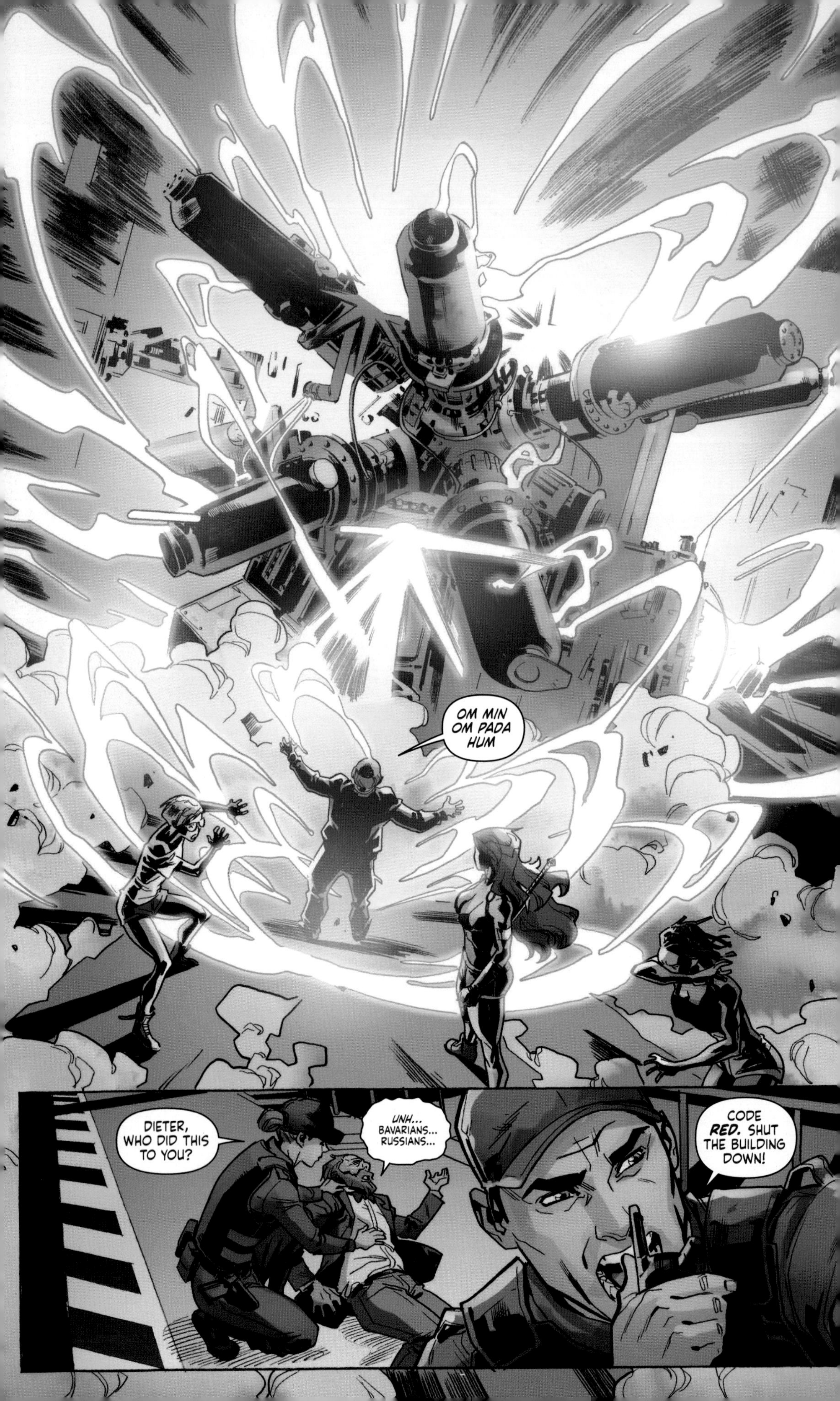
OM MIN OM PADA HUM
DIETER, WHO DID THIS TO YOU?
UNH... BAVARIANS... RUSSIANS...
CODE **RED.** SHUT THE BUILDING DOWN!

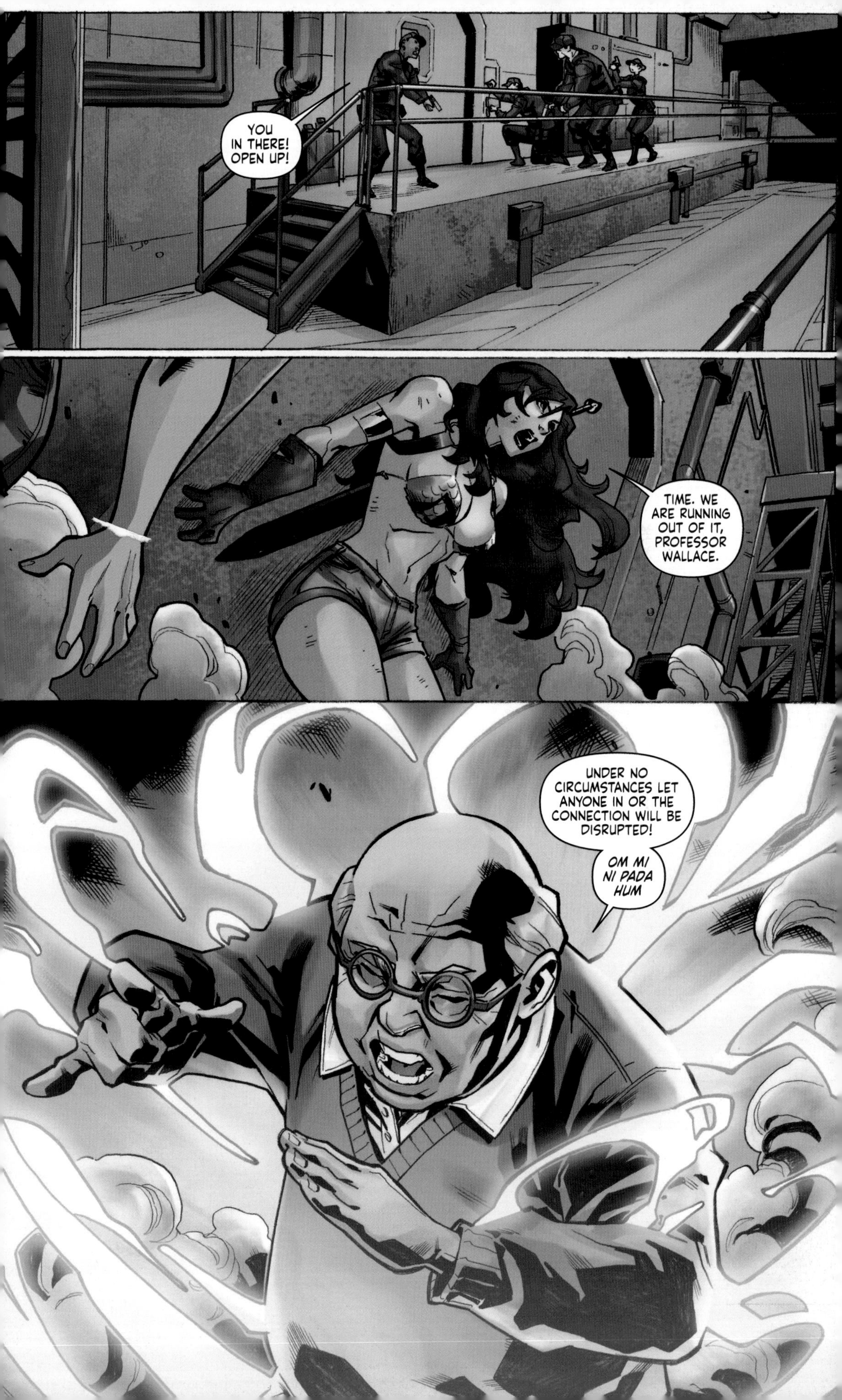

YOU IN THERE! OPEN UP!
TIME. WE ARE RUNNING OUT OF IT, PROFESSOR WALLACE.
UNDER NO CIRCUMSTANCES LET ANYONE IN OR THE CONNECTION WILL BE DISRUPTED!
OM MI NI PADA HUM

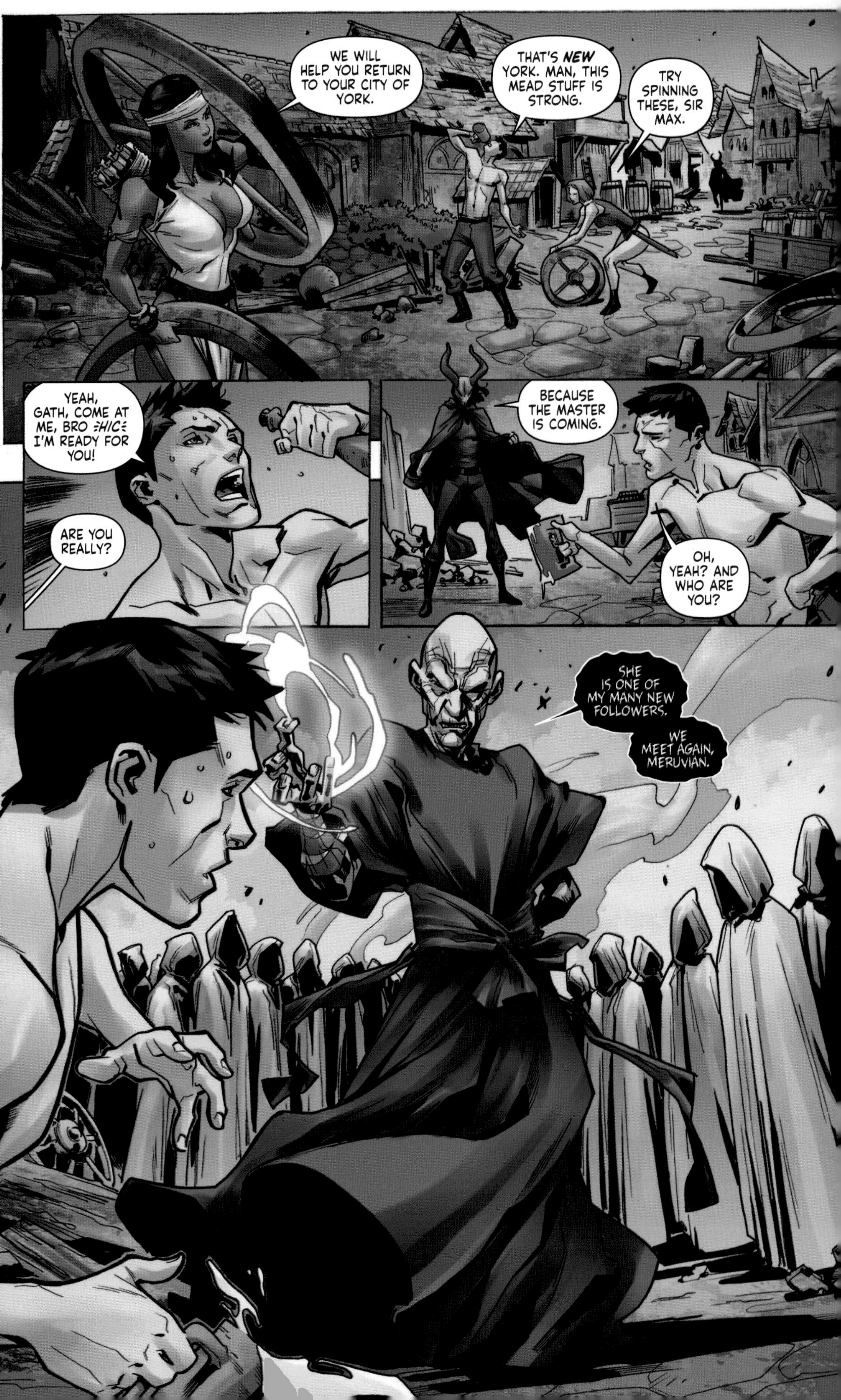
WE WILL HELP YOU RETURN TO YOUR CITY OF YORK.
THAT'S **NEW** YORK. MAN, THIS MEAD STUFF IS STRONG.
TRY SPINNING THESE, SIR MAX.
YEAH, GATH, COME AT ME, BRO *HIC* I'M READY FOR YOU!
ARE YOU REALLY?
BECAUSE THE MASTER IS COMING.
OH, YEAH? AND WHO ARE YOU?
SHE IS ONE OF MY MANY NEW FOLLOWERS.
WE MEET AGAIN, MERUVIAN.

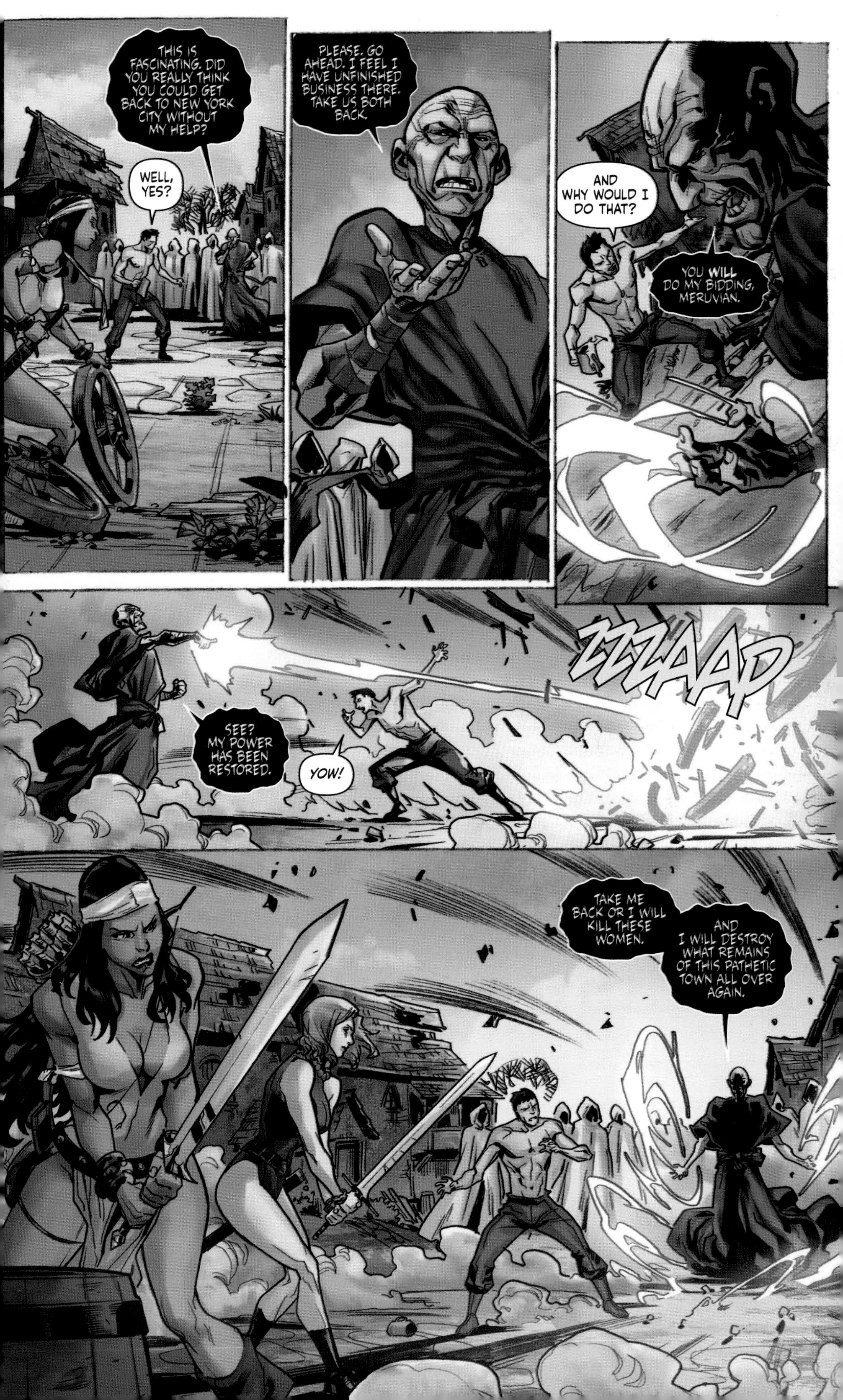
THIS IS FASCINATING. DID YOU REALLY THINK YOU COULD GET BACK TO NEW YORK CITY WITHOUT MY HELP?
WELL, YES?
PLEASE. GO AHEAD. I FEEL I HAVE UNFINISHED BUSINESS THERE. TAKE US BOTH BACK.
AND WHY WOULD I DO THAT?
YOU WILL DO MY BIDDING, MERUVIAN.
ZZZAAP
SEE? MY POWER HAS BEEN RESTORED.
YOW!
TAKE ME BACK OR I WILL KILL THESE WOMEN.
AND I WILL DESTROY WHAT REMAINS OF THIS PATHETIC TOWN ALL OVER AGAIN.

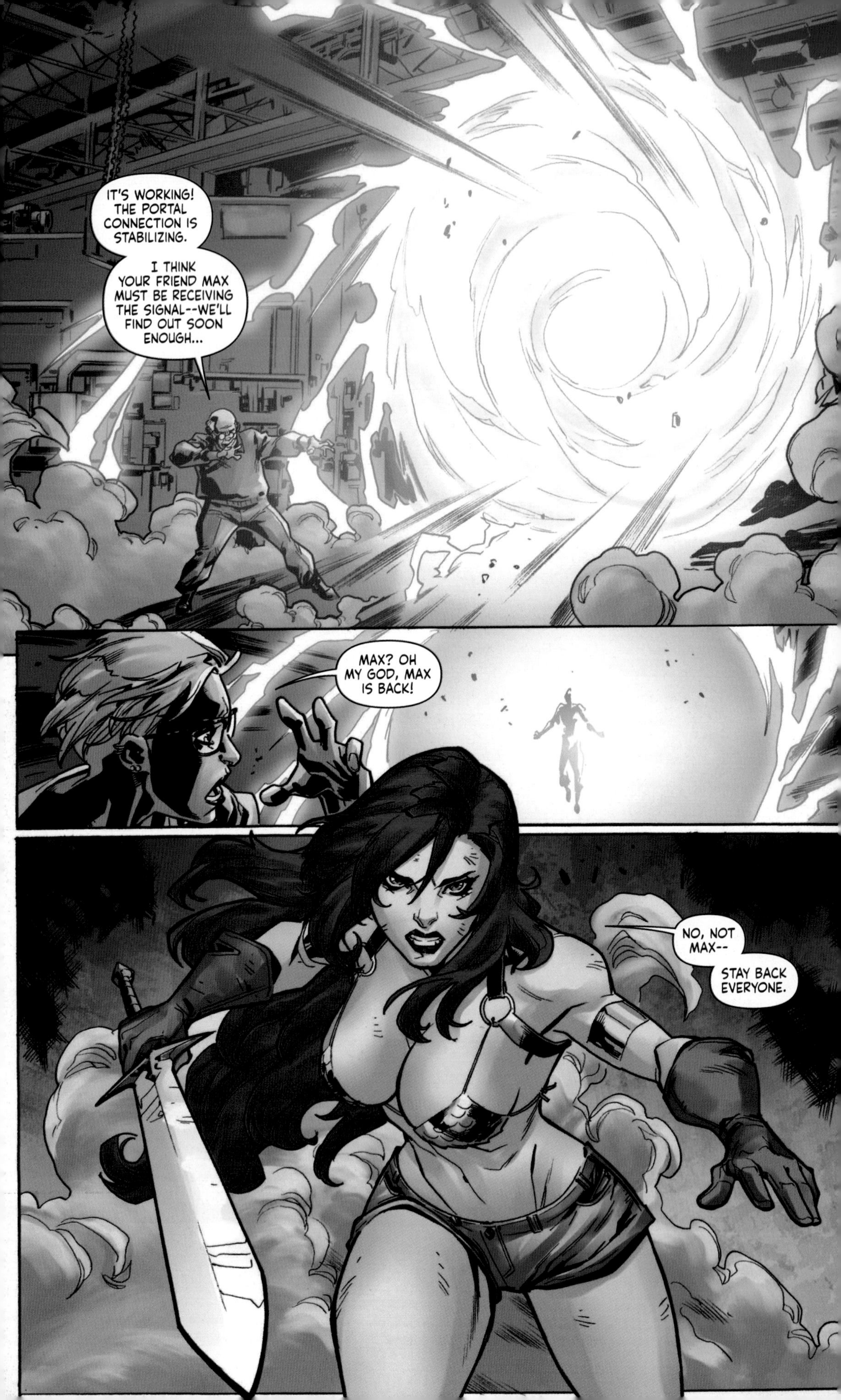
IT'S WORKING! THE PORTAL CONNECTION IS STABILIZING.
I THINK YOUR FRIEND MAX MUST BE RECEIVING THE SIGNAL--WE'LL FIND OUT SOON ENOUGH...
MAX? OH MY GOD, MAX IS BACK!
NO, NOT MAX--
STAY BACK EVERYONE.

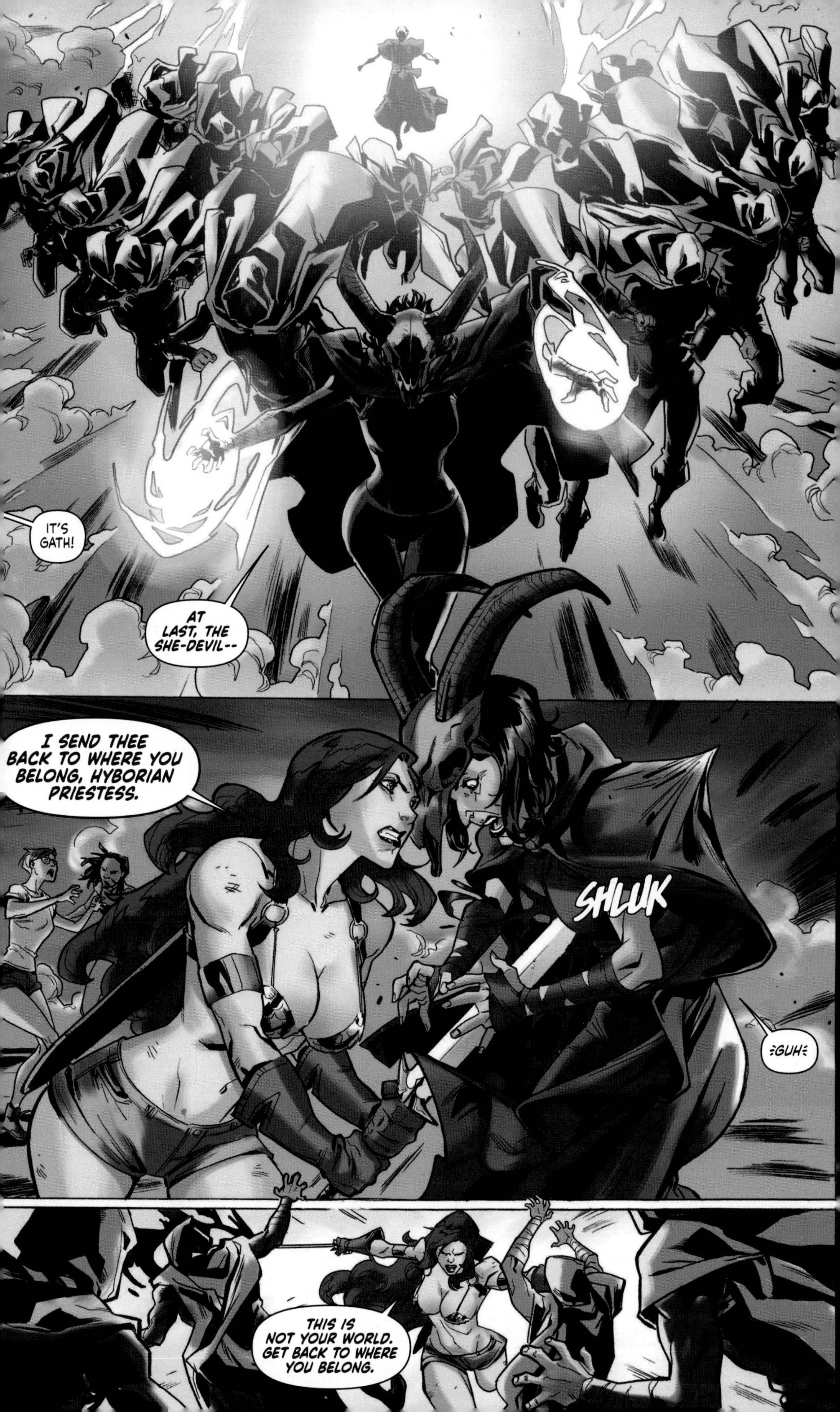
IT'S GATH!
AT LAST, THE SHE-DEVIL--
I SEND THEE BACK TO WHERE YOU BELONG, HYBORIAN PRIESTESS.
SHLUK
GUH
THIS IS NOT YOUR WORLD. GET BACK TO WHERE YOU BELONG.

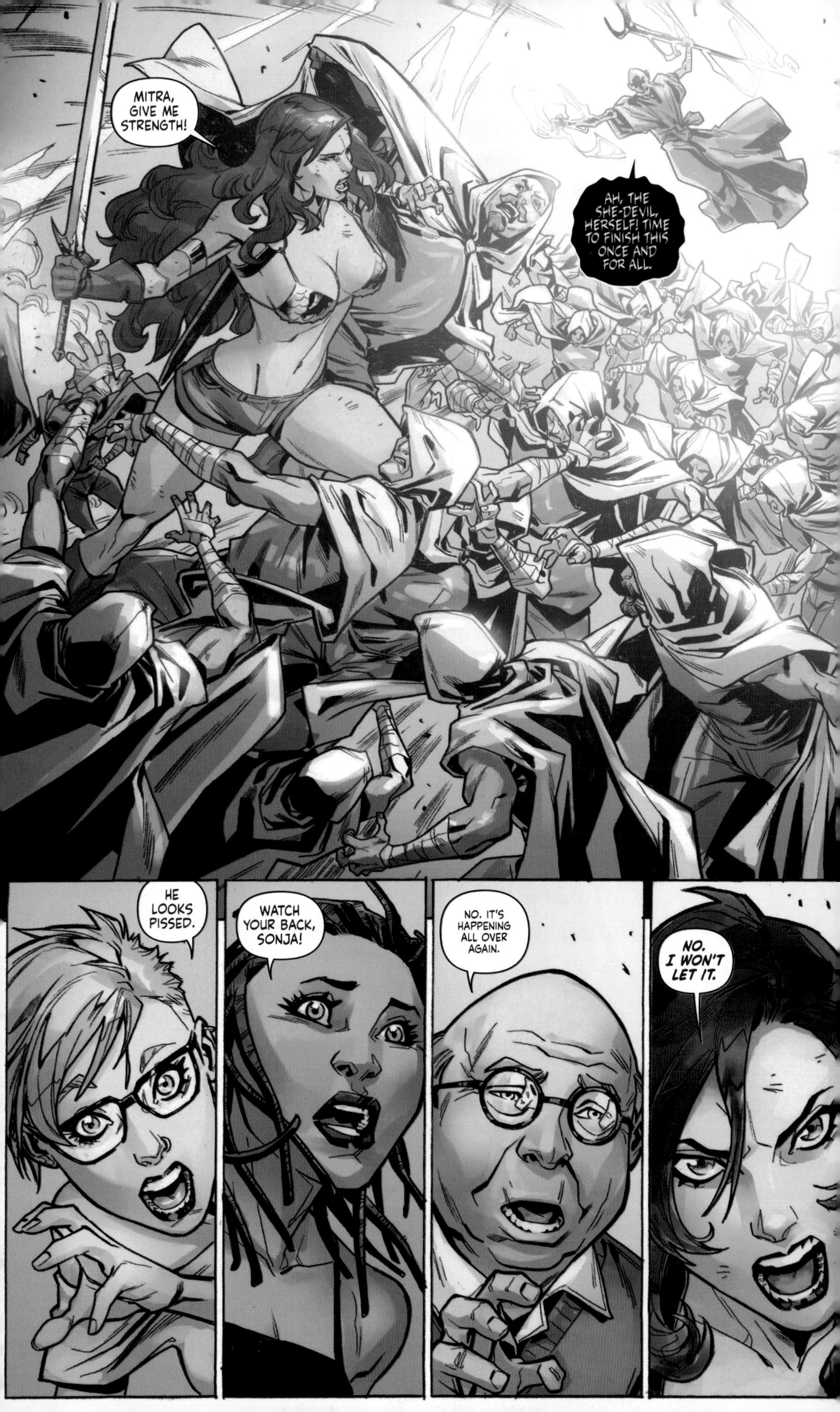
MITRA, GIVE ME STRENGTH!
AH, THE SHE-DEVIL, HERSELF! TIME TO FINISH THIS ONCE AND FOR ALL.
HE LOOKS PISSED.
WATCH YOUR BACK, SONJA!
NO. IT'S HAPPENING ALL OVER AGAIN.
NO. I WON'T LET IT.

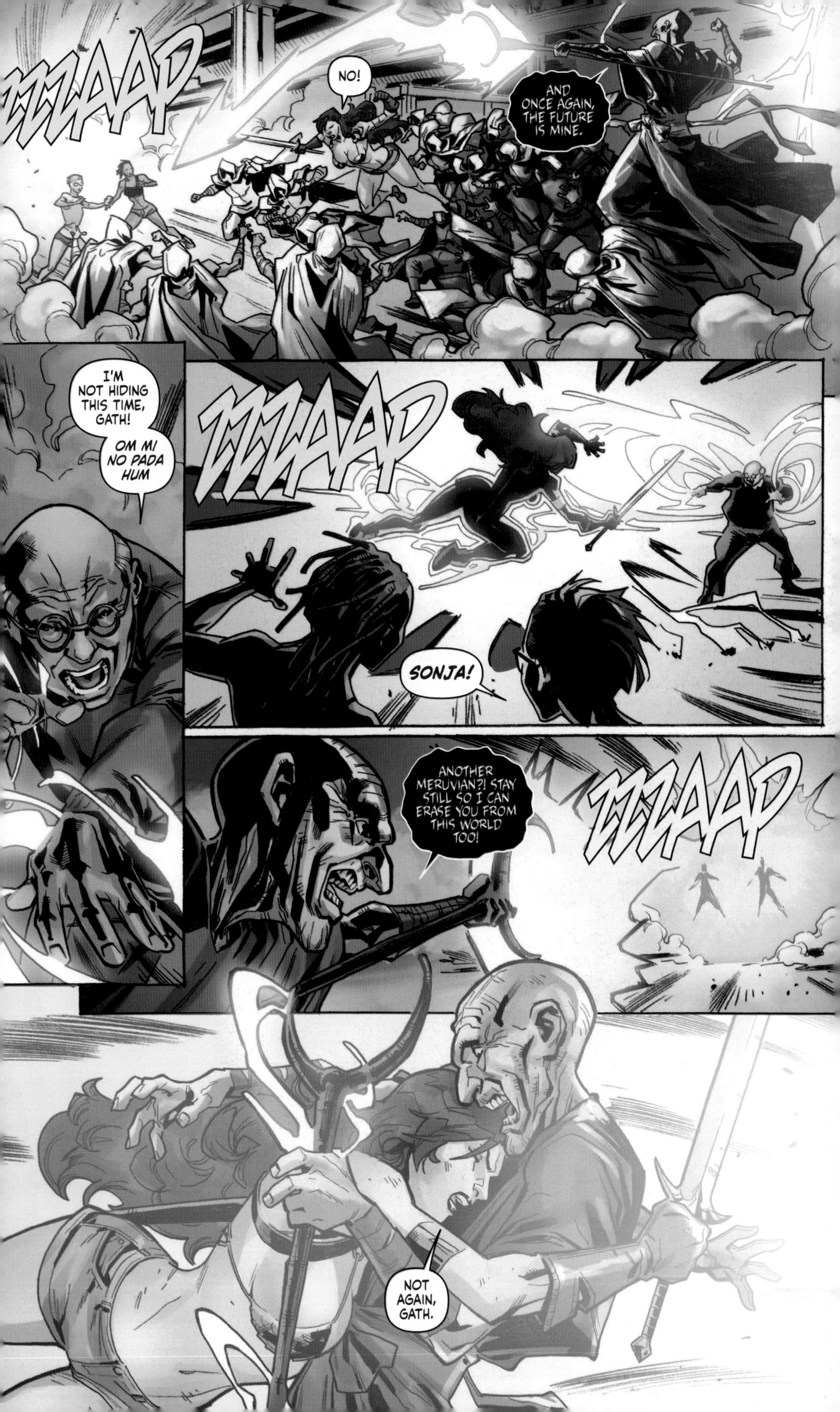
ZZZAAP
NO!
AND ONCE AGAIN, THE FUTURE IS MINE.
I'M NOT HIDING THIS TIME, GATH!
OM MI NO PADA HUM
ZZZAAP
SONJA!
ANOTHER MERUVIAN?! STAY STILL SO I CAN ERASE YOU FROM THIS WORLD TOO!
ZZZAAP
NOT AGAIN, GATH.

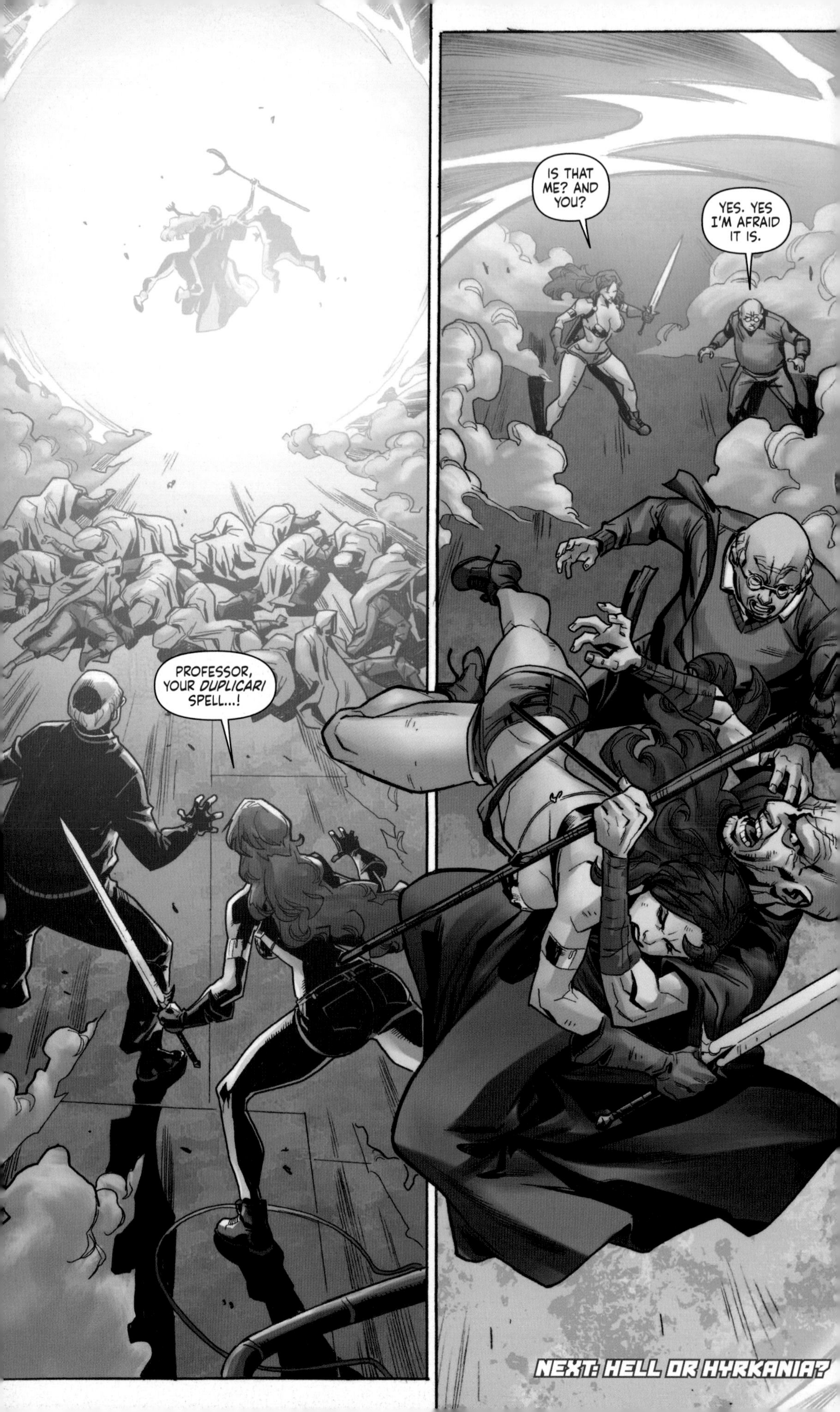
PROFESSOR, YOUR *DUPLICARI* SPELL...!
IS THAT ME? AND YOU?
YES. YES I'M AFRAID IT IS.
NEXT: HELL OR HYRKANIA?

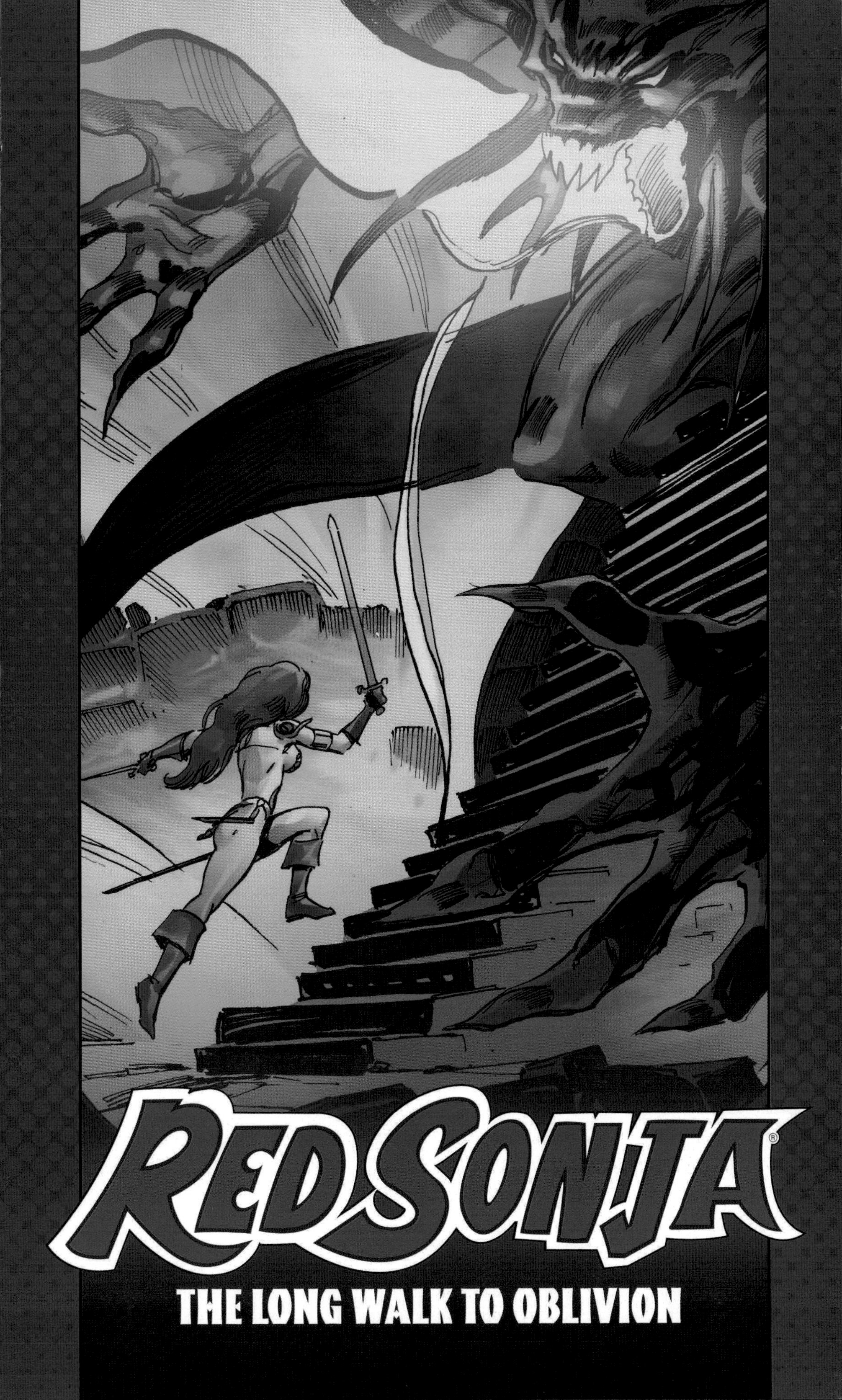

RED SONJA®

THE LONG WALK TO OBLIVION

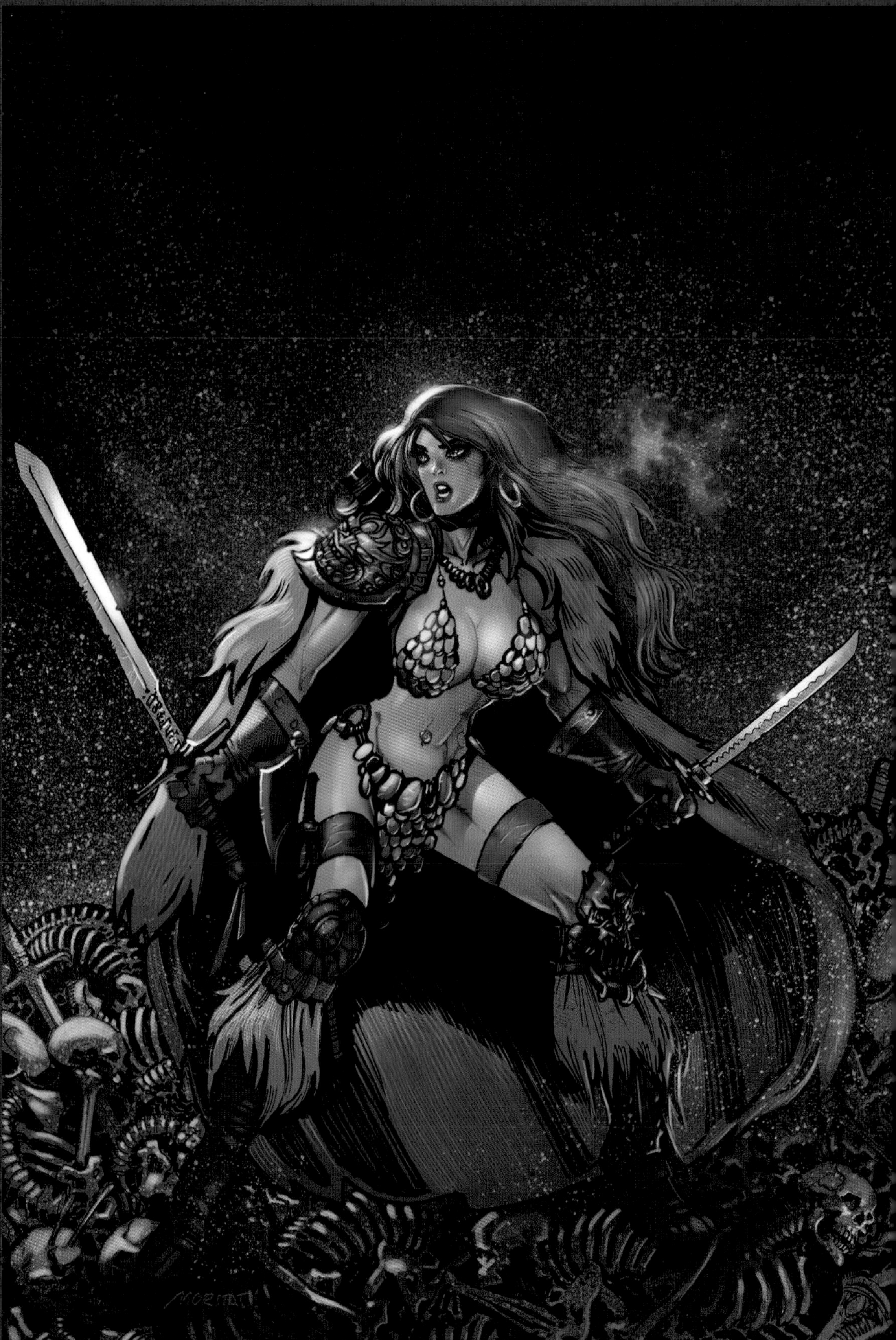

RED SONJA - THE LONG WALK TO OBLIVION:
COVER ART BY **MORITAT**

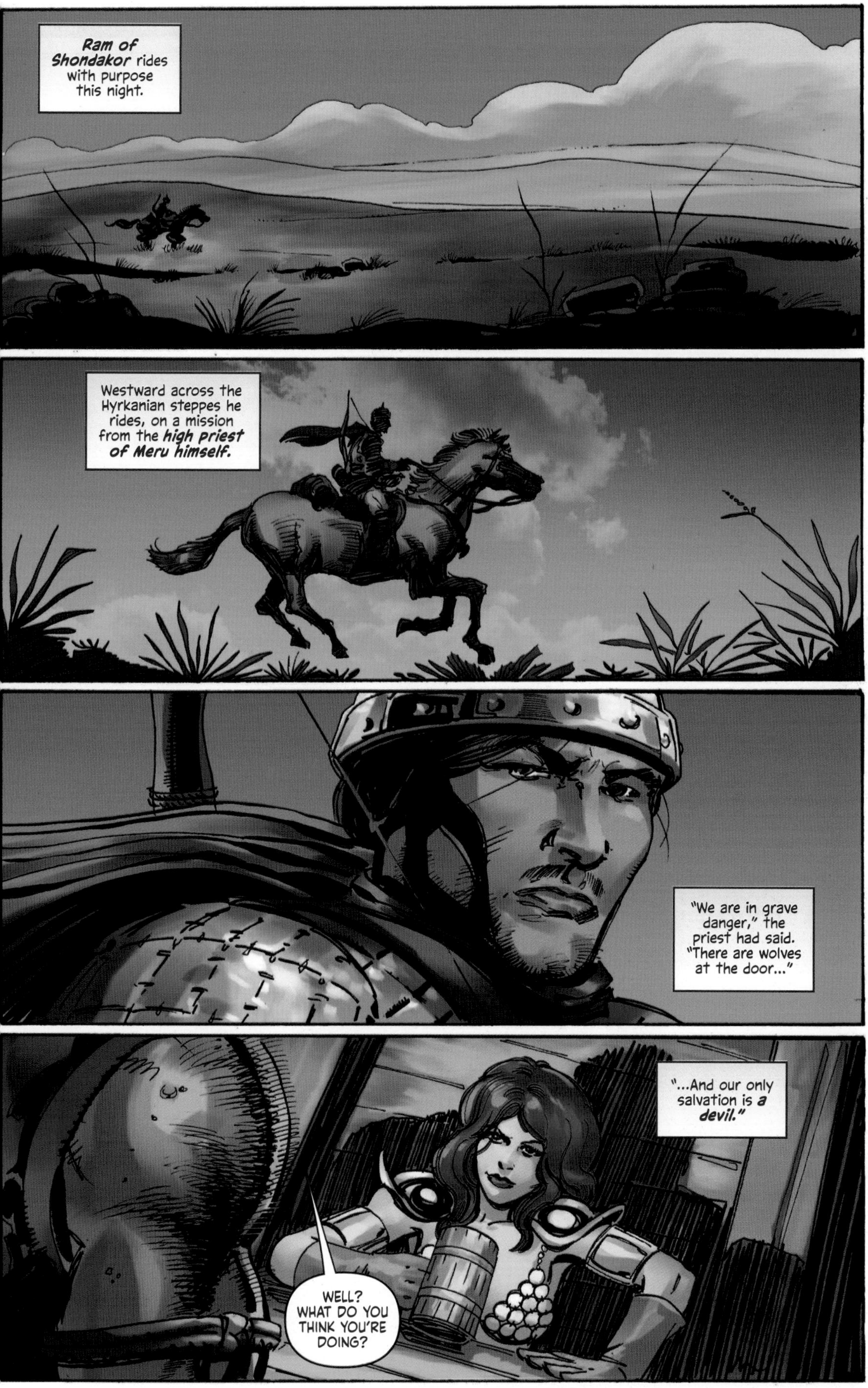

Ram of Shondakor rides with purpose this night.
Westward across the Hyrkanian steppes he rides, on a mission from the high priest of Meru himself.
"We are in grave danger," the priest had said. "There are wolves at the door..."
"...And our only salvation is a devil."
WELL? WHAT DO YOU THINK YOU'RE DOING?

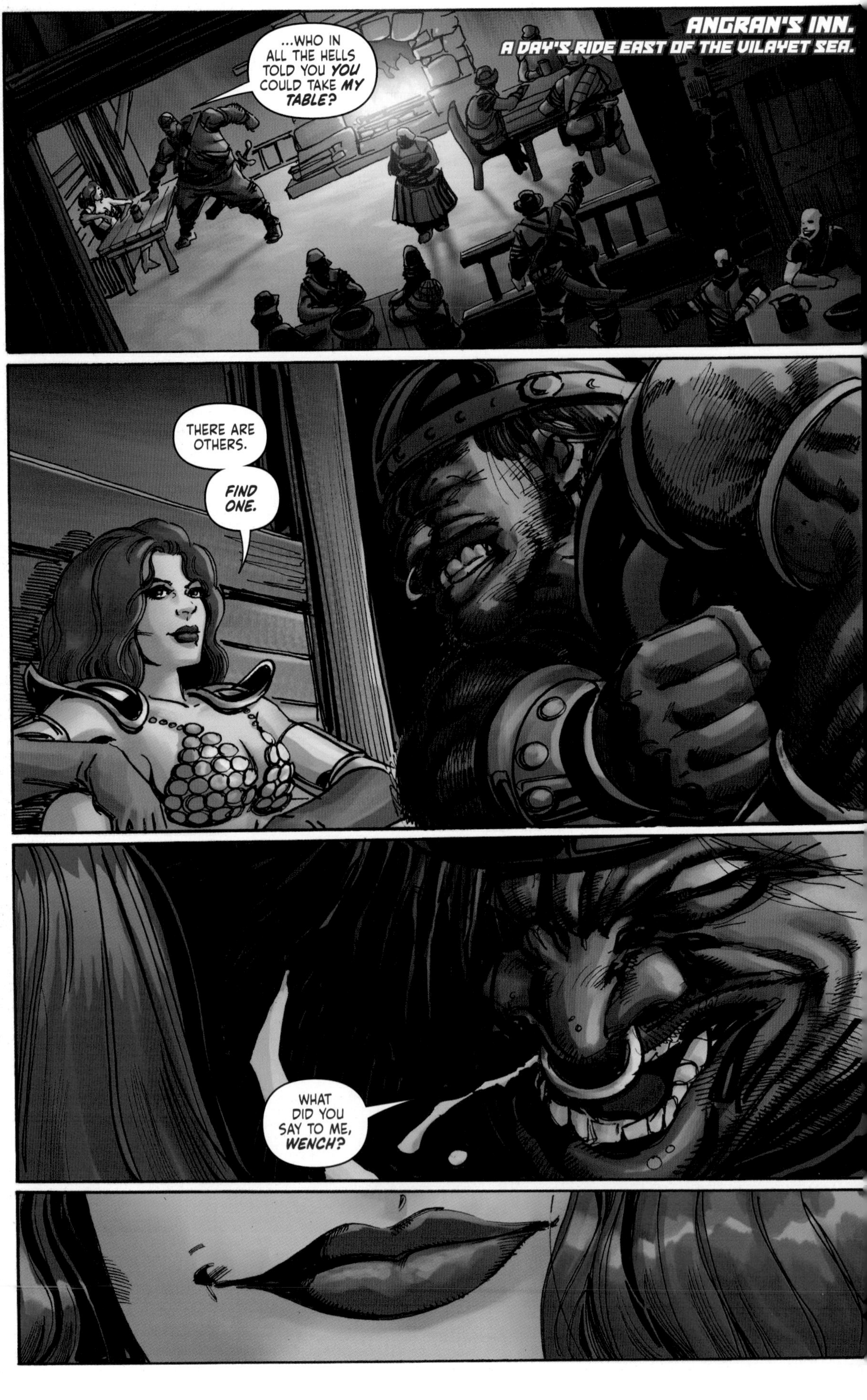
ANGRAN'S INN.
A DAY'S RIDE EAST OF THE VILAYET SEA.
...WHO IN ALL THE HELLS TOLD YOU YOU COULD TAKE MY TABLE?
THERE ARE OTHERS.
FIND ONE.
WHAT DID YOU SAY TO ME, WENCH?

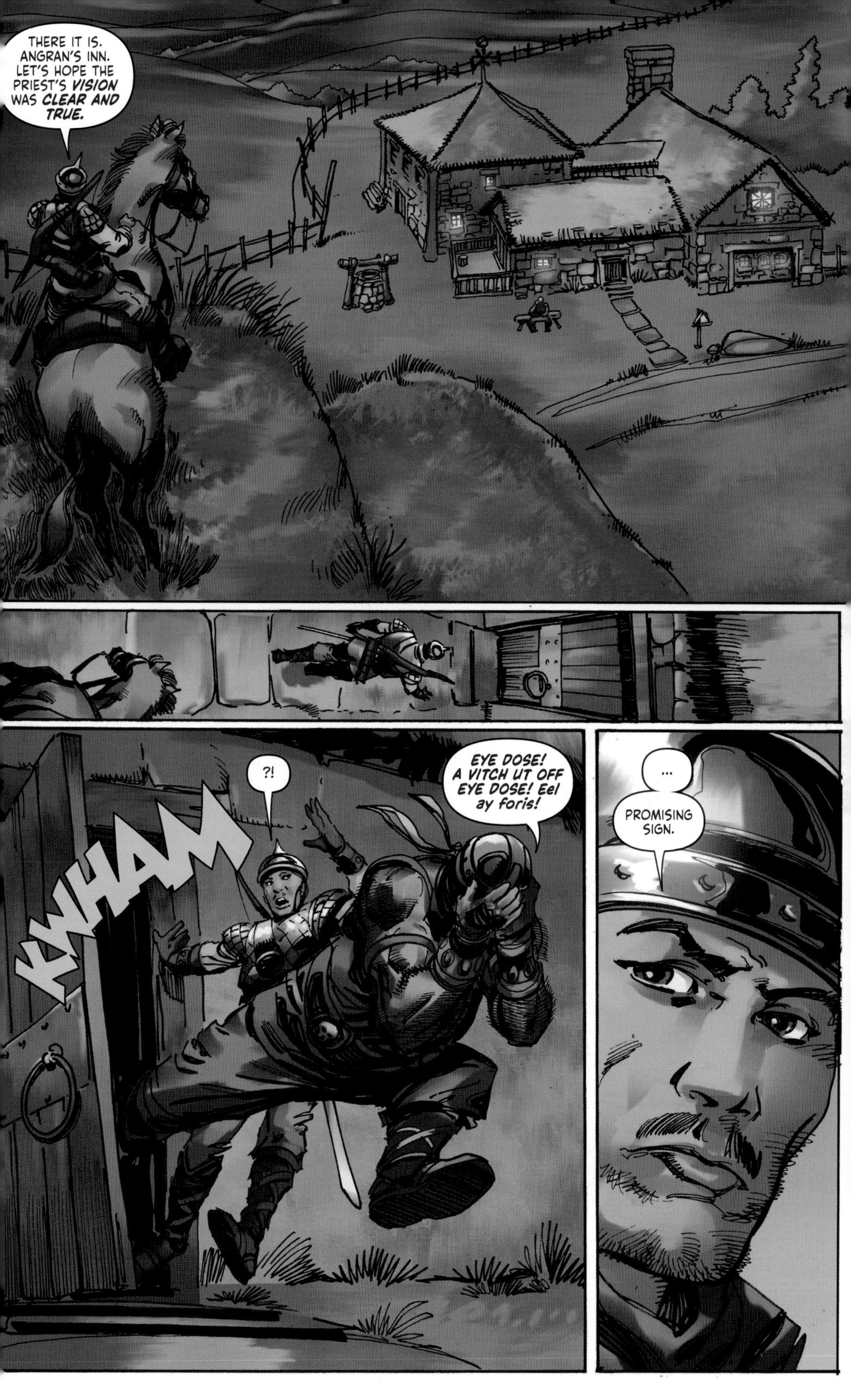
THERE IT IS. ANGRAN'S INN. LET'S HOPE THE PRIEST'S VISION WAS CLEAR AND TRUE.
KWHAM
?!
EYE DOSE! A VITCH UT OFF EYE DOSE! Eel ay foris!
...
PROMISING SIGN.

GREETINGS.

I AM RAM OF SHONDAKOR, AND I'VE BEEN SENT HERE TO FIND THE WARRIOR CALLED RED SONJA. THAT MUST BE YOU.

SQUIIICK

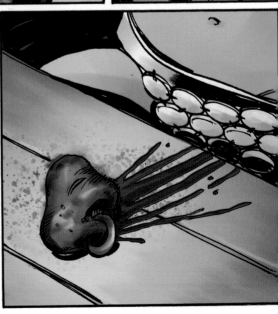

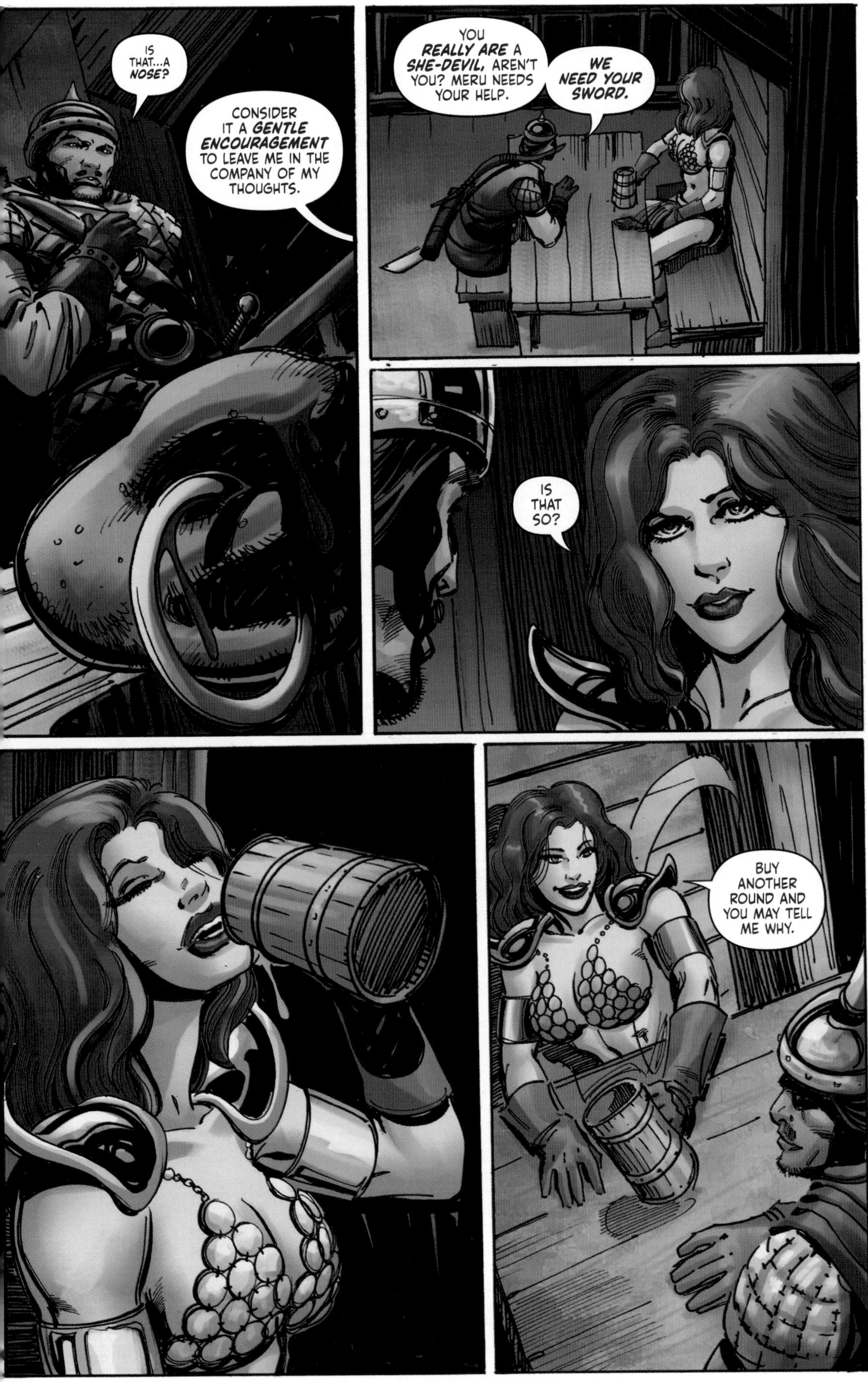
IS THAT...A NOSE?
CONSIDER IT A GENTLE ENCOURAGEMENT TO LEAVE ME IN THE COMPANY OF MY THOUGHTS.
YOU REALLY ARE A SHE-DEVIL, AREN'T YOU? MERU NEEDS YOUR HELP.
WE NEED YOUR SWORD.
IS THAT SO?
BUY ANOTHER ROUND AND YOU MAY TELL ME WHY.

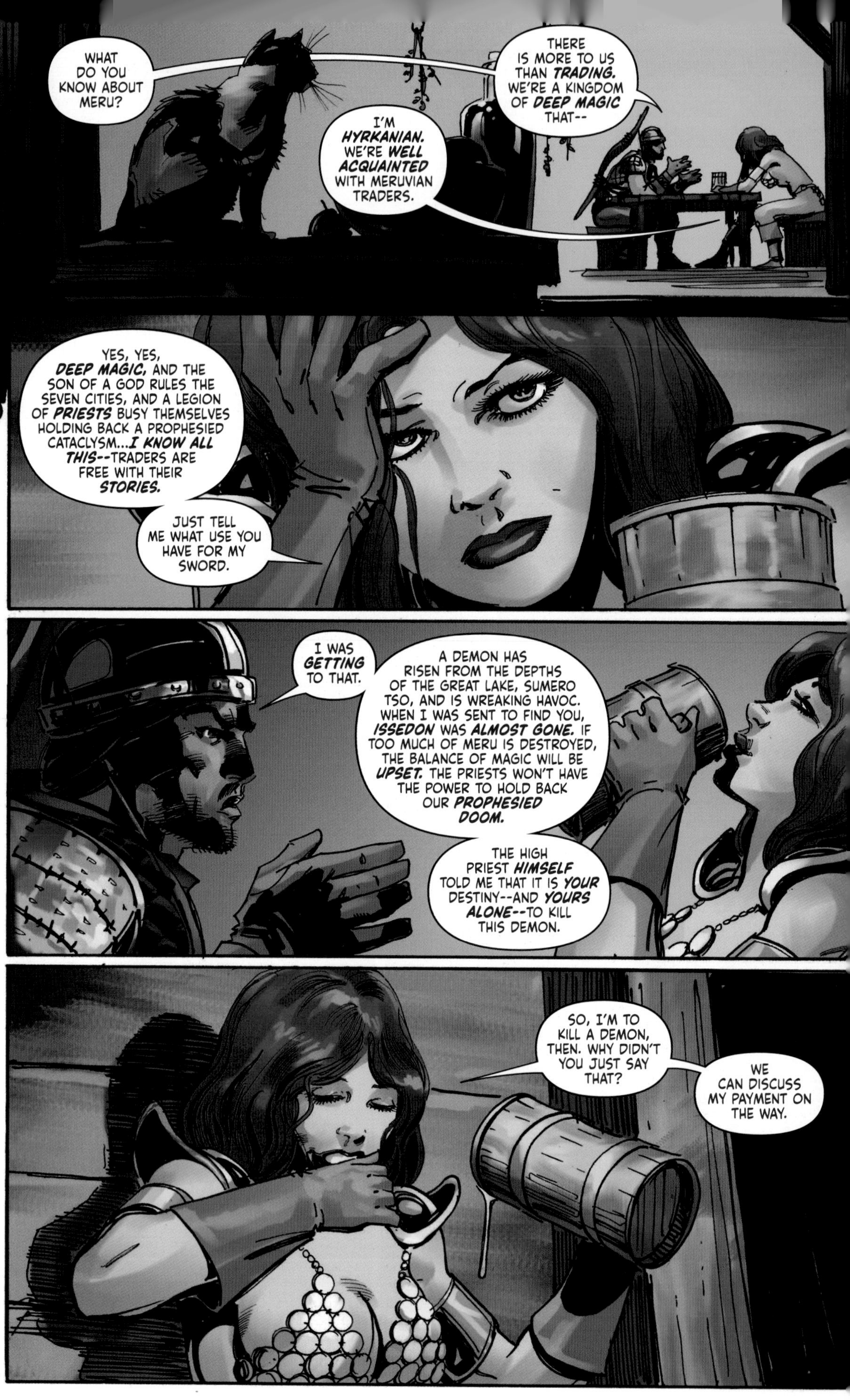

WHAT DO YOU KNOW ABOUT MERU?
THERE IS MORE TO US THAN TRADING. WE'RE A KINGDOM OF DEEP MAGIC THAT--
I'M HYRKANIAN. WE'RE WELL ACQUAINTED WITH MERUVIAN TRADERS.
YES, YES, DEEP MAGIC, AND THE SON OF A GOD RULES THE SEVEN CITIES, AND A LEGION OF PRIESTS BUSY THEMSELVES HOLDING BACK A PROPHESIED CATACLYSM...I KNOW ALL THIS--TRADERS ARE FREE WITH THEIR STORIES.
JUST TELL ME WHAT USE YOU HAVE FOR MY SWORD.
I WAS GETTING TO THAT.
A DEMON HAS RISEN FROM THE DEPTHS OF THE GREAT LAKE, SUMERO TSO, AND IS WREAKING HAVOC. WHEN I WAS SENT TO FIND YOU, ISSEDON WAS ALMOST GONE. IF TOO MUCH OF MERU IS DESTROYED, THE BALANCE OF MAGIC WILL BE UPSET. THE PRIESTS WON'T HAVE THE POWER TO HOLD BACK OUR PROPHESIED DOOM.
THE HIGH PRIEST HIMSELF TOLD ME THAT IT IS YOUR DESTINY--AND YOURS ALONE--TO KILL THIS DEMON.
SO, I'M TO KILL A DEMON, THEN. WHY DIDN'T YOU JUST SAY THAT?
WE CAN DISCUSS MY PAYMENT ON THE WAY.

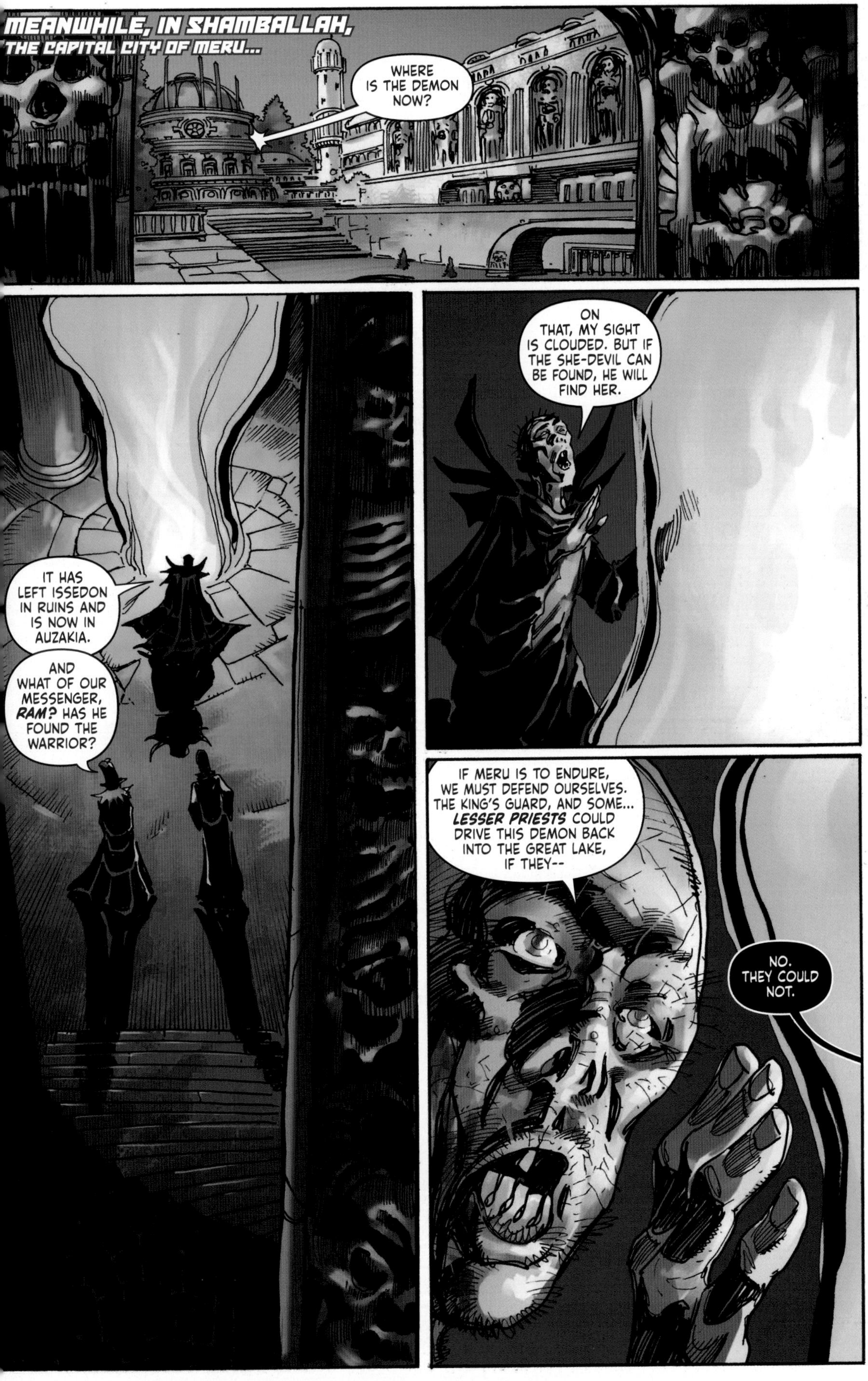
MEANWHILE, IN SHAMBALLAH, THE CAPITAL CITY OF MERU...
WHERE IS THE DEMON NOW?
IT HAS LEFT ISSEDON IN RUINS AND IS NOW IN AUZAKIA.
AND WHAT OF OUR MESSENGER, RAM? HAS HE FOUND THE WARRIOR?
ON THAT, MY SIGHT IS CLOUDED. BUT IF THE SHE-DEVIL CAN BE FOUND, HE WILL FIND HER.
IF MERU IS TO ENDURE, WE MUST DEFEND OURSELVES. THE KING'S GUARD, AND SOME... LESSER PRIESTS COULD DRIVE THIS DEMON BACK INTO THE GREAT LAKE, IF THEY--
NO. THEY COULD NOT.

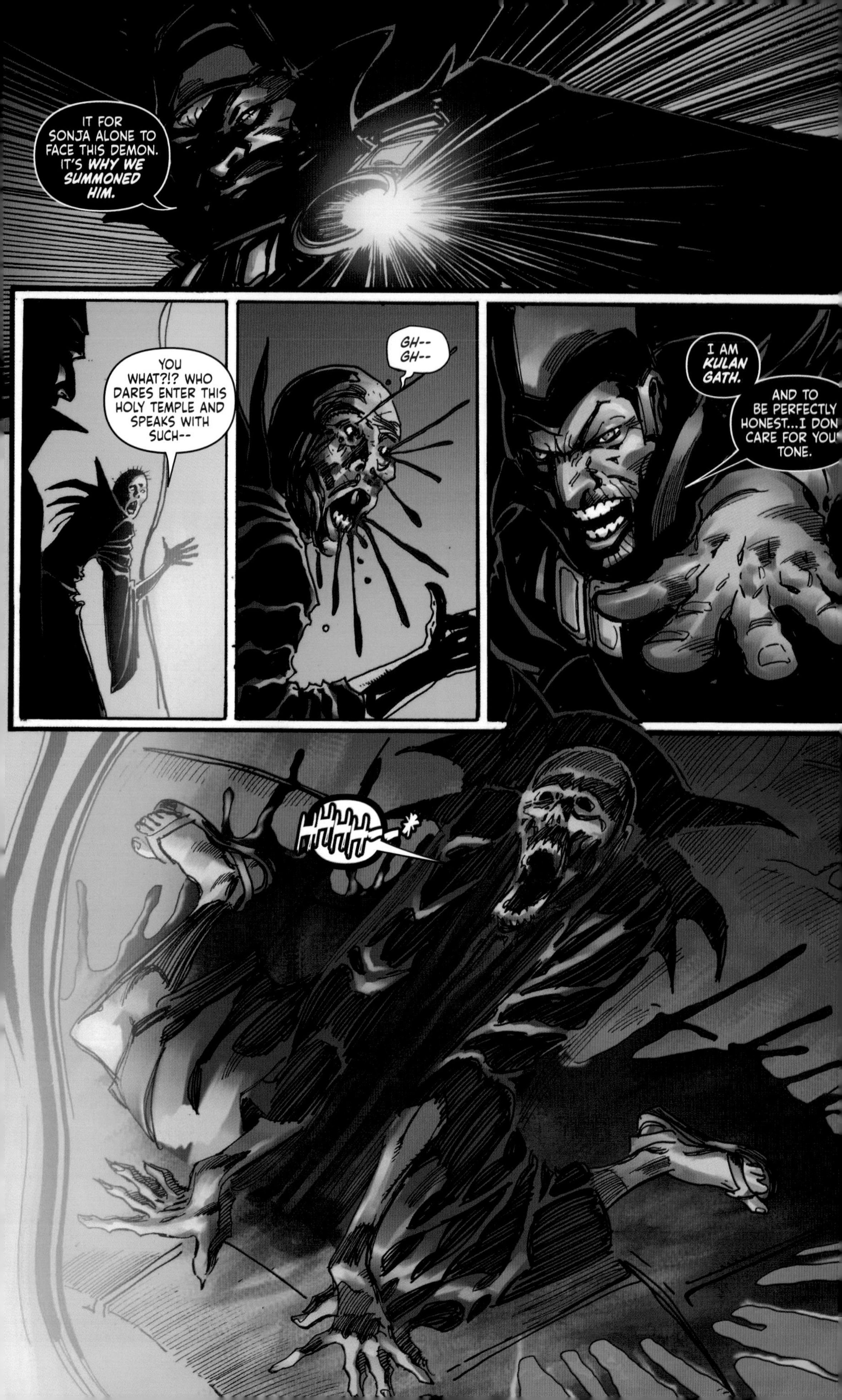
IT FOR SONJA ALONE TO FACE THIS DEMON. IT'S WHY WE SUMMONED HIM.
YOU WHAT?!? WHO DARES ENTER THIS HOLY TEMPLE AND SPEAKS WITH SUCH--
GH-- GH--
I AM KULAN GATH.
AND TO BE PERFECTLY HONEST...I DON CARE FOR YOU TONE.
HHHHH--*

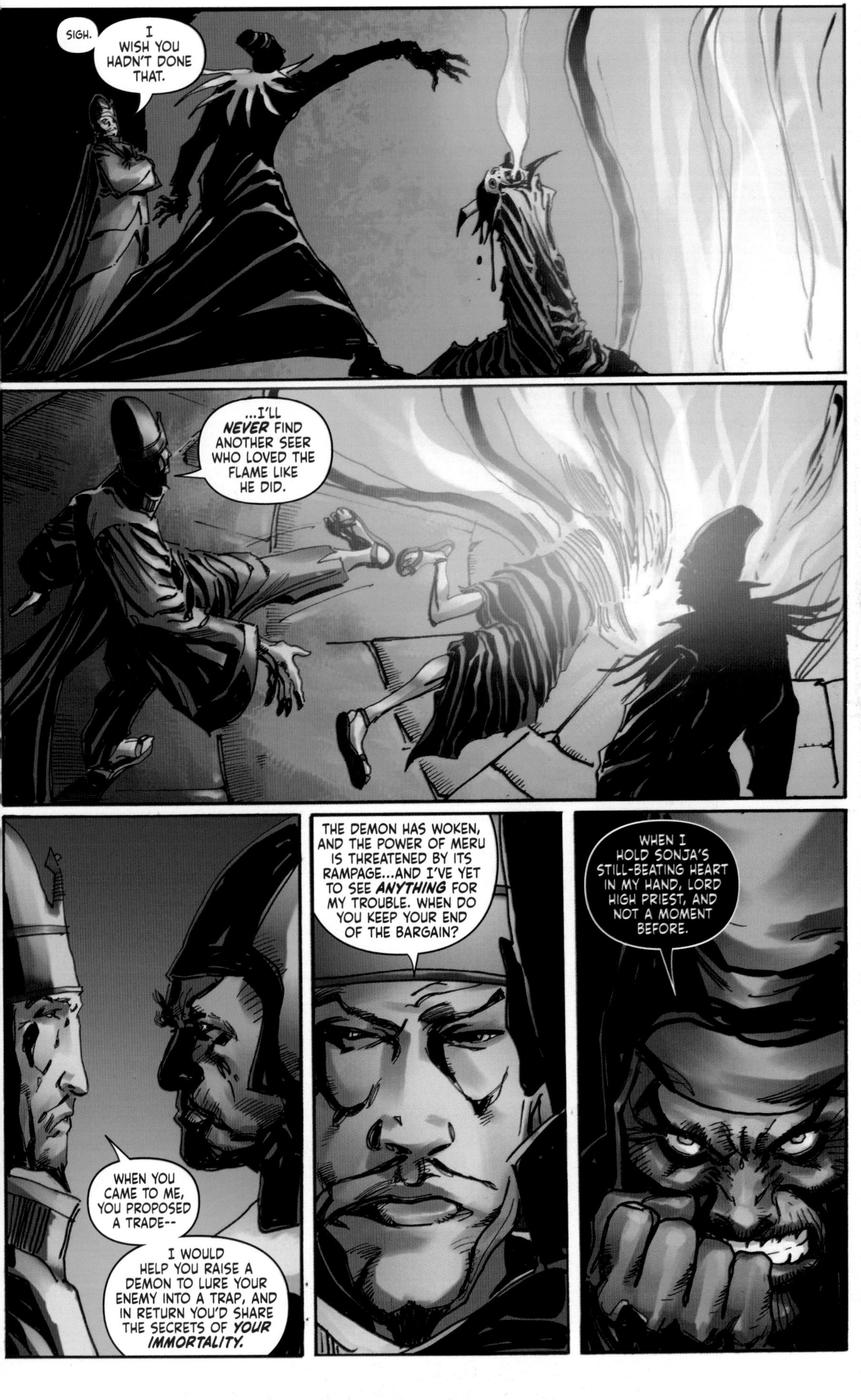
SIGH.
I WISH YOU HADN'T DONE THAT.
...I'LL NEVER FIND ANOTHER SEER WHO LOVED THE FLAME LIKE HE DID.
WHEN YOU CAME TO ME, YOU PROPOSED A TRADE--
I WOULD HELP YOU RAISE A DEMON TO LURE YOUR ENEMY INTO A TRAP, AND IN RETURN YOU'D SHARE THE SECRETS OF YOUR IMMORTALITY.
THE DEMON HAS WOKEN, AND THE POWER OF MERU IS THREATENED BY ITS RAMPAGE...AND I'VE YET TO SEE ANYTHING FOR MY TROUBLE. WHEN DO YOU KEEP YOUR END OF THE BARGAIN?
WHEN I HOLD SONJA'S STILL-BEATING HEART IN MY HAND, LORD HIGH PRIEST, AND NOT A MOMENT BEFORE.

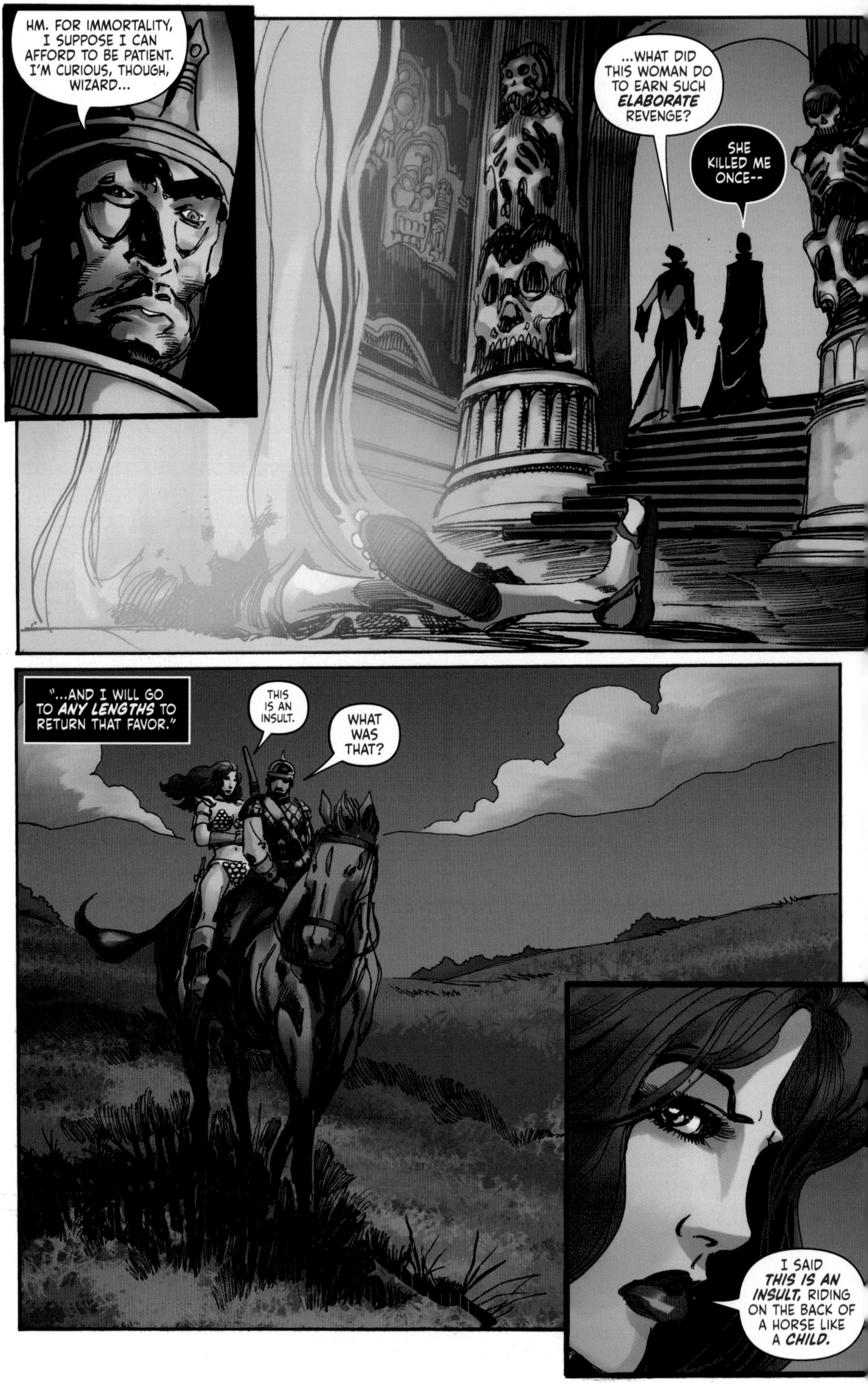
HM. FOR IMMORTALITY, I SUPPOSE I CAN AFFORD TO BE PATIENT. I'M CURIOUS, THOUGH, WIZARD...
...WHAT DID THIS WOMAN DO TO EARN SUCH *ELABORATE* REVENGE?
SHE KILLED ME ONCE--
"...AND I WILL GO TO *ANY LENGTHS* TO RETURN THAT FAVOR."
THIS IS AN INSULT.
WHAT WAS THAT?
I SAID *THIS IS AN INSULT,* RIDING ON THE BACK OF A HORSE LIKE A *CHILD.*

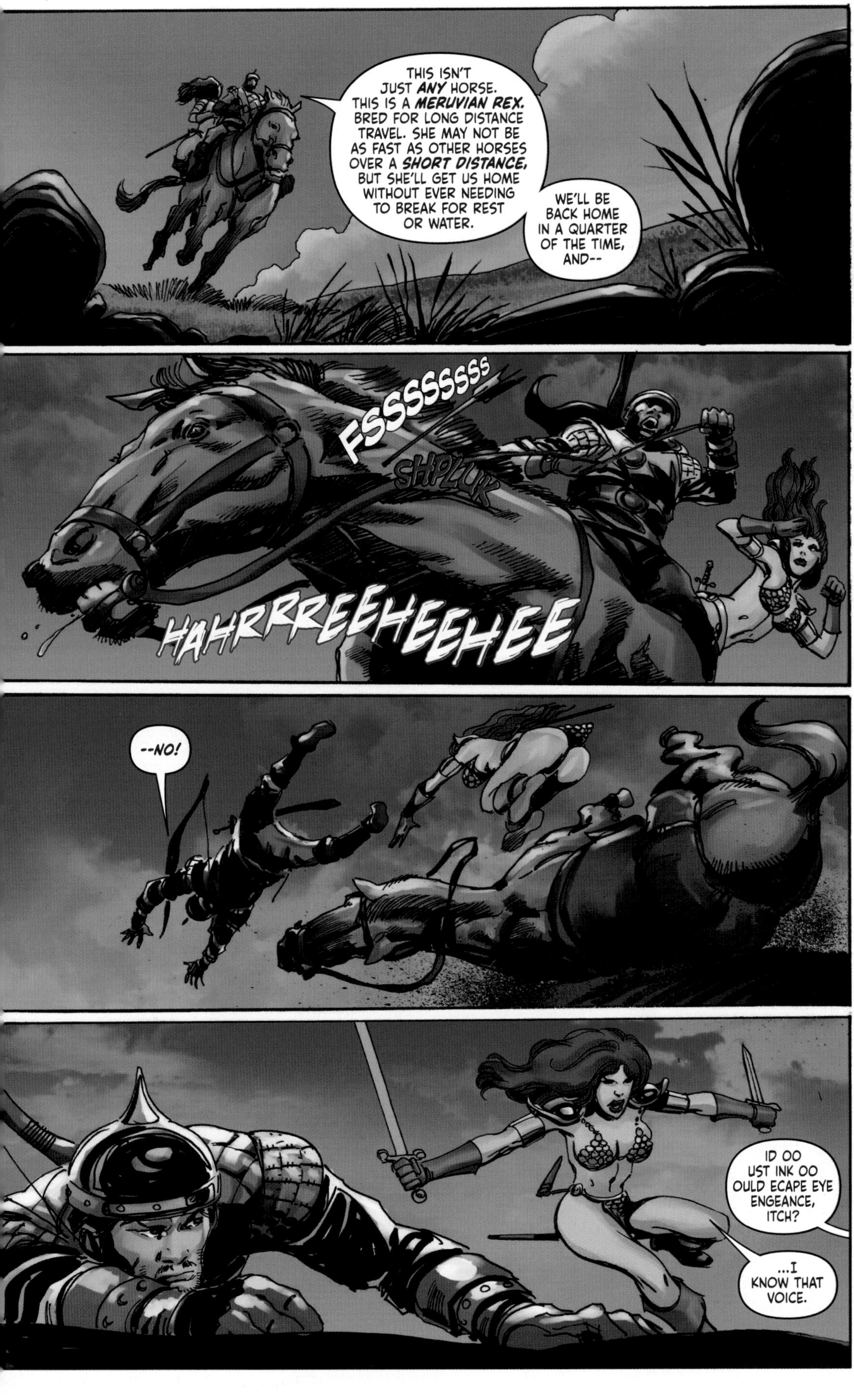

THIS ISN'T JUST **ANY** HORSE. THIS IS A ***MERUVIAN REX.*** BRED FOR LONG DISTANCE TRAVEL. SHE MAY NOT BE AS FAST AS OTHER HORSES OVER A ***SHORT DISTANCE,*** BUT SHE'LL GET US HOME WITHOUT EVER NEEDING TO BREAK FOR REST OR WATER.
WE'LL BE BACK HOME IN A QUARTER OF THE TIME, AND--
FSSSSSSSS
SHPLUK
HAHRRREEHEEHEE
--NO!
ID OO UST INK OO OULD ECAPE EYE ENGEANCE, ITCH?
...I KNOW THAT VOICE.

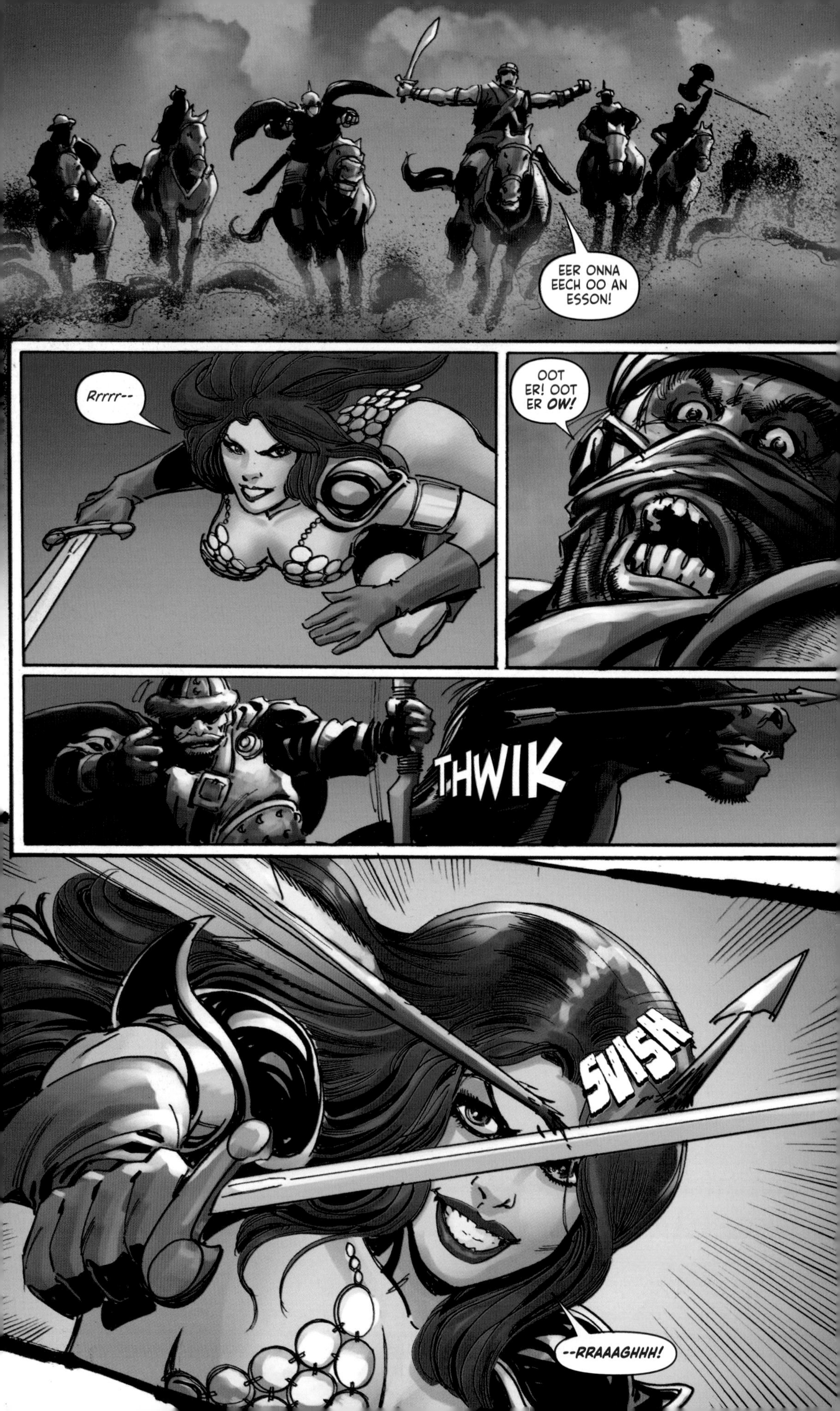
EER ONNA EECH OO AN ESSON!
Rrrrr--
OOT ER! OOT ER OW!
THWIK
SVISK
--RRAAAGHHH!

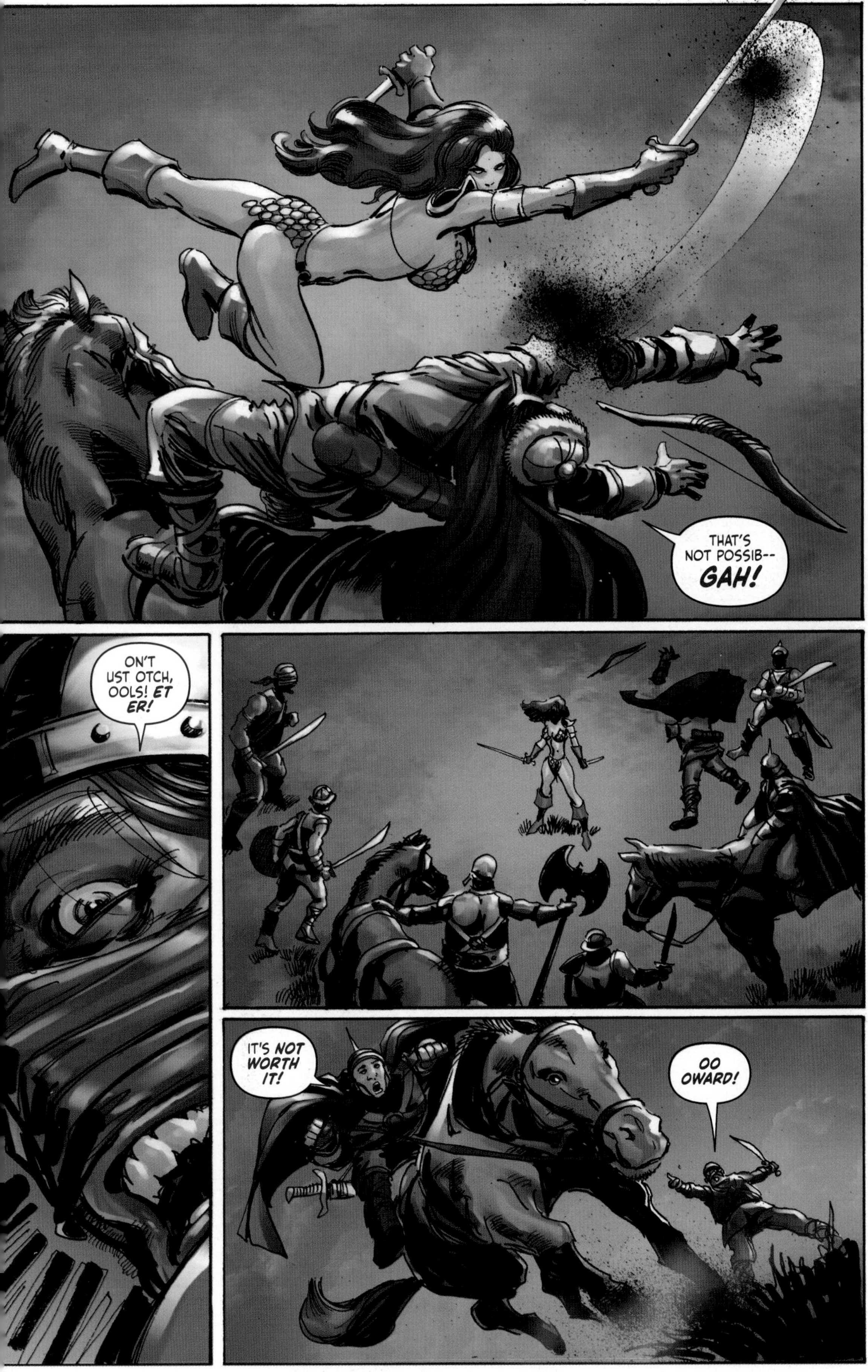

THAT'S NOT POSSIB-- GAH!
ON'T UST OTCH, OOLS! ET ER!
IT'S NOT WORTH IT!
OO OWARD!

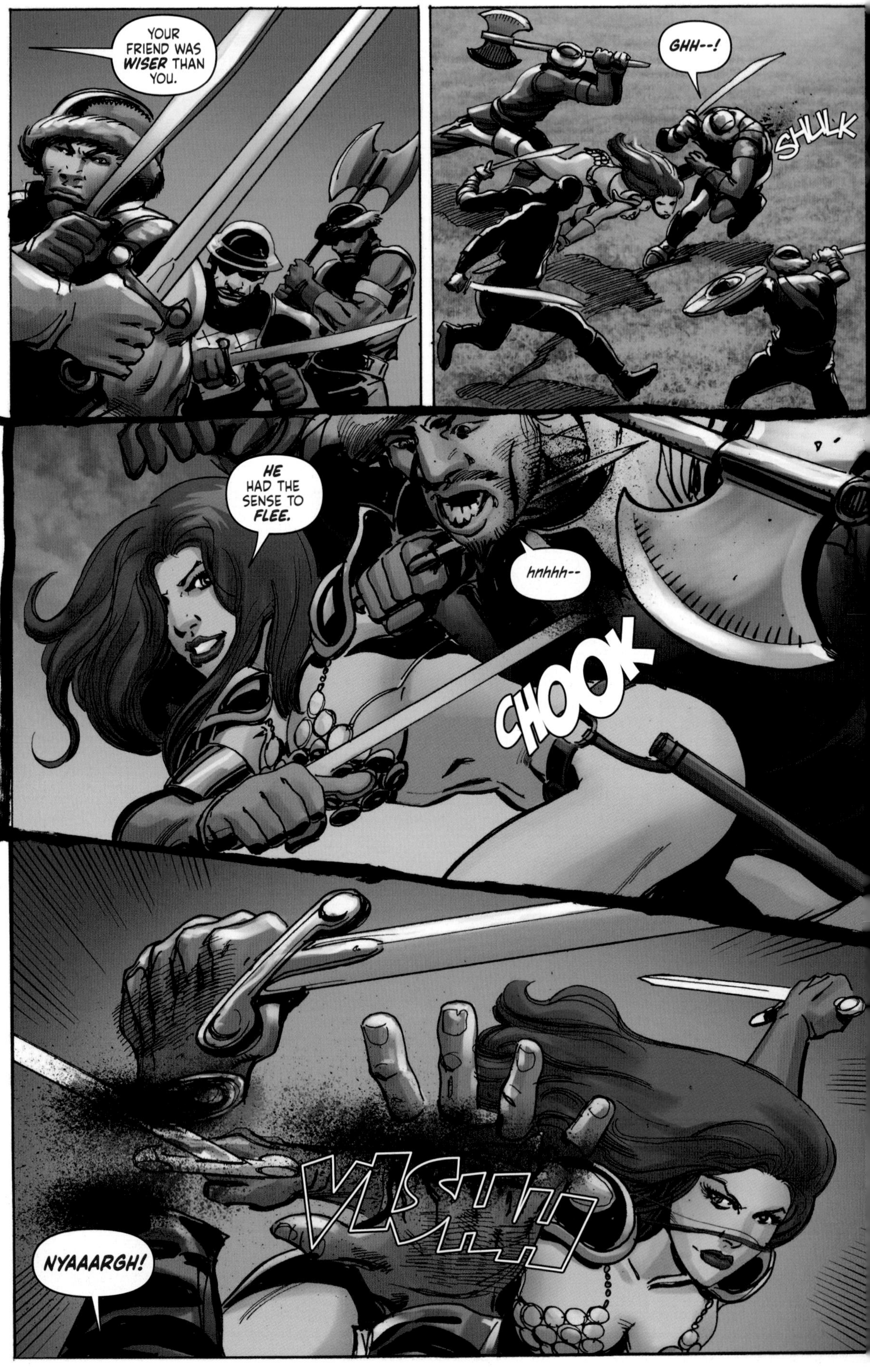
YOUR FRIEND WAS WISER THAN YOU.
GHH--!
SHULK
HE HAD THE SENSE TO FLEE.
hnhhh--
CHOOK
VISHH
NYAAARGH!

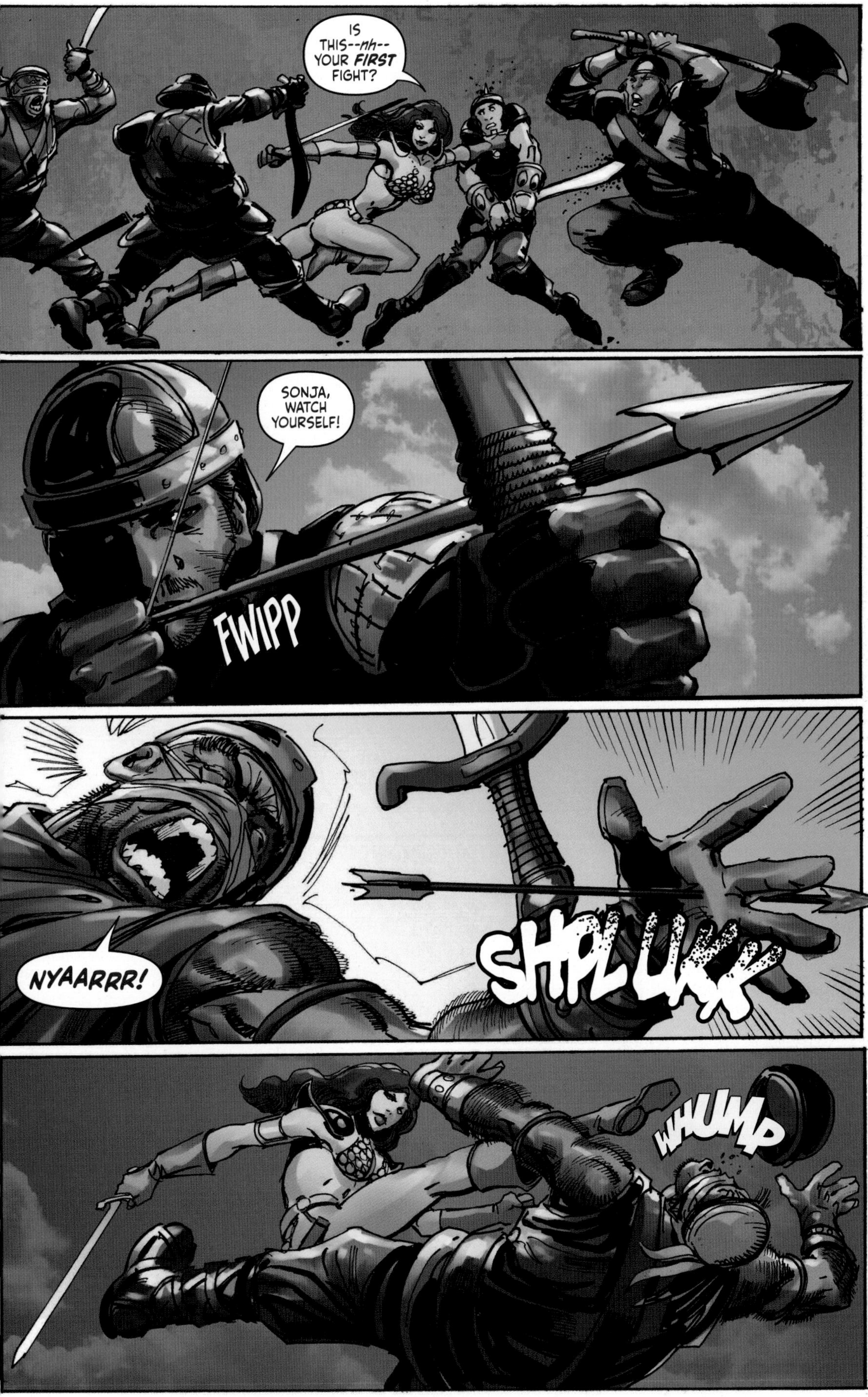
IS THIS--nh--YOUR FIRST FIGHT?
SONJA, WATCH YOURSELF!
FWIPP
NYAARRR!
SHPLUKK
WHUMP

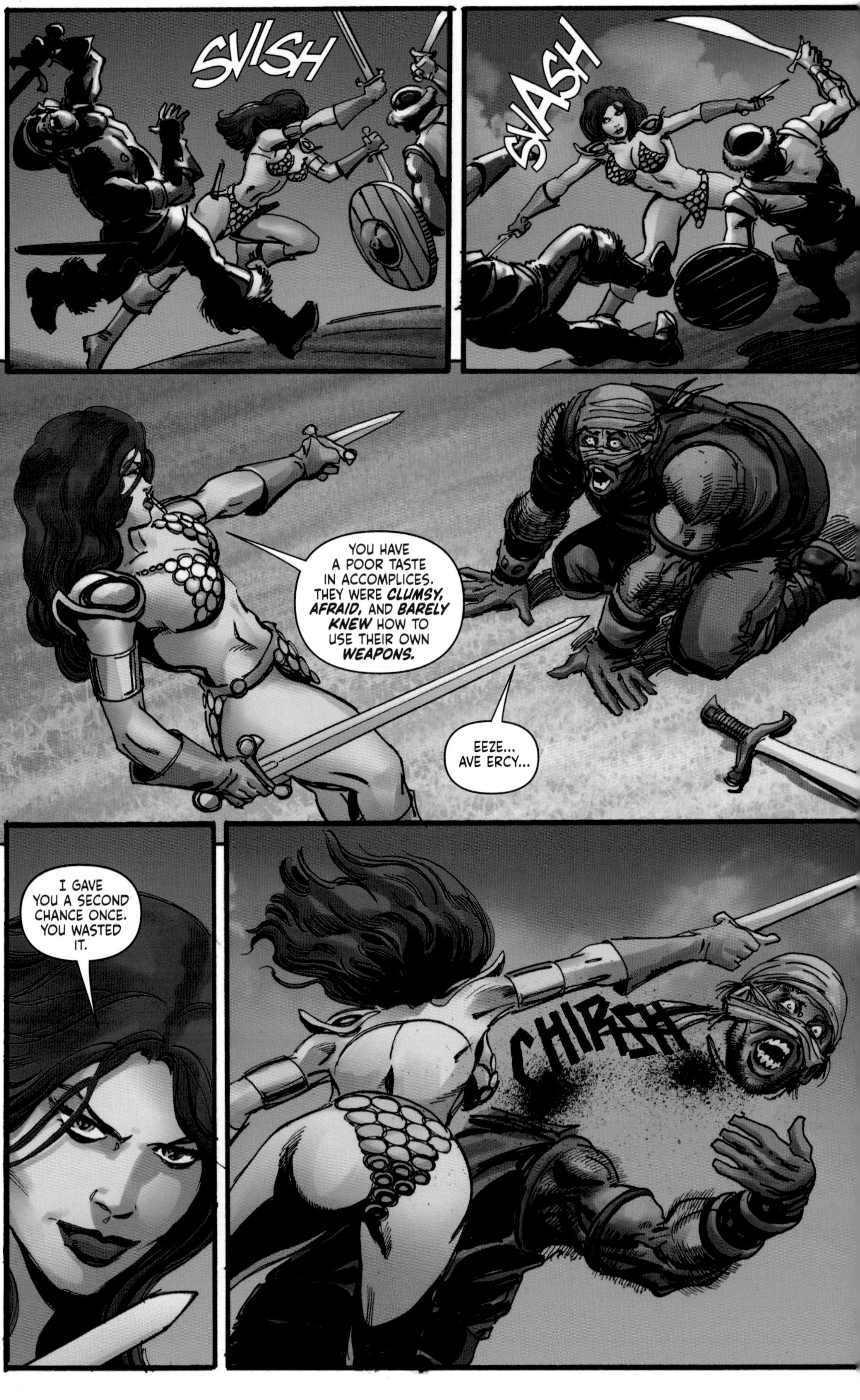
SVISH
SVASH
YOU HAVE A POOR TASTE IN ACCOMPLICES. THEY WERE CLUMSY, AFRAID, AND BARELY KNEW HOW TO USE THEIR OWN WEAPONS.
EEZE... AVE ERCY...
I GAVE YOU A SECOND CHANCE ONCE. YOU WASTED IT.
CHIRSH

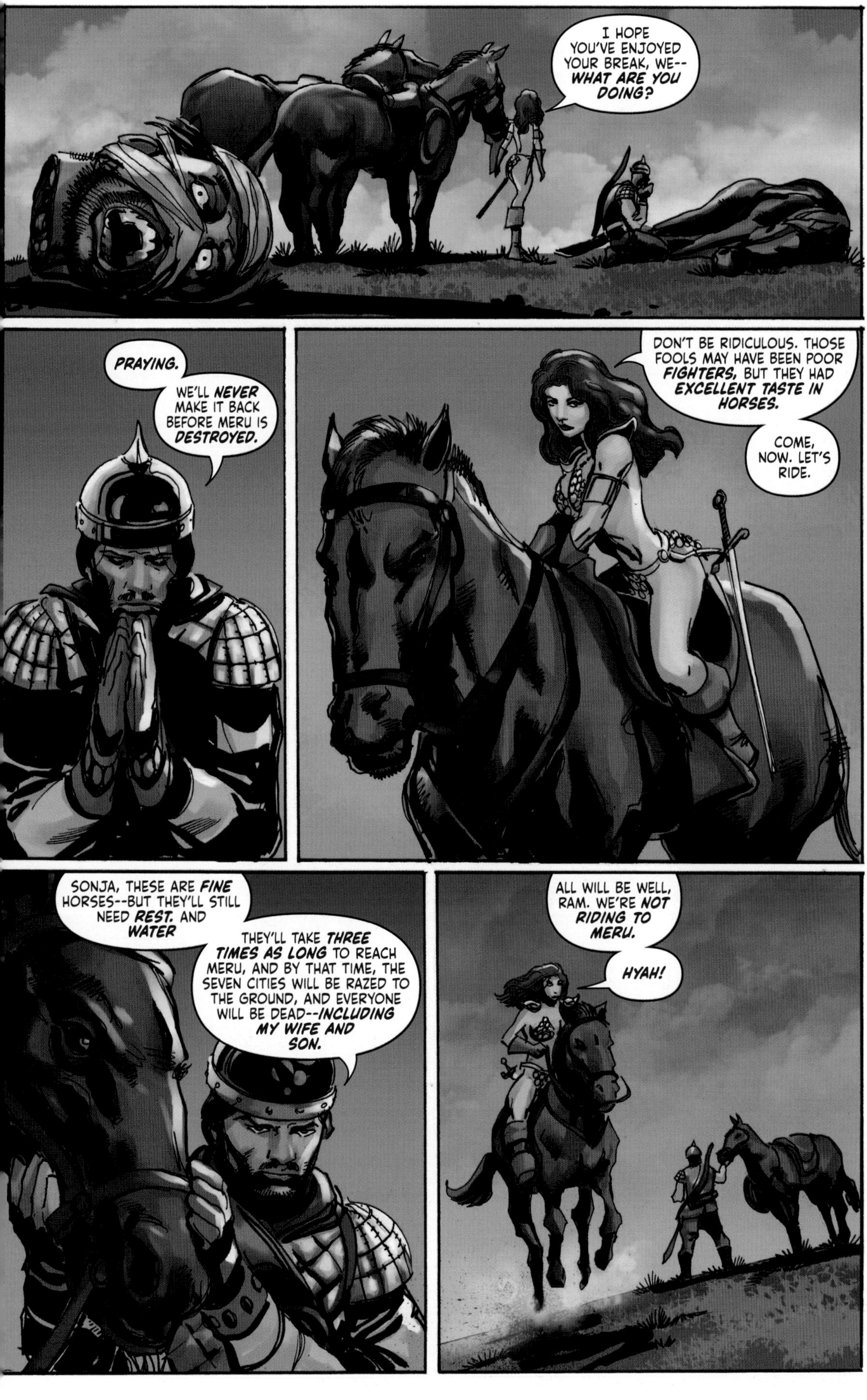

I HOPE YOU'VE ENJOYED YOUR BREAK, WE-- WHAT ARE YOU DOING?
PRAYING.
WE'LL NEVER MAKE IT BACK BEFORE MERU IS DESTROYED.
DON'T BE RIDICULOUS. THOSE FOOLS MAY HAVE BEEN POOR FIGHTERS, BUT THEY HAD EXCELLENT TASTE IN HORSES.
COME, NOW. LET'S RIDE.
SONJA, THESE ARE FINE HORSES--BUT THEY'LL STILL NEED REST. AND WATER
THEY'LL TAKE THREE TIMES AS LONG TO REACH MERU, AND BY THAT TIME, THE SEVEN CITIES WILL BE RAZED TO THE GROUND, AND EVERYONE WILL BE DEAD--INCLUDING MY WIFE AND SON.
ALL WILL BE WELL, RAM. WE'RE NOT RIDING TO MERU.
HYAH!

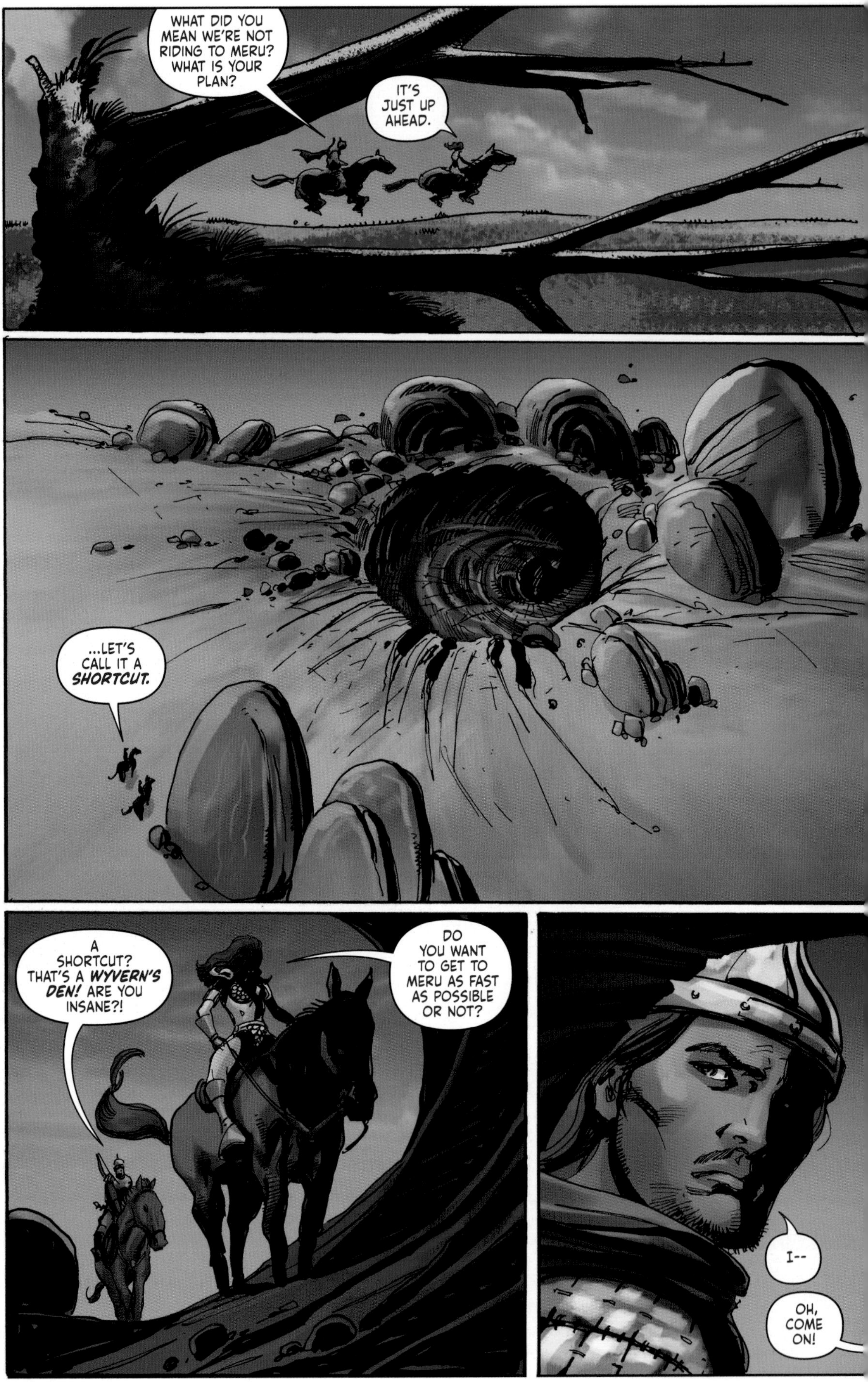

WHAT DID YOU MEAN WE'RE NOT RIDING TO MERU? WHAT IS YOUR PLAN?
IT'S JUST UP AHEAD.
...LET'S CALL IT A ***SHORTCUT.***
A SHORTCUT? THAT'S A ***WYVERN'S DEN!*** ARE YOU INSANE?!
DO YOU WANT TO GET TO MERU AS FAST AS POSSIBLE OR NOT?
I--
OH, COME ON!

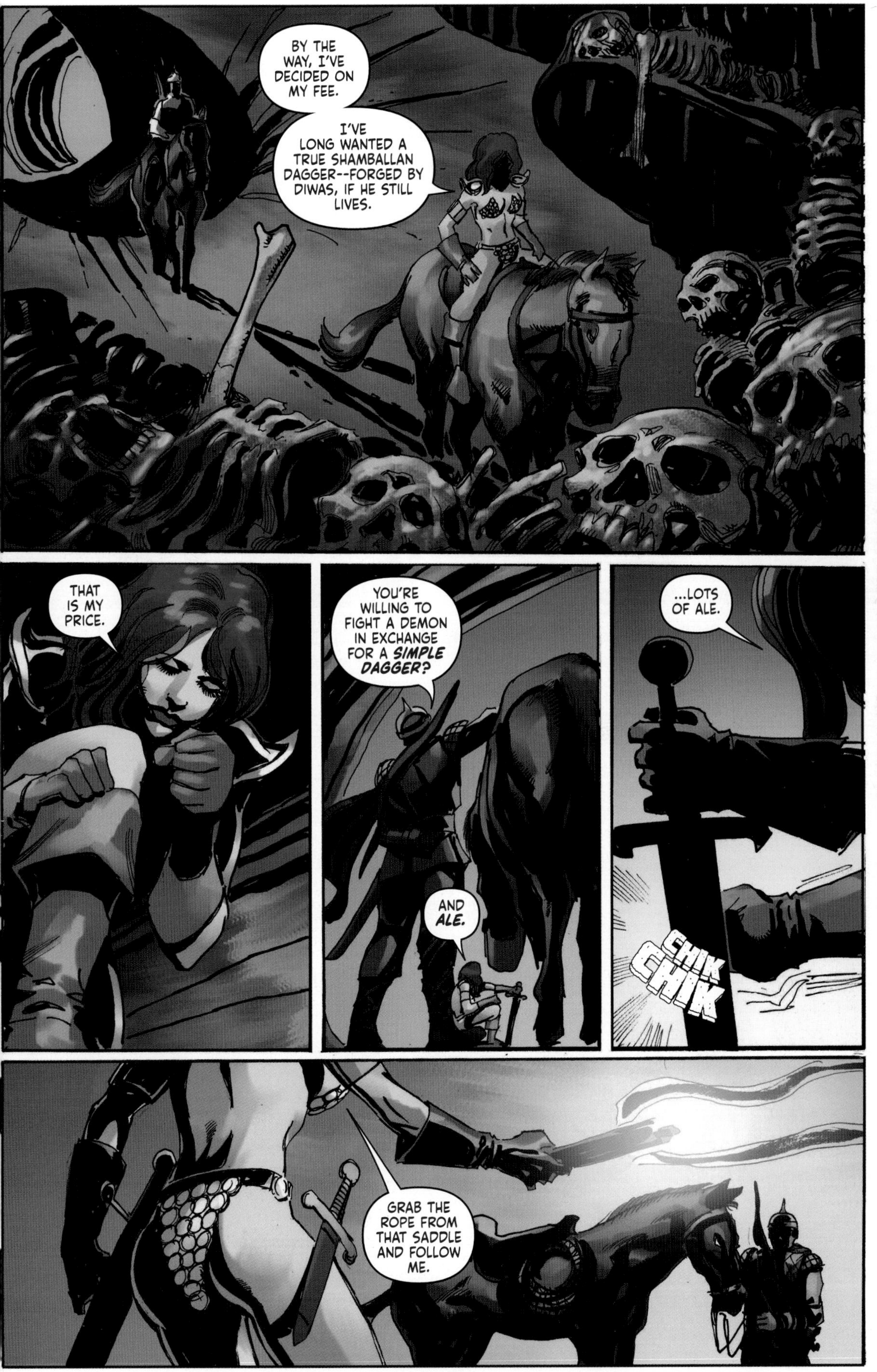
BY THE WAY, I'VE DECIDED ON MY FEE.
I'VE LONG WANTED A TRUE SHAMBALLAN DAGGER--FORGED BY DIWAS, IF HE STILL LIVES.
THAT IS MY PRICE.
YOU'RE WILLING TO FIGHT A DEMON IN EXCHANGE FOR A *SIMPLE DAGGER?*
AND *ALE.*
...LOTS OF ALE.
CHIK CHIK
GRAB THE ROPE FROM THAT SADDLE AND FOLLOW ME.

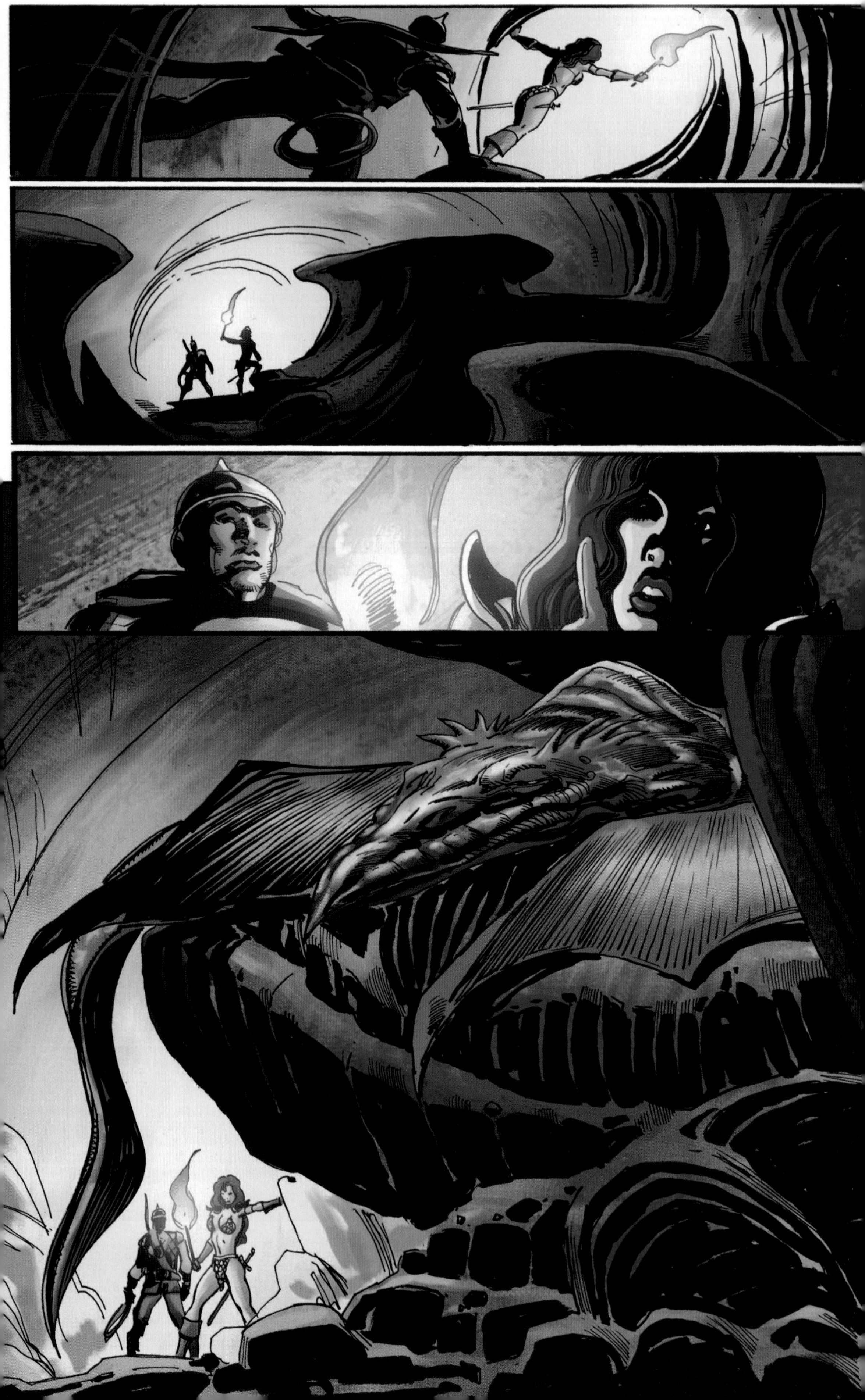

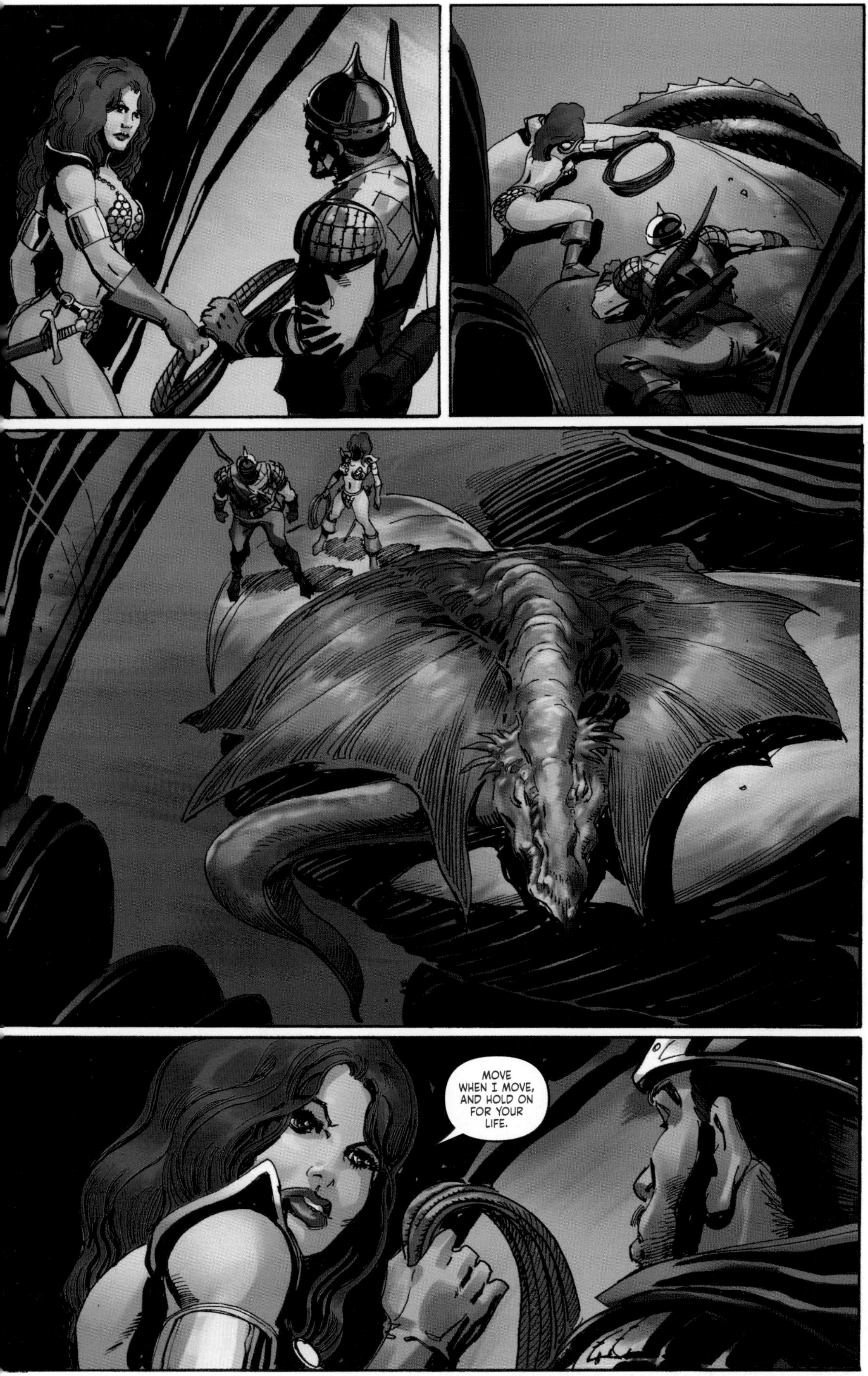
MOVE WHEN I MOVE, AND HOLD ON FOR YOUR LIFE.

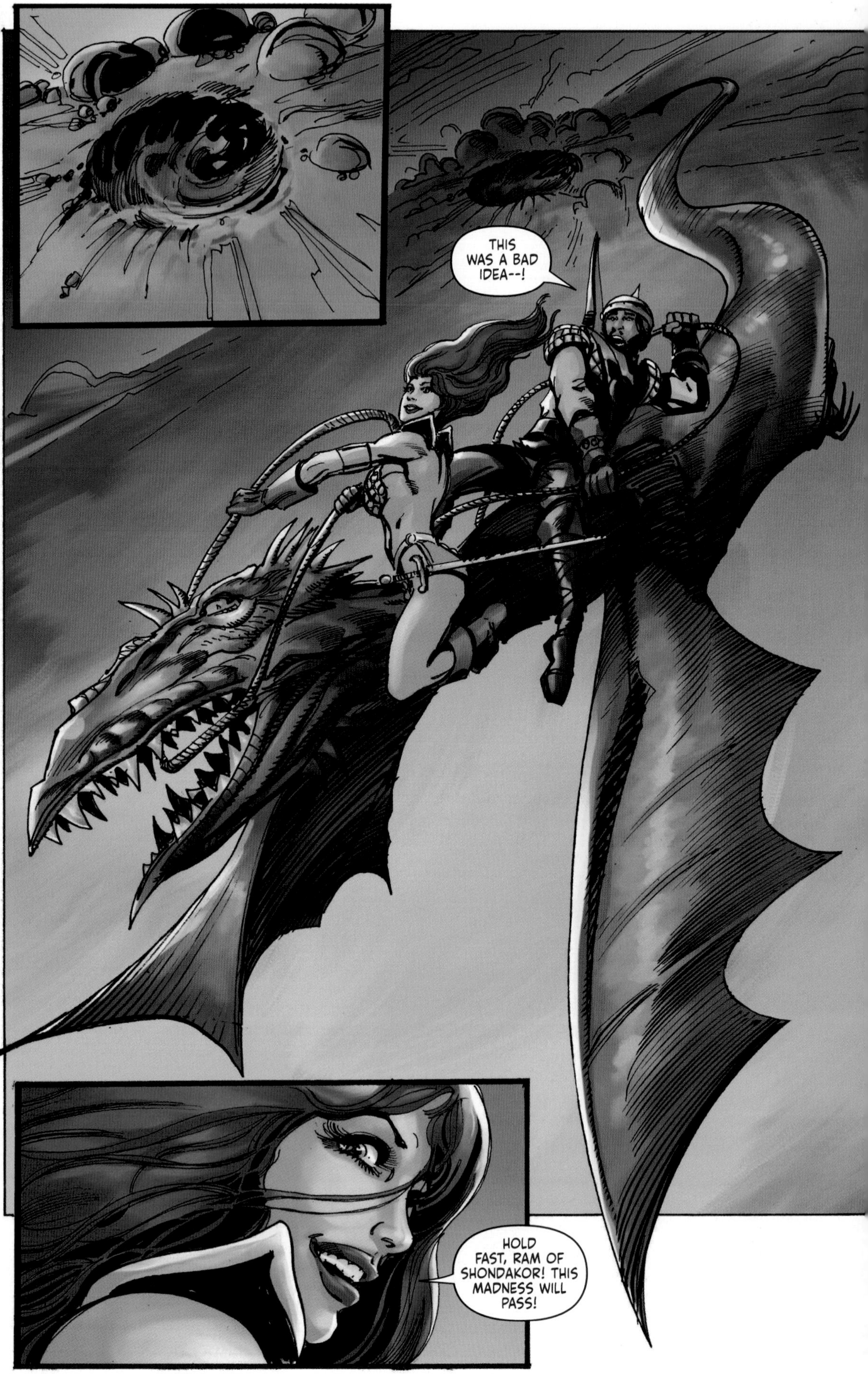
THIS WAS A BAD IDEA--!
HOLD FAST, RAM OF SHONDAKOR! THIS MADNESS WILL PASS!

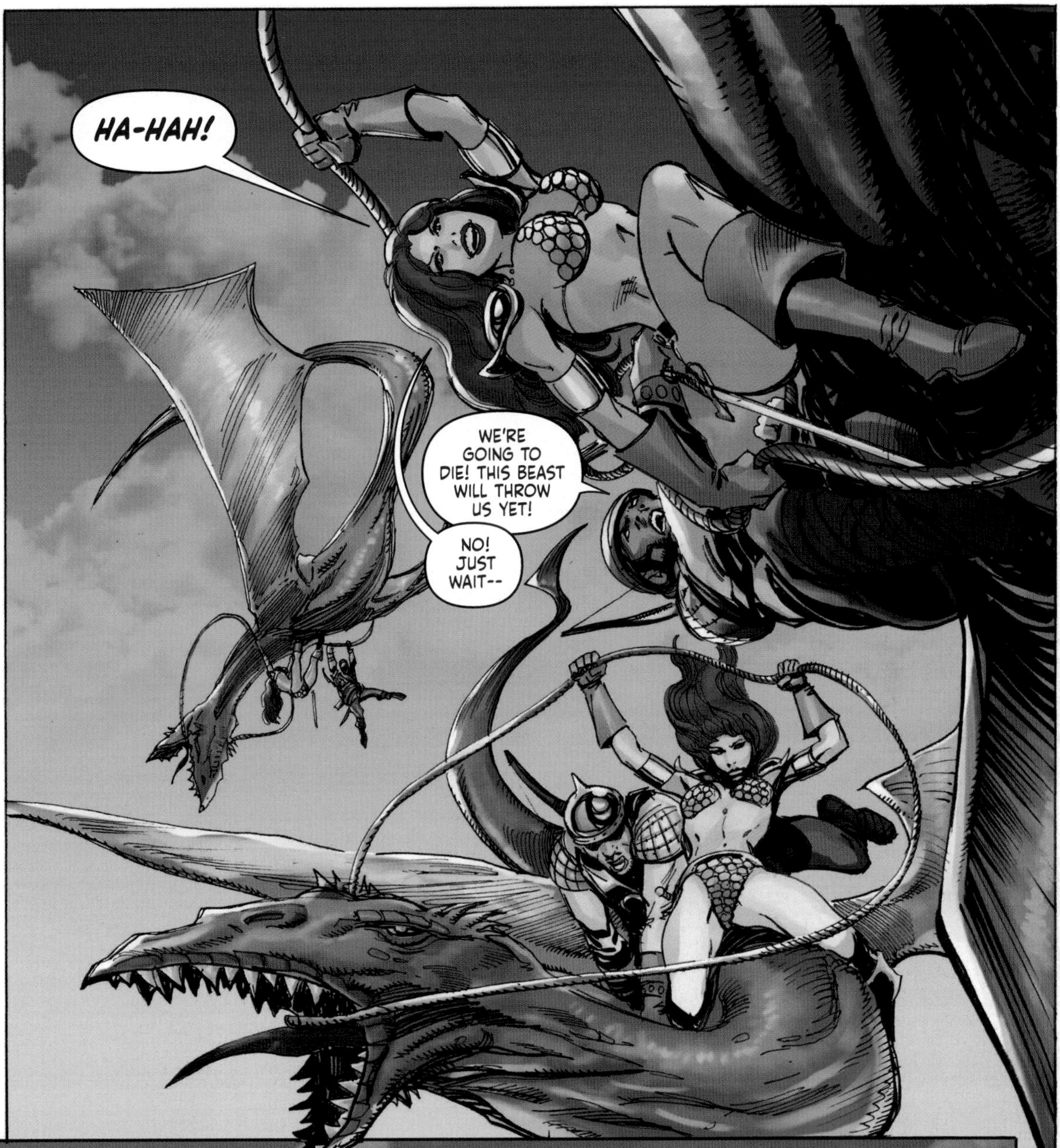
HA-HAH!
WE'RE GOING TO DIE! THIS BEAST WILL THROW US YET!
NO! JUST WAIT--

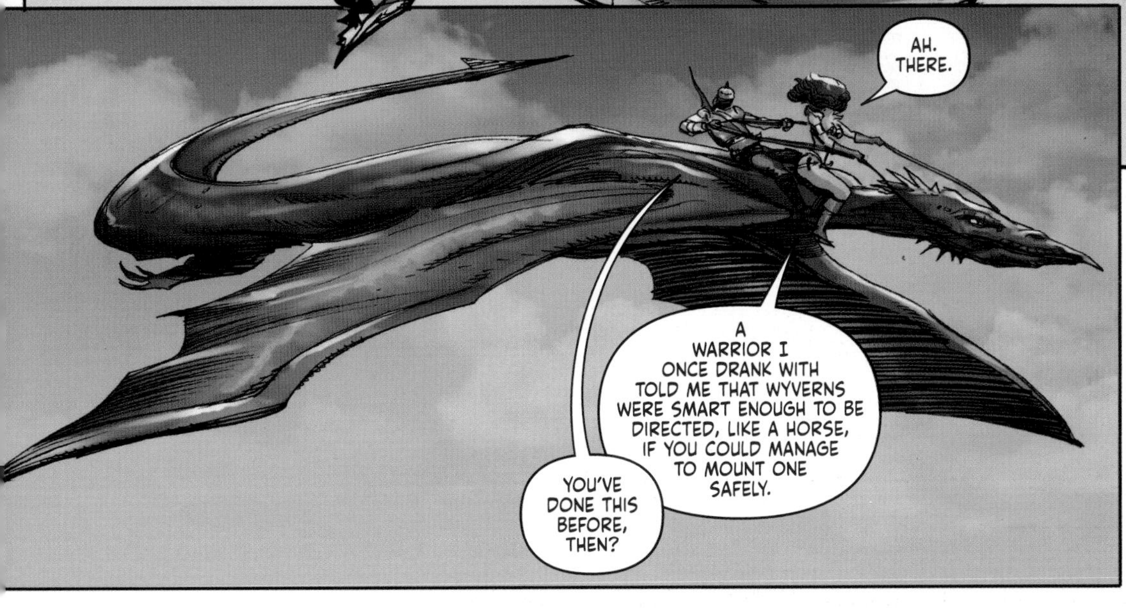
AH. THERE.
YOU'VE DONE THIS BEFORE, THEN?
A WARRIOR I ONCE DRANK WITH TOLD ME THAT WYVERNS WERE SMART ENOUGH TO BE DIRECTED, LIKE A HORSE, IF YOU COULD MANAGE TO MOUNT ONE SAFELY.

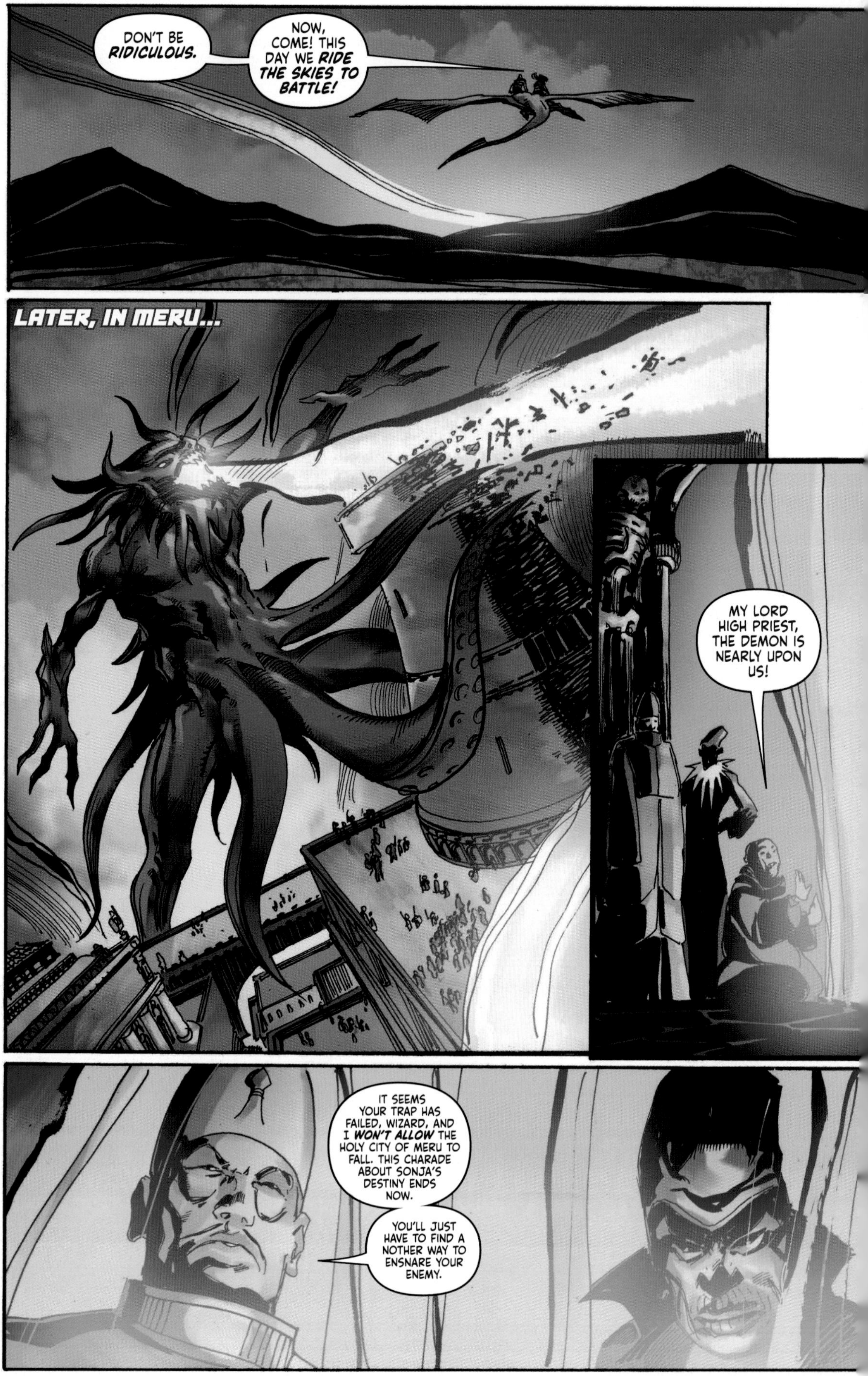
DON'T BE RIDICULOUS.
NOW, COME! THIS DAY WE RIDE THE SKIES TO BATTLE!
LATER, IN MERU...
MY LORD HIGH PRIEST, THE DEMON IS NEARLY UPON US!
IT SEEMS YOUR TRAP HAS FAILED, WIZARD, AND I WON'T ALLOW THE HOLY CITY OF MERU TO FALL. THIS CHARADE ABOUT SONJA'S DESTINY ENDS NOW.
YOU'LL JUST HAVE TO FIND A NOTHER WAY TO ENSNARE YOUR ENEMY.

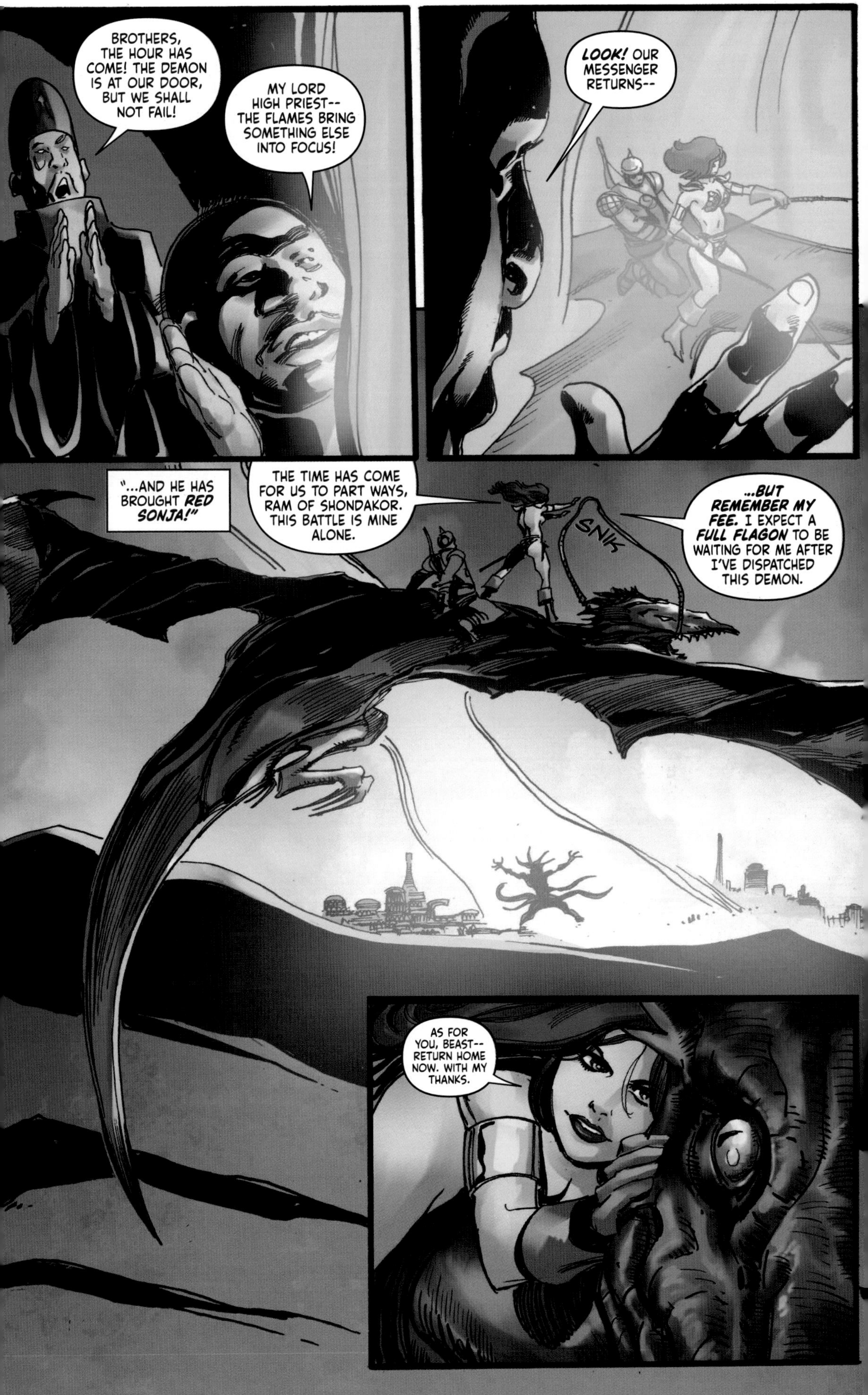
BROTHERS, THE HOUR HAS COME! THE DEMON IS AT OUR DOOR, BUT WE SHALL NOT FAIL!
MY LORD HIGH PRIEST-- THE FLAMES BRING SOMETHING ELSE INTO FOCUS!
LOOK! OUR MESSENGER RETURNS--
"...AND HE HAS BROUGHT RED SONJA!"
THE TIME HAS COME FOR US TO PART WAYS, RAM OF SHONDAKOR. THIS BATTLE IS MINE ALONE.
SNIK
...BUT REMEMBER MY FEE. I EXPECT A FULL FLAGON TO BE WAITING FOR ME AFTER I'VE DISPATCHED THIS DEMON.
AS FOR YOU, BEAST-- RETURN HOME NOW. WITH MY THANKS.

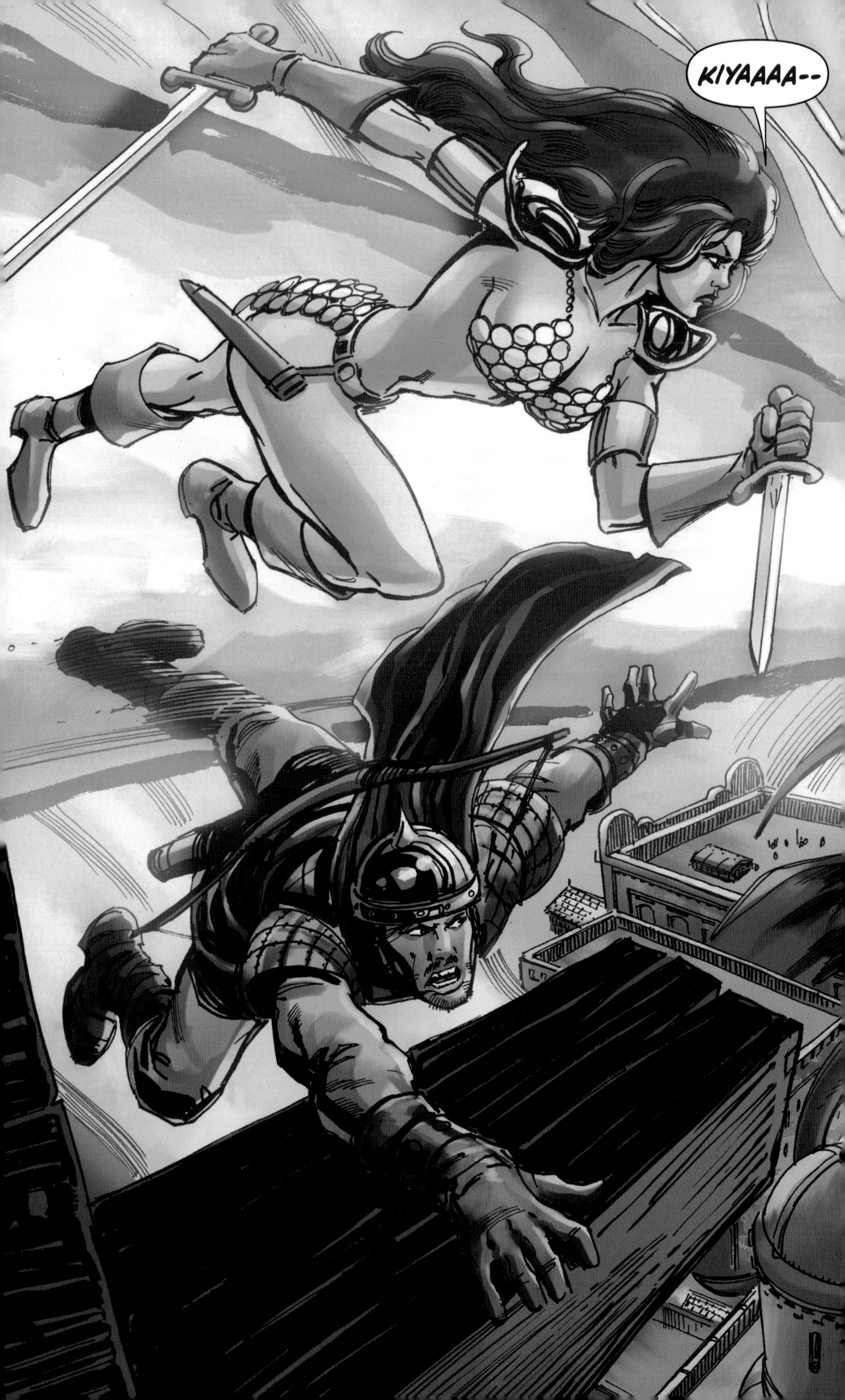
KIYAAAA--

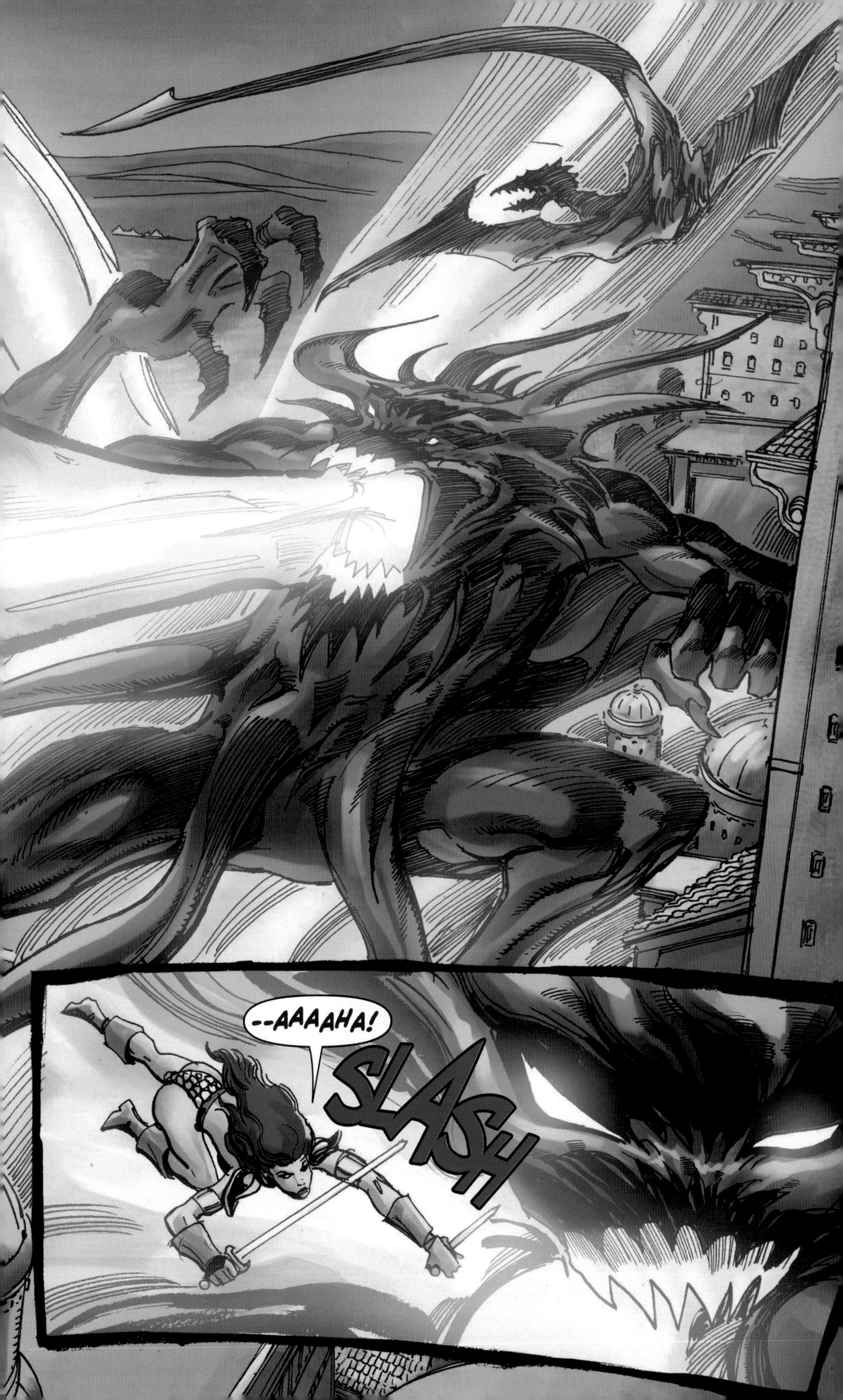
--AAAAHA!
SLASH

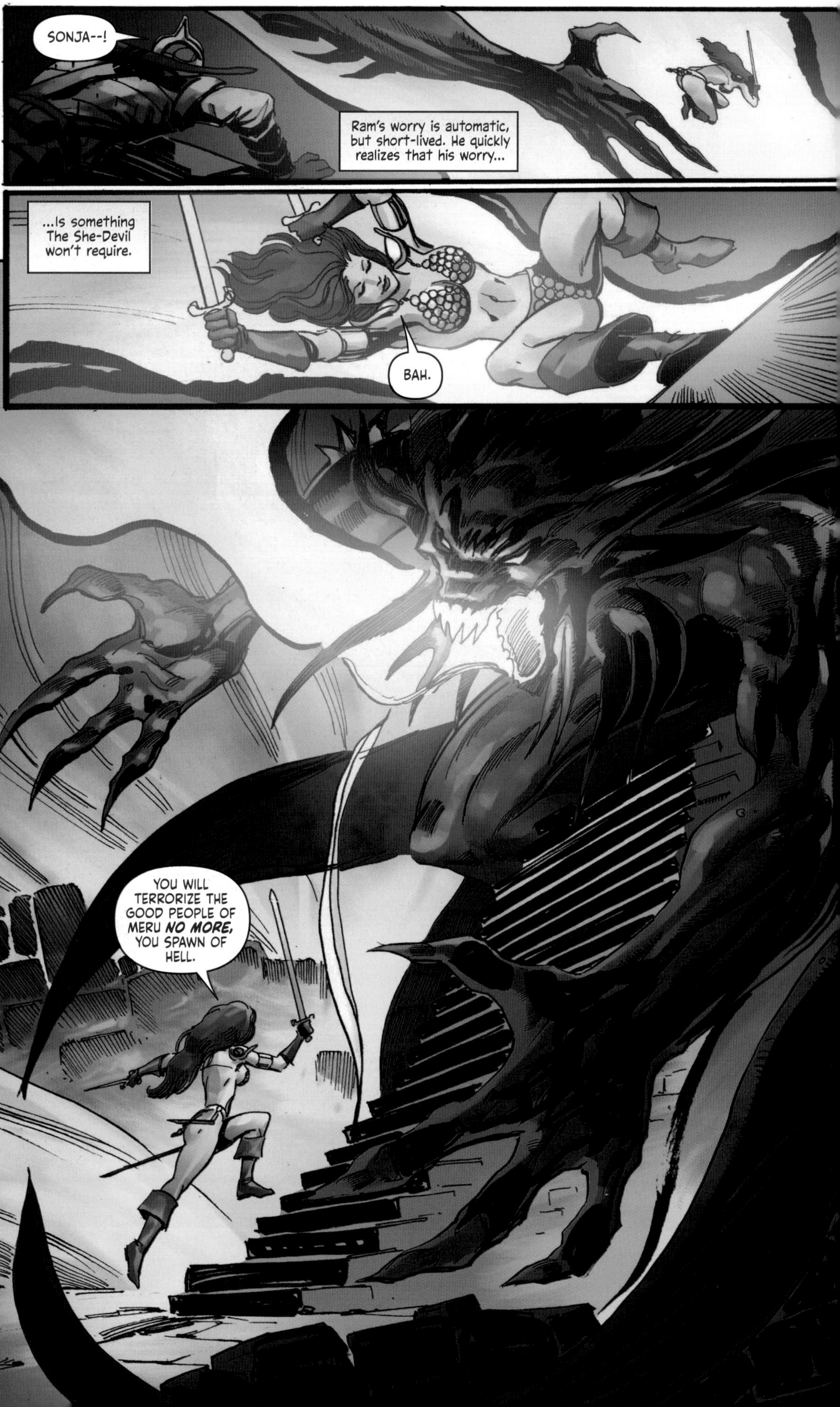
SONJA--!
Ram's worry is automatic, but short-lived. He quickly realizes that his worry...
...Is something The She-Devil won't require.
BAH.
YOU WILL TERRORIZE THE GOOD PEOPLE OF MERU **NO MORE,** YOU SPAWN OF HELL.

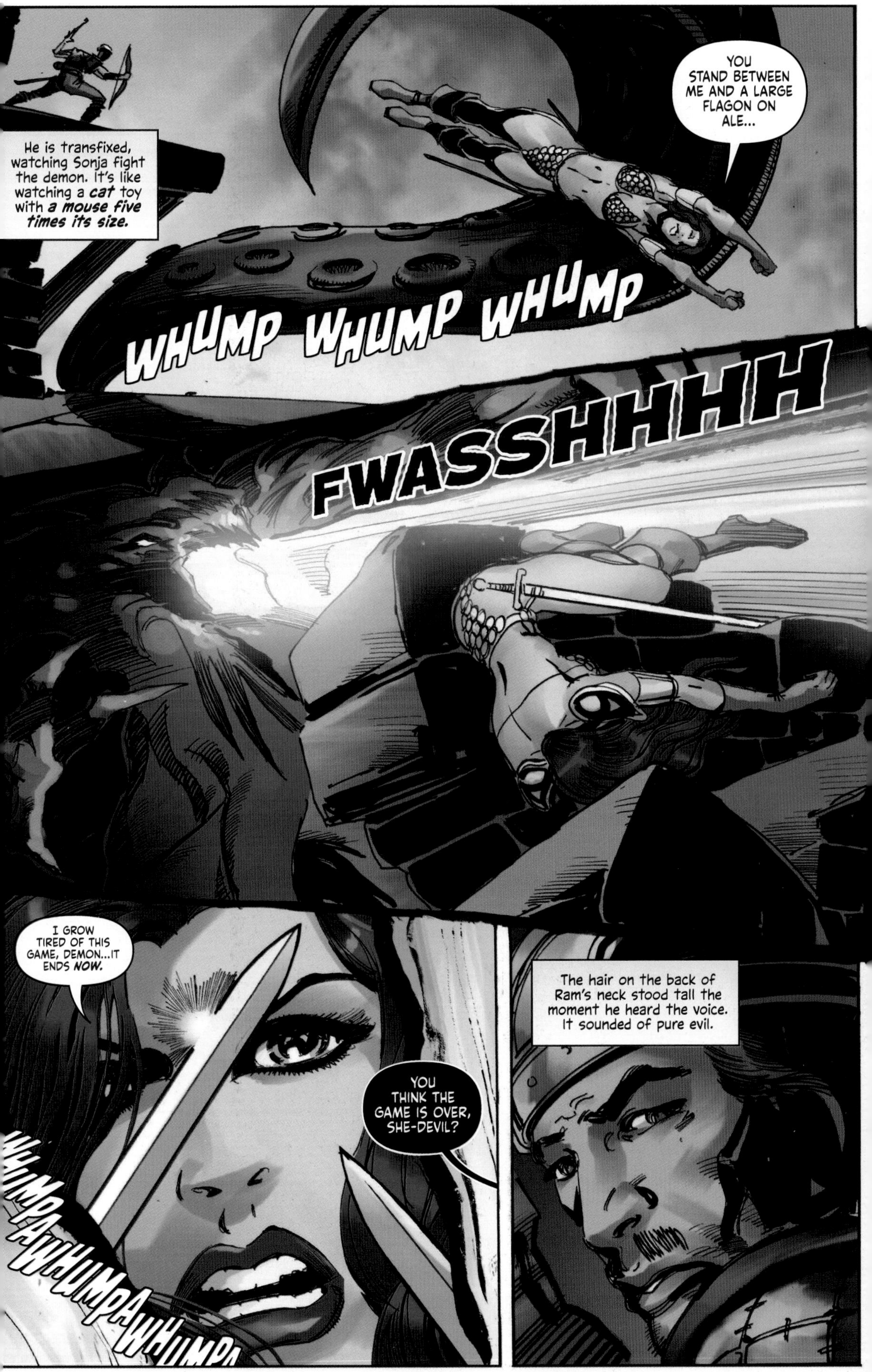
He is transfixed, watching Sonja fight the demon. It's like watching a *cat* toy with ***a mouse five times its size.***
YOU STAND BETWEEN ME AND A LARGE FLAGON ON ALE...
WHUMP WHUMP WHUMP
FWASSHHHH
I GROW TIRED OF THIS GAME, DEMON...IT ENDS ***NOW.***
YOU THINK THE GAME IS OVER, SHE-DEVIL?
The hair on the back of Ram's neck stood tall the moment he heard the voice. It sounded of pure evil.

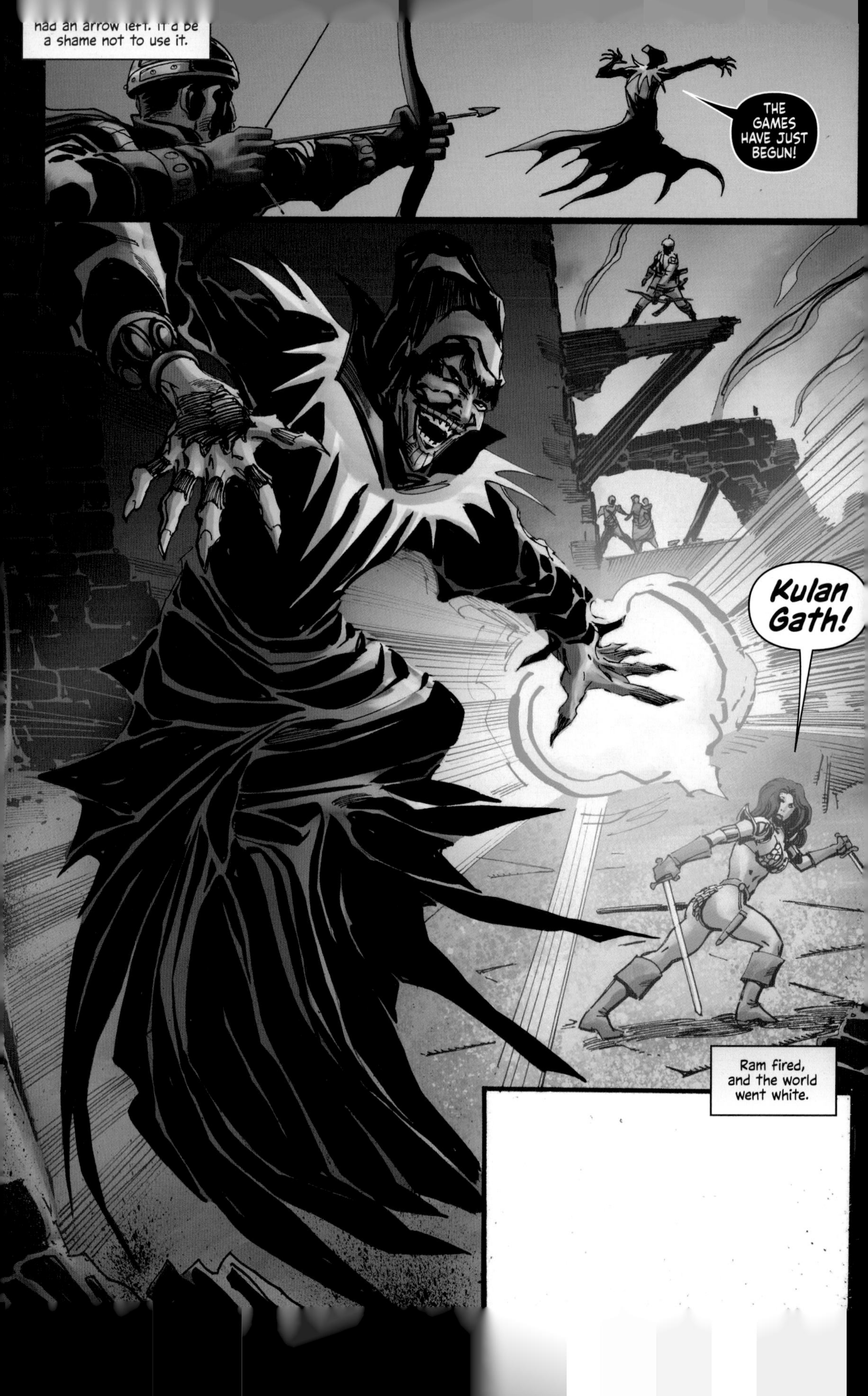
had an arrow left. It'd be
a shame not to use it.
THE GAMES HAVE JUST BEGUN!
Kulan Gath!
Ram fired, and the world went white.

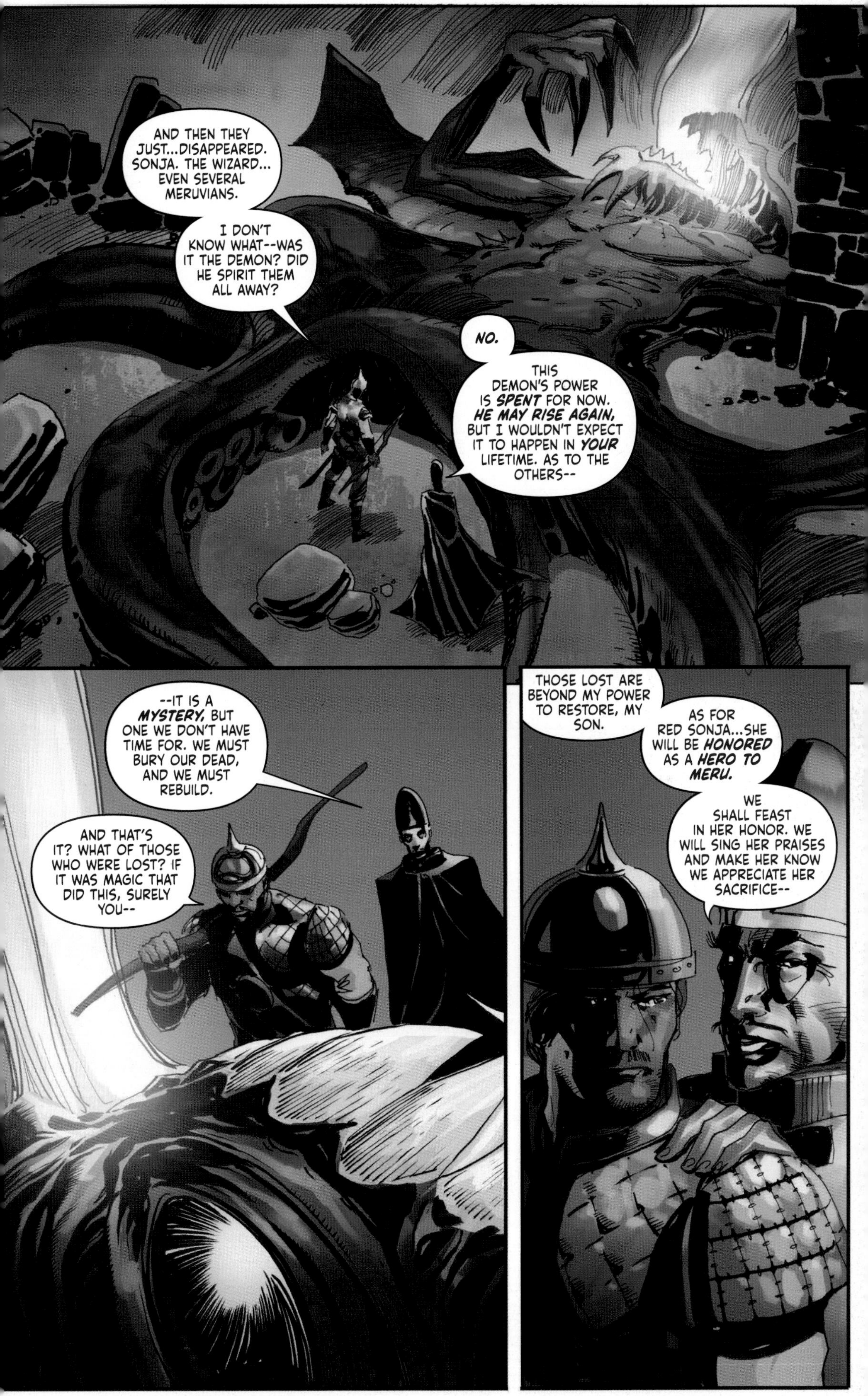
AND THEN THEY JUST...DISAPPEARED. SONJA. THE WIZARD... EVEN SEVERAL MERUVIANS.
I DON'T KNOW WHAT--WAS IT THE DEMON? DID HE SPIRIT THEM ALL AWAY?
NO.
THIS DEMON'S POWER IS SPENT FOR NOW. HE MAY RISE AGAIN, BUT I WOULDN'T EXPECT IT TO HAPPEN IN YOUR LIFETIME. AS TO THE OTHERS--
--IT IS A MYSTERY, BUT ONE WE DON'T HAVE TIME FOR. WE MUST BURY OUR DEAD, AND WE MUST REBUILD.
AND THAT'S IT? WHAT OF THOSE WHO WERE LOST? IF IT WAS MAGIC THAT DID THIS, SURELY YOU--
THOSE LOST ARE BEYOND MY POWER TO RESTORE, MY SON.
AS FOR RED SONJA...SHE WILL BE HONORED AS A HERO TO MERU.
WE SHALL FEAST IN HER HONOR. WE WILL SING HER PRAISES AND MAKE HER KNOW WE APPRECIATE HER SACRIFICE--

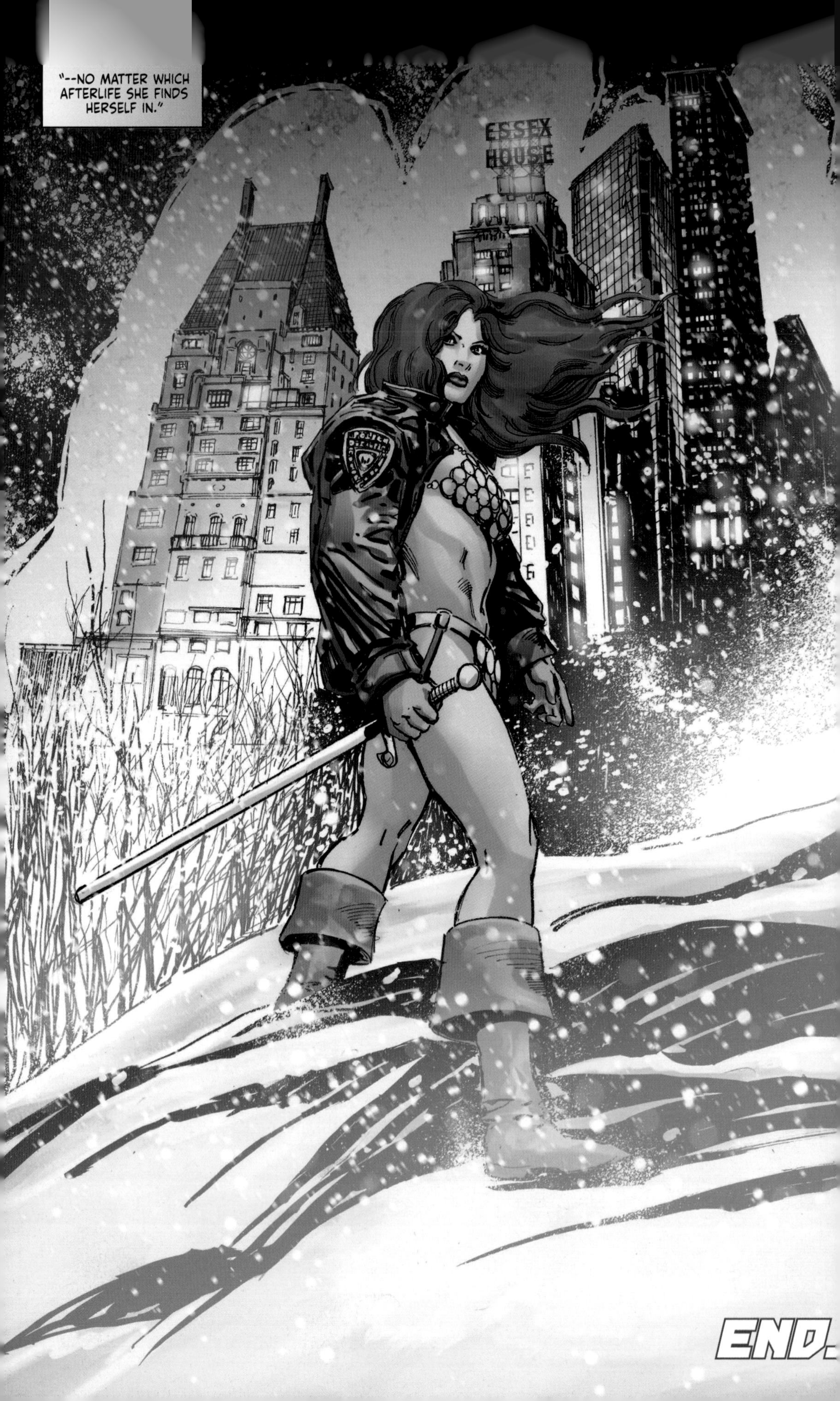
"--NO MATTER WHICH AFTERLIFE SHE FINDS HERSELF IN."
ESSEX HOUSE
END.

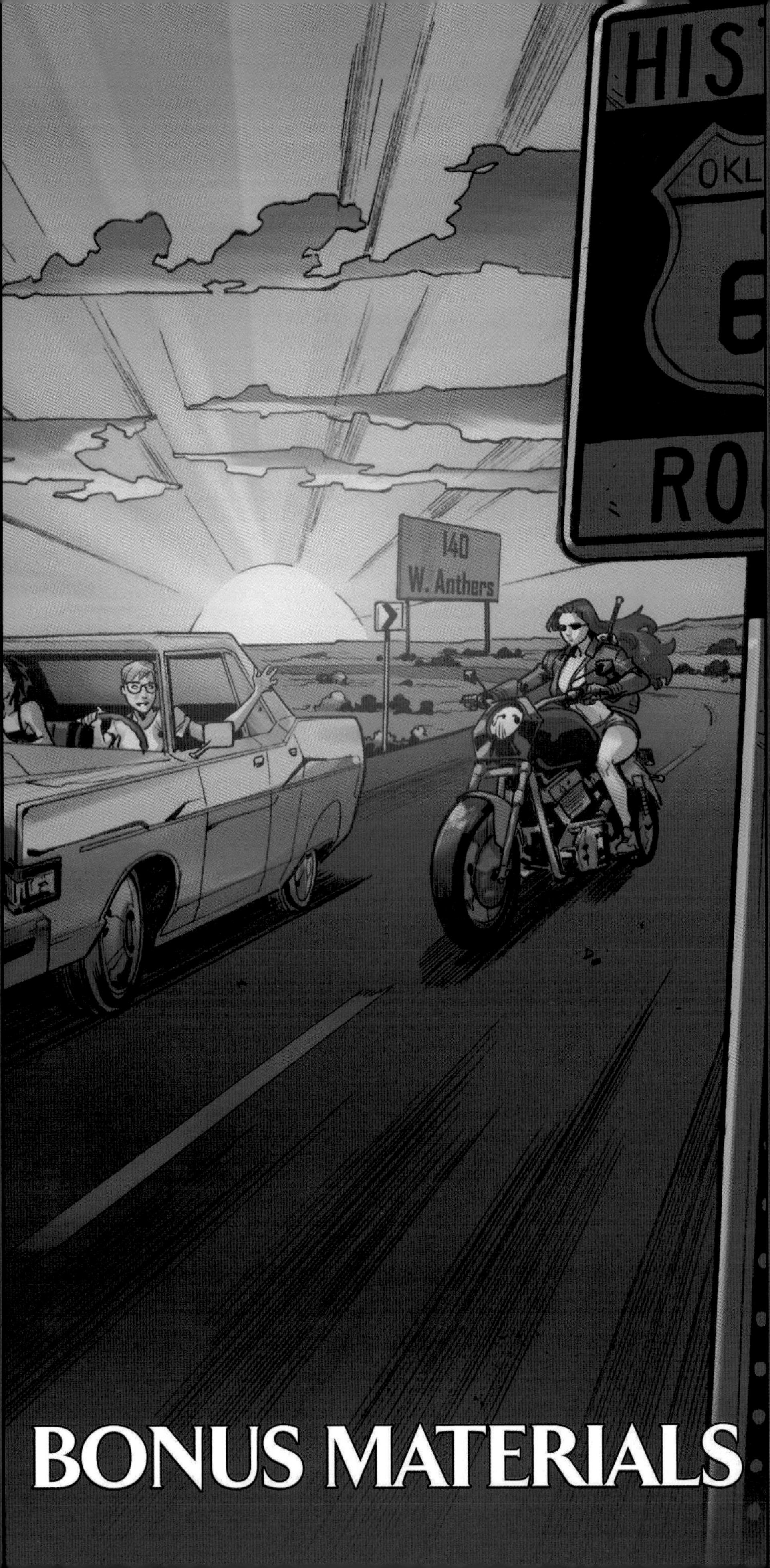
140
W. Anthers

BONUS MATERIALS

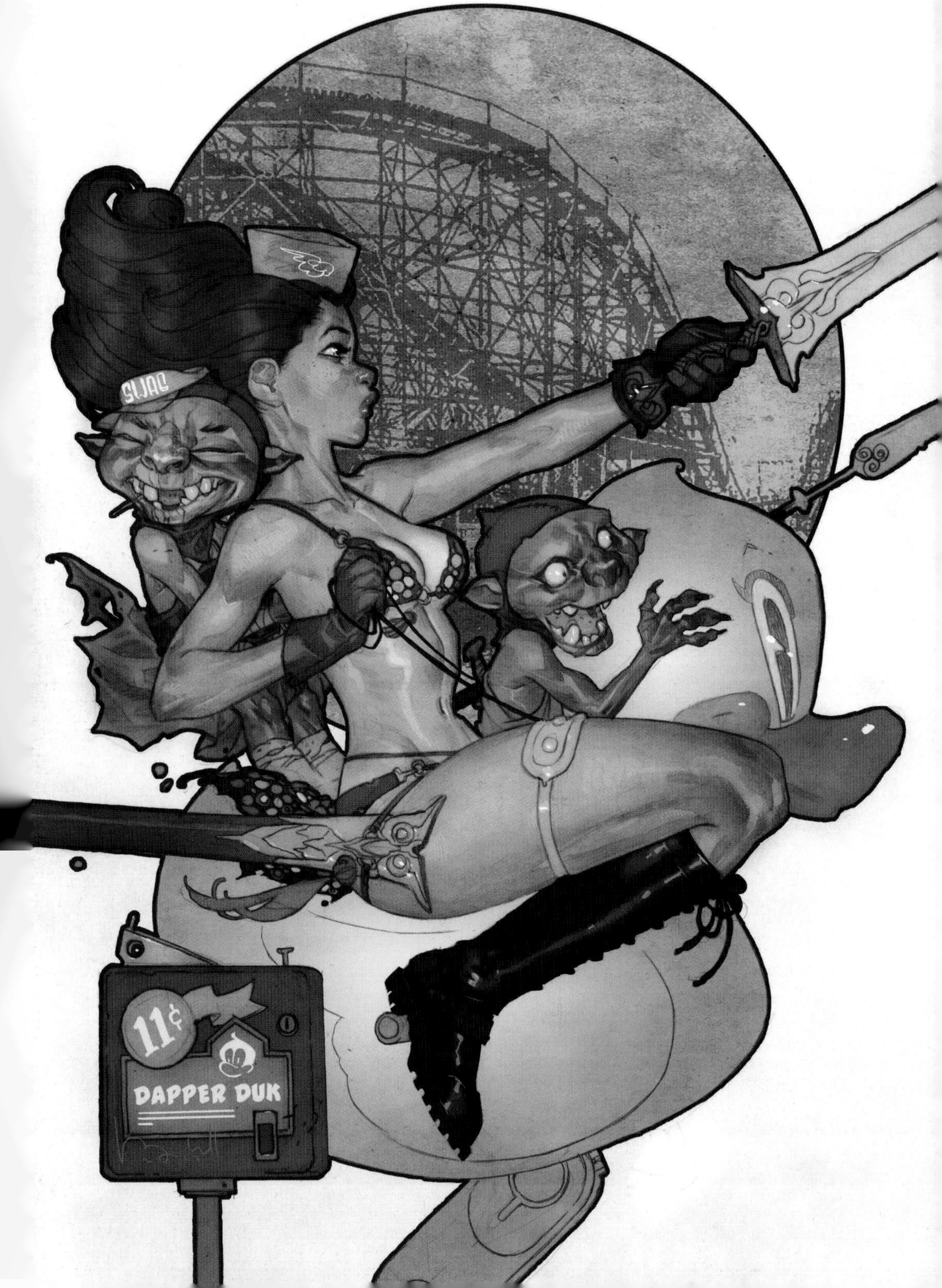
SWAG
11¢
DAPPER DUK

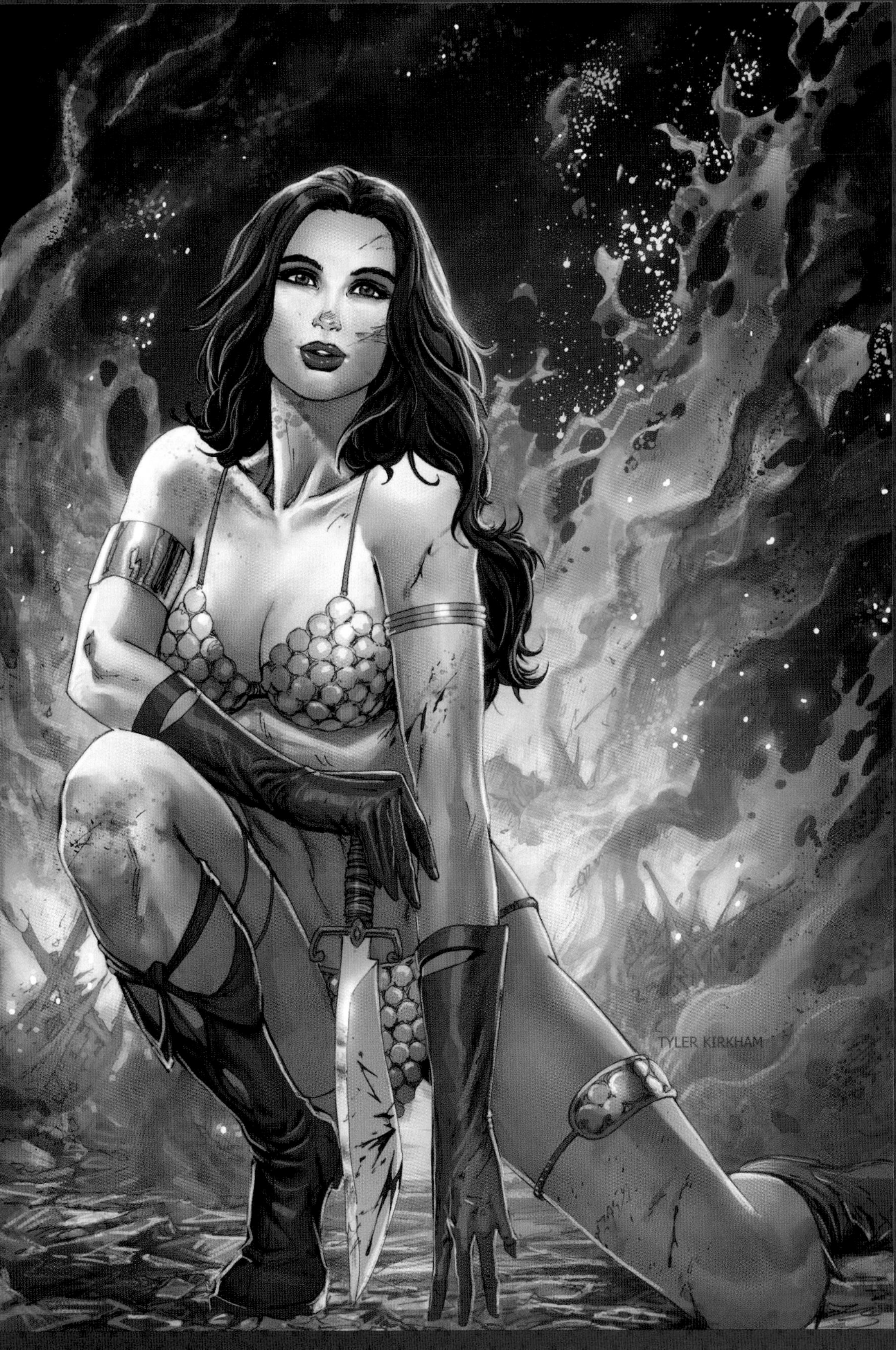
TYLER KIRKHAM

ISSUE #7: COVER ART BY TYLER KIRKHAM, COLORS BY ROMULO FAJARDO

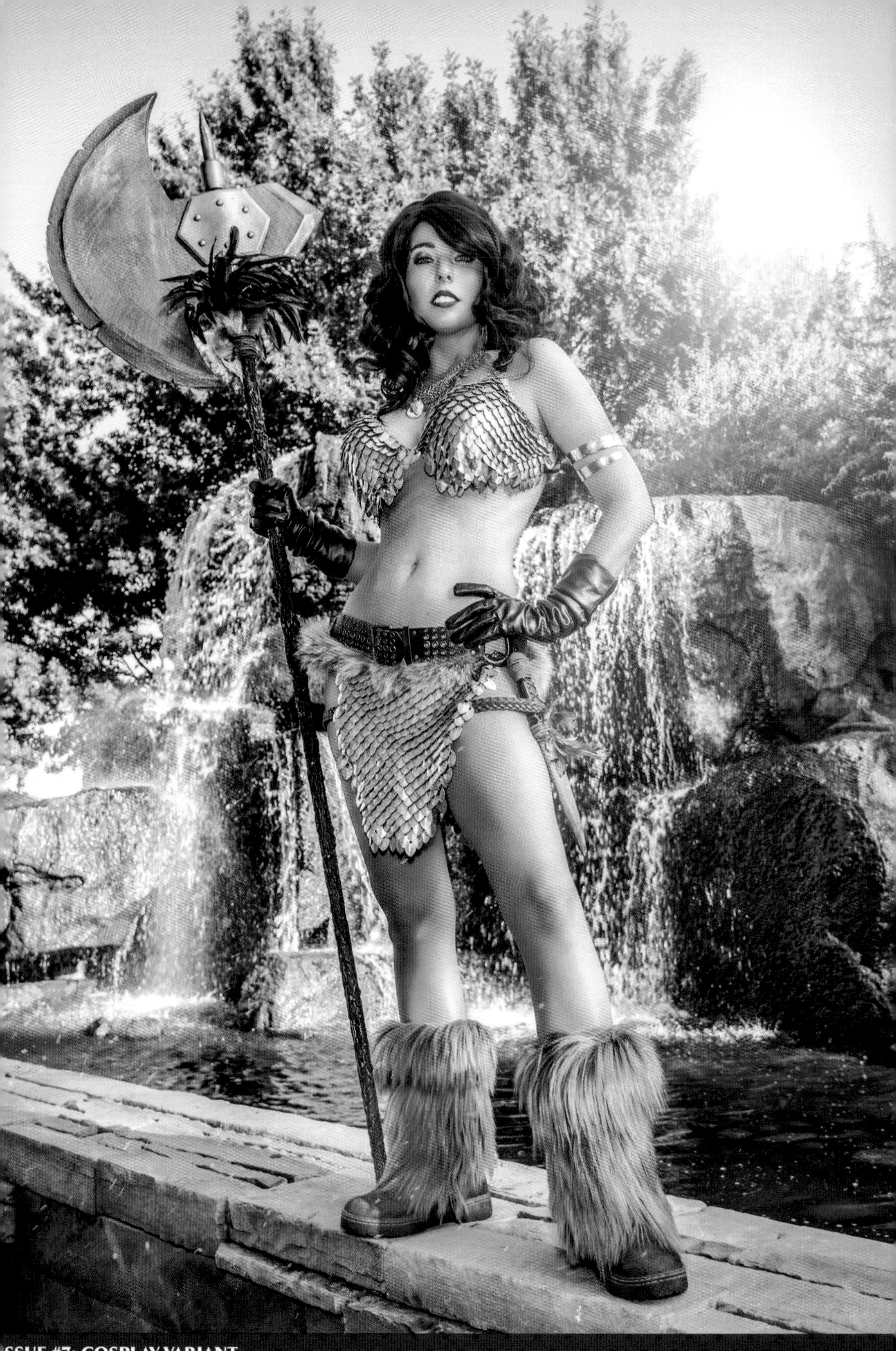

SSUE #7: COSPLAY VARIANT

MODEL: KRYSTLE STARR (TWITTER: @THEKRYSTLESTARR), PHOTOGRAPHER: DAVID NGO

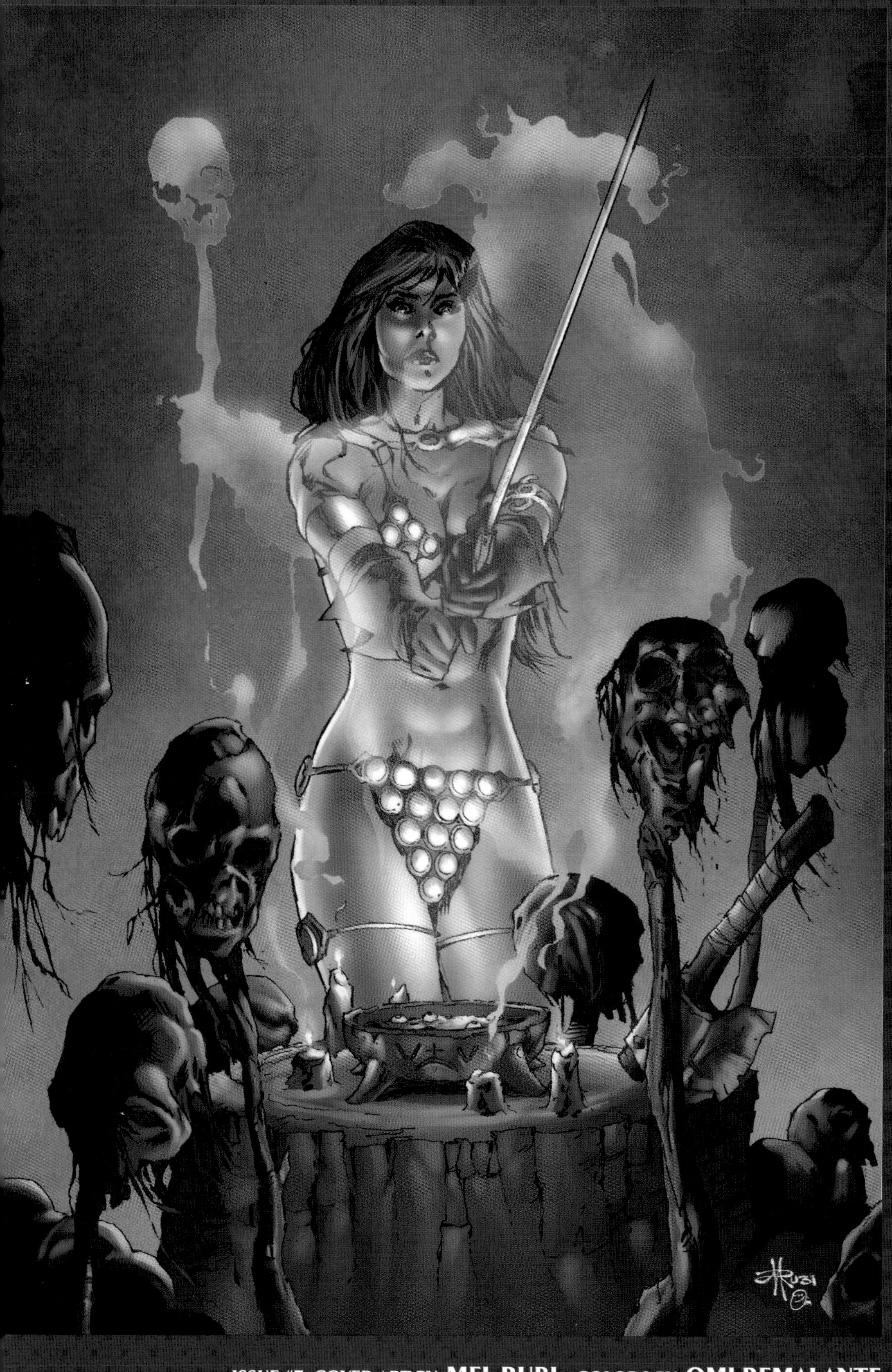

ISSUE #7: COVER ART BY MEL RUBI, COLORS BY OMI REMALANTE

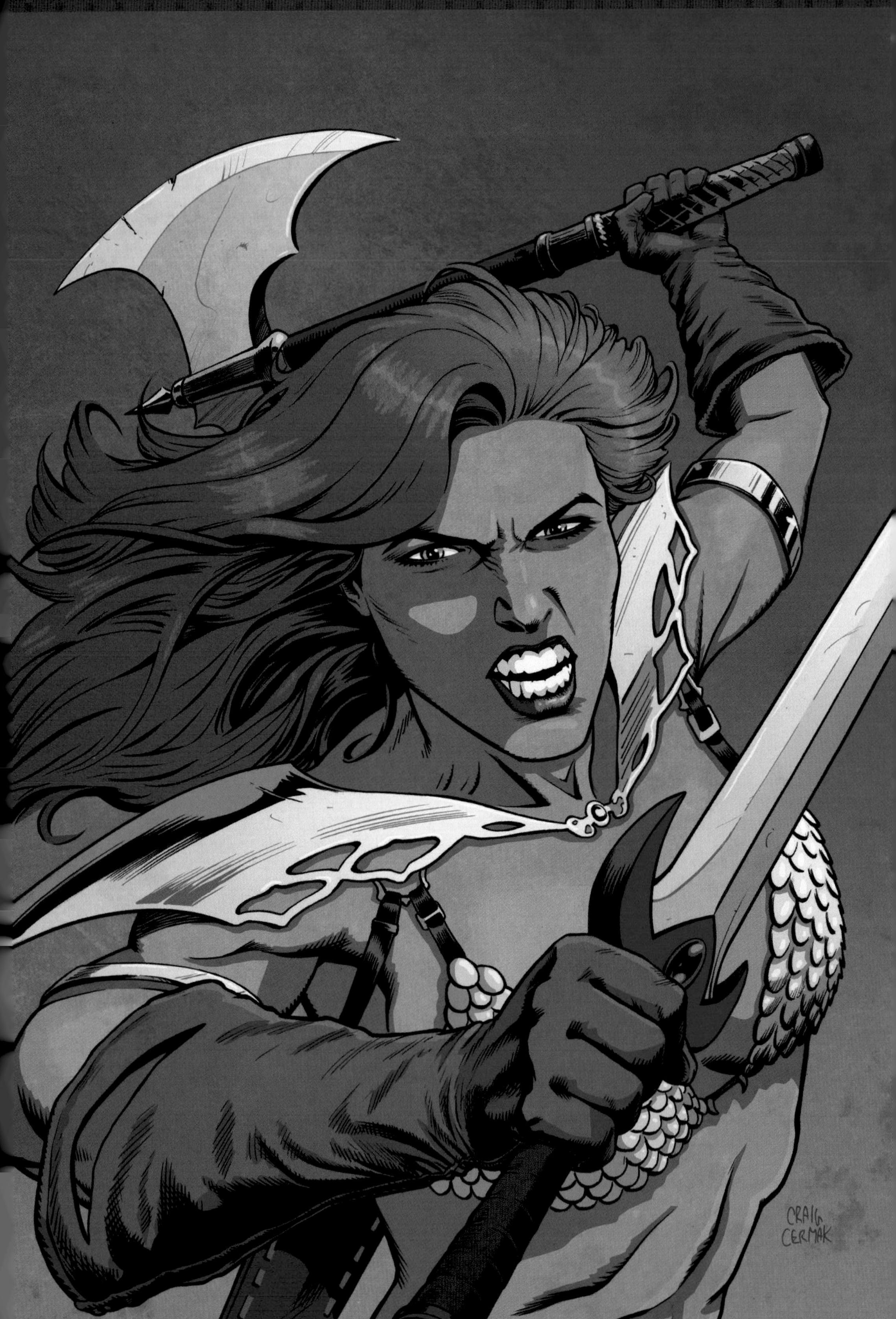
CRAIG
CERMAK

ISSUE #7: GROUPEES EXCLUSIVE COVER
ART BY CRAIG CERMAK COLORS BY CHRIS O'HALLORAN (GROUPEES.COM)

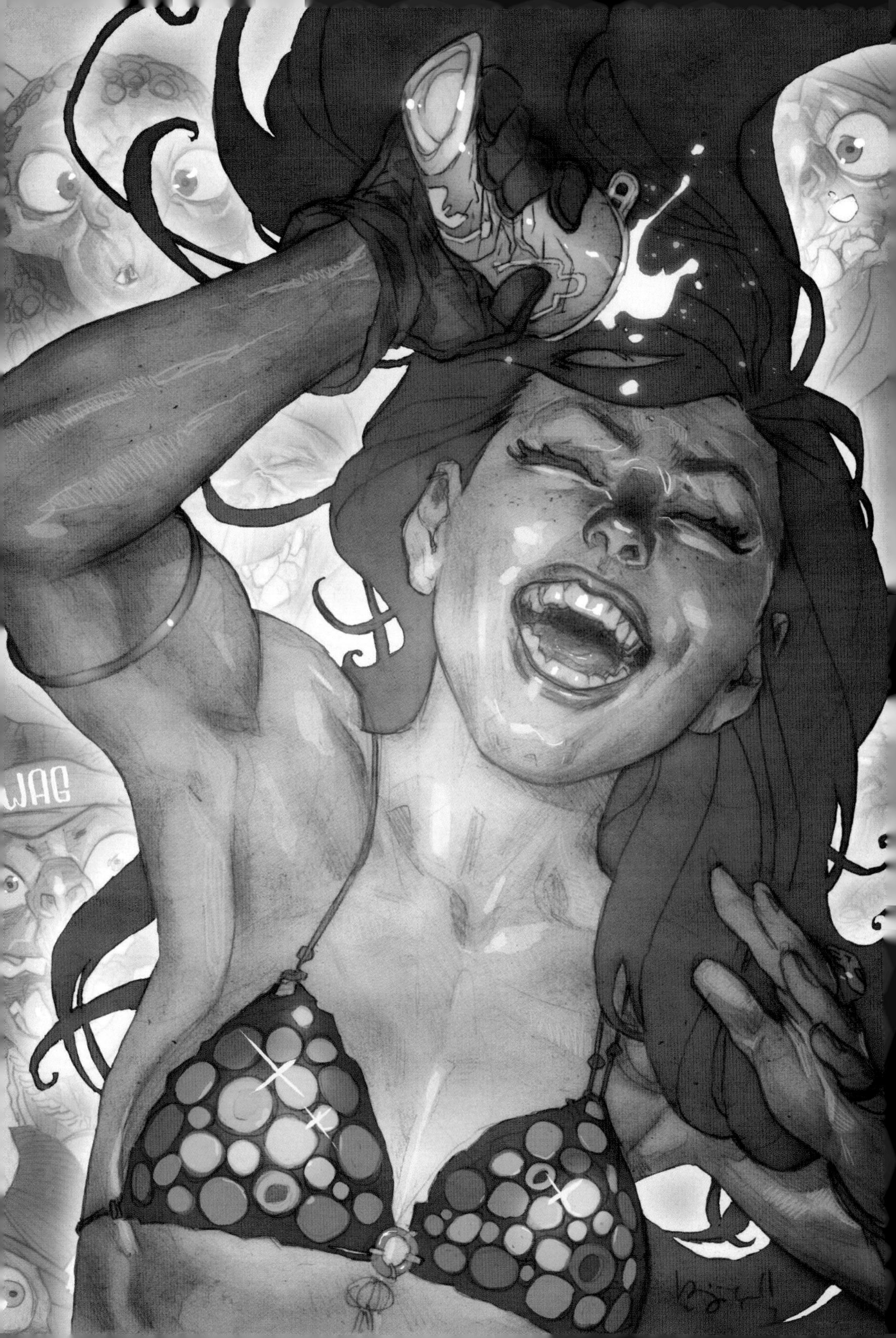
WAG

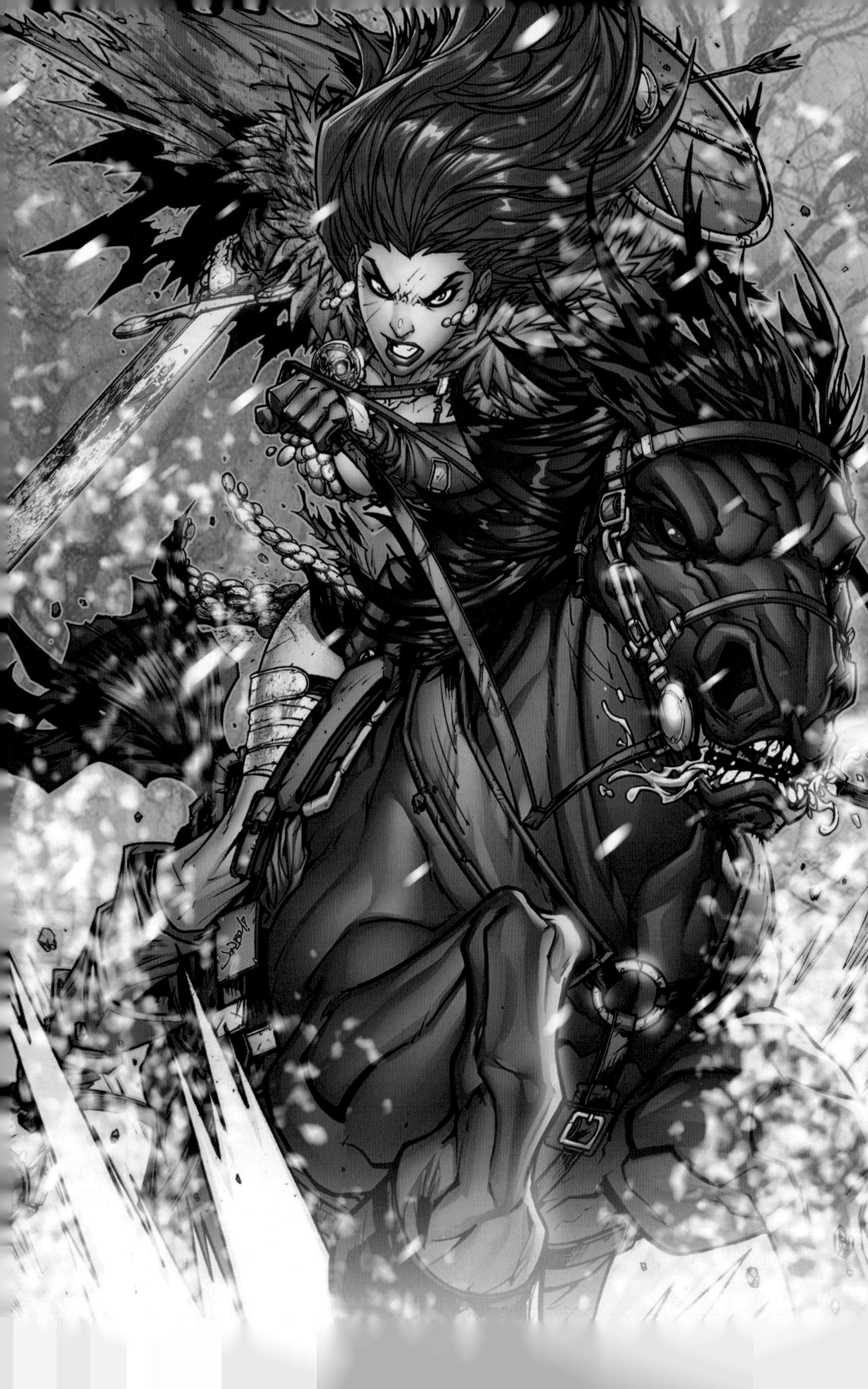

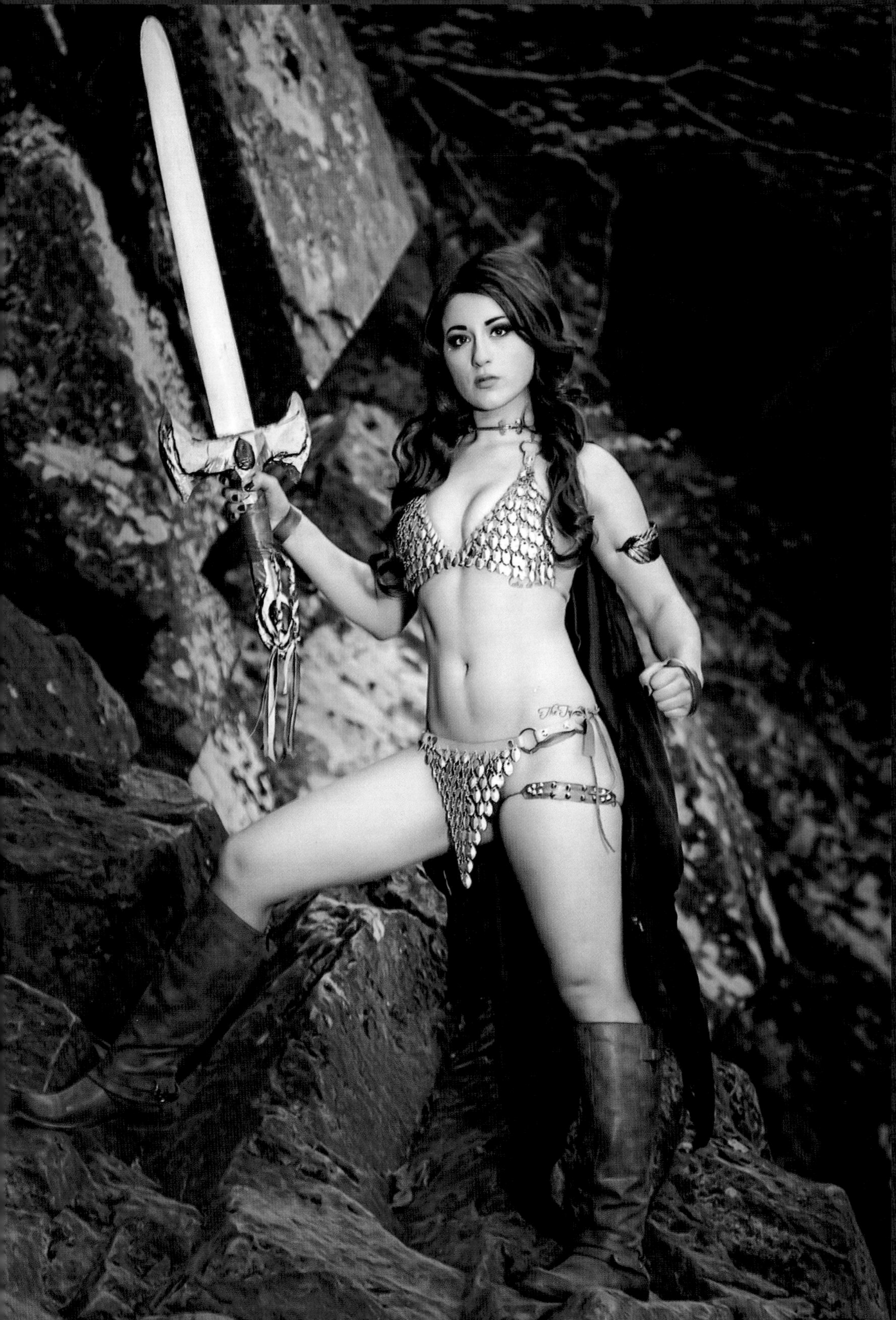

ISSUE #8: COSPLAY VARIANT
MODEL: AMANDA KITSON (TWITTER: @THEKITCANDELA)

COVER GALLERY

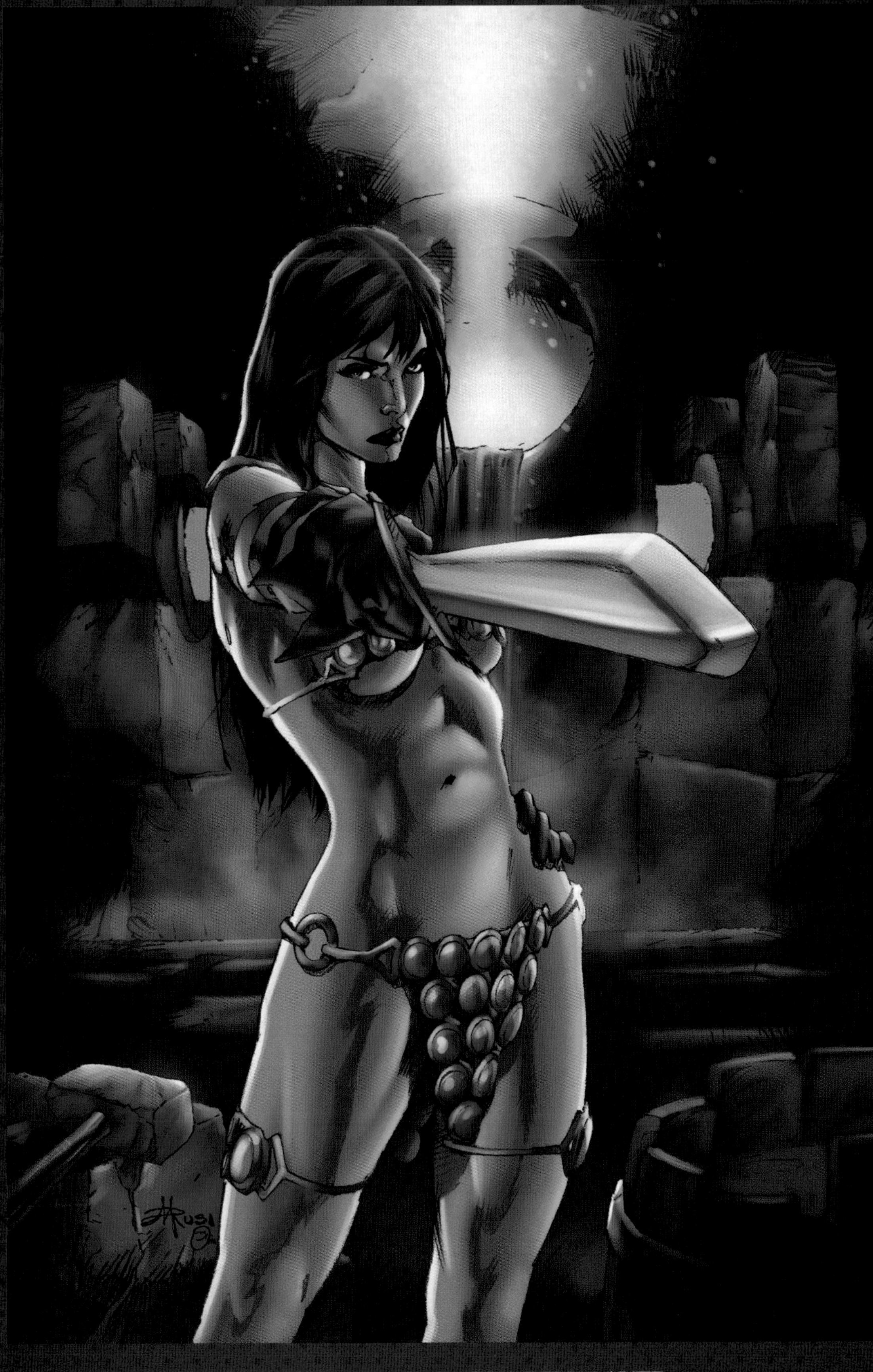

ISSUE #8: COVER ART BY **MEL RUBI**, COLORS BY **OMI REMALANTE**

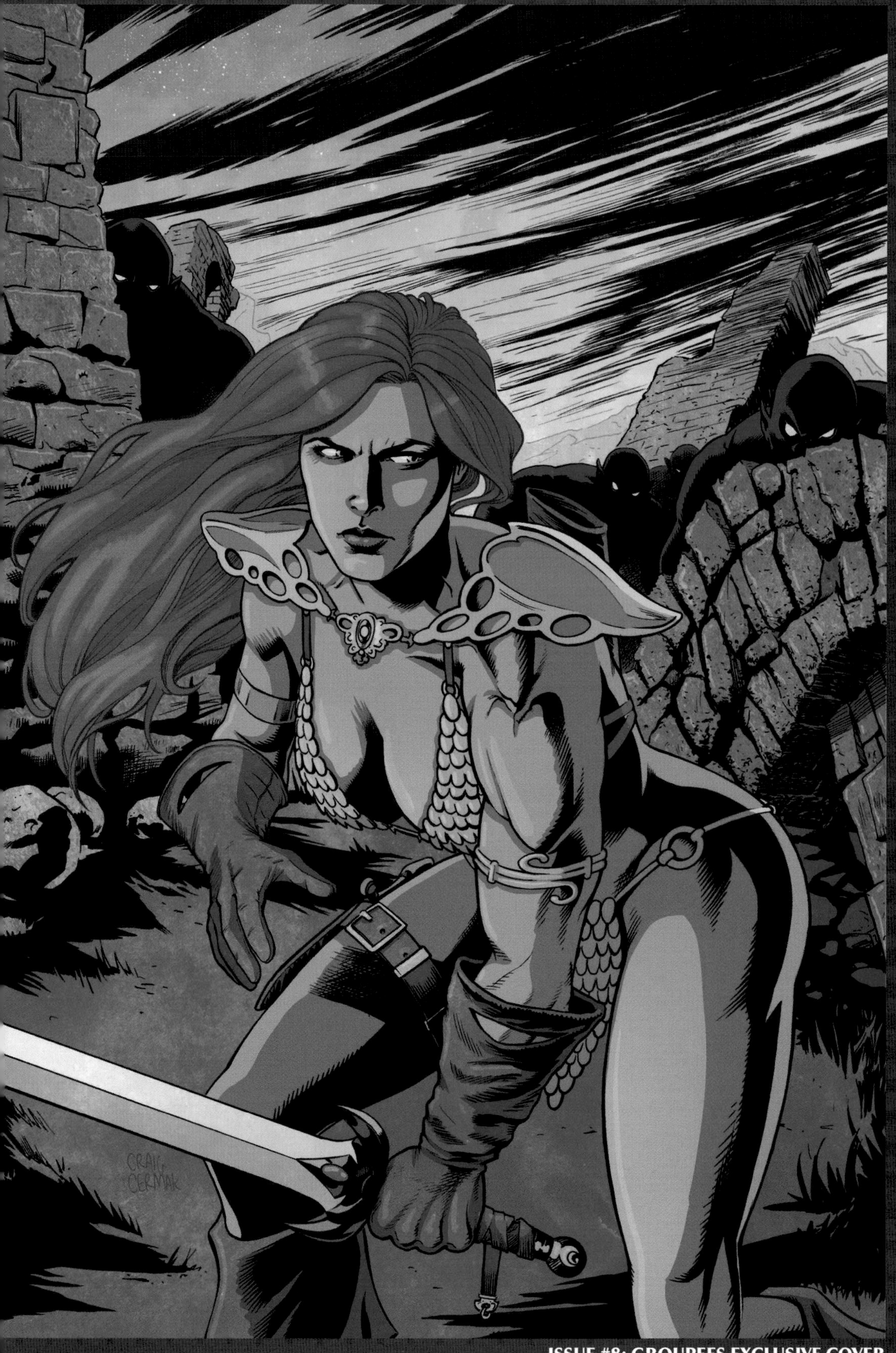
CRAIG
CERMAK

ISSUE #8: GROUPEES EXCLUSIVE COVER
ART BY CRAIG CERMAK, COLORS BY CHRIS O'HALLORAN (GROUPEES.COM)

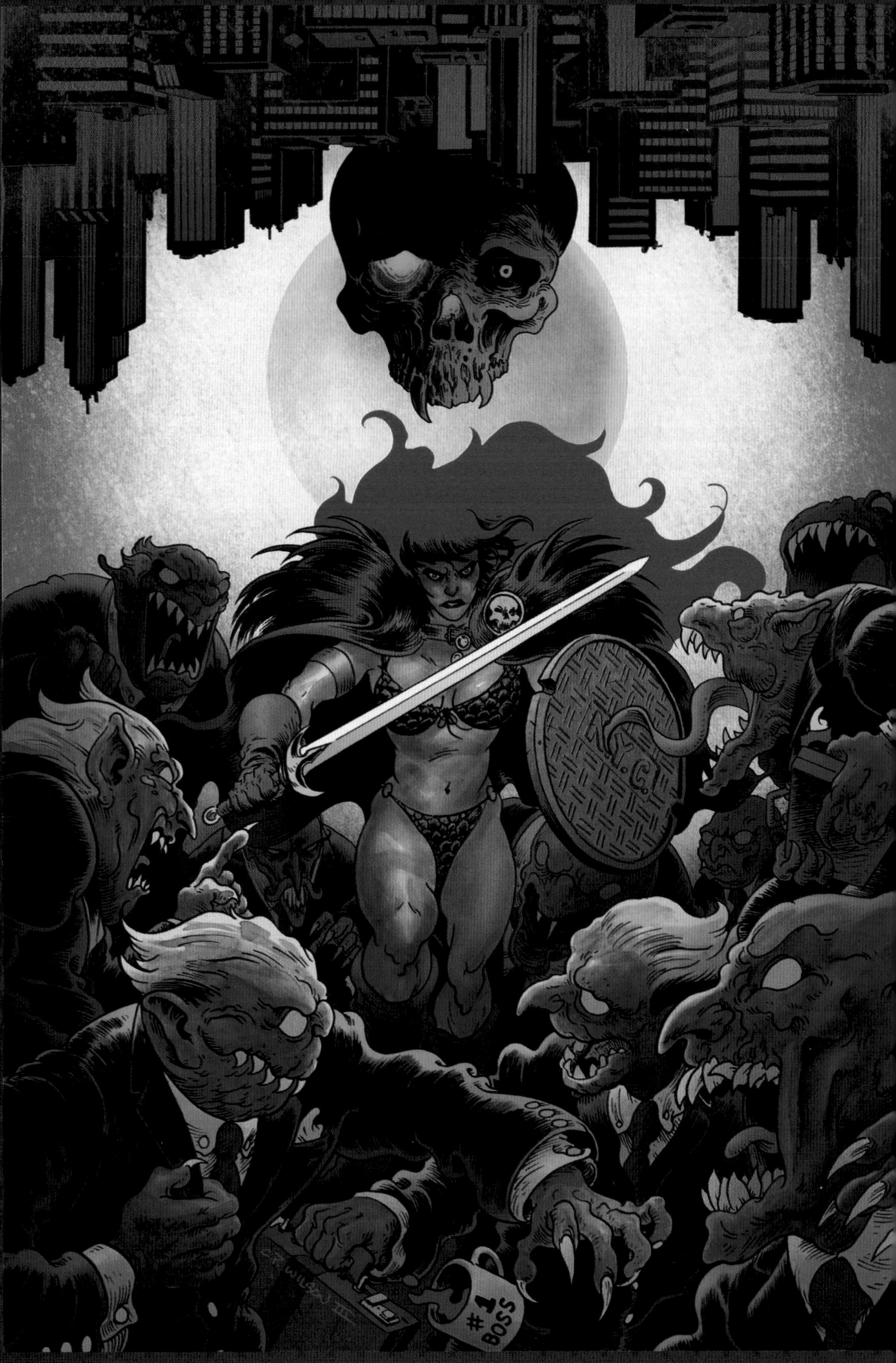
#1
BOSS

ISSUE #9: COVER ART BY **CP WILLIAMS III**

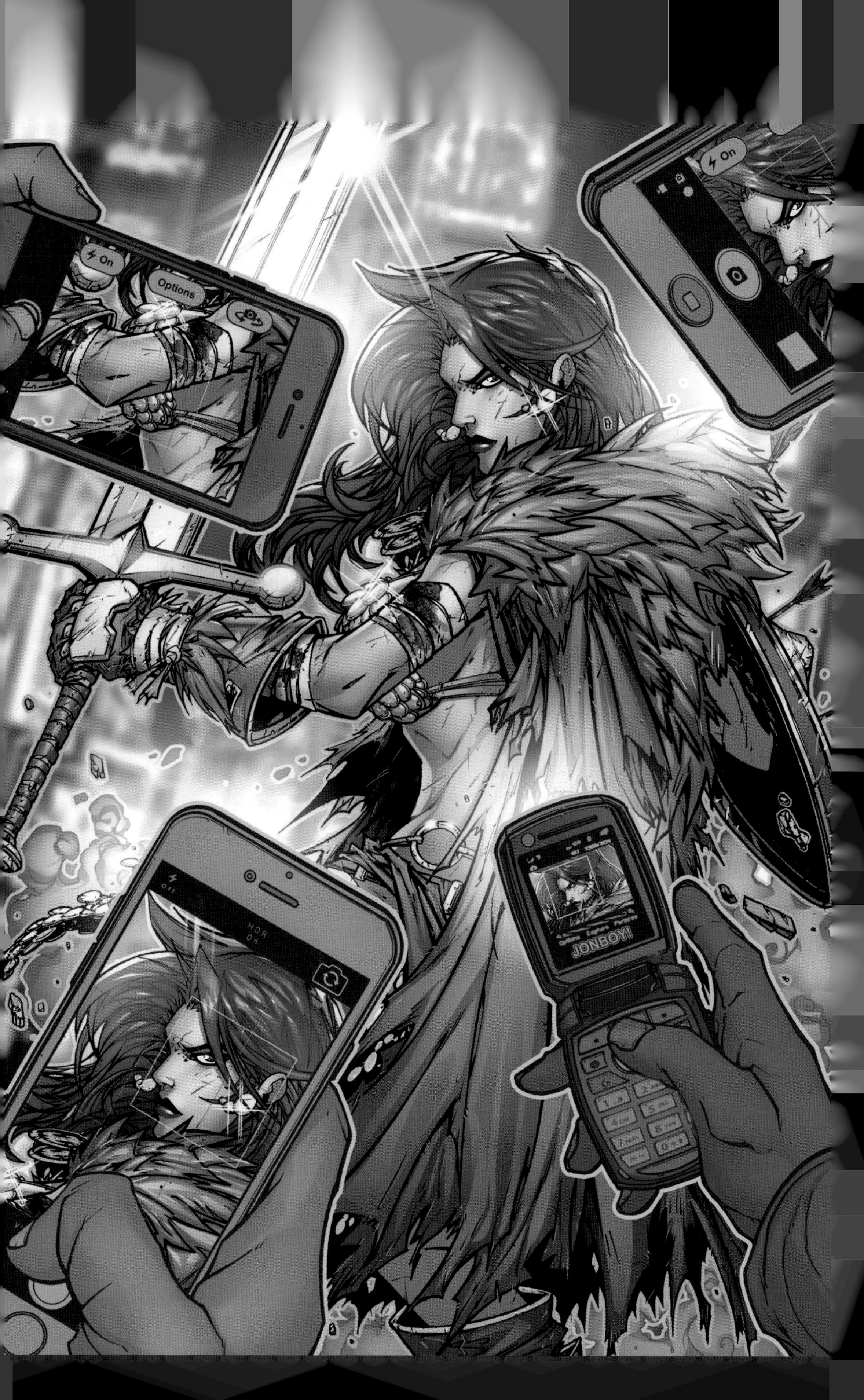
On
Options
On
JONBOY!

COVER GALLERY

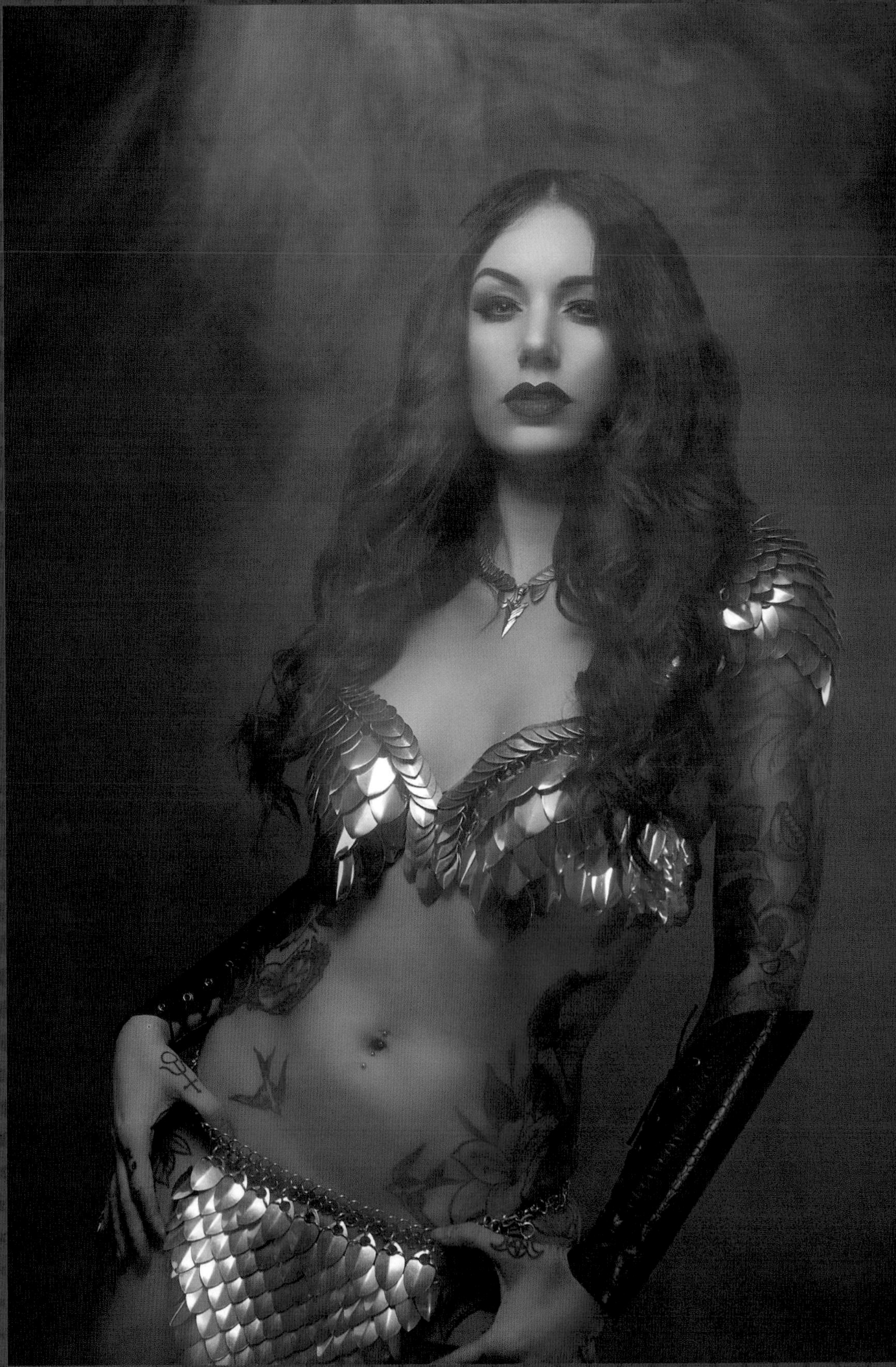

ISSUE #9: COSPLAY VARIANT
MODEL: CERVENA FOX (TWITTER: @CERVENAFOX), PHOTOGRAPHER: KEELY WEIS

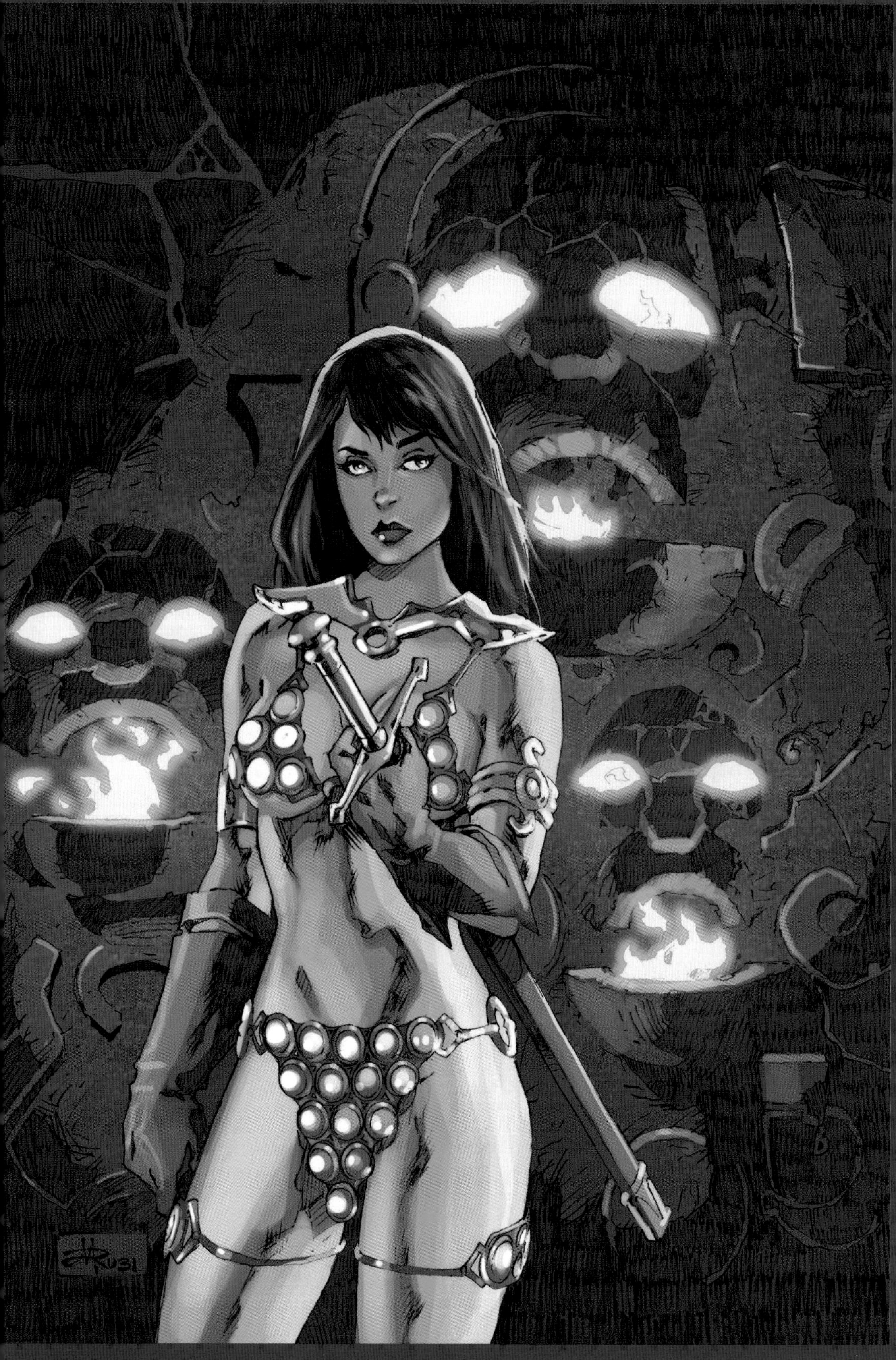
RUBI

ISSUE #9: COVER ART BY **MEL RUBI**, COLORS BY **OMI REMALANTE**

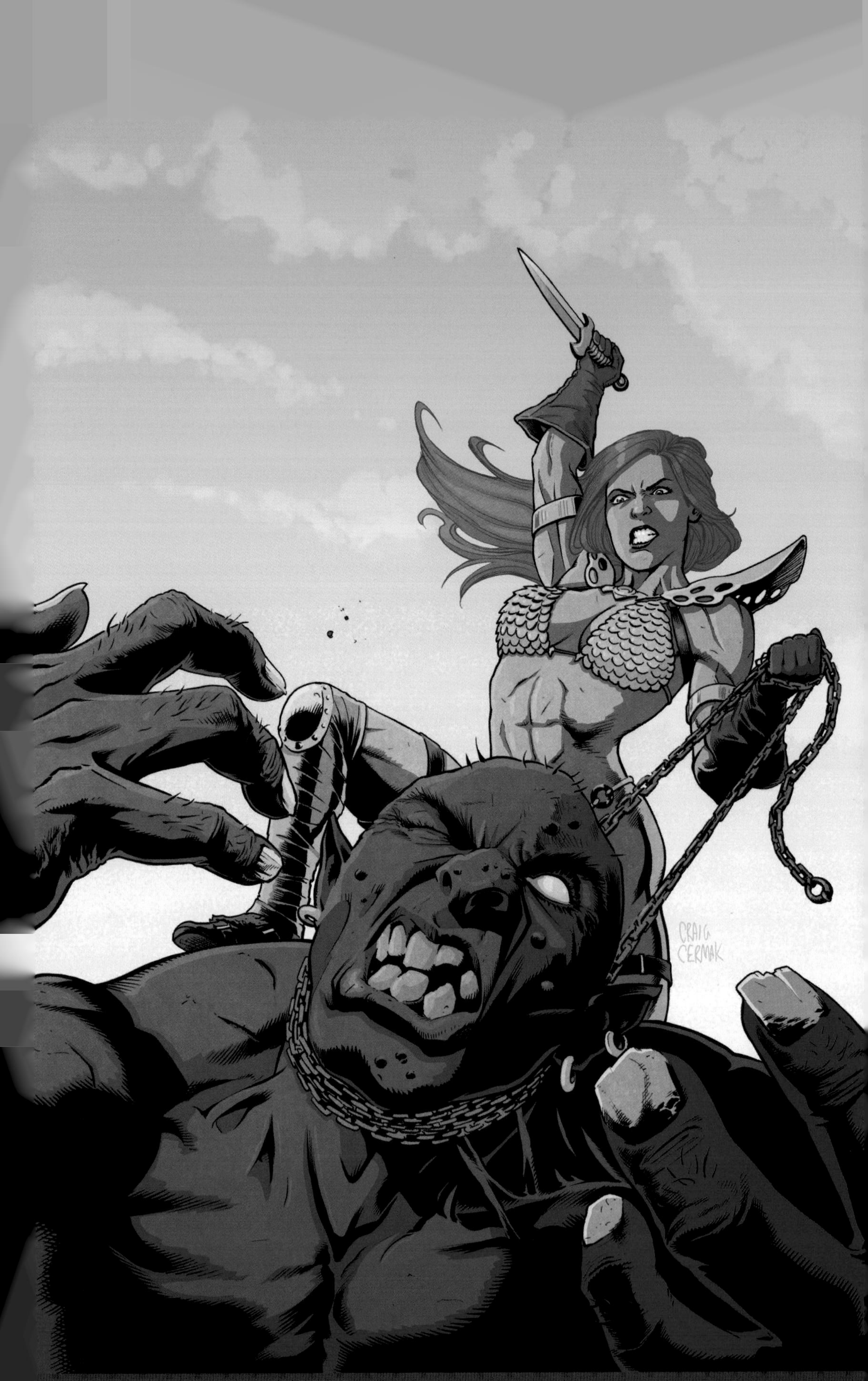
CRAIG
CERMAK

SSUE #9: GROUPEES EXCLUSIVE COVER
ART BY CRAIG CERMAK, COLORS BY CHRIS O'HALLORAN (GROUPEES.COM)

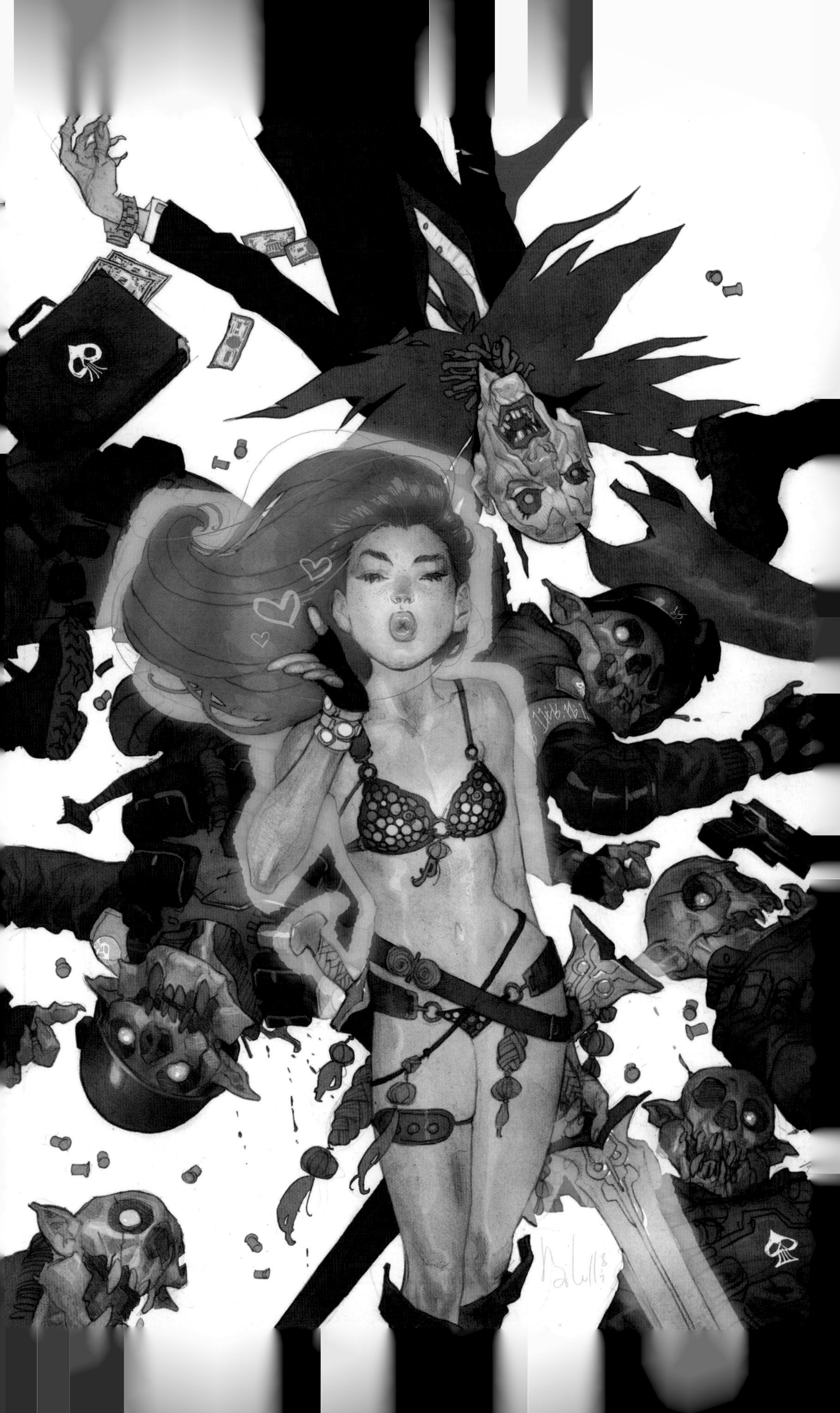

COVER GALLERY

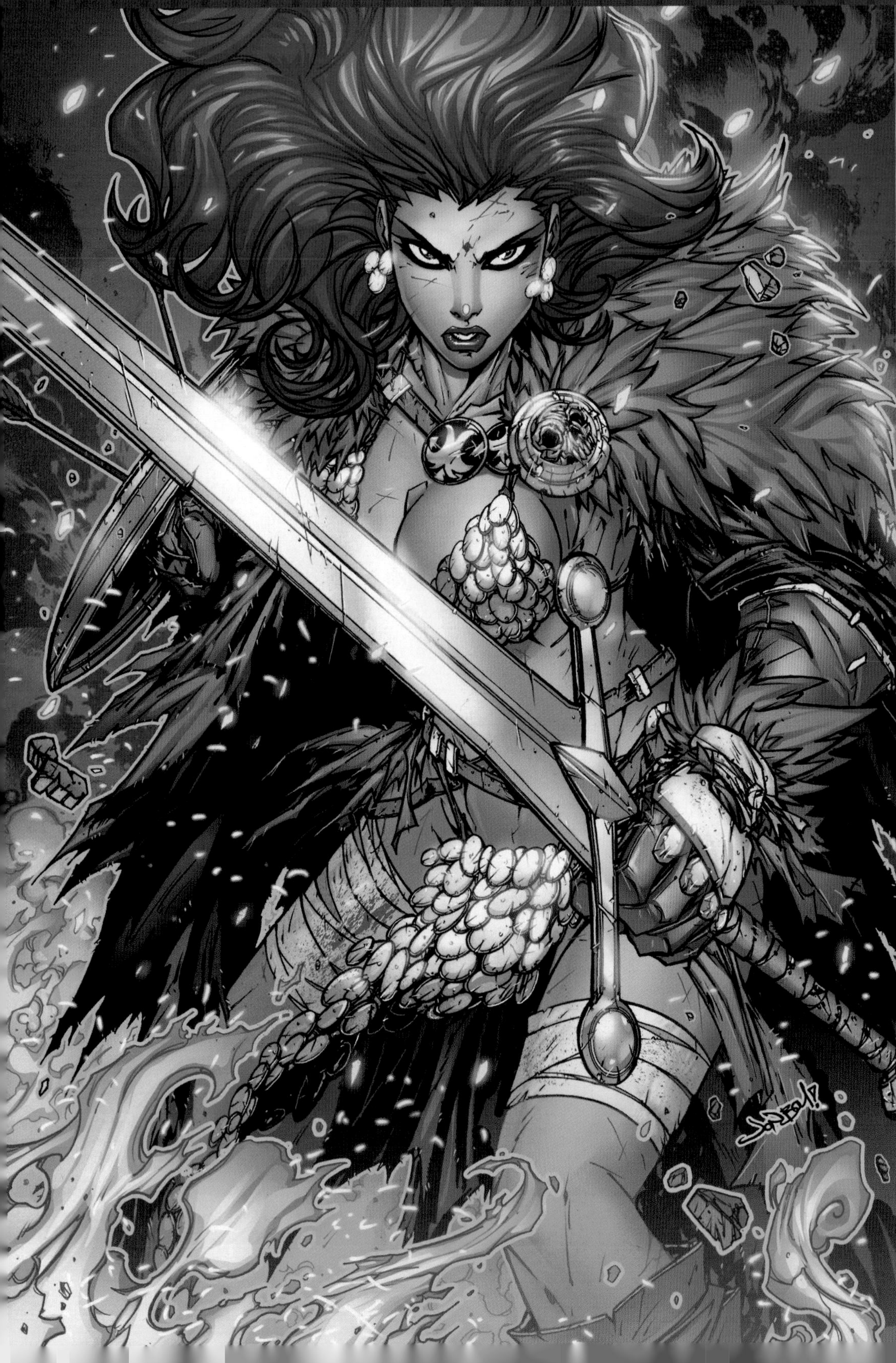

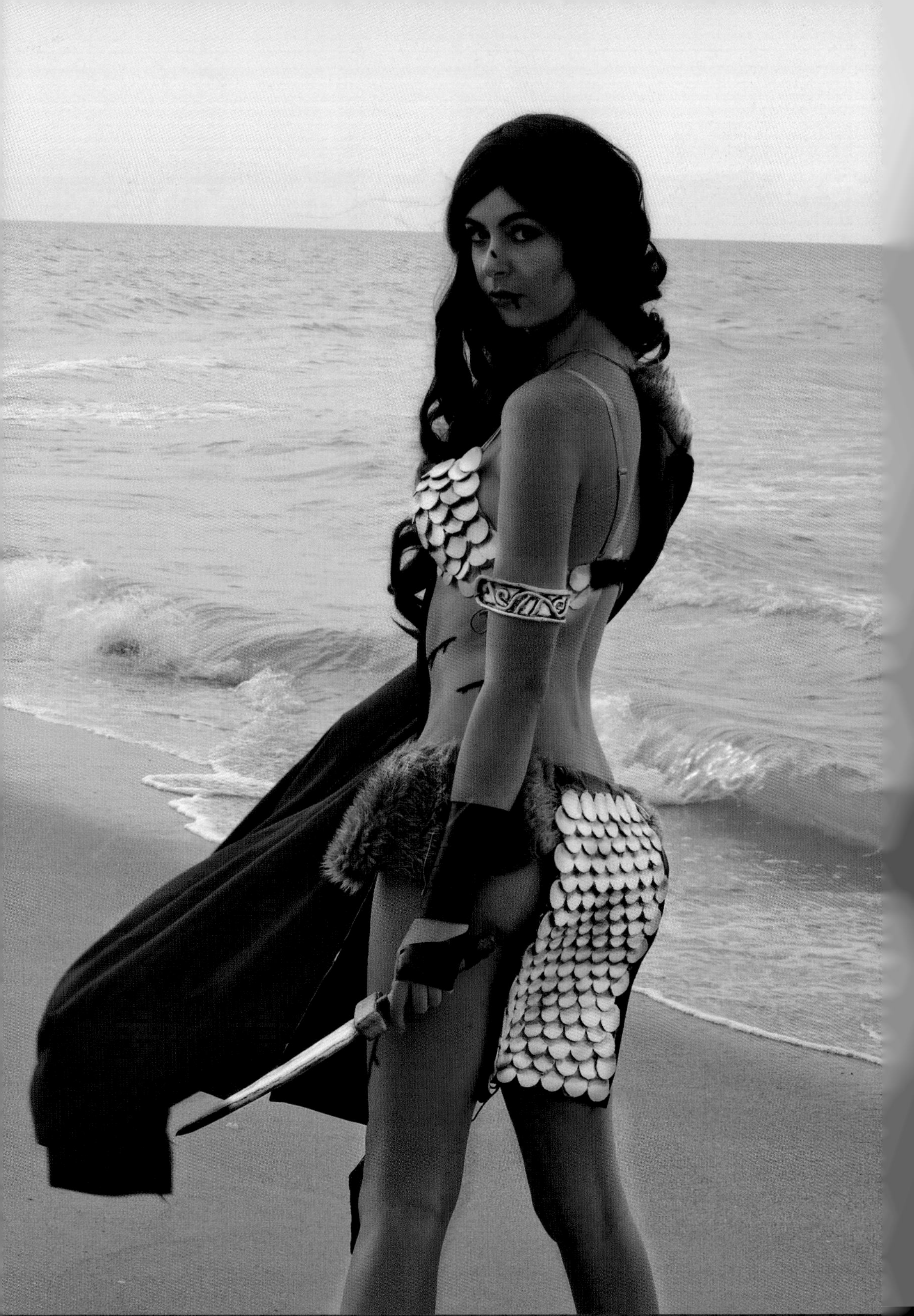

ISSUE #10: COSPLAY VARIANT

COVER GALLERY

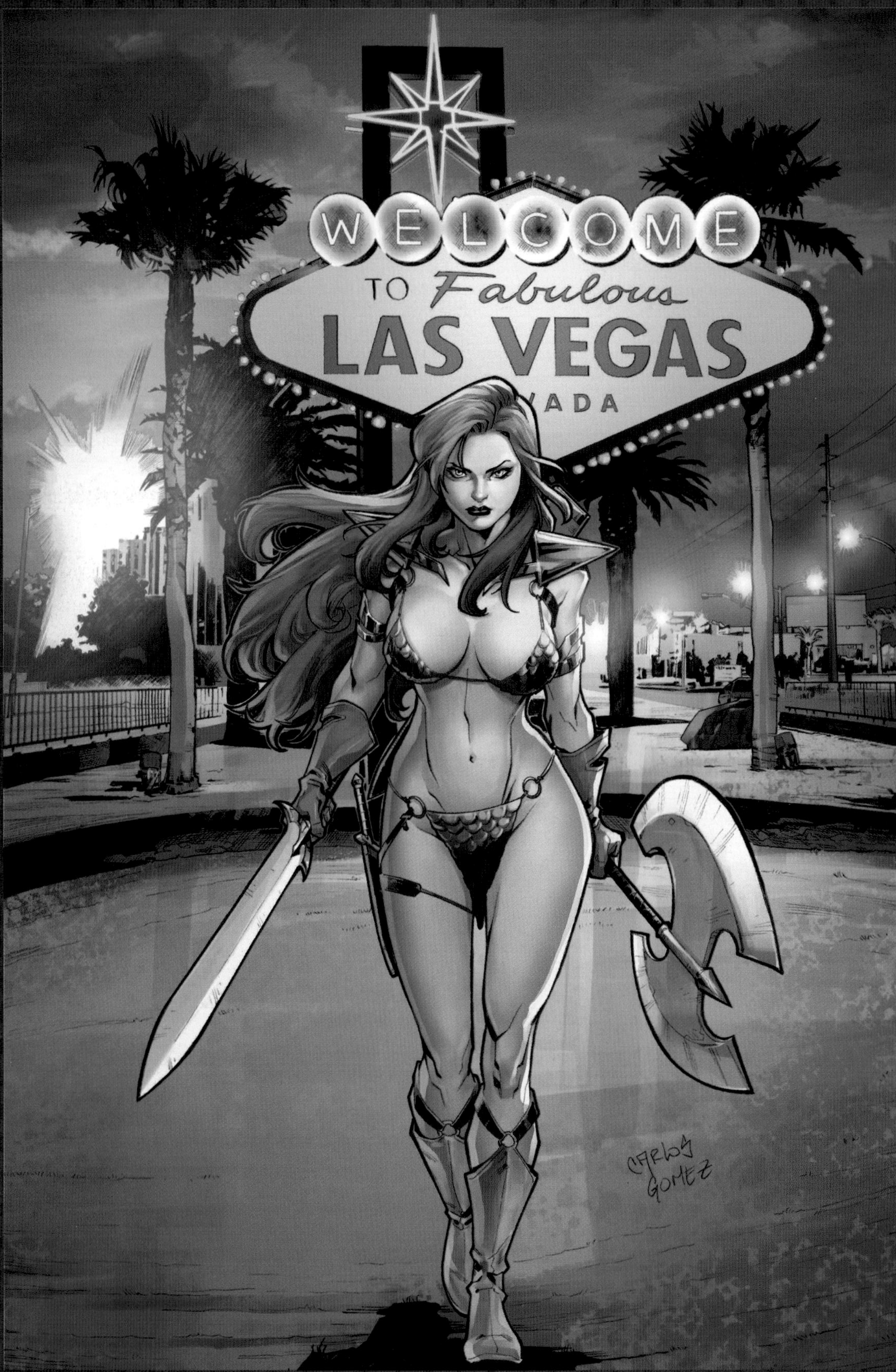
WELCOME
TO Fabulous
LAS VEGAS
VADA
CARLOS GOMEZ

ISSUE #10: COVER ART BY **CARLOS GOMEZ**, COLORS BY **MOHAN**

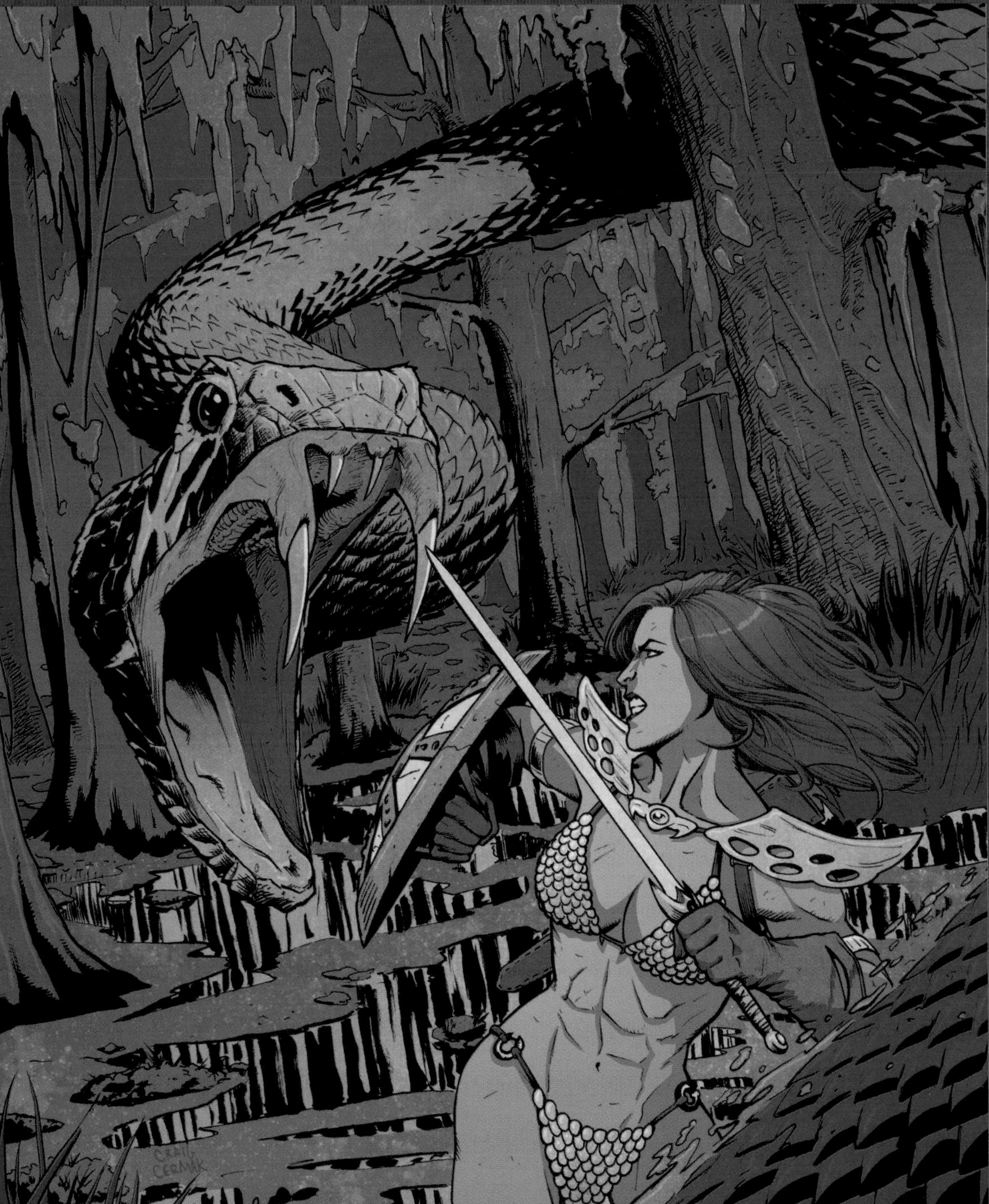
CRAIG CERMAK

ISSUE #10: GROUPEES EXCLUSIVE COVER
ART BY CRAIG CERMAK, COLORS BY CHRIS O'HALLORAN (GROUPEES.COM)

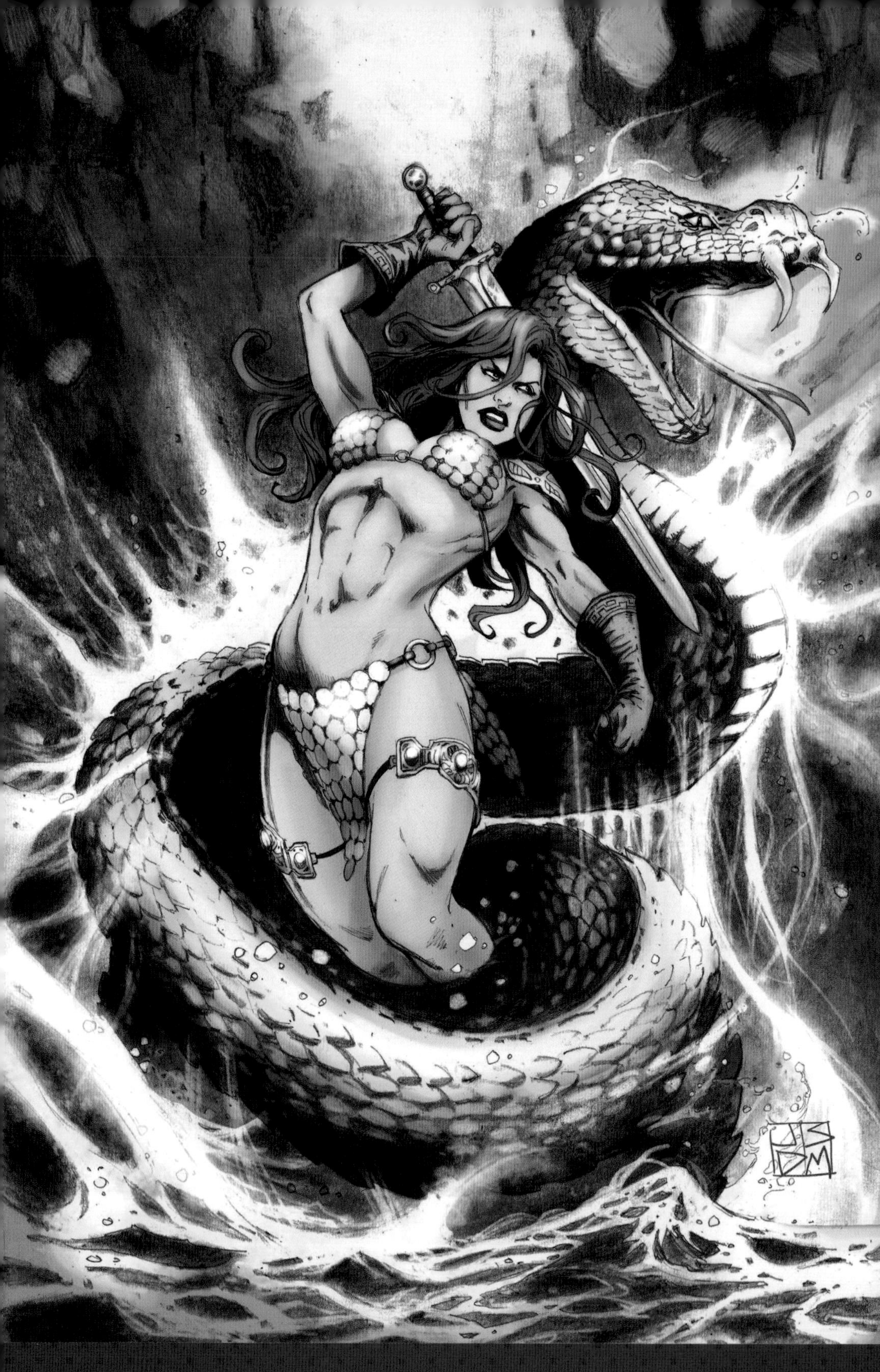

SSUE #11: COVER ART BY JAN DUURSEMA COLORS BY SIAN MANDRAKE

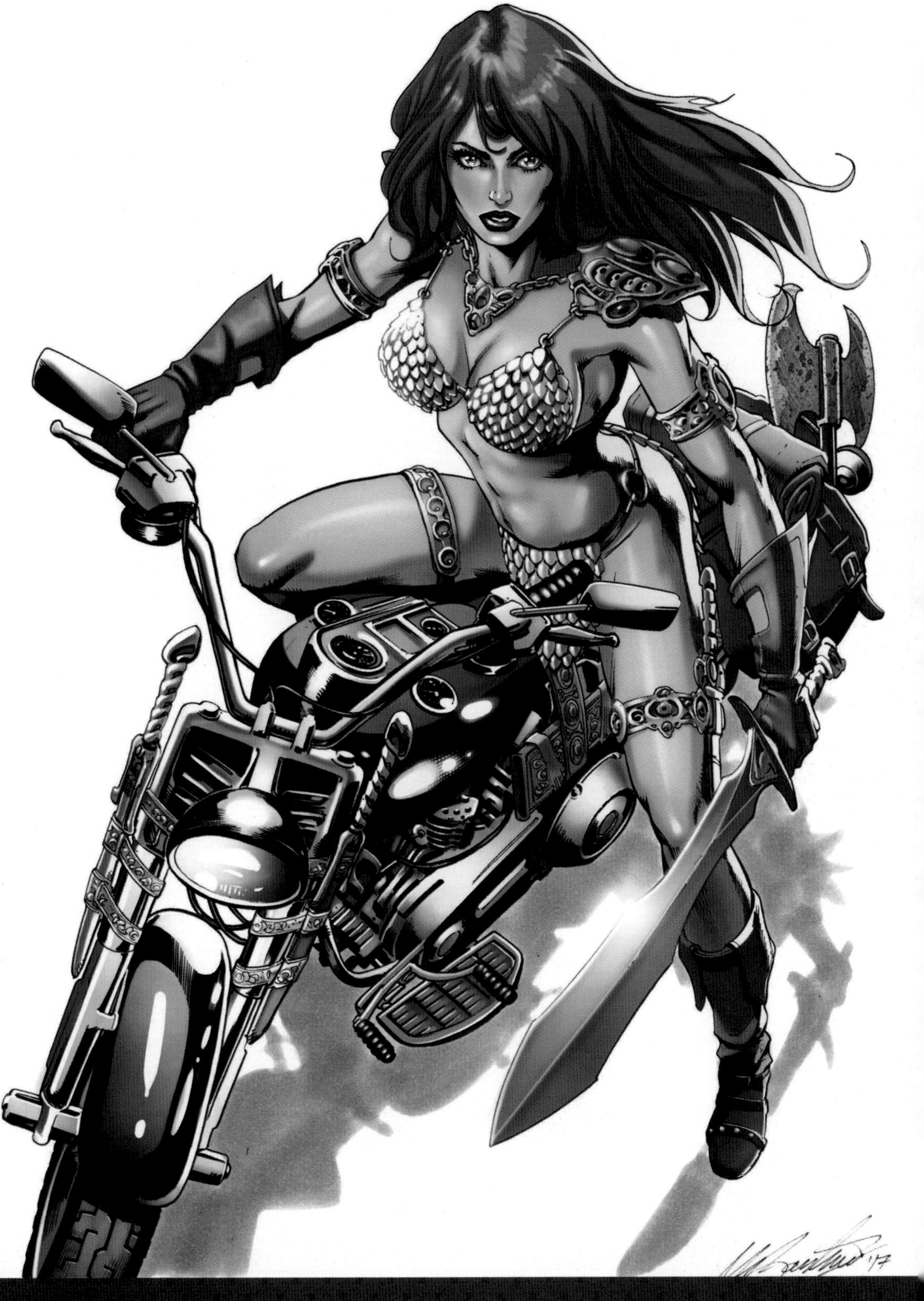
Santucci '17
ISSUE #11: COVER ART BY MARCO SANTUCCI, COLORS BY MARIACRISTINA FEDERICO

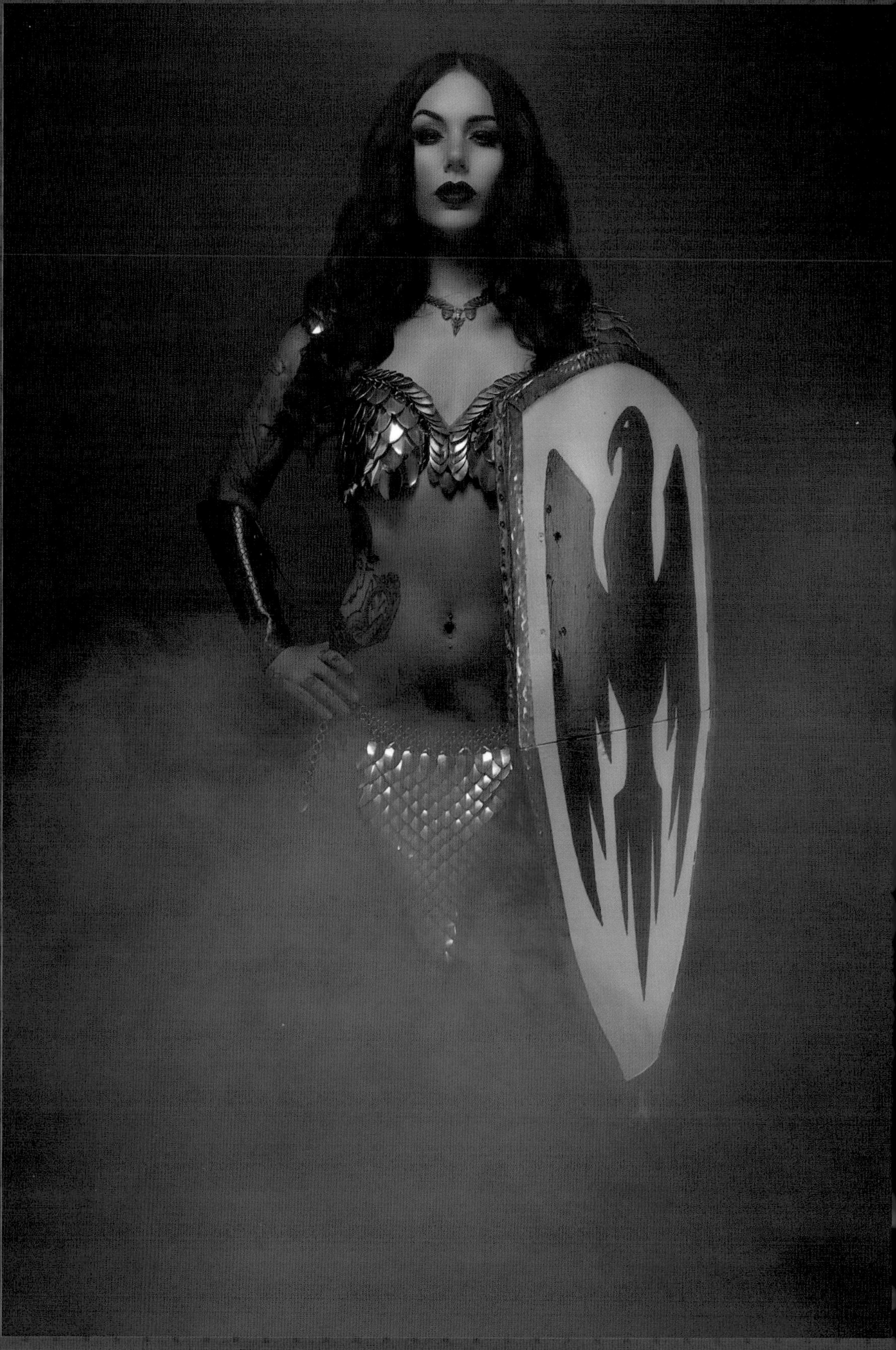

ISSUE #11: COSPLAY VARIANT
MODEL: CERVENA FOX (TWITTER: @CERVENAFOX), PHOTOGRAPHER: KEELY WEIS

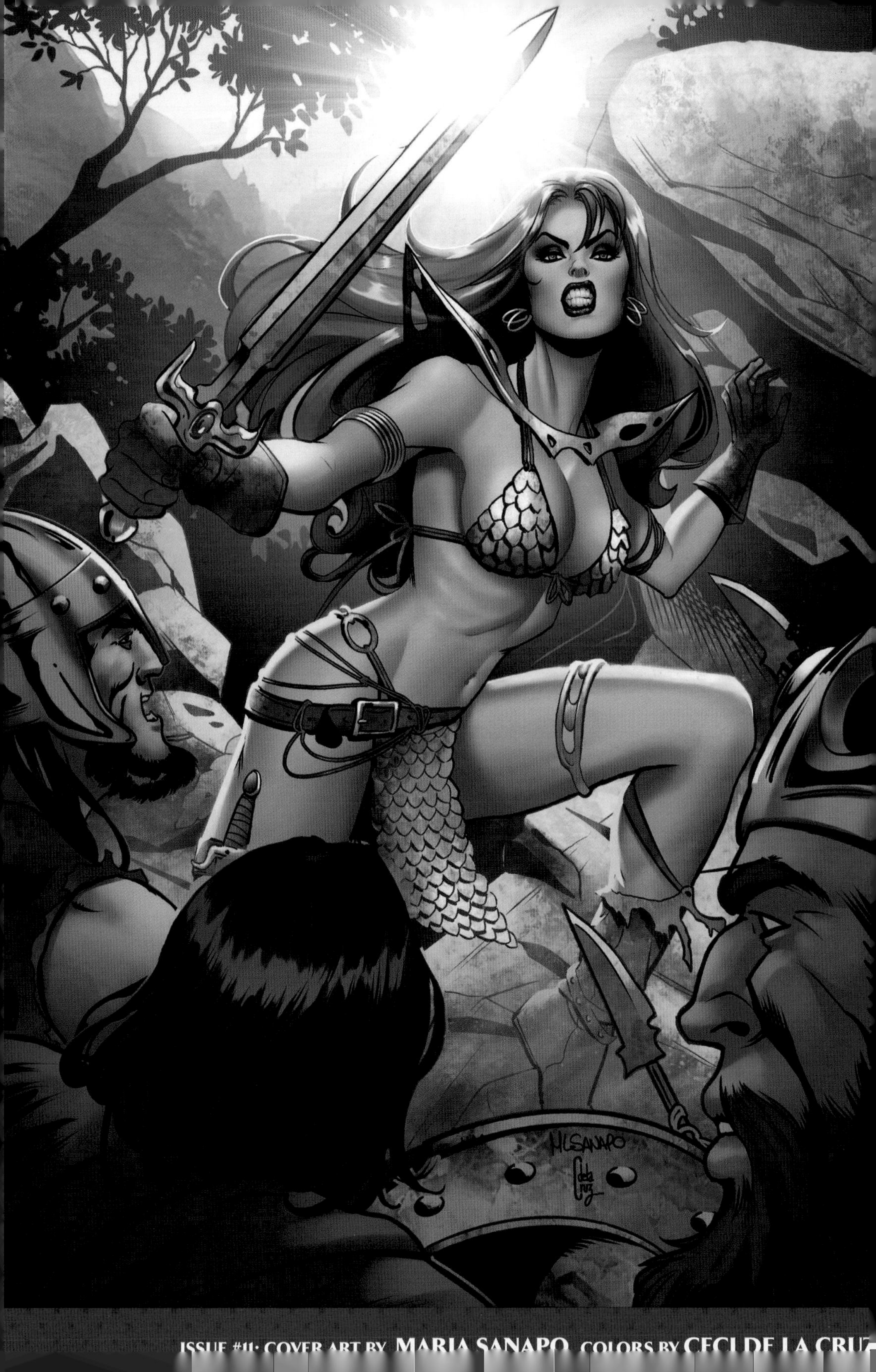
MLSANARO
CdelaCruz

ISSUE #11: COVER ART BY MARIA SANAPO, COLORS BY CECI DE LA CRUZ

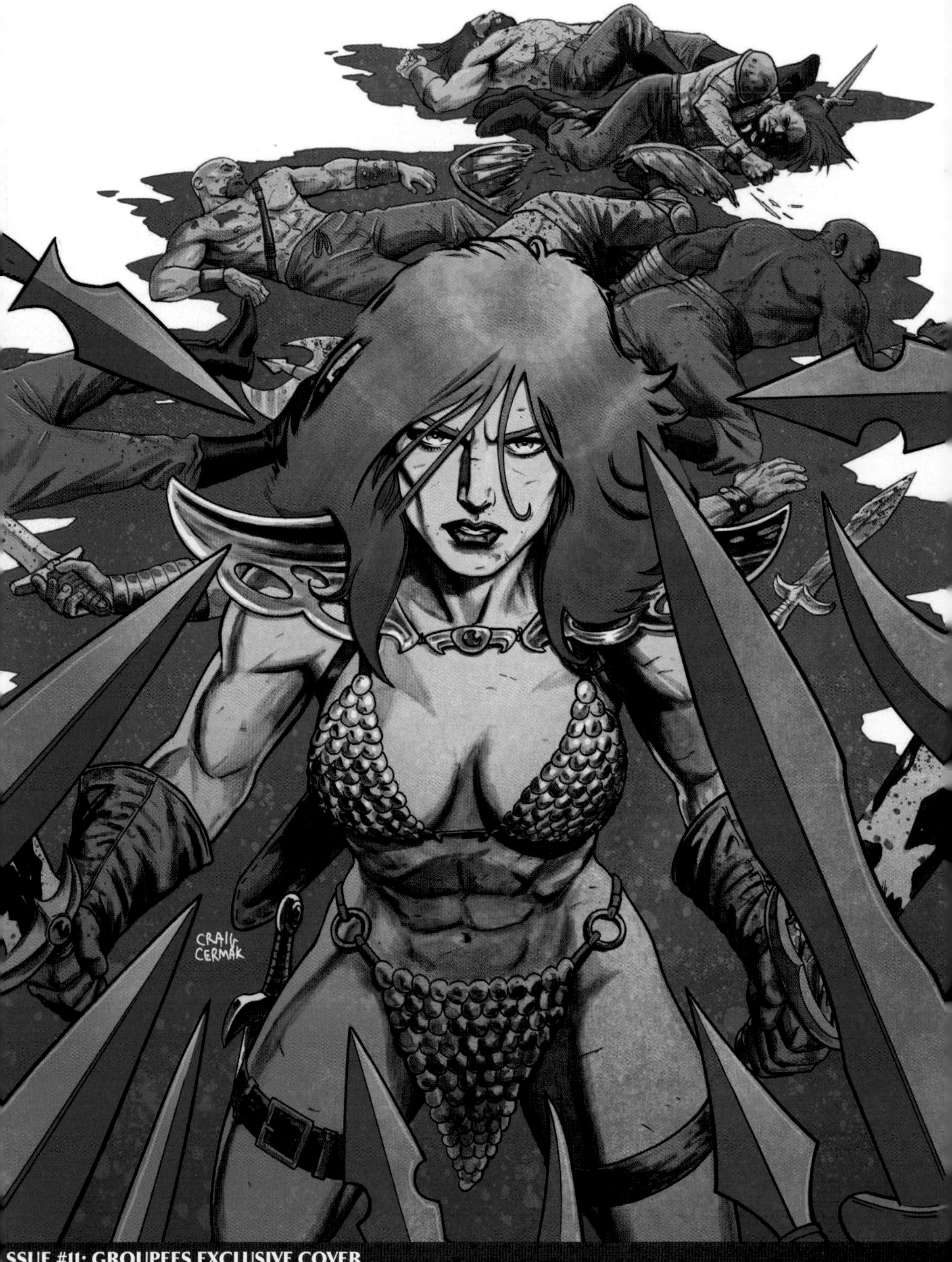
CRAIG
CERMAK

ISSUE #11: GROUPEES EXCLUSIVE COVER
ART BY CRAIG CERMAK, COLORS BY CHRIS O'HALLORAN (GROUPEES.COM)

RED SONJA FAN ARTIST SPOTLIGHT

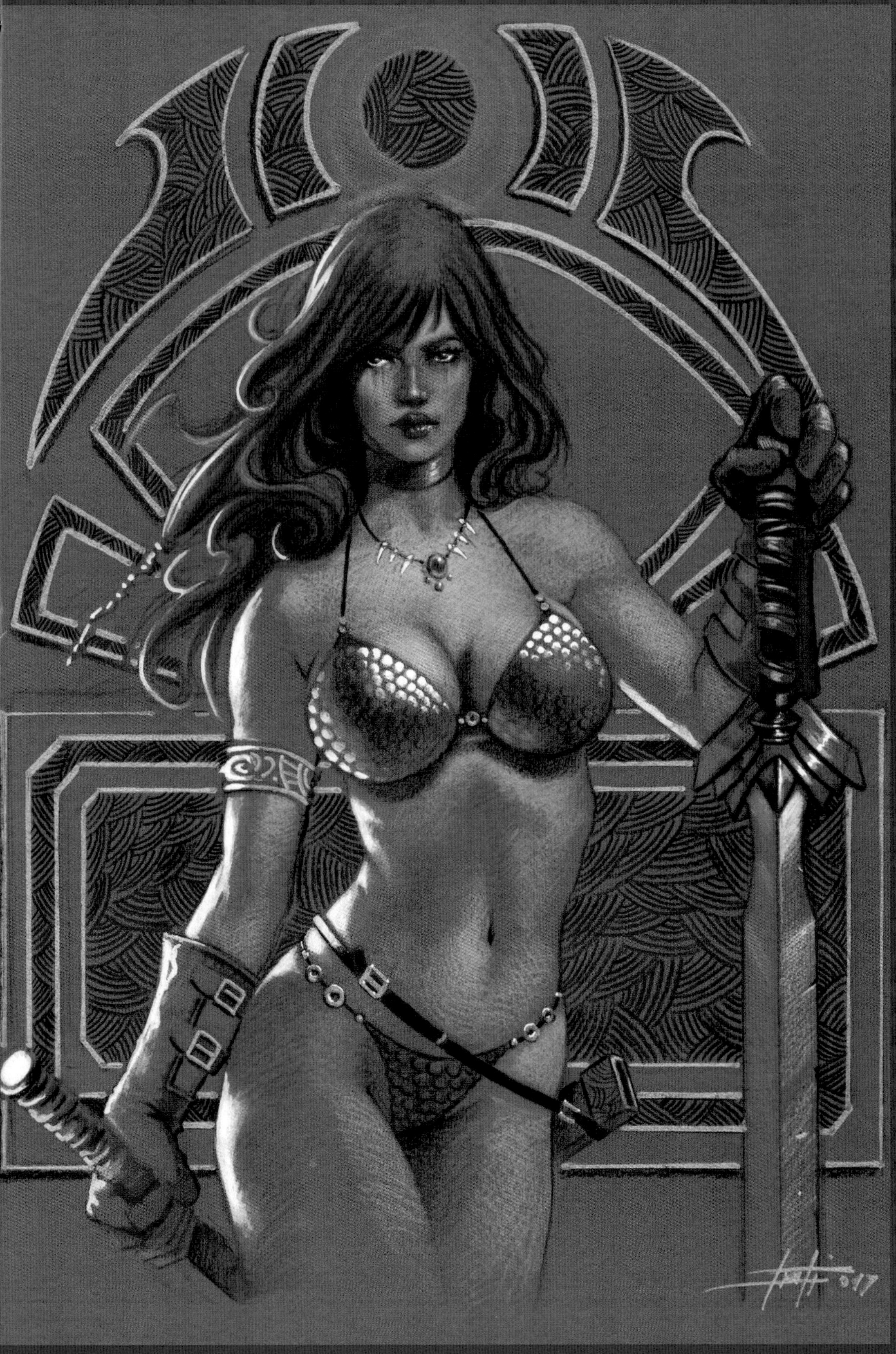

ART BY **LUCA STRATI**

RED SONJA FAN ARTIST SPOTLIGHT

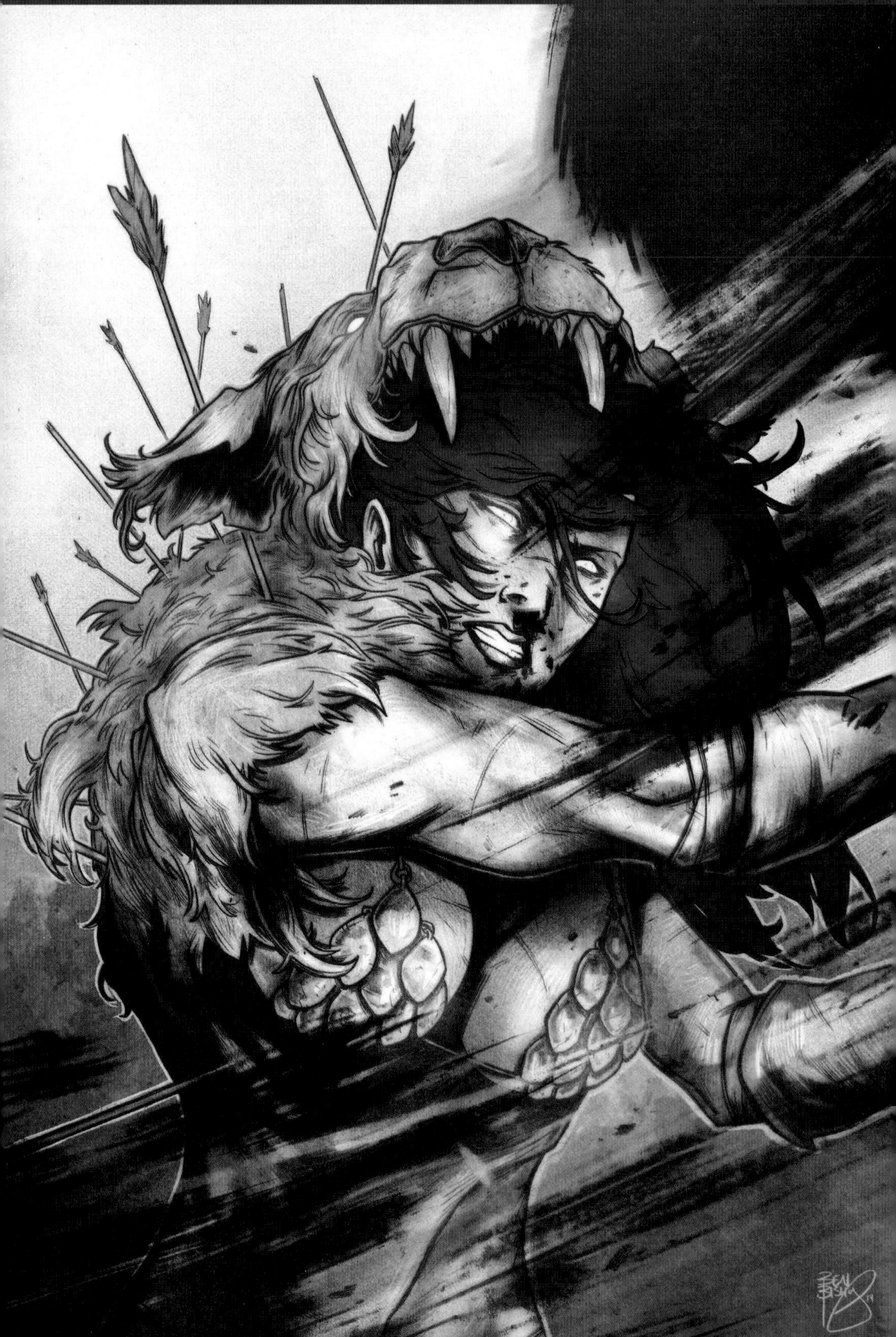

ART BY BEN BISHOP

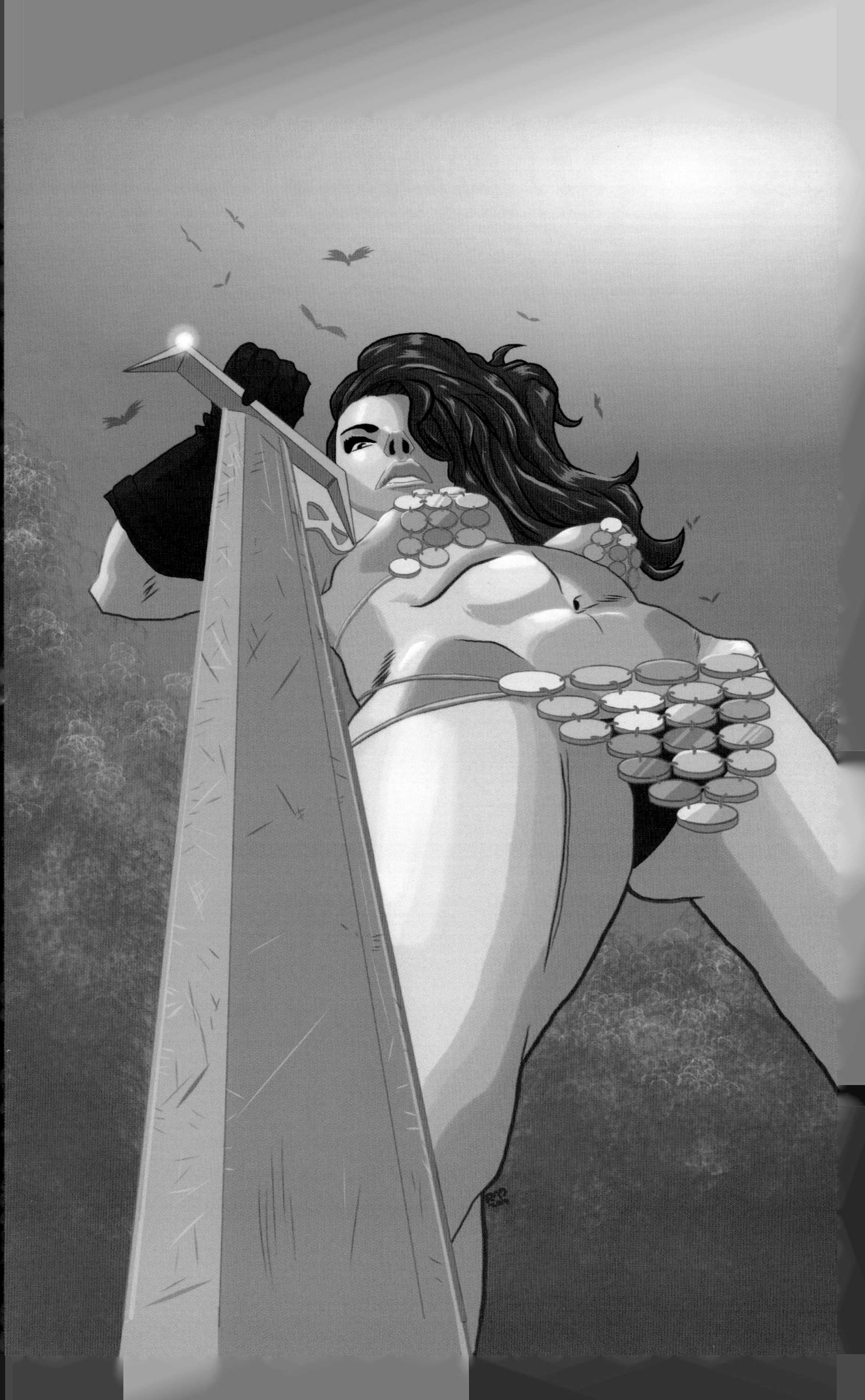

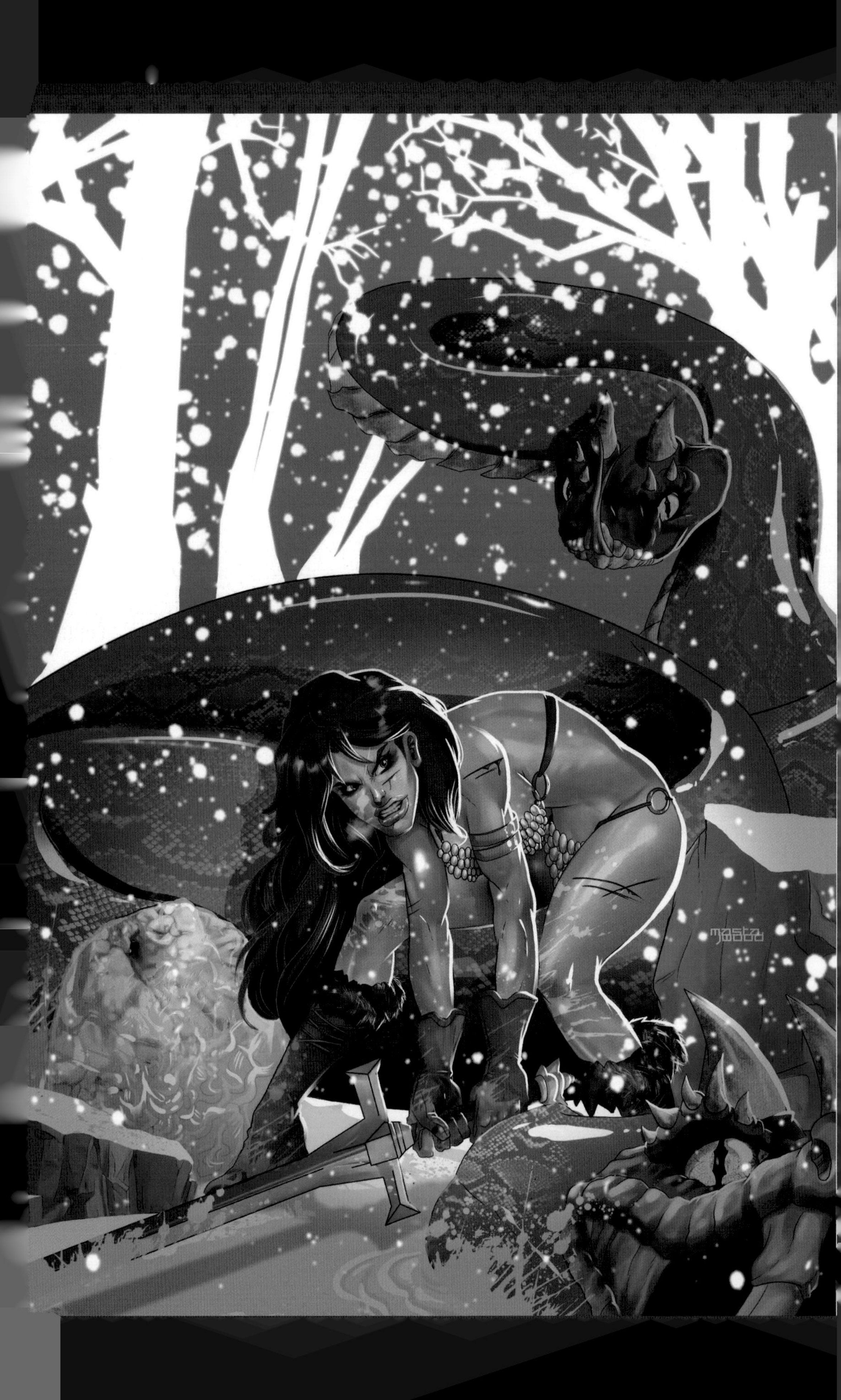

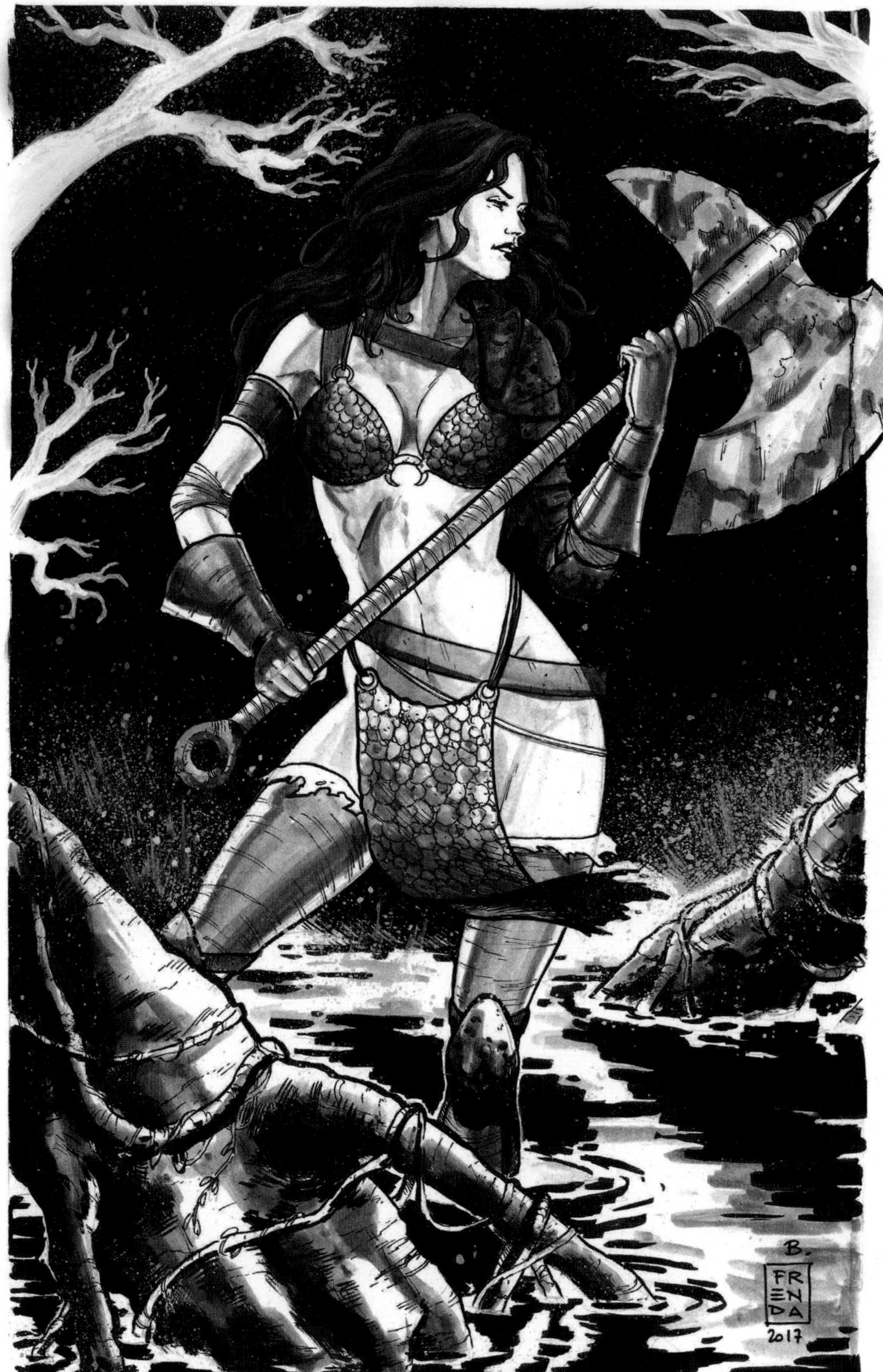
B. FRENDA
2017

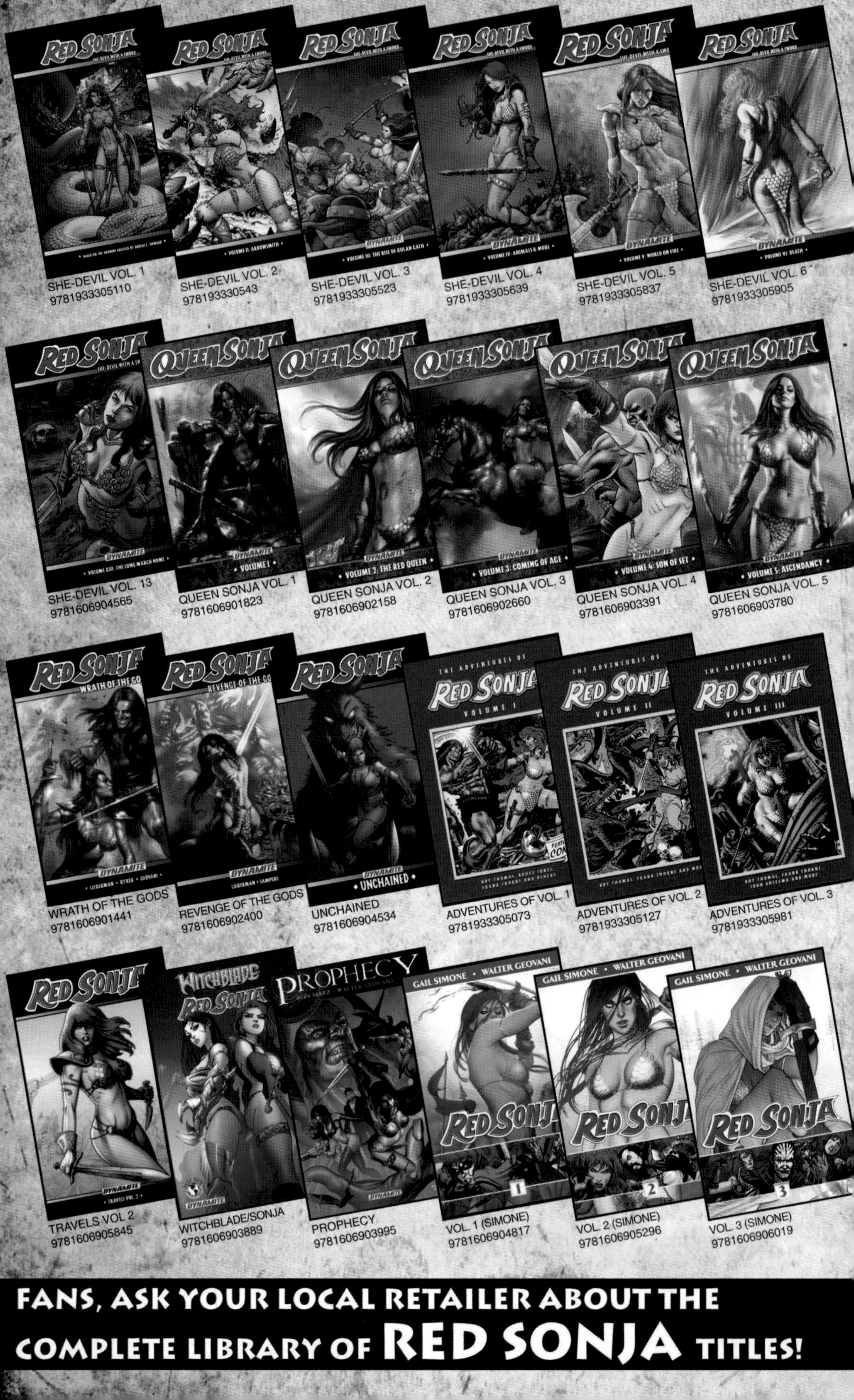
SHE-DEVIL VOL. 1
9781933305110
SHE-DEVIL VOL. 2
9781933330543
SHE-DEVIL VOL. 3
9781933305523
SHE-DEVIL VOL. 4
9781933305639
SHE-DEVIL VOL. 5
9781933305837
SHE-DEVIL VOL. 6
9781933305905
SHE-DEVIL VOL. 13
9781606904565
QUEEN SONJA VOL. 1
9781606901823
QUEEN SONJA VOL. 2
9781606902158
QUEEN SONJA VOL. 3
9781606902660
QUEEN SONJA VOL. 4
9781606903391
QUEEN SONJA VOL. 5
9781606903780
WRATH OF THE GODS
9781606901441
REVENGE OF THE GODS
9781606902400
UNCHAINED
9781606904534
ADVENTURES OF VOL. 1
9781933305073
ADVENTURES OF VOL. 2
9781933305127
ADVENTURES OF VOL. 3
9781933305981
TRAVELS VOL 2
9781606905845
WITCHBLADE/SONJA
9781606903889
PROPHECY
9781606903995
VOL. 1 (SIMONE)
9781606904817
VOL. 2 (SIMONE)
9781606905296
VOL. 3 (SIMONE)
9781606906019
FANS, ASK YOUR LOCAL RETAILER ABOUT THE
COMPLETE LIBRARY OF RED SONJA TITLES!

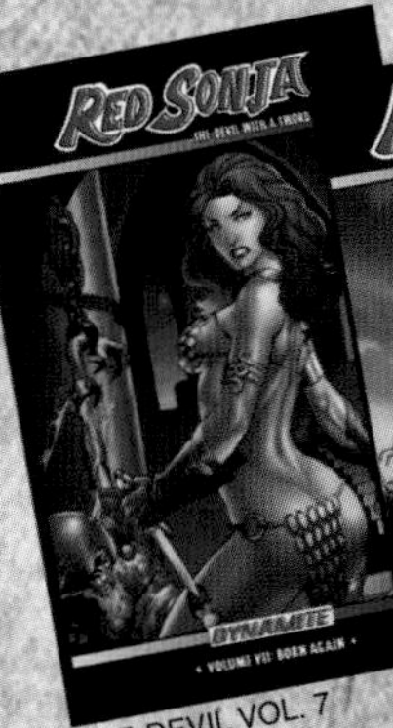
RED SONJA
DYNAMITE

SHE-DEVIL VOL. 7
9781606900116

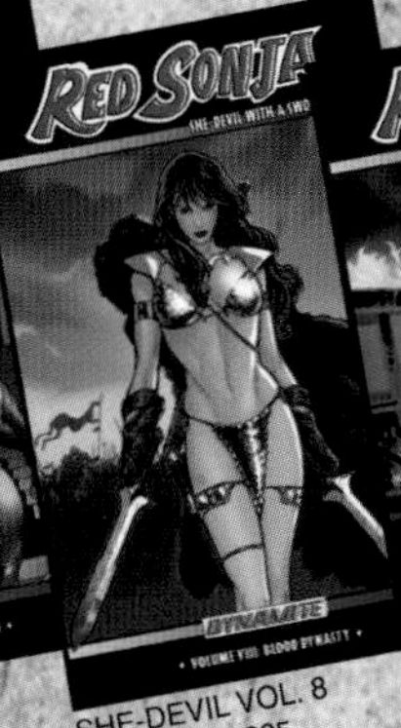
RED SONJA
DYNAMITE

SHE-DEVIL VOL. 8
9781606900635

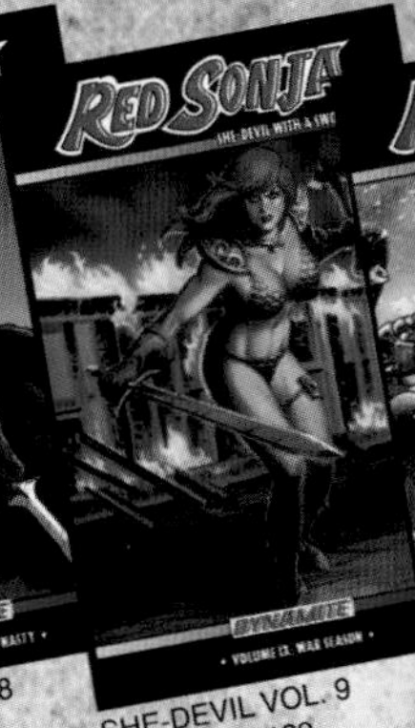
RED SONJA
DYNAMITE

SHE-DEVIL VOL. 9
9781606901120

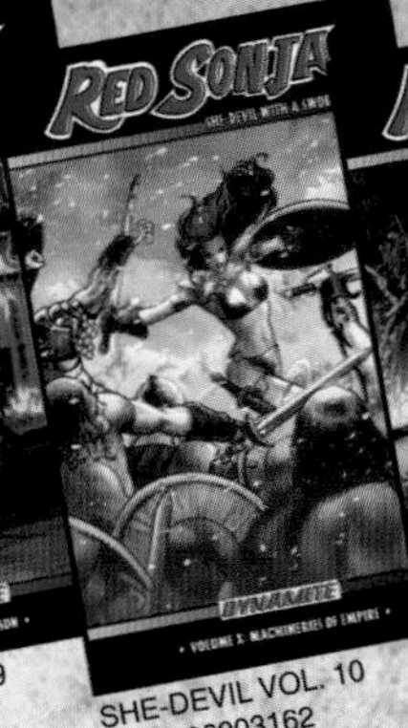
RED SONJA
DYNAMITE

SHE-DEVIL VOL. 10
9781606903162

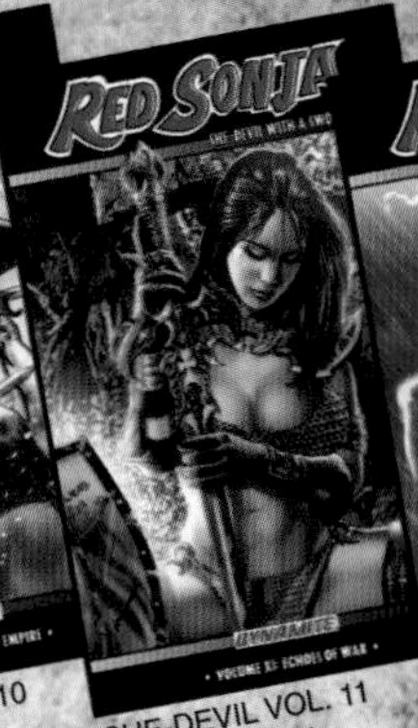
RED SONJA
DYNAMITE

SHE-DEVIL VOL. 11
9781606904091

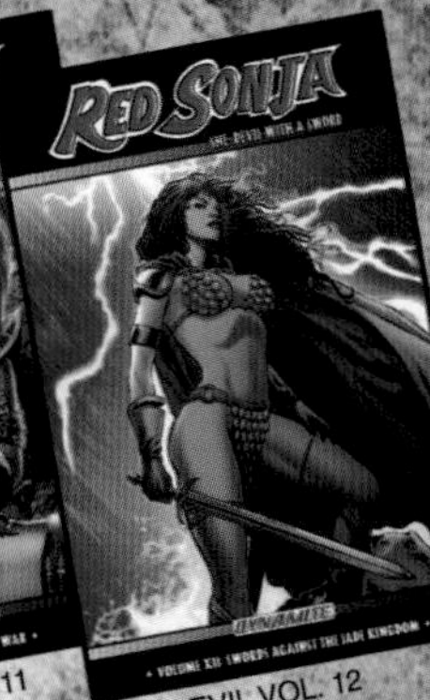
RED SONJA
DYNAMITE

SHE-DEVIL VOL. 12
9781606904428

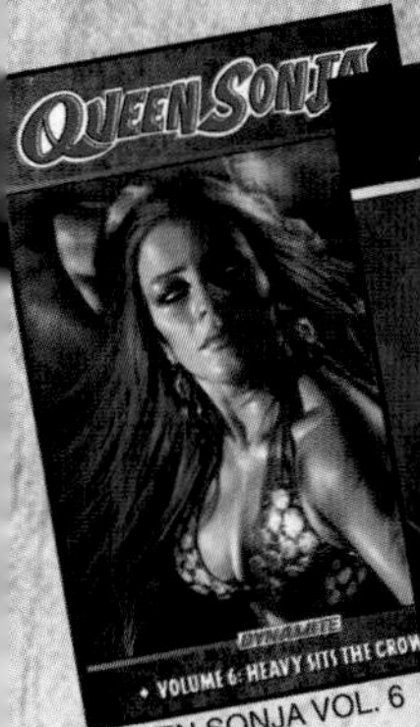
QUEEN SONJA
DYNAMITE

QUEEN SONJA VOL. 6
9781606904022

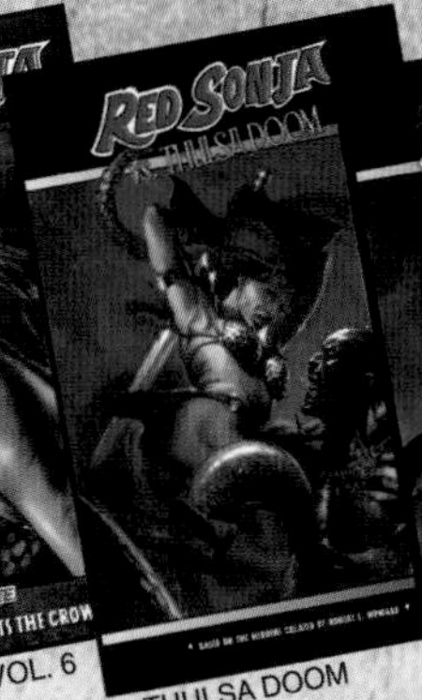
RED SONJA

vs THULSA DOOM
9781933305967

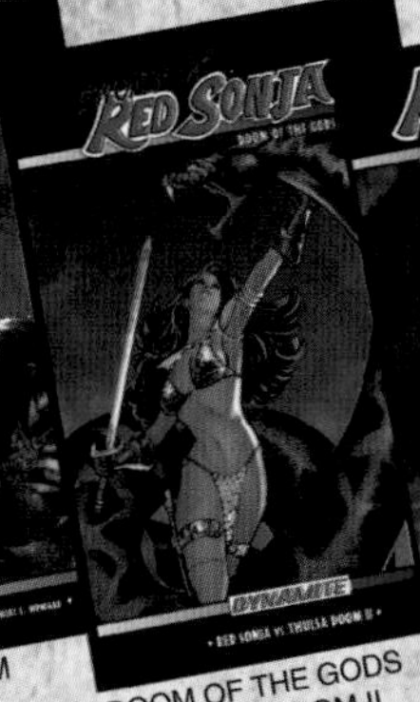
RED SONJA
DYNAMITE

DOOM OF THE GODS
vs THULSA DOOM II
9781933305769

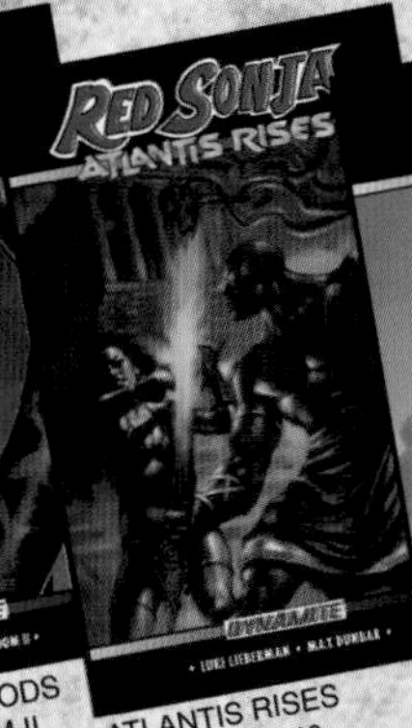
RED SONJA
ATLANTIS RISES
DYNAMITE

ATLANTIS RISES
9781606903940

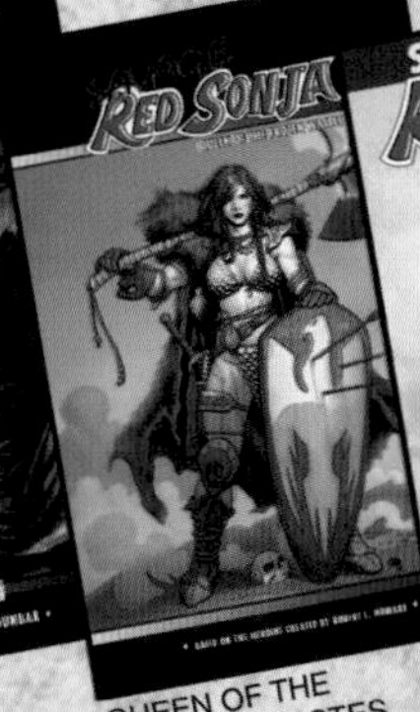
RED SONJA

QUEEN OF THE
FROZEN WASTES
9781933305387

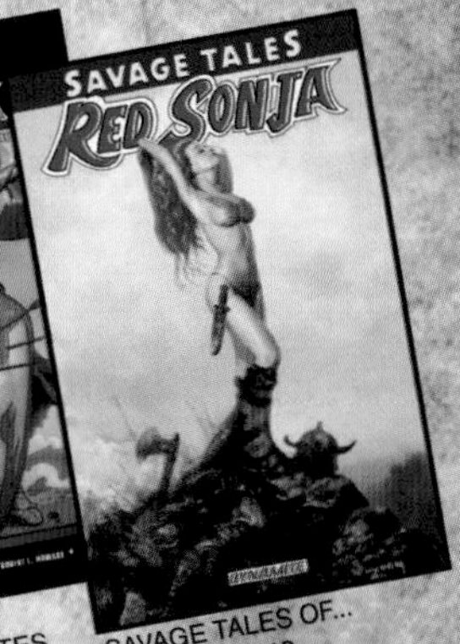
SAVAGE TALES
RED SONJA

SAVAGE TALES OF...
9781606900819

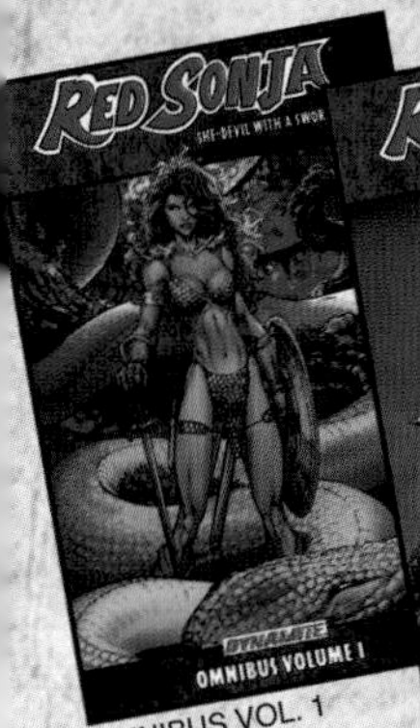
RED SONJA
DYNAMITE
OMNIBUS VOLUME 1

OMNIBUS VOL. 1
9781606901014

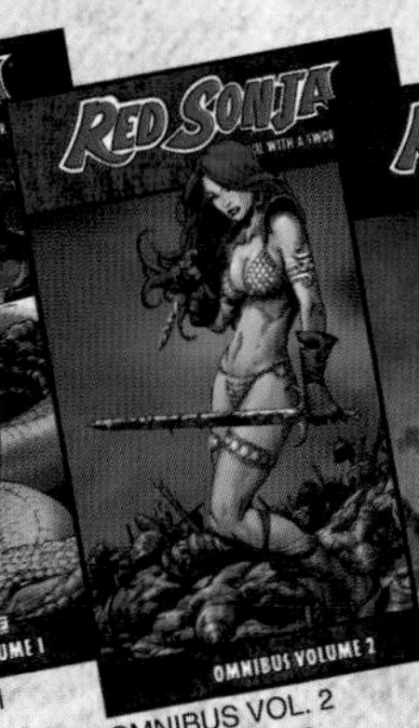
RED SONJA
OMNIBUS VOLUME 2

OMNIBUS VOL. 2
9781606902318

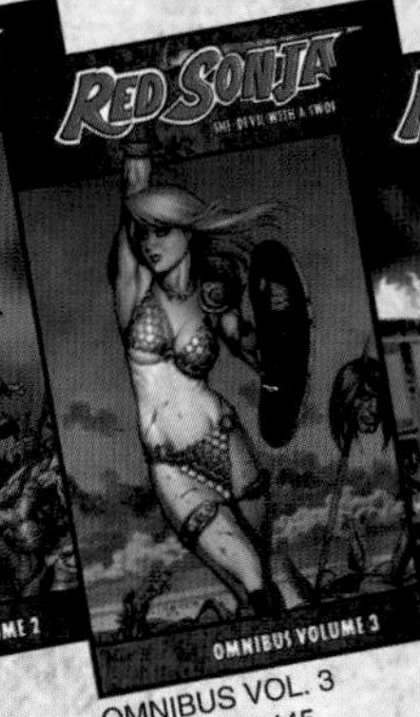
RED SONJA
OMNIBUS VOLUME 3

OMNIBUS VOL. 3
9781606903445

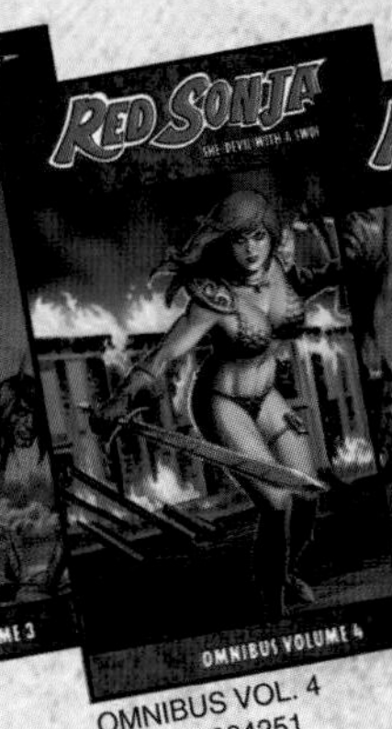
RED SONJA
OMNIBUS VOLUME 4

OMNIBUS VOL. 4
9781606904251

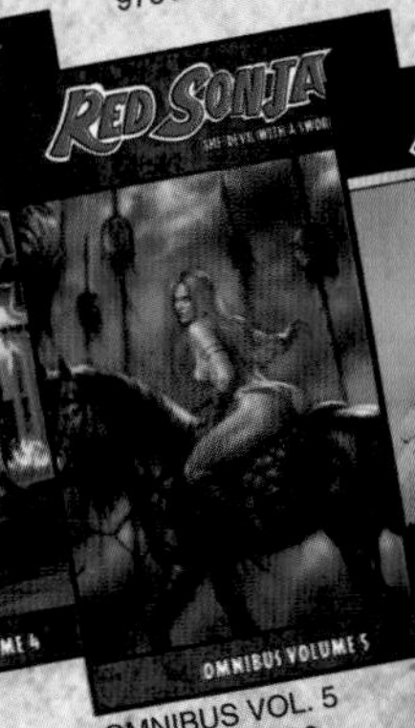
RED SONJA
OMNIBUS VOLUME 5

OMNIBUS VOL. 5
9781606904886

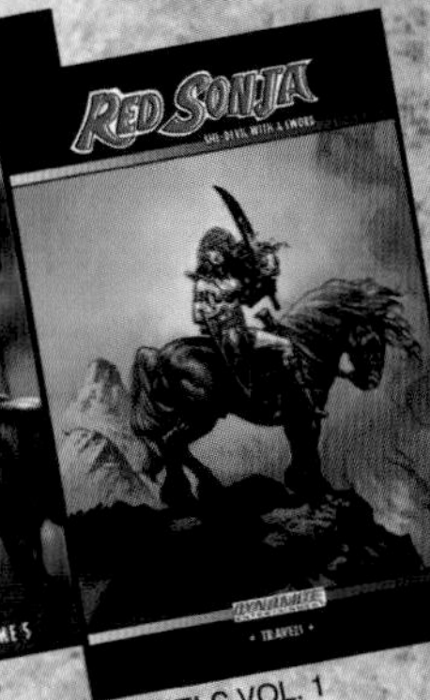
RED SONJA
DYNAMITE

TRAVELS VOL. 1
9781933305202

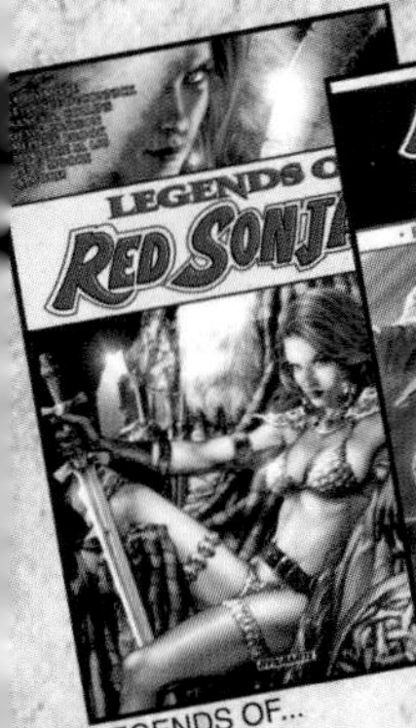
LEGENDS OF
RED SONJA
DYNAMITE

LEGENDS OF...
9781606905258

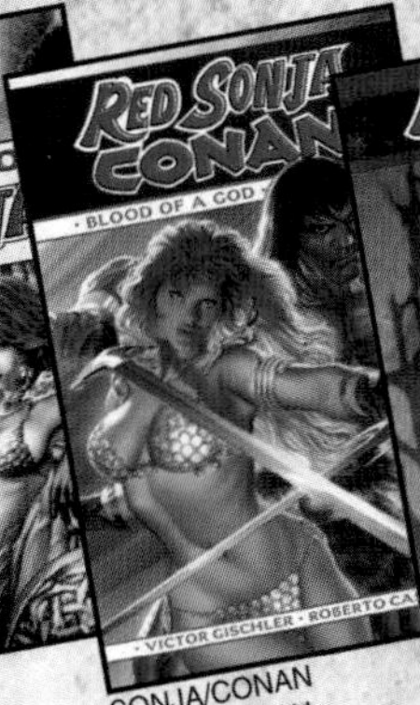
RED SONJA
CONAN
BLOOD OF A GOD

SONJA/CONAN
9781606908211

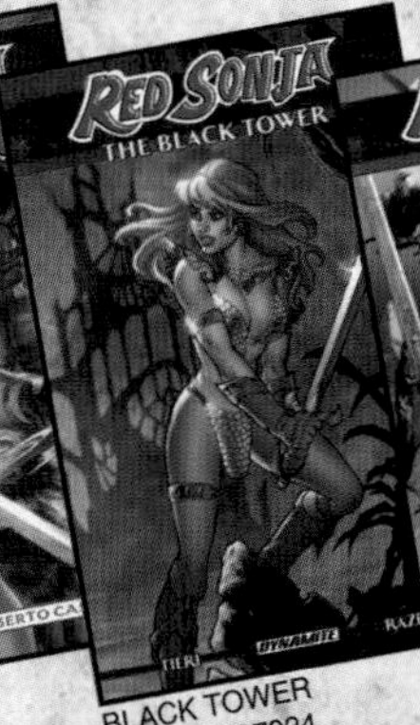
RED SONJA
THE BLACK TOWER
DYNAMITE

BLACK TOWER
9781606907924

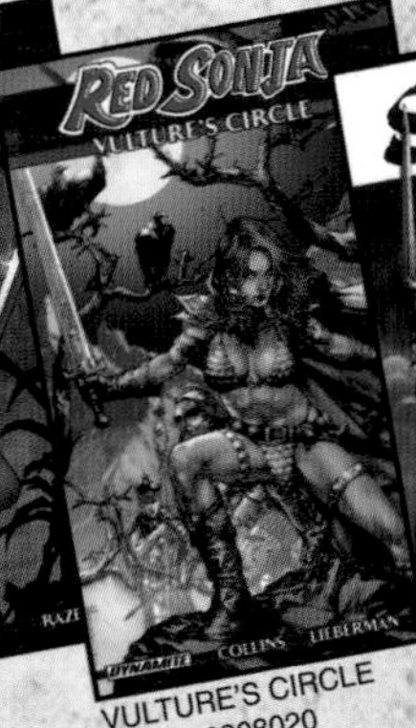
RED SONJA
VULTURE'S CIRCLE
DYNAMITE
COLLINS
LIEBERMAN

VULTURE'S CIRCLE
9781606908020

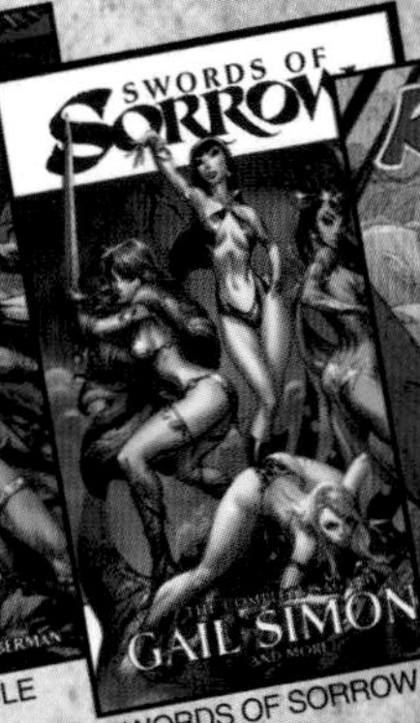
SWORDS OF
SORROW
GAIL SIMONE

SWORDS OF SORROW
9781606908068

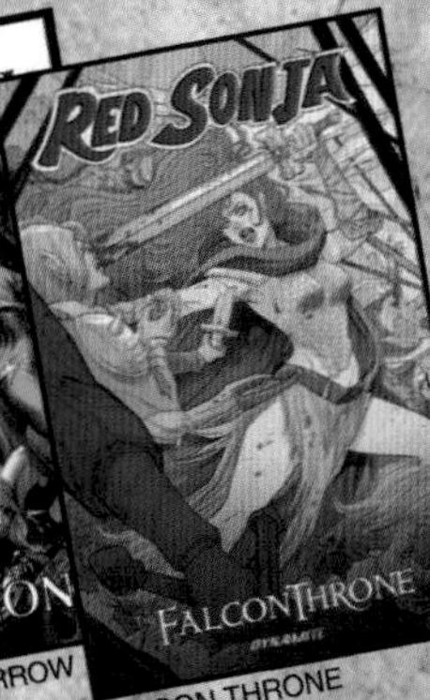
RED SONJA
FALCON THRONE
DYNAMITE

FALCON THRONE
9781524101152

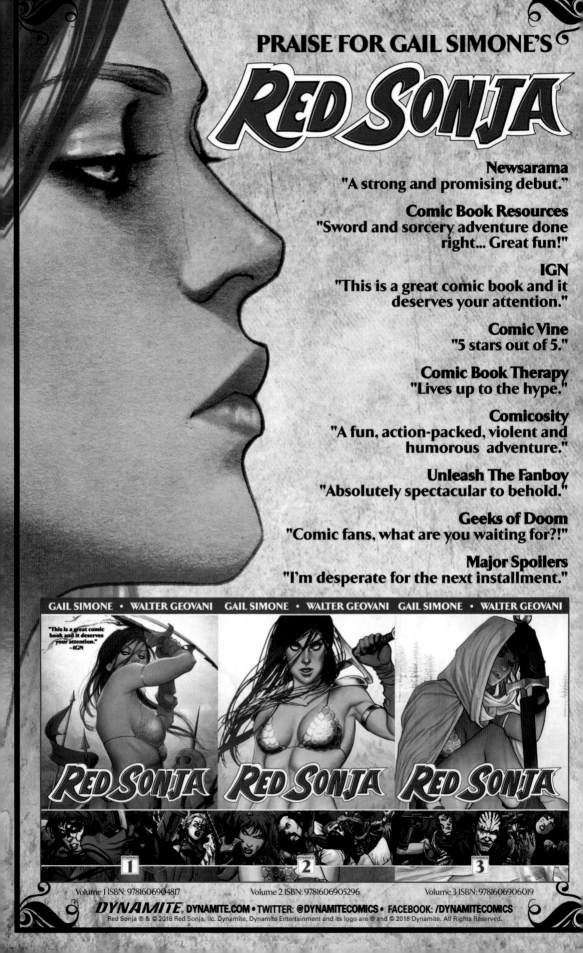

THE SHE-DEVIL WITH A SWORD TAKES MANHATTAN!

CARLOS GOMEZ
AMY CHU
RED SONJA
DYNAMITE
WORLDS AWAY

"SLICK STORYTELLING AND STRONG VISUALS MAKE THIS BOOK A WINNER IN ANY TIME. ABSOLUTELY RECOMMENDED."
SciFi Pulse

"RED SONJA JUST MAY BE ONE OF THE STRONGEST PROPERTIES DYNAMITE IS PRODUCING. THIS IS A GREAT JUMPING ON POINT."
All-Comic

"DYNAMITE HAS A SURE-FIRE HIT HERE AND WITH A CREATIVE TEAM OF AMY CHU AND CARLOS GOMEZ AT THE HELM THERE IS NO TELLING JUST HOW AMAZING THIS IS GOING TO GET."
Outright Geekery

Written by **AMY CHU** (Poison Ivy, Kiss)
Drawn by **CARLOS GOMEZ** (The Dresden Files)

IN STORES NOW
Available in Print & Digitally

DYNAMITE. www.dynamite.com
/dynamitecomics @dynamitecomics

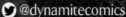

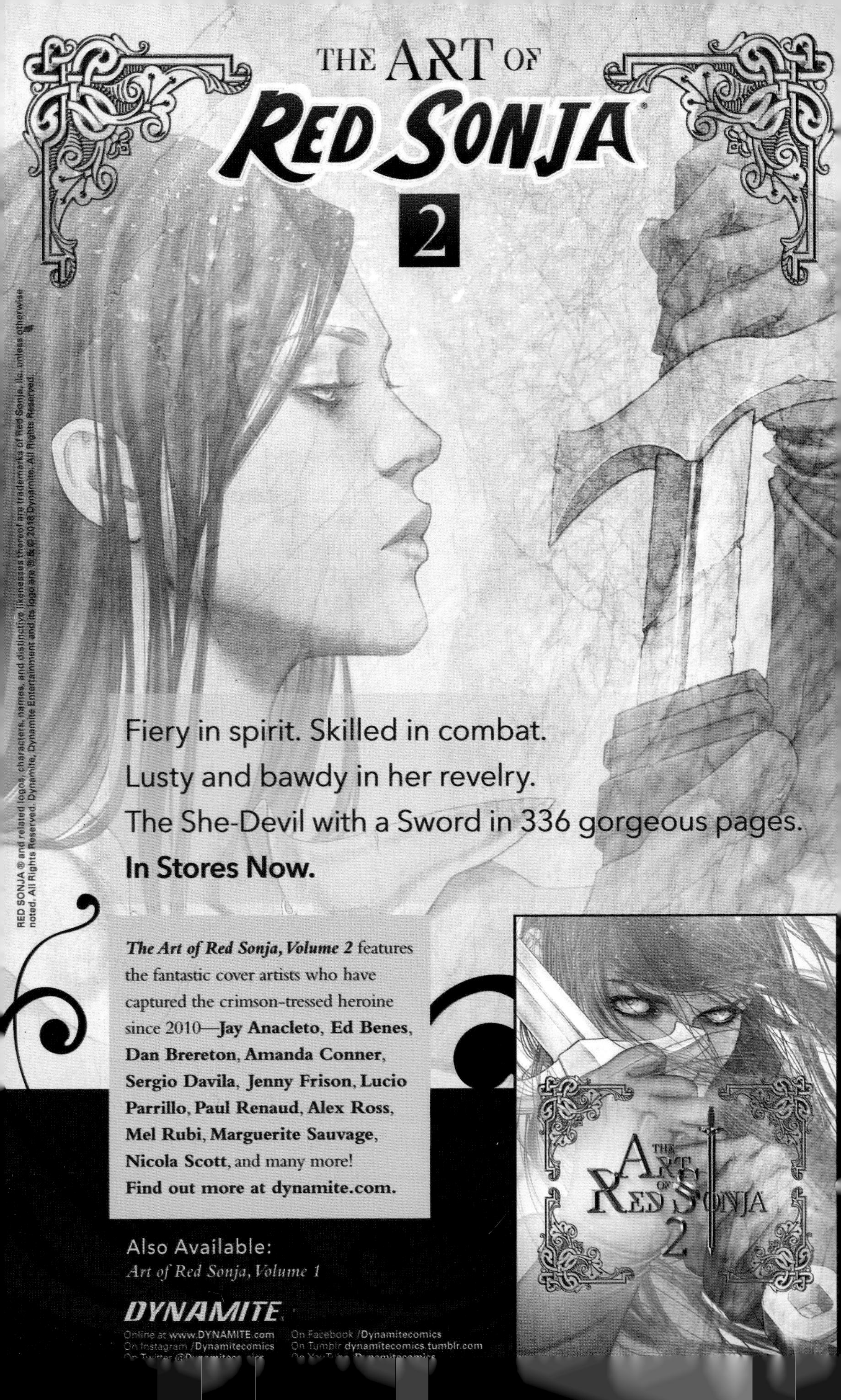
THE ART OF
RED SONJA®
2
Fiery in spirit. Skilled in combat.
Lusty and bawdy in her revelry.
The She-Devil with a Sword in 336 gorgeous pages.
In Stores Now.
The Art of Red Sonja, Volume 2 features the fantastic cover artists who have captured the crimson-tressed heroine since 2010—Jay Anacleto, Ed Benes, Dan Brereton, Amanda Conner, Sergio Davila, Jenny Frison, Lucio Parrillo, Paul Renaud, Alex Ross, Mel Rubi, Marguerite Sauvage, Nicola Scott, and many more!
Find out more at dynamite.com.
Also Available:
Art of Red Sonja, Volume 1
DYNAMITE
Online at www.DYNAMITE.com
On Facebook /Dynamitecomics
On Instagram /Dynamitecomics
On Tumblr dynamitecomics.tumblr.com
THE ART OF RED SONJA 2
RED SONJA ® and related logos, characters, names, and distinctive likenesses thereof are trademarks of Red Sonja, llc. unless otherwise noted. All Rights Reserved. Dynamite, Dynamite Entertainment and its logo are ® & © 2018 Dynamite. All Rights Reserved.